TM

Guild Press of Indiana, Inc.

Indianapolis, Indiana

Rebel Sons of Erin

A Civil War Unit History
of the
Tenth Tennessee Infantry Regiment (Irish)
Confederate States Volunteers

By
Ed Gleeson

With a Foreword By
Dr. Herschel Gower
Biographer of Colonel Randal W. McGavock

Maps by Richard Day
The Lewis Library, Vincennes University
Vincennes, Indiana

Guild Press of Indiana
6000 Sunset Lane
Indianapolis, IN 46208

Guild Press of Indiana, Inc.
6000 Sunset Lane
Indianapolis, IN 46208

Printed in the United States of America

Library of Congress Number
93-078167

ISBN 1-878208-24-1

The dust jacket cover was designed from a photograph taken by June Dorman of the Tenth Tennessee Infantry regimental flag (73.27) in the collection of the Tennessee State Museum. Thanks are due to Mr. Stephen D. Cox of the Museum staff for his cooperation in this matter. Jacket designed by Jeane Gaiennie of *Real Quack Designs*, Alexandria, Virginia. The cover illustration was done by Pietri Freeman, Richmond, Virginia.

iv

Table of Contents

Area and Battle Maps

List of Photographs

The photographs of the twenty-seven Civil War generals used in this book are re-printed with the permission of the Library of Congress. The photograph of Griffin is used with the permission of *Confederate Veteran Magazine.* The photographs of Heiman, McGavock, Morgan, Clark, and Gibson are used with permission of Herschel Gower; the photograph of Malone was provided by John M. Vaugh III; the photograph of Bliemel is the property of Father Peter J. Meaney.

A MEMORIAL

"The Sons of Erin, the 10th Tennessee Infantry Regiment, was one of the most colorful outfits in the entire Confederacy."

Thomas Connelly,
Army of the Heartland, p. 38.

This book is dedicated to the memory of Irish-American Confederate Army of Tennessee historian Thomas Lawrence Connelly, who died January 18, 1991, at the age of fifty-one.

FOREWORD

Let me say that I have no professional qualifications for writing a foreword to this impressive history of the Tenth Tennessee Regiment (Irish), C.S.A. I learned long ago that I have no talent for reporting military maneuvers, battles big or small. The knack for bringing to life the daily lot of the common soldier and looking at combat from his angle of vision is a gift denied me and I very much regret the denial.

However self-prejudicial in these matters, I can add that from 1954 to 1960 I put in many hours with Jack Allen editing the journals of Randal McGavock and putting together McGavock's biography. That narrative became the preface to his journals in the volume *Pen and Sword.* Those six years were happily spent listening to him, traveling with him, sleeping, eating, and drinking with him. It was the same kind of intimacy that Ed Gleeson has had with the colonel and each of his men in the Tenth Tennessee.

Finally, in 1960, I felt I had pulled McGavock the student, McGavock the lawyer and politican, and McGavock the social lion out of the past and endowed him with new flesh and bones as nearly as I could. But I also knew that "Randy Mac" the Confederate was poorly served in my narrative. Randal deserved better treatment, especially during the war years. His followers, the Sons of Erin, those little Irishmen with big brawn, healthy appetites for food and drink and a good fight, deserved better treatment too.

This is another way of saying that all of them have lodged heavily on my conscience for thirty-five years. Thanks to Ed Gleeson and the exciting account that follows, Randal McGavock and the lads of the Tenth Tennessee have finally come into their own. I can now announce that fact and applaud the achievement. In fact, I can finally be at ease.

It is clear from his meticulous documentation that Ed Gleeson has pursued his subjects with the investigative skills of a professional. It is doubtful that any scrap of evidence has eluded him in his relentless (perhaps obsessive) quest.

And it is a matter of poetic justice that after he had exhausted all the official records, scoured the archives, delved into every source available that Gleeson had the good luck of the Irish to come by the long forgotten diary of Private Jimmy Doyle. The account of receiving it in 1991 from Mrs. Margaret Bailey, 93, a resident of Boston and a granddaughter of a slave, is another testimonial to Irish luck showered on a determined scholar.

As Gleeson points out, the two diaries complement each other—the colonel's and the private's—and the two voices begin to sound in our ears as they tell their tales. All the sounds of the regiment come across first-hand—Irish voices, advancing hoofbeats, musket fire, cannon bombardments. There is even the ominous quiet of a cease-fire before the bullets start up again.

Gleeson also knows how to bring home to us the underlying paradoxes and devastating ironies that a war produces: slaughter and death to the right of the men and scenes of grim comedy and horseplay to the left.

> *Shattering beams and timbers, the ball filled the air with splinters fine as needles, pricking and stabbing the Northerners through their clothes, though in the grim excitement of it all, they weren't aware of this until they felt the blood running down into their shoes.*

So in addition to making vivid and thus memorable the images of war, the author knows how to express a concerned narrator's compassion. For example, in reporting the tragedy of Erin Hollow, Tennessee, Gleeson notes the forest fire that threatened the recovery of the wounded and the bodies of the dead by their helpless comrades. Afterward:

> *Soldiers on both sides congregated in the valleys and by the creek, discussing the events of that afternoon. The Sons of Erin mingled with the Galena [Illinois] lead miners; they were,*

after all, not natural enemies. Shortly the young men in blue and gray were ordered back to their own lines, and the cease-fire was lifted. Immediately the sharpshooters were at each other again.

These passages are but two that point to the merits of this book.

Finally, this history sets an indelible example for regimental histories to come. It will continue to evoke the memory of the tall, red-haired McGavock and his colorful Irish lads with all their courage and cussedness. Ed Gleeson has bestowed upon them their final triumph. He has mustered the men, called the roll, and set them marching down the years.

Herschel Gower
May 12, 1993

CIVIL WAR INFANTRY UNITS

The basic infantry unit in both armies was the volunteer company. Most companies were state units: some companies were Federalized units. The men of a particular farm district or town would recruit themselves into a company and elect their own three officers: a captain, a first lieutenant, and a second lieutenant. The ideal company would have one-hundred men, but some sparsely populated rural areas would post companies with as few as fifty or sixty men. Once the companies were formed, they would report to a central training camp, where they would be organized into battalions and regiments.

Infantry battalions, rarely deployed in Union service, were sometimes deployed in Confederate service. A battalion consisted of two or more companies commanded by a major, assisted by the captains of the companies. The ideal battalion would have five companies totaling five-hundred men, but some battalions were as small as two companies of one-hundred fifty men. Battalions, like companies and regiments, could be detached for fort duty, or attached to larger infantry units.

The basic fighting unit was the regiment, consisting of more than five companies or two battalions, and commanded by a full colonel, assisted by a lieutenant colonel, a major, and the captains of the companies. The ideal regiment would have ten companies totaling one thousand men, but some regiments would be as small as seven companies totaling six-hundred men.

In the Confederate Army between two and seven regiments formed a brigade, commanded by a brigadier general, assisted by his own personal staff and the colonels of the regiments. The ideal brigade on both sides would have had five regiments consisting of a thousand men each, but such numbers were seldom achieved, especially in Confederate service. At the beginning of the war an average brigade might consist of four regiments of two thousand men, whereas at the end of the war, the remnant of that same brigade might have as few as two-hundred men left on its active roster.

Divisions consisted of two or more brigades; corps consisted of two or more divisions; armies consisted of two or more corps; departments or theatres of operation consisted of two or more armies. From the brigade level on up, there were some differences between Union and Confederate command structure.

In Confederate service, brigades were commanded by brigadier generals, divisions by major generals, corps by lieutenant generals, and armies by full generals. In Union service, brigades were commanded by full colonels, divisions by brigadier generals, corps and armies by major generals. U. S. Grant was the only lieutenant general in Union service.

Policies regarding the ranking of officers differed greatly in the Richmond and Washington war departments. On the whole, Confederate officers were over-promoted, while Union officers were under-promoted. For instance, the Confederates had seven full generals: Cooper, A.S. Johnston, Lee, J.E. Johnston, Beauregard, E.K. Smith, and Hood. The Federals had none at all.

By the end of the war, a Confederate officer with the rank of major general might be commanding the remnant of a division consisting of eight-hundred men, while a Union officer with the lesser rank of brigadier general might be commanding an army corps of eighteen-thousand men. The last appointed brigadier in Confederate service, Theodore Brevard of Florida, never, at any time, commanded more than one-hundred men on a battlefield.

The way in which the opposing armies identified their larger infantry units was entirely different. The Federals used a precise numbering system: for example, the Third brigade of the Second division of the Fifteenth corps. The Confederates used the names of their commanding officers: for example, Gregg's brigade of Johnson's division of Hood's corps.

For the sake of both a full understanding and simplicity, this book identifies all the infantry units on the field, along with the numerical strength of those units, in its various battle descriptions.

Introduction

During the 1940s, I discovered that I had many Irish relatives. During the 1950s, I discovered that some of my Irish ancestors had come to Chicago from Ireland via South Kentucky and North Middle Tennessee. During the 1960s, I discovered that some of them had supported the Southern Confederacy. During the 1970s, I discovered that there had been an entire Tennessee Confederate outfit of Irish immigrants and Irish-Americans, known as the Tenth Tennessee Infantry Regiment of Volunteers (Irish). During the 1980s, I developed an urge to research this unit of Irishmen who called themselves the Sons of Erin, and during the 1990s I finally found it possible to complete the project.

At first it was my firm contention that I knew quite a lot about the American Civil War. I didn't. My reading had been limited to descriptions of the heroic deeds of men who had "seized the colors" and made "gallant charges" against heavily defended enemy positions. Now, however, I know just a very little about most of the soldiers of the real Civil War. And, knowing the contributions average soldiers made on both sides, I determined to tell the story of the Tenth Tennessee the way they saw it.

These were the men who marched, marched some more, dug trenches, slept on the ground, got hot and cold and wet, ate indigestible food when it was available, never had a change of clothes, drank dirty water, used bushes for bathroom facilities, buried the bodies of their fallen comrades, got sick from unsanitary conditions, and risked their lives for the Northern industrialists, Southern plantation owners, politicians and high-ranking military professionals, whose self-serving interests had started the insane conflict in the first place.

Unit histories have a somewhat different approach to Civil War research than that of other works. The style of this book may not be necessarily typical of what is considered to be modern Civil War scholarship. The book had to be constructed from a few original nineteenth century manuscripts left by soldiers like Private Jimmy Doyle, who wrote about their own experiences. I make no apologies about the somewhat strange contents of these eyewitness accounts; I wished to include them because they told the story, too. My responsibility was to separate the Irish blarney from the facts, and I hope I have done so.

In the midst of the naval battle of Fort Donelson, for instance, a few of the infantry pickets on duty from the Tenth Tennessee warmed themselves by getting drunk. This obviously had no effect on the bombardment. It is included here because it was the only experience of those few men in that particular battle. In the midst of the chaos at Chickamauga, one of the bloodiest battles in American history, the Irish regimental mess mules, carrying rations for the men, were escorted across the creek by Commissary Sergeant Barney McCabe. Since the survivors had to eat, McCabe was simply doing his job; it is included here because it was the experience of that one man in that particular battle.

Most of the Irishmen didn't write their memoirs, because they couldn't write. Down through the years college professors and their students haven't huddled in rooms with long tables to examine unpublished manuscripts about the Tenth Tennessee. Though there was a long-standing myth of the unit as being the "Bloody Tenth"—the oft-wounded, well-known Confederate Irish regiment—it was a vague myth. Between 1865-1905, very little was written on the subject. Since 1905 next to nothing has been written on the subject.

To tell the story of the Tenth Tennessee, to explore the vague myth, my task was to make maximum use of every tidbit of information from muster rolls, service records, pension applications and a few eyewitness reports. Every grim and gritty fact, important and unimportant, is contained somewhere in this book. Battle descriptions from Army Official Records and camp stories from the personal accounts are interwoven in the exact sequence that they occurred, all the way from the most sublime to the most ridiculous. All of this, I hope, provides the reader with a realistic overview of common soldiers caught up in the Western theatre of the Civil War.

To analyze the myth and separate it from the reality of the factual Irish regiment one must go back to two key accounts done decades after the war—those of Captain Lewis R. Clark and Private Patrick M. Griffin. Both of them, drawing on a few happenings and inaccurate published stories during the war, actually believed their Irish regiment suffered an unusally high rate of casualties. It didn't. The soldiers of every war, of course, routinely think that their unit was afflicted worse than other units. One of my responsibilities was to identify the enduring myth, explain where it came from and set the record straight, all the while remaining empathetic about the ordeals of battle-tested troops.

For me, finally, the story of the factual Irish regiment became much more interesting than the Irish regimental myth. These Sons of Erin played their own part in the drama that was the Confederate war effort. Probably they were unique.

A large majority of the 732 members of the Tenth Tennessee were either Irish immigrants from the seven counties of Southern Ireland (modern Republic of Ireland) or first generation Irish-Americans, whose parents had been immigrants from the seven counties. These men were Catholic, for the most part, and lived in the small all-Irish Tennessee settlements in Nashville, Clarksville, McEwen and Pulaski.

What made this Confederate Irish unit different from most of the many Union Irish units was the diversity reflected in the highly visible minority and the "Irish" unity forged in the unit in spite of diversity. There were the Scotch-Irish Presbyterians and Anglo-Irish Episcopalians, whose heritage was from Northern Ireland. And, as in most units involved in engineering work, there was a sprinkling of Germans.

Union Army Irish units consisted almost exclusively of Irish-Catholic immigrants. Irish units in the Confederate Army consisted almost exclusively of native-born Protestants of Northern Irish descent. The unusual fact with the Tenth Tennessee is that even though it was a conglomerate of various Irish groups, the Irish identity was just as strong or stronger than it was with any Irish unit on either side. More importantly, that Irish identity marked the performance of the unit throughout the whole war.

In the accounts of the Tenth Tennessee there is not a single word of friction reported in regards to nationalism, religion, or ethnic origin. The unity and tolerance demonstrated by these Sons of Erin one-hundred-and-thirty years ago has not been matched by the folks over on the Emerald Isle to this very day.

The three central figures in this story are, in order, Colonel Randal W. McGavock, a fourth-generation Scotch-Irish American Presbyterian and Mason, Colonel Adolphus Heiman, a Lutheran German immigrant from Prussia, also a Mason, and Father Emmeran Bliemel, a Catholic Benedictine monk-priest and German immigrant from Bavaria who became chaplain. All three of these men were much loved by the enlisted men. Such a combination of characters would have been highly unlikely in any of the regiments of the Union Irish Brigade.

As for the enlisted men, they did their duty with style. Because of the fact that they were consistently deployed as skirmishers and rear guards, the Confederate Sons of Erin left a good, but not outstanding combat record behind them. Their finest quality was perseverance. In spite of betrayal, imprisonment, disease and participation in nearly all of the Western campaigns, some of the Irishmen made it all the way through until the bitter end, from Fort Henry to Bentonville.

I have grown fond of every single one of the "lads," saints and scoundrels alike. While everything about their war record will be forgotten eventually, the camaraderie, determination and enduring Irish spirit of the Tennessee Sons of Erin should be remembered as a unique heritage from the Confederate side of the War Between the States.

Ed Gleeson
Oak Lawn, Illinios
St. Patrick's Day
Wednesday, March 17, 1993

ACKNOWLEDGMENTS

My thanks go to Dr. Herschel Gower, Professor Emeritus of English, Vanderbilt University, Nashville, now a resident of Dallas, Texas, for his detailed information about Randal McGavock and for his many letters of support; to Father Peter J. Meaney, a Benedictine from Morristown, New Jersey, for detailed information about Father Emmeran Bliemel and for his encouragement; to Mrs. Margaret Bailey, Boston, Massachusetts, who at ninety-three graciously and helpfully responded to my letter in the May, 1991 issue of *Civil War News.*

I also appreciate the help of Mr. Timothy Burgess of White House, Tennessee and the Middle Tennessee Civil War Round Table, for the casualty, death and burial records of the Tenth Tennessee. Thanks also to Dr. John McGlone of the *Journal of Confederate History* for his historical review of the manuscript.

My appreciation goes to Mr. Edwin C. Bearss, chief historian of the National Park Service, United States Department of the Interior, Washington, D.C. for his notes and papers concerning the battles of Fort Donelson and Raymond, Mississippi. Thanks are also due to Mr. Michael Countess, Hendersonville, Tennessee, a research historian for the military and pension records from the Tennessee archives; Mr. Benjamin Franklin Cooling, chief of the Special Histories Branch, Office of Air Force History, Washington, D.C., for his assistance with the battles of Fort Henry and Fort Donelson; Mr. Howard Michael Madaus, of the Milwaukee Public Museum, for his explanation of the Tenth Tennessee regimental battle flag; Dr. George Levy, Roosevelt University, Chicago, for his Camp Douglas governmental records and notes; Ms. Susan Hormuth of Washington, D.C. for the photos from the Library of Congress; Father Harry J. Walsh, Jr. chaplain of the Tenth Tennessee reenactment group of Delavan, Wisconsin, for his advice, counsel and consistently strong support.

Mr. John M. Vaughn III, of Boca Raton, Florida, who supplied letters and a photograph of Clarence C. Malone and the workers at the reference desk at the Oak Lawn Public Library, who ran the volumes of the Army Official Records back and forth, are also due thanks, as are all the members of the staff of Oakwoods Cemetery, Chicago.

Finally, thanks to Nancy N. Baxter, Publisher of Guild Press of Indiana, for taking a risk on a fifty-year-old rookie writer.

PREFACE

It was a mild, clear morning in September of 1861. Colonel Adolphus Heiman, an architect from Nashville, was in command of troops whose task was to construct Fort Henry on the Tennessee River. Because of a lack of raw materials, many of the soldier-workers were standing around idle, talking and laughing, which caused the colonel to have one of his famous bursts of agitation.

There were at least two problems. First, Heiman was a Prussian immigrant who shouted curses in his native German tongue. Second, the enlisted men were Irish immigrants who spoke in brogue as thick as the hide on Commissary Sergeant Barney McCabe's mess mules. The language barrier was insurmountable. Even when the German used his version of English, the Irishmen claimed that they could communicate only in "Gaelic."

The commanding officer continued to curse and the lads continued to ignore him. It was an average day in the lives of a group of rather atypical Southerners in rebellion against the government of the United States.

Chapter One
Seven-Hundred-Twenty-Five Lads

The Sons of Erin: the St. Patrick's Club

Randal William McGavock was in some ways an unlikely leader for Irish laborers. A fourth-generation Southern American, scholar, lawyer, writer, politician and soldier, he was descended from Scotch Highlanders who had emigrated to Northern Ireland in James I's transplanting of Protestants among the Catholic Irish. He was born August 10, 1826, the fifth child of Jacob and Louisa McGavock, who dabbled in plantations, commercial real estate, tobacco, cotton and horses in three states and were social leaders in the growing town of Nashville. Among the senior McGavocks' closest friends were Mr. and Mrs. James K. Polk, of Columbia, Tennessee, who would become President and First Lady.[1]

In addition to being dashing, tall, and handsome, with flaming red hair, the youthful McGavock was also a good student and enjoyed trying his hand at writing prose from time to time. After graduating from the University of Nashville, he took a leisurely year off before entering the Harvard School of Law in September, 1847.

Although law student McGavock did not have them as instructors, the Harvard faculty at that time included Edward Everett, Henry W. Longfellow and Oliver Wendell Holmes. Lectures were sometimes presented by Henry David Thoreau and Ralph Waldo Emerson. During his tenure at Cambridge, McGavock listened politely to speeches from New England abolitionists, probably wondering at the intensity of their Northern political views and quite naturally finding his own typically Southern views conflicting with theirs.

Randal seems to have had no conflict with the beautiful women of the Boston area, however; he was romantically involved with Miss Lemira Ewing of New Haven and Miss Maria A. Gould of Boston. Miss Gould was named by *The Boston Bee* as the most lovely belle in all of New England.[2]

The Boston Daily Evening Transcript informed its readers that Mr. McGavock of Nashville was fond of attending gala balls,[3] and it was at this time that the Nashville aristocrat established a reputation for courting the ladies and then stopping short of the altar.

On February 21, 1849, Randal McGavock completed his one-and-a-half year's stay at Harvard. On his way back home, he appears to have attended the inauguration of President Zachary Taylor. McGavock's return to Tennessee in the spring occurred at about the same time that James and Sarah Polk were also returning from their four years in the executive mansion.

The young lawyer opened up an office on Cherry Street, but he seems rarely to have practiced his profession. His social life was active if not frenetic; soon he was devoting himself to a passionate love affair with Nashville's lovely Fanny Jane Crutcher. This relationship lasted better than a year and ended in a near-marriage. The courtship was broken off on Christmas Day of 1850 with no explanation in his journal other than he "had lost his one great chance at happiness."[4]

"Having no entangling alliances or particular object" to bind him to Nashville, McGavock went abroad for eighteen months, where he courted fair damsels with titles and once beat off an attack by river pirates in Egypt.[5]

Ironically, he was unimpressed with Ireland. McGavock didn't much care for the seven counties of the south. In his faithful companion the journal, he made the point that Northern Ireland was inhabited with people "descended principally from the Scotch, who have inherited to a considerable degree their habits of industry and frugality."[6] In the "desolation" that was the southern counties, he found no such industriousness or frugality. This view, of course, he would have shared with any other Scotch-Irish descendent of the Northern counties. He seems not to have attributed any of the apathy and squalor he saw to long years of English absentee ownership and other economic and political mismanagement. It was, of course, the fact. From the 1730s on, grinding poverty and lack of opportunity had sent thousands of Irishmen, both from north and south, to his own state, and a sizeable contingent occupied an Irish district in Nashville.

In 1853 McGavock moved into the arena of Tennessee Democratic party politics. His career proceeded slowly, possibly retarded by the attention he was continuing to pay to social obligations.

He was engaged to Miss Lizzie Bonner of Fayetteville, Tennessee; that engagement and near-marriage was followed immediately by another one, involving Miss Lydia Smith of Nashville.This near-marriage didn't last very long, because at a "Grand Fancy Ball" in Macon, Tennessee, he met Miss Ophelia Nisbet. "With this lady I had quite a flirtation," he reported in his journal.[7]

In 1855 McGavock began to build a broader base of out-of-town interests, including Miss Annie Grundy of Kentucky and Miss Sallie Faulkner of Virginia.

At the age of twenty-nine, the dashing Democrat decided that it was in his own best interests to get married once and for all.

The chosen young lady was a petite, flirtatious, ravishingly beautiful maiden from East Tennessee, who was, like him, a Presbyterian of Scotch-Irish descent.

She was five feet two inches tall and had light brown hair with gold tints. Her blue eyes might have been colored for a china doll. She was little and graceful and her dresses were bright-colored.[8]

A sensation at any social gathering, her magical Southern name was Seraphine (pronounced Ser-a-fin-a) Deery, and she was known to her family as "Seph."

In the face of doubters among his friends and his own

family, Randal jumped at this new "one great chance at happiness" and married Seph Deery two weeks after he proposed.The date was August 23, 1855, at her home in Allisona, Tennessee. The wedding was followed by a honeymoon trip to Boston.

The year after the wedding saw the political career of the future colonel of the Sons of Erin begin to take shape. Appointed by the governor as a member of the Democratic Central Committee of Tennessee, he toured the Nashville area campaigning for the national ticket headed by James Buchanan of Ohio. The 1856 presidential race was a three-way tug-of-war, as Democrats, Know-Nothings, and a new group calling themselves the Republicans, struggled for votes of traditional agricultural states and the newly emerging urban centers.

The candidate of the new Republican party was John C. "The Pathfinder" Fremont, of California, later to be a somewhat-less-than-successful Union general. In order to expand their national base, the Know-Nothings were determined to offer their own candidate.

Traveling the length of the country, they selected the Honorable Millard Fillmore of New York, who had already held the office of President—completing the term of Taylor when "Rough and Ready" had expired from an overdose of milk and cherries. Neither anti-Catholic nor anti-foreign, Fillmore doesn't seem to have been able to understand his own Know-Nothing party's platform.

With zest and merriment, Democrat McGavock rode to the hamlets of Middle Tennessee, hammering away at Fillmore and the Know-Nothings, and sending some side-swipes the way of John Fremont while he was at it. While still cultivating the big wigs of the state party, McGavock was for the first time gathering his own constituency. He had begun to cultivate a newly emerging voting block—the Irish of Tennessee. He realized they would soon be a factor to be reckoned with because of their numbers alone, and they liked him. Young, red-haired, and outspoken against the bigots, McGavock seemed to be "one of the lads" and did not dispel the image that he was "true Irish."

McGavock and the other Central Committee fellows were all pleased when Buchanan and the Democrats swept the federal and state elections. Fillmore carried just one state. "We carried the state by a large majority, which compensated me amply for my humble labors in the canvass," McGavock said.[9]

McGavock's next goal was the Democratic nomination for a seat in Congress, and when it went out of his grasp, he decided to run for the office of Mayor of Nashville.[10]

A mid-nineteenth century mayoral race in Nashville was simplicity itself. The campaign started on the first Saturday of September, and following three weeks of campaigning, the election was held on the last Saturday of the month to fill an office whose term was exactly one year. All speeches were made on street corners or in halls, with expenses limited to those incurred for the printing of hand-bills. Most of the candidates were Democrats, and no matter how many candidates ran or how close, run-offs weren't considered. The winner was the man who got the most votes.

Only adult, white male citizens, of course, could run; 10,000 men lived in Nashville in 1858 and about 9,000 could vote. Seph and Randal, still childless after three years, lived with his parents in a house at Cherry near Union Street.

McGavock remembered the curious constituency he had wooed and won during the presidential race: he began to think about the Irish vote for himself. Irishmen could vote, and Irishmen were loyal. For political reasons he joined the local St. Patrick's Club, where the lads drank whiskey and beer, exchanged a few interesting stories, listened to a little home-made music and sang songs.

It was here that he first met Jimmy Morrissey, Matt Brown and Marty Gibbons. Here Mike Carney played his harmonica; here Jimmy Doyle told his jokes. They were all young fellows in their twenties, some first, some second generation Irish-Catholic laboring men of the city, who were helping to raise the brick mercantile shops in the downtown and provide carpentry skills for the blossoming residential areas where fashionable people like McGavock's parents lived. The lads were only too eager and willing to serve as precinct captains.

The McGavock supporters in the St. Patrick's Club called themselves the "Sons of Erin." "Randy Mc" was a nickname which they gave their political champion, the adopted "Irishman" they were beginning to admire. During the summer of 1858 the Sons of Erin marched together for the first time, knocking on doors, providing voter registration information.[11]

On Saturday, September 4, four candidates entered the race, their names being Clemons, Godshill, Hale, and Singelton. For two weeks McGavock listened to the negative ramblings of this quartet and made up his mind. Finally, he threw his hat into the ring officially on Saturday, September 18, exactly one week before the election.

"Randy Mack," as he was now being universally referred to by the lads at the drinking club, may well have been the first mayoral candidate in Nashville history to announce his intentions at an Irish wake. The deceased was a member of the St. Patrick's Club, a lad by the name of R. O'Kane, whom McGavock eulogized in true Irish fashion in his journal and for the mourners who stood around the casket toasting their departed friend with good Irish whiskey. It seems that on the evening of Tuesday, September 17, only one train passed through Cowan, and Mr. O'Kane somehow managed to get himself run over by it. "He was killed while standing on the railroad tracks near Cowan. A cleverer man never lived," McGavock said.[12] It was a dramatic start for one of the most colorful one-week urban political crusades in American history.

Never overly modest, the candidate described his own activities as a "blaze of action."[13] By days he sallied forth, dressed in a green coat, riding his horse "Tenth Legion," waving his hat, shaking hands. By nights he would travel by open carriage and make speeches, drawing listeners to him by the force of his personality, ignoring his four opponents as if they didn't exist.

Accompanying the candidate in the evenings was the St. Patrick's Club Irish Band, led by professional musician Jimmy Morrissey, followed by many non-professional musicians from the tavern.

Any time a heckler started up on the candidate, the band would break right in with a popular tune like "St. Patrick's Day in the Morning." But even when "Randy Mack" himself couldn't be present, his faithful lieutenants of the Sons of Erin passed out handbills emblazoned with shamrocks and messages of Irish support.[14]

The day before the election was a non-stop, twenty-four-hour campaigning whirlwind. After speech-making, McGavock visited Mrs. O'Sullivan's Irish Boarding House on Front Street and Joe Dolin's saloon on Market Street. At midnight the candidate's beautiful wife, Seph, joined the festivities, accompanying her husband to a formal ball on Capitol Hill, and then popped in at an "Irish ball near the depot." "We were out all night," was all that McGavock could write.[15]

On election day Seph, looking stunning as usual, met Randal in the morning, so that she would appear with him as he voted. In a very close race, the last few votes to be counted came from the Irish district. At about 6:30 p.m. a din of noisy joy could be heard all over town. It was the St. Patrick's Club Irish Band, rendering their version of a victory march.

The race was decided by ninety-three votes, with McGavock getting close to 2,000 votes, about 1,400 of which came from the one big predominantly Irish neighborhood.[16] Irish-Americans had elected their first big city mayor, though the truth of it was that the champion of these poor people was a Southern-bred aristocrat, who was about as Irish as Millard Fillmore.

7

Later that same evening Mayor-elect and Mrs. McGavock were driven in an open carriage to the hall on College Hill, where they attended another ball! The Sons of Erin presented a top hat dyed green to their hero, who danced with it on his head all night long.[17]

Rising early the next morning, as they did every Sunday, the new first couple of Nashville attended the 9:00 a.m. services at the First Presbyterian Church. With somber music drifting out from the church organ, they strolled in, arm-in-arm, to be greeted by a few polite nods from the congregation, the vast majority of whom had voted for Clemons, Godshill, Hale, and Singleton. The incongruity of the moment did not escape the fun-loving McGavock, who gave his wife "a wee bit of a wink."[18]

Mayor McGavock turned out to be a reformer of sorts, setting up the Robertson Association, a group of wealthy gentlemen who contributed food, shelter, and health care to the poor, while cleaning out the filth of the workhouses, and moving the homeless off the streets.[19] No doubt his own acquaintance with those in the poorer Irish sections, where the workhouse was no novelty, had helped him understand the poverty of his city better.

The young mayor's most controversial decision involved the creation of two new city offices—the Poor of the City Department and the Free Negro Affairs Department. Endearing himself forever to the Irish community, he gave some police and fire jobs to Irishmen.

Surely, though, McGavock's best remembered contribution to Nashville was to its social life. Randal McGavock, 32, 6' 2" and immaculately groomed, and Seph, 23, 5' 2", trim and elegant, must have set an all time record for gala balls hosted. The highlight may well have been the weekend of June 17 and 18, 1859. Nashville was visited by the Savannah, Georgia

Artillery Marching Band; and the gala included a concert, a banquet, a boat trip, fireworks, several fired salutes, the illumination of the capitol building, and a special presentation of an engraved silver pitcher to the beaming first couple.[20]

A month later McGavock announced that he wasn't running for re-election, offering no reason. The truth was that Nashville wasn't big enough to hold his higher ambitions.

At the Democratic State Convention in Nashville on January 18, 1860, the Honorable Randal W. McGavock was selected as one of the ten voting delegates to the National Convention, which was to gather that April in Charleston, South Carolina. It was a convention of note, as the country the founding fathers had put together began to rend itself apart in the first in a series of South Carolina secessions. Eight Southern states (not including Tennessee) walked out, splitting the Democratic party right down the middle.

Senator Stephen A. Douglas of Illinois emerged as the candidate of the Northern Democrats, and incumbent Vice-President John C. Breckinridge of Kentucky became the eventual choice of the Southern Democrats. It was a party disaster waiting to happen. Disappointed, the ex-mayor of Nashville, very much a moderate himself, returned home to chart out his own personal course of action in a sectional schism that threatened to become a war.

Though he very much hoped for a peaceful solution to the differences between North and South, McGavock left no doubt about his being a Southerner, loyal through and through. Throughout the summer and fall of 1860, he campaigned just as hard for Breckinridge as he had for Buchanan in 1856.

The Douglas-Breckinridge split gave the Republicans a less-than-majority plurality. Southerners held little hope of reconciliation with the hard-nosed Westerner who was the Republican President-elect—Abraham Lincoln. McGavock's concern was about something he called "Democracy of the South," and the "right of secession," which were just another way of saying "states rights."[21]

There were so many mixed feelings among Tennesseans that the state legislature in Nashville called for a non-binding popular referendum. The secessionists were led by incumbent Governor Isham G. Harris, the unionists by U.S. Senator (and former governor) Andrew Johnson, of Greeneville, East Tennessee. When the vote was held on February 9, McGavock again experienced defeat. Unionism won overwhelmingly 91,803 to 24,749 with the absolutely solid support of the mountainous eastern counties.

Fort Sumter in Charleston Harbor fell on April 14, and the next day President Lincoln made one of the few political mistakes of his presidency, sending out a call to Tennessee to join with the other states still of the Union in raising 75,000 militiamen for ninety-day service.

Because the President's edict was perceived as high handed, it caused many of the important fence-sitting Tennesseans to switch sides in the secession debate. It was at this time that Randal McGavock announced his intentions to join the pro-Confederate Tennessee Home Guards. The state legislature pulled Tennessee out of the Federal Union on May 6, as the tenth of the eleven states that became known as the Southern Confederacy. A new referendum on June 10 supporting the decision carried 105,511 to 47,338, with most of the dissenting votes coming from east of Knoxville.[22] Like the nation, Tennessee was divided.

The Sons of Erin: the Company

As political pros, Governor Harris and Committeeman McGavock were always looking for ways to improve their weakest links. When it came to recruits for the state militia, the weakest link in Middle Tennessee was Nashville's Irish community. Sentiment for military service from the Irish ranged from indifference at best to pro-Union at worst. There were several reasons for this. First, some of the Irish were recent immigrants, unwilling to part with what they considered to be their newly found homeland. In addition, most of the lads didn't understand the sectional issues. Some couldn't even tell you where Washington and Richmond were. Then, too, these immigrants were part of America's poorest class and held fast to the traditional European hostility toward the wealthy upper classes. Southern slave owners were perceived by the anti-slavery new arrivals to be the most arrogant and lazy of the hated rich folks. To defend their way of life would be ridiculous.

Finally, because their accents and customs made them different, and because they knew they were frowned on by the rest of the communities, the Irish were clannish. They had forged their own strong loyalties and support systems which worked. Why should they join a military mission that would take them away from their community, to stand side by side with the men who looked down on them? The Irishmen, anyway, were most hesitant to fight in a war that might pit Irishmen from the North against Irishmen from the South. If you were Irish, you were Irish. What was "the Southern cause" anyway when compared to the brotherhood forged by religious and national affinities that went back over a thousand years?

McGavock had the perfect solution. As Nashville's most visible Irish-American, he would form a company of all-Irish volunteers. In this way he could use both his own popularity and Irish clannishness to foster the Southern cause, not to mention his own career. He would utilize his home-made political organization from 1858, the St. Patrick's Club—Irishmen like Jimmy Morrissey, Matt Brown, Marty Gibbons, Mike Carney the harmonica player, Jimmy Doyle and the other lads from the tavern.

The focus was Irish pride, the idea that the Irishmen were as good as anyone when it came to toasting company spirit, banging on drums, blowing into bagpipes, parading around with flags and fighting the enemy. The nickname of the Irish company was to be, of course, the Sons of Erin. When recruitment began, the lads lined up without hesitation. Seph McGavock organized the wives into the Ladies Soldiers' Friend Society, a Confederate patriotic group that

11

featured celebrity Sarah Polk, widow of the late President, who ironically, had been pro-Union.

The company flag the ladies designed and sewed, as large as a banner, was outlined in kelly-green on a light green background with a gold harp, maroon trim, and white lettering. Above the harp were the words: "Sons of Erin." Below the harp, "Where Glory Waits You" was inscribed. [23]

Not too surprisingly, the Irishmen's "Randy Mack" was elected captain of the Sons of Erin. Since the lone Irish company was the fourth of sixteen units organized at Nashville in April of 1861, it was officially designated as "D" Company, Tennessee Home Guards (state militia).

Captain McGavock spent his evenings studying military manuals and his days recruiting young Irishmen for D Company, which met at Cheatham's store on College Street and drilled each afternoon at 5:00 p.m. to the fife of Jimmy Morrissey and to the drum of a seventeen-year-old youngster by the name of Patrick M. Griffin.

The other recruits included Thomas "Long Tom" Connor, who was not only tall, but a seasoned hunter and best rifleman of the lot and Thomas Feeney, five feet, eight inches, with black hair and grey eyes. "Crazy Tom" Feeney, as he was called, had dived off a bridge into a creek that was dry as a bone when he was a boy, and the lads at the St. Patrick's Club claimed his head had never been the same after that.[24]

Some of the other original Sons of Erin were: John Duffy, Frank Nelligan, Jack Kennedy, Jimmy Collins, Ed Fahey, Mike Gallagher, Denny O'Neill, Mickey Ryan, Brian Connolly, Bill Quirk, Paddy McCormick, Charlie Berry, Pat O'Brien, Eddie Kelly, Jimmy Flanagan, John Curley, Pete Joyce, Jack Quigley, Dennis Murphy, Danny Driscoll, John Sullivan, and Johnny Sullivan.

In three weeks Captain McGavock had 124 Irishmen recruited, enough to be considered a full company. On May 9 D Company was mustered (sworn) into the Tennessee State Militia for a period of one year, under the command of Isham Harris, governor of the state.[25] On May 25, better than two weeks before passage of the ordinance of secession, Harris gave the Sons of Erin an assignment appropriate for day laborers in Nashville—he sent them to help construct two inland river forts to be named Henry and Donelson.

Before the lads took off on the steamer *B.M. Runyon,* many of the women-folk of Nashville came out to bid them farewell. Patrick Griffin's mother and his auburn-haired girl-friend were there to tearfully wave goodbye. As the boat took off on its seventy-mile journey north down the Cumberland River, the St. Patrick's Club Irish Band played that old favorite, "The Girl I Left Behind."[26]

"Crazy Tom" Feeney seems at that point to have jumped overboard, ostensibly because he began thinking about the girls he left behind him. The captain of the meager vessel was visibly upset about having to stop and fish one of the "soldiers" out of the drink and warned against any more tomfoolery. The band switched to that popular tune, "Gary Owen."

But after Tom Feeney jumped overboard again, the steamboat captain was angered, and Captain McGavock himself settled the matter by taking the addle-brained recruit aside for a talk.[27]

The new company was heading into a cauldron of activity as the nation, ripped apart, struggled for the great rivers which were its central arteries of transportation and had to be held for strategic reasons in the war. Though they may not have realized it, the Irishmen were going to build the defense of two of the most important rivers which flowed into the great Mississippi system. Both the Cumberland and the Tennessee flowed south to north, instead of the usual way, and their geography played a vital part in the way the campaign built around them developed.

Actually the two "inland rivers," or "twin rivers," part of a system of water highways of the West, were almost as vital to the Southern cause as was the Mississippi River itself.

The rivers were the gateway to Nashville, supply center and railroad depot and the heart of the munitions industry which produced critical war materials for the South.

Fort Henry and Fort Donelson were going to be located in North Middle Tennessee, twelve miles apart, near the Kentucky border. Fort Henry was right on the Tennessee River just to the west of Nashville. It would be difficult for the Confederates to hold Nashville if Fort Henry fell to the Federals.

Fort Donelson was being raised on the Cumberland River, and Nashville was also right on the Cumberland. So it would be absolutely impossible for the Confederates to hold Nashville if Fort Donelson fell to the Federals, and all of Middle Tennessee would eventually fall. In short, the two forts were valuable Southern real estate, and the struggle for them would be the first important landmark test in the Western theatre of the war.

Ahead for the Sons of Erin loomed a good deal of swamp muck, back-breaking rock-digging, malaria, and bad military management in about as hot, disease-laden and boggy a piece of real estate as lay in the new Confederate States of America.[28]

At that time, of course, McGavock and the rest had little inkling of the military import and unpleasant dangers of the places to which they were headed; the lads simply settled down in the steamboat and began a routine of card playing, joke-telling and (when they could) drinking that continued the early activities of the St. Patrick's Club. The spirit of that place carried over a long time for them.

The Sons of Erin: the Regiment

McGavock, of course, was only one of several unusual personalities who were to be connected with the Sons of Erin.

14

The governor of Tennessee gave command of new Forts Henry and Donelson to Adolphus Heiman. He was a man the Irishman came to respect and even revere.

Heiman, a mechanical engineer who had been designing steam and hot-air systems for insane asylums, had been born in Potsdam, Prussia, on April 17, 1809, as the son of the Superintendent of Guards for the summer palace of the Prussian King.[29]

The young Adolphus had as his tutor the famous intellectual Alexander Von Humboldt, who instructed his pupil in English, math, science, architecture, engineering and stone masonry. With Humboldt's letter of introduction in his pocket, Heiman traveled to America in 1834, at age twenty-five, and settled in Nashville, where there was a small German community. After distinguished service in Mexico as a major of Tennessee volunteers, Heiman went into the construction business, building both public structures and fine, elegant homes.

In addition to his other projects, Herr Heiman experimented in bridge construction. His wire extension bridge over the Cumberland, completed in 1853, collapsed in 1855.

Among his friends were Jacob McGavock, the father of Randal McGavock and Dr. John Berrien Lindsley, the brother-in-law of the captain of the Irish company. Heiman and McGavock, interestingly enough, had clashed in the smoke-filled rooms of the Nashville political scene—Heiman the Whig and McGavock the Democrat shouted each other down at a few town meetings.

When the Civil War began, Adolphus Heiman was commissioned a full colonel of engineers in the Tennessee Home Guards. As the commanding officer at both inland river forts, he had about 350 laborers under his stern, watchful eye, most of whom were Irish. It was to his command that the former St. Patrick's Club-political marching society, now militia company, was heading.[30]

The final destination for the Sons of Erin was the town of Dover, Tennessee, a short hike away from Fort Donelson.

Colonel Heiman already had his Irishmen busily engaged in defensive preparations, running his 350 lads back and forth between the forts. Scouting reports were coming in from all over that the Federals were amassing forces in Missouri, Kentucky, and all along the Ohio River. Defenses would have to be mounted, the forts completed. The reinforcements (Sons of Erin) then on the march towards the fort areas would enable Heiman to meet the Union challenge by running about 475 Irishmen back and forth between the forts.[31]

"Uncle Dolph" was what the Irishmen affectionately named the fifty-two-year-old German when they met him.[32] They found him difficult to understand, and of a volatile temperament·when he grew frustrated, but ultimately reliable. On May 29, 1861, at Fort Donelson, Heiman formed his crew into an undersized regiment, officially registered as the Tenth Tennessee Infantry Regiment of Volunteers (Irish), Home Guards (state militia). Nine other state regiments had been formed in numerical sequence.

The new militia regiment adopted both the nickname, Sons of Erin, and the colorful green standard of D Company. As was the custom, the lads of the Tenth were free to elect their own officers. With the help of some of his old precinct workers, politician McGavock was elected lieutenant colonel, second in command, under Heiman. The Nashville political squabbles were behind the two men, and under the necessities of the moment, McGavock and Heiman began to work smoothly together.

The top two officers worked out an arrangement to their mutual satisfaction. Colonel Heiman's role was that of construction foreman. Lieutenant Colonel McGavock's role was that of field commander. Although the German was officially in charge, he referred all regimental matters to the Scotch-Irish leader. Heiman did not drill or train the Irish lads in any military capacity; and as far as camp life went, McGavock was in practice the *de facto* officer in command.[33]

All Heiman cared about was a full day's work for a full day's pay, and with McGavock in charge, he got it. In turn, McGavock was allowed to turn the Irishmen loose without too much notice when it came time for the work details to be finished.[34]

On July 1, leaving Fort Donelson alone and unfinished, Colonel Heiman marched the Sons of Erin twelve miles due west to Fort Henry. As Lieutenant Colonel McGavock arrived at Fort Henry mounted on his horse, Tenth Legion, and took a look over the Tennessee River shoreland, he came to the instant realization that the whole project was off on an impossible foot. The fort was being constructed on the wrong side of the river![35]

Fort Henry sat right on the Tennessee-Kentucky border on the east (Tennessee) bank of the Tennessee River. The west bank was on the soil of Kentucky, a state still in the Union; on the opposite shore there was a heights which would have been perfect for a river fort. But Heiman had been directly ordered by Governor Harris not to build over there because of "Kentucky sovereignty."

Orders were orders and Heiman began building his rude, rock-log fortress on the low marshy side of the river, subject to flooding whenever it rained.

The back-breaking labor of tree-felling, rock-hauling and emplacing began. One of the problems that surfaced immediately was that Adolphus Heiman wasn't especially good at communicating. Not only did the colonel speak with a pronounced German accent, but when agitated, he ran around waving his arms and swearing in German.

McGavock found he had to often translate, mediate and frequently smooth over during the daily grind which was beginning to constitute a good deal of the military regimen of the Tenth Tennessee.[36]

The Sons of Erin awakened each morning at 4:00 a.m. to the sound of the bugle and the calling of the roll. Morning routine consisted of marching and digging rifle pits under the guidance of Lieutenant Colonel R. W. McGavock. Later in the morning the Irishmen would go over to the fort and cart stones and logs around, while doing some more digging, under the guidance of Colonel A. Heiman. Then they would

17

return to camp, respond to afternoon roll-call, march, and dig some more, and gladly settle down for evening mess.[37]

The Tenth Tennessee was living, thriving, actually, on its Irishness. Tell the lads where they should be, give them the shovels or the weapons and the rally cry. They would take it on the trust of Randal McGavock, their leader. It was in that same spirit that the O'Neills, O'Boyles, McGuires and McGuinesses rallied when legendary leaders from the Race of Conn called them to rise against Henry VIII's invasions, King James I's settling of the Scotch, and Cromwell's intrusions into Ireland.

Clannishness would see them through. In the counties of the mother country, clan leaders could count on thousands of kinsmen to come out of hidden crofts on short notice if their way of life was threatened, as for instance at the Battle of the Boyne. It made no difference to the Tennessee lads that the McGavocks hadn't come from the same glen, and were, in fact, on the enemy side of those encounters.

The Sons of Erin had to work hard to preserve that easy conviviality which was a part of their outlook on life. Hard work raised a great thirst in those who practiced the ancient Irish custom of friendly, frequent drinking. Amazingly, whiskey was not readily available on the Tennessee side of the river, so the lads would come out of their tent crofts and take rowboats out of the fort sally port and cross the river into Kentucky, where moonshine was plentiful.

The Sons of Erin had identical twin brothers from Heiman's original crew. They were Morris (Mo) and William (Willie) Fitzgerald. These bearded Irishmen had come up the hard way as immigrant orphans in the workhouses of Nashville. Both wore mud-covered, ten-gallon hats and frowned a lot. Their accents were a strange conglomerate of Irish and Tennessee dialects—"Tenth Tennessee" became "Tinth Tinnissee."

Private Jimmy Doyle figured out a way to tell them apart: "Willie's long, ratty-looking brown beard was most of the time dirtier than Mo's long, ratty-looking brown beard."[38]

The twins were dubbed the "Fighting Fitzgeralds," not from any resolve on the brothers' part to get at the Yankees, but merely as a description of the relationship they shared with each other.

On one seemingly quiet summer's evening in July of 1861 at Peggy's Tavern, Kentucky, the Fighting Fitzgeralds started a brawl.

Returning home from Peggy's Tavern, Mo and Willie ended up in the same rowboat. They began arguing about drinker's rights on a whiskey jug they were sharing. About midway out Willie decided to drown Mo by holding his head under the Tennessee River. The boat turned over, which proved to be a considerable problem, since neither could swim. Pat Griffin, Marty Gibbons, "Crazy Tom" Feeney, and Mike Carney, the harmonica player, managed to pull them to safety before the currents carried them away to Paducah. The next day the Fighting Fitzgeralds were assigned by Lieutenant Colonel McGavock to two six-hour shifts of digging and hauling fifty-pound rocks around the swamps of the river valley.

As a general principle, McGavock dismissed the nights out at Peggy's Tavern as a necessary diversion. It was his theory that "lads must be lads." On occasion during that summer, he made a few Dover-to-Nashville-to-Dover trips for the purpose of recruiting more Irishmen for the regiment.

Once while he was gone, Heiman grew impatient with the wild living of the Sons of Erin. Colonel Heiman proclaimed Kentucky to be off limits. Lads didn't need to be lads to that extent; he had the rowboats smashed, not a very good idea strategically for his command.

There was, however, a stashed rowboat, and the Sons of Erin took turns going for whiskey, drawing lots for the rowing job. On August 10 the honor fell to Patrick Sullivan and Timothy Tansey of I Company, a pair of farmboys from downstate Pulaski. Before their return voyage they secured their cargo of four large jugs to the rowboat.

A squall suddenly overtook the two, with waves so high that the pair thought for sure that their time had come. "Bejabbers, Paddy, and the boat will be overturned and we will lose our whiskey," Tim said to Paddy. "We sure and we won't. We will drink it and save it," Paddy said to Tim.[39] Drink it they did; with the refreshment adding to their courage and strength, they reached the shore safely.

By the end of the summer, McGavock had rounded up enough recruits for an official Confederate regiment, although the reinforced Sons of Erin were still smaller than most Civil War regiments at that early stage of the war. At Fort Henry on September 1, 1861, 720 officers and men, plus five non-combatants were mustered into regular Confederate service.

The official identification remained Tenth Tennessee Infantry Regiment of Volunteers (Irish). The Irish reference is exactly as it appeared in Richmond war department documents and suggests similarity to the designation "Colored" used in the Union service.[40] Clearly the Irishmen were to be thought of as different.

There were ten companies, all with their own elected officers. McGavock's original D Company became H Company, without thirty-two of the original 124 lads who did not re-register, including Matt Brown and Jimmy Morrissey. Heiman, as local commander of both forts, was officially the colonel. McGavock was again elected lieutenant colonel, with William Grace, a tall and energetic lad from Nashville, as major, third in the staff line of command.[41] Colonel Heiman and Lieutenant Colonel McGavock kept the same arrangement as before, which, in effect, gave McGavock permanent regimental command.

What percentage of the regiment was "mere" Irish as opposed to Northern Irish? Today names like Jones and Smith make ready assignment of nationality impossible. However, based on individual service records, it seems safe to assume that between eighty and ninety percent of the lads were immigrants from the southern counties or sons of immigrants from those counties. For instance, eyewitnesses Doyle and Griffin were both Tennessee-born sons of Irish immigrants who had come to Middle Tennessee during the potato famine in the 1830s and 40s. In none of the accounts, however, was there any talk of going back to the "Old Sod," as happened with the Irish in Federal service. For a variety of reasons, the Tenth Tennessee was thoroughly American-Irish.

Since the elected staff chaplain, recommended by non-Catholics Heiman and McGavock, was a Catholic priest, it can be assumed that Catholics comprised the largest group, making the Sons of Erin one of the two predominately Irish-Catholic infantry regiments out of the 669 infantry regiments in the Confederate Army. The other was the Sixth Louisiana, a unit of Irishmen from the docks of New Orleans.

All ten companies in the Tenth Tennessee were overwhelmingly Irish, but obvious Anglo names like Anderson, Ellis, Jepperson, and Winston also appear in all ten. Many of the commissioned officers were non-Catholics who could trace their ancestry back to Northern Ireland. This has nothing to do with prejudice, since all officers were elected. The natural tendency was to elect the organizers, several of whom were Scotch-Irish friends of McGavock, like Captain Saint Clair Morgan, who was popular with the lads.

The muster roll for the Tenth Tennessee at Fort Henry reads like a clan map of Ireland. There were twenty-four Sullivans, fifteen Connolys, thirteen Kellys, nine Murphys, nine Ryans, seven Joyces, six Farrells, six O'Donnells, six Rileys, five Morans, five O'Briens, five McLaughlins, five Mahoneys, four Doughertys, four Flahertys, four Harringtons, four O'Neills, four O'Sullivans, four Roaches, four Walshes, four Quinns. There were three Monohans, a Monihan, two Donohoes, two Donohos and an O'Donohou.

Tenth Tennessee Officers

(Top Left) Captain Lewis R. Clark of Tennessee.
(Top Right) Captain Thomas Gibson of Tennessee.
(Center) Colonel Randal W. McGavock of Tennessee.
(Bottom Left) Captain Saint Clair Morgan of Tennessee.
(Bottom Right) Captain Clarence C. Malone of Mississippi.

THE TENTH TENNESSEE INFANTRY
REGIMENT OF VOLUNTEERS (IRISH) C.S.A.[42]

Staff And Field Officers
Colonel Adolphus Heiman
Lieutenant Colonel Randal W. McGavock
Major William Grace

Appointed Support Staff
First Lieutenant John Handy, Adjutant
First Lieutenant Lafayette McConnico,
Assistant Adjutant
Second Lieutenant Randal G. Southall, Courier
Second Lieutenant William F. Beatty, Drillmaster
Master Sergeant John Ames, Assistant Drillmaster
Master Sergeant John W. McLaughlin, Quartermaster
Sergeant Felix Abby, Commissary Officer
Sergeant Bernard McCabe, Commissary Officer
Corporal James Hayes, Standard Bearer

Non-Combatant Staff
Father Henry Vincent Browne O.P., Chaplain
Doctor Dixon Horton, Surgeon
Doctor Joseph M. Plunket, Surgeon
Doctor Alfred Voorhies, Surgeon
Doctor D. F. Wright, Surgeon

Elected Company Officers (Line Officers)

A Company (McEwen)
Captain John G. O'Neill
First Lieutenant James McMurray
Second Lieutenant James White
Brevet Second Lieutenant William Michael Burke

B Company (Nashville)
Major William Grace
Captain Leslie Ellis

First Lieutenant R. W. McAvoy
Second Lieutenant William Isaac Poe
Brevet Second Lieutenant William Gleason

C Company (Nashville)
Captain John H. Anderson
First Lieutenant Henry Carter
Second Lieutenant William F. Beatty
Second Lieutenant L. P. Hagan

D Company (Clarksville)
Captain William M. Marr
First Lieutenant Lynch B. Donoho
Second Lieutenant Henry Monroe
Brevet Second Lieutenant Edward Ryan
Brevet Second Lieutenant William Dwyer

E Company (Nashville)
Captain John Archibald
First Lieutenant W. S. Flippin
Second Lieutenant George A. Diggons
Brevet Second Lieutenant Oliver H. Height
Brevet Second Lieutenant James P. Kirkman

F Company (Nashville)
Captain Saint Clair Morgan
First Lieutenant William Moses Hughes
Second Lieutenant John S. Long
Brevet Second Lieutenant J. N. Bradshaw

G Company (Nashville)
Captain Boyd M. Cheatham
First Lieutenant William Sweeney
Second Lieutenant Bartley Dorsey
Brevet Second Lieutenant Aloysius Berry

H Company (Nashville)
Lieutenant Colonel Randal W. McGavock

Captain William Ford
First Lieutenant Robert Joynt
Second Lieutenant Randal G. Southall
Brevet Second Lieutenant James Finucane

I Company (Pulaski)
Captain Lewis T. Waggoner
First Lieutenant John Handy
First Lieutenant Lafayette Mc Connico
Brevet Second Lieutenant William McCoy

K Company (Nashville)
Captain Samuel M. Thompson
First Lieutenant Joseph Phillips
Second Lieutenant John W. Bryan
Brevet Second Lieutenant Robert Erwin

The Tenth Tennessee was young: all in the regiment were under forty except for Heiman, and the youngest of all was the non-registered drummer boy of the all-Clarksville D Company, Daniel McCarthy, just turned fourteen.[43]

Becoming official Confederate soldiers didn't change the routine very much. It was still marching and digging with McGavock, carting logs and stones for Heiman. Dull routine or not, there definitely were some advantages in being in the regiment whose lieutenant colonel was a rich fellow. Fancy new uniforms, bought personally by McGavock, arrived in September. The new look gave the lads the appearance of Tennessee Zouaves. The jackets and pants were Confederate gray, with a scarlet line running down the pants legs. The hats were gray with scarlet trim, and best of all, the insides of the jackets, as well as the shirts, were bright scarlet. The commissioned officers also got crimson and gold trimming on their jacket sleeves. The enlisted men took good care of the jackets for a while; but Fort Henry was still hot in the fall. Soon the area was swarming with ditch diggers in bright red shirts which stood out for miles around.[44]

The construction project that the Sons of Erin were involved with at Fort Henry on the Tennessee was moving at a snail's pace, while over on the Cumberland, Fort Donelson was making no progress at all; there was still absolutely nobody over there. In September Governor Isham Harris sent a single man, Captain Jesse Taylor, a trained veteran of the U. S. Navy, to help with the placement of guns at Fort Henry.[45]

On October 7 Heiman sent McGavock over to Fort Donelson, with A, D, and I companies of the Tenth Tennessee to assume command. These were the three companies recruited from outside of Nashville, consisting of Irishmen from McEwen, Clarksville, and downstate Pulaski. Previously there had been no Confederates between the Union Army on the Ohio River and Nashville. After the arrival of three companies of the Sons of Erin, there were some 225 Irish Rebels between the Union Army on the Ohio River and Nashville.[46]

The commanding general responsible for this inadequate and potentially very dangerous state of affairs was Major General Leonidas Polk, 55, of Louisiana. Polk was then a two star army general who was also an ordained Episcopal bishop. He had been the West Point roommate and close personal friend of President Jefferson Davis, who had given him command of all Confederate troops in the West. As Southern commander, Polk's main duty was to defend the Big Three Rivers, the Mississippi, and the two inland rivers, the Tennessee and the Cumberland.

Unfortunately, Polk became so preoccupied with protecting his own garrison at Columbus, Kentucky, on the Mississippi, that he refused to send men and materials to Heiman or McGavock.[47]

On September 15 the President officially replaced Polk with General Albert Sidney Johnston, a move which both McGavock and Heiman viewed as salutary. In reality Johnston merely superseded Polk, who retained command of the "Big Three" rivers.

In October Colonel Heiman at Fort Henry warned General Polk that if supplies didn't arrive in time for the troops to do substantial building on the forts, when the seasonal rains came in January and February, both rivers would rise high enough for Federal gunboats to slip in and take over, almost unopposed. A few days later, Lieutenant Colonel McGavock at Fort Donelson backed up his colonel with a plea of his own, believing he might have some luck because General Polk was a relative of family friend, the late President James K. Polk. "We must have a regiment in here at once . . . .. Even the companies I have are poorly armed . . . .. If you could furnish us with better equipment, I would be much pleased," was what McGavock dispatched.[48]

Nothing happened. In November Johnston somehow managed to complicate matters even worse than they already were. He made two appointments that were in direct conflict with each other.

Major Jeremy Francis Gilmer, 43, was an army engineer from Savannah, Georgia. General Sidney Johnston sent him in to oversee the construction of fortifications at Paducah, Kentucky; Russellville, Kentucky; Dover, Tennessee; Clarksville, Tennessee; and Nashville, Tennessee. This command was referred to as the Clarksville District.

Brigadier General Lloyd Tilghman (pronounced Tillman), 45, was an army engineer from Paducah. Johnston sent him in, along with 4,600 untrained and poorly armed troops, to command all construction and military operations at both inland river forts, superseding but not replacing Heiman. "Dutch" Tilghman arrived at Fort Donelson on November 27 and divided his forces between the two places, sending McGavock and his three companies back to Fort Henry with Heiman and the seven Nashville companies of the Sons of Erin, giving both forts about 2,650 men each. This new arrangement proved to be less than satisfactory. Major Gilmer was from then on under-equipped and the supplies he did receive did not go to the river forts.[49]

General Sidney Johnston's Army Department
Central and Eastern Districts, 1861-1862

OHIO

IND.

ILL.

KENTUCKY

MO.

Bowling
Green

Hopkinsville

Burkesville

Dover

Clarksville

Nashville

Mississippi R.

Tennessee R.

NORTH
CAROLINA

Memphis

TENN.

Chattanooga

0 25 50 75 100

Miles

At about this same time, a group of North Alabama citizens sailed north downriver to Columbus to personally appeal to Bishop-General Polk to strengthen the defenses along the Tennessee River. Remarkably, Polk told them to go home, raise a home guard unit, and defend the river themselves![50]

Belmont, Missouri, was almost directly across the Mississippi from Columbus, Kentucky, with a ferry running between the two. If Belmont and the west bank of the river fell into Federal hands, then the east bank and the garrison at Columbus would have to be evacuated, leaving the Mississippi open to gunboats all the way down to southwest Tennessee. But the signs for controlling the river looked good for the Confederates. On November 7 at Belmont, an obscure Union brigadier by the name of U.S. Grant was driven back to Cairo by one of Nashville's Irish-American favorite sons, hard drinking, two-fisted Brigadier General Benjamin Franklin Cheatham, 41.[51]

Instead of reassuring General Polk that his own troops were able to defend the area, and freeing him up to send help to the river forts, General Grant's aggressiveness had the bishop-general holed up in his own garrison. In what had become almost a pathological obsession to defend Columbus, Polk decided to retire into a state of siege.

In the Clarksville District, Albert Sidney Johnston decided to delay the construction of Fort Henry on the east bank of the Tennessee in favor of building a new fort—Fort Heiman—on the west bank, something that should have been done six months earlier. The original "Kentucky sovereignty" issue had become a moot point by this time.

So General Tilghman was ordered to stop work on the east bank of the Tennessee and pack everything over to the west bank. At this point, of course, it was discovered that Colonel Heiman had smashed the boats. The Sons of Erin had to build new rowboats.[52]

The result of these changes in plans was that it almost guaranteed that not a single Confederate fort would be finished in time for the rainy season. There seemed to be no complaints from the Irish regiment, however, which found itself on the Peggy's Tavern side of the river.

Not that the lads of the Tenth Tennessee would have much time to indulge in festivity. They were going to have to take their fill of digging and marching in whatever fort they were stationed—at least for the immediate future. It was time to do whatever they could to get the forts really operative—the Northern threat was looming larger every day.

Gen. Sidney Johnston's Army Dept.
Western District, 1861-1862

ILLINOIS

MISSOURI

St. Louis

Cairo

KY.

Belmont

columbus

New Madrid

TENN.

ARKANSAS

Memphis

Little Rock

MISSISSIPPI

LOUISIANA

Yazoo
City

Vicksburg

Jackson

0   25   50   75   100
Miles

Chapter Two

Escape

Christmas Cheer

In the middle of December Lieutenant Colonel Randal W. McGavock was making plans for Christmas. The leader of the Sons of Erin thought his lads had worked hard, particularly on the new and trying Fort Heiman project. They were in need of some additional treats.With this in mind, he set out for Dover to make purchases with his unlimited personal credit. Against the wishes of Colonel Heiman, he had arranged with some Kentucky bootleggers to secure a generous amount of local moonshine, the only sort of whiskey available.[1] On the morning of December 23, then, a heavy supply wagon pulled out of a warehouse headed west on the Dover road. Four of the lads of the Sons of Erin, Denny Grogan and Pat Carberry of B Company, and Billie McCready and Mike Quinihan of I Company rode shotgun.

Jimmy Doyle's diary mentions the load of Christmas cheer that came out of the wagon: hams, turkeys, geese, ducks, cans of sardines, and crackers in wooden boxes, plus a surprising variety of coats, shoes, hats, and blankets.[2]

The extra, festive Christmas rations would be prepared by one of the most popular Irishmen in the regiment—Commissary Sergeant Bernard "Barney" McCabe.

On Christmas morning, Mass was celebrated in the fort by Father Henry Vincent Browne, the Dominican regimental staff chaplain of the Tenth Tennessee. Browne was a New Yorker who had been a convert to both Catholicism and the Rebellion. Some of General Tilghman's staff chaplains and officers provided other Christian services. However, a surprising number of Colonel Joe Drake's Mississippi Baptists attended the Mass.[3]

During the day the food and refreshments were shared as long as they lasted. "Randy Mack" and the Sons of Erin hosted all the others, who wandered back and forth between the camp sites and the fort.

The articles of clothing were dispensed among the lads who needed them the most. Drummer boy Danny McCarthy of Clarksville was presented with a pair of shoes which he really needed. Danny was known to be a poor child, and those were the first new shoes he ever had. In fact, his widowed mother had not been able to buy much of anything for him, in spite of her strong desire to do so. As it was Danny sent his $15 per month pay back home. The gift helped to offset the fact that the boy was away from home at Christmas for the first time.[4]

The Christmas spirit was so strong at Fort Henry that day, Doyle reported, that not even the Fitzgeralds started a fight.

In the evening, around a campfire, a hastily organized choir was rehearsed by a well liked officer, John G. "Gentleman Johnny" O'Neill, the captain of A Company. O'Neill was a mature, twenty-one-year-old native of Ireland, who had a lordly accent and well respected leadership style. Danny McCarthy danced, Mike Carney accompanied on the harmonica, and First Lieutenant Lafayette McConnico was a true sensation as a soloist.

The choir was a "wee bit" lacking in harmony but outstanding in volume. Hymns and carols were sung by Morley O'Shea and Pat Walsh of A Company, John Tully of B Company, Mike Sullivan of C Company, Marty Maloney and Denny O'Sullivan of E Company, Paddy Blye and Jesse Dunigan of F Company, Jack McGurty of G Company and Tim Leary of I Company.

Christmas had brought a huge gift, if you could call it that, to the door of General Albert Sidney Johnston. The dignified, fifty-eight-year-old Texan had been a top lieutenant of General Sam Houston in the Republic of Texas and had served as commanding officer of General Robert E. Lee in the Second U.S.

Cavalry. His foremost friend was Jefferson Davis, and Davis had presented his friend with a command that included the states of Kentucky, Tennessee, Missouri and Arkansas. This was the Confederate Army's Department of the West, or simply Department No. 2.

General Johnston's Christmas gift came with a bagful of problems. At the start of that new year of 1862, the Federals had two large armies poised to strike Johnston's command. On top of the western part of Confederate Department No. 2 was the Union Army of the Mississippi, about 60,000 men strong under the command of Major General Henry Halleck, 46, of California. On top of the eastern part of Confederate Department No. 2 was the Union Army of the Ohio, about 50,000 men strong under the command of Major General Don Carlos Buell, 43, of Ohio.[5]

To oppose these forces General Johnston had some 27,000 rag-tag volunteers scattered about. One half was unarmed. The other half was armed with squirrel guns, fowling pieces, and "Tower of London" flintlock muskets that had been used by General Andrew Jackson in the War of 1812![6] In addition to the thinly spread troops, Johnston had also inherited a list of subordinates: capable Generals William J. Hardee, Simon B. Buckner, Bushrod R. Johnson and Lloyd Tilghman. He also found himself commanding a quartet of commanders about whom history has been less kind: Generals G. B. Crittenden, John B. Floyd, Gideon Pillow and Felix Zollicoffer.

What Jefferson Davis needed on the Western front was a magician, not a general. The troubles were intensified by the fact that the Confederate President was totally preoccupied with the war on the Eastern front and the losing game of European diplomacy. He sent a good friend into a bad situation and wouldn't or couldn't give him any help.

General Johnston faced reality with considerable patience. (Some might say slowness.) On January 22, 1862, at his Bowling Green, Kentucky, headquarters, he learned from reading *The Louisville Democrat* that the entire right wing of his army had collapsed. This had occurred at Cumberland Gap, (called the Battle of Mill Springs, Kentucky) where the Cumberland River serves as a boundary for the states of Kentucky, Tennessee and Virginia. There a division of almost 4,000 Southerners commanded by Generals Crittenden and Zollicoffer were crushed by a division of General Buell's army commanded by Brigadier General George H. Thomas, a Union-loyal Virginian.

With his right (east) flank gone, the only soldiers then east of Johnston were wearing blue jackets. President Lincoln could launch a two-pronged assault from north and east, using the coordinated armies of Halleck and Buell, which is exactly what he had intended all along. All that Johnston could do was protect his left and center.

To the west was the Missouri District, later called the Department of the Trans-Mississippi, commanded by Major General Earl Van Dorn and Brigadier General Sterling Price.

The Confederate center had realistic hopes for survival. The problem was that Johnston, made insecure by lack of knowledge about where Buell's 50,000 Federals actually were, was starting to catch the same disease that was gripping General Polk in Columbus—siege mentality. The end result of all of this was that the Clarksville District continued to be neglected, especially the two inland river forts, and time was running out.[7]

On Wednesday, January 29, 1862, black clouds massed in the skies over Forts Henry and Heiman, and it began to rain and rained hard all day long; the Tennessee River was rising. Half-forts would be a more accurate description for what had been built. General Tilghman had given up on the less than half-finished Fort Heiman and was across the river, on the east bank, again working on the still incomplete Fort Henry. Nothing had changed: Tilghman, Heiman, McGavock, and the other Confederate officers continued to face problems of no commitment at the command level, no materials, and inadequate personnel.[8]

On the morning of the heavy rain, the bugle had

sounded for the Sons of Erin at 4:00 a.m., as usual. At morning roll call, McGavock had cited four lads for distinguished service: Willie Muldoon and Tom Slattery of B Company, Mike Laffey of G Company, and Paddy Kearnes of K Company. Because of a missing diary page, their meritorious deeds remain unknown. If the distinguished service wasn't involved with the heavy construction they had been doing, it should have been: the workers at the river forts had continued their back-breaking labor even as the Union threat loomed; in fact, they had accelerated it.

Later that day Mo and Willie Fitzgerald got into another of their altercations. "Crazy Tom" Feeney egged them on by asking who was the oldest and continued to mutter afterwards that the brothers had fought the "Battle of the Womb."[9]

On Thursday, January 30, the rain continued. Fort Henry was taking in a ton of water, while Fort Heiman was dry as a bone. Colonel Heiman himself, irritable and short-tempered, spent all day supervising the placement of sandbags.

The Irish-born regimental mess sergeant, Barney McCabe, 28, of B Company, was uncharacteristically irritable himself, and even profane. He was experiencing difficulties. It was better than one-hundred yards from the fort to the Tenth Tennessee encampment. With all the rain and mud, heavy-set McCabe was having his troubles getting supplies hither and yon.[10]

General Tilghman supplied McCabe with two extra mules to assist with the heavy load, a pair the regiment had named George and Herm. In the deep mud the pair managed to get their feet tangled together and fell into a mud puddle. The mess sergeant tried to help them up, and had to pull and haul at them until they finally came out and delivered the miserable food supplies which were being issued by this time to the river forts.[11]

For McGavock, the coming of the rainy season meant more than just quartermastering troubles. It meant the days of marching and digging would soon be history. The Yankees were coming.[12]

As commanding general of all Federal forces in the West, Henry Halleck was responsible for the two Western armies, Buell's and his own. He was remaining stationary at his headquarters in St. Louis, eager and willing to let General Polk remain stationary in Columbus, Kentucky.

General Halleck was passed off by almost everyone who ever came to really know him in the war as a light-weight bureaucrat who did not even know his own limitations. He did, however, have sense enough to know that he needed to do something soon, or get fired like the other two generals President Lincoln had already tried in the West. Halleck desperately needed a personal victory. And he had just the right man in mind to move on Fort Henry.

Twice within three days during that January of 1862, Brigadier General U.S. Grant, 39, of Galena, Illinois, had asked his superior to let him go south up the Tennessee River and take Fort Henry, using a combination of army and navy power. Halleck had dismissed the idea as "madness."

However, the Union commanding general needed to even the score on Don Carlos Buell, who had technically been in command at Cumberland Gap. Also, Federal intelligence reported (inaccurately) that General P.G.T. Beauregard was coming west to reinforce Sidney Johnston with three brigades of fifteen regiments.

If Grant failed, Halleck could sit back and let his subordinate take the blame. If Grant succeeded, Halleck, as his commander, would take the credit. On Thursday, January 30, General Halleck wired General Grant: "Make your preparations to take and hold Fort Henry. I will send you written instructions by mail."[13] Sam Grant didn't need to wait for the mail. He was off and running.

On Friday evening, January 31, 1862, some of the lads of the predominantly Irish-born, Catholic, all-Clarksville, Montgomery County D Company had to do picket duty south of the fort on the river near Paris Landing, Tennessee. The hardy lads included Dan Daley, Larry Landrigan, Owen Keenan, Josh Macey, and W. S. "Lunny" Lunn, all of whom were former employees of the Clarksville Iron Works. (Lunn, a blacksmith, was one of the few native born non-Catholics in the Clarksville Company.)[14]

The cold, wet, and irritable sentinels vocally expressed their displeasure with army life. A pair of local pro-Union farmers passed through, and a few heated words were exchanged over the constitutional right of secession.

On Saturday, February 1, Confederate scouts reported some Yankee cavalry movement in the Paducah area. Also that day a pro-Rebel Kentucky farmer presented the Sons of Erin with several complimentary jugs of his own special swill, overproof and very strong. The men began immediately to drink the concoction. As the dedicated reporter of meaningless camp news, Private Doyle reported the following as inebriated: Paddy McGivney, Connie O'Donnell, and Garrett O'Hara of A Company; Paddy Carmudy and Paddy Garraghan of B Company; Paddy Riley and Hugh Tonney of C Company; Paddy O'Keefe of D Company; Jerry O'Donahou of E Company; Paddy Boyle, Joe Moriority and Jack Purcell of F Company; Wally McAvellay of G Company; Harry McGinnis of H Company; and Coleman Connolly and Ducan Duffey of K Company.[15]

The heavy drinking reported about the Tenth Tennessee is not an Irish stereotype; it was the reality. Certainly the Irish drinking tradition from the mother country and the scant respect for the "muckety mucks" of the army contributed to the frequent drinking, on and off duty. Irishmen depended on their social drinking to get them through the daily lives of hard-working laborers. There is no evidence to suggest that regimental drinking hindered the performance of regimental duties; in fact, it sometimes may have helped.

Whether or not the Sons of Erin and other Irish soldiers of the Civil War drank more than the soldiers of any other ethnic group is difficult to determine. On both sides the battle against drinking was a constant one, and in periods of inactivity or stress or when the weather was bad, the drinking was worse. One thing is for sure; the Sons of Erin made no effort to cover up their fondness for the jugs.

Throughout that first weekend of February, scouting reports were coming to Fort Henry that some sort of an enemy advance was imminent.[16] Rumors were rife that battle was inevitable. On Sunday morning, February 2, Father Henry Vincent Browne celebrated Mass in the fort for the members of the Tenth Tennessee, asking for the Lord's favor in the coming battle and a return to peace. Nearly all of the lads of the Irish regiment, of all denominations, attended that last Fort Henry Mass on the Tennessee River. Missing were the lads listed by Doyle, who were hungover.

Cairo is the small town at the bottom tip of the arrowhead that is the state of Illinois. At Cairo, the Mississippi and Ohio rivers come together, while at Paducah, Kentucky, directly east of Cairo, the Ohio and Tennessee rivers flow together. Cairo, then, was a direct water link to Fort Henry.

General Grant's plan of attack against Fort Henry called for a coordinated three-pronged army-navy operation south up the Tennessee River from Cairo through Paducah to the fort. To accomplish this deed, "Old Brains" Halleck had given him two full infantry divisions of 15,000 men, and some artillery and cavalry scouts. Troop transports would move the detached army corps. The navy consisted of seven gunboats manned by 2,500 soldiers converted into sailors.[17]

The navy squadron and the two army divisions were commanded by General Grant's top three subordinates, all of whom were considerably older than the commanding general. As supplied by General Halleck, the list was headed by Navy Commodore Andrew Hall Foote, 56, of Connecticut.

Deeply and puritanically religious and one of the few true abolitionists in Union service, Foote was a navy veteran of forty years with an outstanding record.

Brigadier General Charles Ferguson Smith, 55, of Pennsylvania, commanded Grant's Second infantry division. C. F.

40

Smith, a man who was literally a legend in his own time, had been for many years the Commandant of Cadets at West Point, and professional soldiers on both sides revered him. "By all odds the handsomest, stateliest, most commanding figure I have ever seen," was what soldier-writer Lew Wallace wrote about him.[18]

Brigadier General John Alexander McClernand, 50, of Illinois, commanding Grant's First division, was a horse of a different color. Here was a man who was a legend in his own mind. A civilian political appointee, "Blackbeard" had exchanged his seat in Congress for a brigadier's star. General McClernand's personal ambition stood out in an era filled with ambitious men. Firmly he held the belief that after the war "aggressive" and successful military commanders would find the road to political advancement. He was, therefore, willing to take chances—with his men's lives. Grant didn't like the fellow at all and was convinced he needed watching.[19]

The plan to take Fort Henry was simple and bold. From intelligence reports, General Grant knew some but not all of the factors he needed to know: one missing piece of information was the range of the Confederate guns. So the first order of business was a navy reconnaissance probe. The commanding general had to know where to safely land his transports. Should he disembark at a site three miles north of the fort, or at a site nearly four and a half miles away? Once that factor had been determined, the operation would proceed. Phases one and two would be simultaneous.

General McClernand's First division of 9,000 men would land on the east bank of the Tennessee River and march south to Fort Henry. General C. F. Smith's Second division of 6,000 would land on the west bank and march south to Fort Heiman. In the third phase, Commodore Foote would sail his seven gunboats south up the river and knock out the Rebel guns in the fort. And while all of this was going on, Union cavalry scouts would be keeping track of Confederate infantry movements.[20]

The moment was ripe for Grant's advance; the rainy

Brigade Commanders of the Sons of Erin

(Top Left) Brigadier General John Gregg of Texas.
(Top Right) Brigadier General Robert C. Tyler of Tennessee.
(Center) Colonel Adolphus Heiman of Tennessee.
(Bottom Left) Brigadier General Thomas Benton Smith of Tennessee.
(Bottom Right) Brigadier General Joseph B. Palmer of Tennessee.

season would allow the transports and boats to move at ease up the swollen river. Of course it might be said that the same rain that was so good for sailors might not be all that advantageous for foot soldiers, and that this was one aspect of the plan that seems to have been overlooked.

Colonel Heiman Versus the United States Navy

On Monday, February 3, 1862, General Grant's troop transports were on the move from Cairo to Paducah, while his gunboat fleet was headed south up the Tennessee River from Paducah toward the Confederate garrison at Fort Henry and the Sons of Erin. Several types of cannon defended the hastily built log and stone fortress: there was a squat, stubnosed howitzer-like cannon that fired fifty-pound balls—the columbiad, it was called. There was also a rifled cannon which could be accurate and deadly, as well as smoothbores without as much accuracy as the rifled ordnance.

General Lloyd Tilghman had only 2,659 Confederate soldiers to throw up against General U.S. Grant's 17,500 army and navy Federals. Tilghman, however, was well organized and logically divided his forces into two brigades, with both getting whatever was available.

His division was organized as follows:

First Brigade (Colonel Adolphus Heiman of Tennessee), consisted of the three largest infantry regiments, that is, the Tenth Tennessee, the Forty-Eighth Tennessee, the Twenty-Seventh Alabama, plus a small battery of four guns, and a small battalion of cavalry. Total of 1,444 men.

Second Brigade (Colonel Joseph Drake of Mississippi), Consisted of the three smallest infantry regiments, that is, the Fourth Mississippi (Drake's own unit), the Fifteenth Arkansas, and the Fifty-First Tennessee, plus all the heavy artillery with seventy-five gunners inside the fort, a small battery of three guns outside the fort, two companies of regular cavalry, and one small detachment of cavalry scouts. Total of 1,215 men.[22]

Five miles south of Fort Henry was Paris Landing, one mile south was the Charlotte road, one mile north was the Dover road, three miles north was Panther Creek, and finally a little better than four miles north was a place called Bailey's Ferry.

On the morning of Tuesday, February 4, 1862, the position of the six Confederate infantry regiments was confused. The Tenth Tennessee and the Fourth Mississippi were bivouacked near their rifle pits. Sitting over in the roofless shell that was Fort Heiman were the Twenty-Seventh Alabama and the Fifteenth Arkansas. Down at Paris Landing the Forty-Eighth and Fifty-First Tennessee regiments formed the Confederate left flank. Why General Tilghman wished a left flank at all is not clear; not a single Federal had ever been spotted south of the fort.

Tilghman himself wasn't present at Fort Henry. The previous day he had gone over to Fort Donelson to check out what was going on over there with the other half of his command. He encountered no activity there, but remained anyway.[23]

At about 3:00 a.m., Lieutenant Colonel Randal W. McGavock was startled out of a less-than-restful sleep by small arms fire. Hesitantly peering out his tent, the first thing that he noticed was that, in addition to being pitch dark, it was also pouring rain, as it had been almost continually since January 29. The shots were from the Confederate sentinel across the river at Fort Heiman, who was in turn relaying a signal from the pickets up at Bailey's Ferry. Three shots meant the menacing approach of three Union gunboats, and three shots it had been.[24]

McGavock woke his courier and cousin, Second Lieutenant Randal G. Southall, whose task was to make his way down a muddy track on horseback to Paris Landing to bring up the two Tennessee regiments. What McGavock could not do was to bring over the two regiments from across the river. Only Colonel Heiman, as acting fort commander could do that, and he was reluctant to act without the knowledge of General Tilghman, who, of course, was not around.

"Randy Mack" had the bugle sounded, and cheerfully greeted the lads with a special message. "The boys from the northwestern waters are coming," he said, which seems to have been his way of referring to Illinois and Indiana troops.[25]

By 5:00 a.m., the Sons of Erin and the Mississippians were standing at battle alert in the rain and mud in the rifle pits. When courier Southall returned from his mission, he found McGavock in his tent, sitting on his almost submerged sleeping bag with a blanket over his head, writing something into his notebook.

The efficient courier saluted formally and properly informed his commanding officer that the two Tennessee regiments were about to arrive on their rickety old boats, the *Boyd* and the *Dunbar*. McGavock got up and put an arm around the young officer's shoulder, grinning from ear to ear. "Better go tell that old German buzzard that our friends from the northwestern waters are about to pay us a visit," was what he ordered.[26]

McGavock's message to Heiman wasn't needed. The Prussian colonel was already barking out orders inside the fort. In fact the gunners hadn't slept any better than the infantrymen; there was more water in the fort than in the tents. The first level had taken in two feet of river and the Tennessee was rising every minute.

The gun crews were soon in place, with five men assigned to each one of the eleven functioning cannon, one columbiad, one rifled gun, and nine smoothbores. Colonel Heiman then sent a message to General Tilghman at Fort Donelson, informing him that the blue-clads were in the process of advancing, a premature pronouncement. General Grant and Commodore Foote were stalling for time before making the probe, trying to land a few cavalry scouts at Bailey's Ferry, all in the dark and fog and pouring rain.[27]

Southern scouts hadn't been able to supply much information, for the simple reason that there wasn't much happening to report about. Not satisfied, Heiman ordered McGavock to send out reconnaissance patrols. Shortly after 7:00 a.m. the lieutenant colonel sent B Company under Captain Leslie Ellis up the east bank of the river, and C Company under Captain John Anderson over the Dover Landing and up the west bank.

Heiman positioned the Fourth Mississippi and the other eight companies of the Sons of Erin in the rifle pits, supported from behind by the Forty-Eighth and the Fifty-First Tennessee regiments, all pointed north, leaving the Twenty-Seventh Alabama and the Fifteenth Arkansas across the river, supposedly to "protect" Fort Heiman. Cavalry Captain John Milner of Heiman's brigade, with his single company, was moved inland to the east in order to occupy the small roads leading from Bailey's Ferry, a mission made almost impossibly difficult because of the flooded swamps and lack of visibility.

Nervously keeping busy, Heiman ordered Colonel Joe Drake forward, with two of his companies and with one smoothbore and one gun crew, to the farthest rifle pits, three-quarters of a mile north of the fort, to serve as a sort of right flank, protecting the Dover road. Unfortunately, the cannon fell into a swamp hole and couldn't be rescued.[28]

By now Heiman expected some decisive results from the twelve torpedoes (mines) that he had carefully placed in the river north of Bailey's Ferry. He was to be disappointed; rains had elevated the river so high that all dozen of the contraptions were rendered useless. Northern sailors fished them out of the water, disarmed them and kept them for trophies.

Union gunboats started to shell the Confederate "forces" in the neighborhood of Bailey's Ferry at 9:00 a.m. No one out there was actually in range, except for a few of Milner's men who quickly got out of the way. Ellis and Anderson and the lads of B and C companies returned up to their waists in mud to report what Milner's courier had already reported—some Yankee horse soldiers had landed. Still, there might be respite—there wasn't yet a single infantry transport in sight.

Water had risen to nearly two feet over the sandbags

that had been dumped at the foot of the fort, and McGavock was one of the few Southerners who could stand upright without drowning.[29]

But the weather wasn't playing favorites. The Union troopers couldn't get any closer to Fort Henry than Panther Creek, which flowed in and out of the river, east and west, but was so swollen that the crossings on both sides were submerged. They and their animals were stuck. Scouts on both sides of the river had to travel inland and find a way to move south, and men and animals slumped and plugged along through the mire.[30]

The only fellows to benefit from the downpour were the soldiers-converted-into-sailors of the United States Navy. From his guest seat aboard the flagship, Essex, General Grant was viewing the scene and making plans for movement south up the river.[31]

By 11 a.m. that dark morning, the Sons of Erin had already been standing and/or marching in the rain for eight hours. Heiman had his gunners move the ammunition away from the water to the parapet walls, making the potential of a direct hit more deadly than ever. Apparently still experiencing a case of nerves and loneliness at the top of fort command, Heiman sent another message to Tilghman suggesting the potential seriousness of the situation.

Finally at 12:00 high noon, all seven Federal boats came in sight some two miles north of Fort Henry, "belching black smoke." They formed a double line across the river, with the four ironclads in a single row, followed by the three wooden warships. Then the *Essex*, piloted by Commander William D. "Dirty Bill" Porter, with Grant and Foote aboard, moved to the point position, making it a 1-3-3 formation.[32]

Inside the fort, everything was in a state of readiness, with one problem existing, and that was major—nine of the eleven Confederate guns were out of range of the Union boats. Heiman was anticipating that the boats would move up, but they didn't. Grant was still looking back at the east bank, waiting for his scouts to appear, not knowing that they were trapped at the north side of Panther Creek.

By 12:30 Heiman had not been able to gain any information on possible Northern strength. The Union boats sat on the water motionless, like sleeping ducks, and the gray-clad scouts had nothing to report. For all that Heiman knew, General Halleck's army of 60,000 might be out there somewhere in the woods, reinforced by General Buell's 50,000.

Knowing that the enemy hadn't landed any infantry units *by river*, Heiman took a calculated risk, and sent McGavock and the Sons of Erin north along the east bank on another reconnaissance patrol.[33] The Irishmen complained about a "phony war" in the mud and fog and rain but stumbled through the sodden underbrush anyway.

At 1:00 p.m., Tuesday, February 4, 1862, the Civil War came to Middle Tennessee. Ten hours after having first been spotted, the Northern gunboats opened fire with both solid shot and exploding shells, a fire that was immediately returned by the two big Southern guns.[34]

The Sons of Erin, marching through the mud, stopped and watched, like spectators at an athletic contest. McGavock kept them moving, anxious to discover if there were any hidden Yankees out in the woods. Suddenly, a big grin appeared on the lieutenant colonel's face.[35] At the same time McGavock was grinning, Heiman was whooping and yelling along with the crew of the rifled cannon on top of Fort Henry.

At the exact time that Colonels Heiman and McGavock were enjoying themselves at the sight of the firing, General Sam Grant was lying flat on his back in the boiler room of the Essex, calmly puffing on a cigar. A vital piece of intelligence—

the very one he had needed, concerning the enemy's artillery range—had been supplied when an exploding shell came crashing into the bridge of the flagship, knocking the commanding general down a flight of stairs. Imperturbable as always, Grant, who was unhurt, realized that he had better be safe than sorry. He needed to land his infantry transports back at Bailey's Ferry instead of up at Panther Creek.

At 1:30 Commodore Foote advanced his flotilla to within 1,700 yards of the fort, and opened up with all fifty-four of his guns concentrated at the artillery positions on the walls. He had hoped to come under the range of the two big Rebel guns, but Colonel Heiman skillfully adjusted the sights.[36] From the closer range the nine smoothbores got into the action, bouncing their overweight bowling balls off the hulls of the ironclads.

Amidst the gun-smoke and noise and rain and fog, one of the clamps of the columbiad broke. Fearing that the cannon would implode, Heiman ordered it shut down, transferring the gun crew to the smoothbores. Frustrated at the turn of events, the Prussian colonel waved his fists at the Yankee boats, swearing in German at the top of his voice.

At about 1:45 a Union shell landed directly in the fort, but there was so much water in the place that it never did explode.[37] General Grant had seen and heard enough. At 2:00 p.m., to the cheers of the Sons of Erin and other Rebels, Flag Officer Foote turned his gunboats around, went north down the Tennessee River, and tied-up about eight miles away.

Opposing points of view emerged almost immediately and debate continued among historians: that the one hour artillery bombardment of February 4 was a Confederate military victory, or that it was a successful Union probe. Actually, both points of view were accurate. Heiman's gunners expressed their correct opinion on the subject by shouting for joy and throwing their hats around. Grant, rightly believing he had successfully completed the first phase of his plan, ordered his infantry in from Paducah. And the distressed Heiman sent yet another courier over to Fort Donelson to try to find out why Tilghman was still there.

> *I was satisfied that we could not hold the fort on the heights opposite [Fort Heiman], and that it would be prudent to move the forces [two regiments] from there to Fort Henry, but I did not want to take responsibility without the order of General Tilghman,*

Heiman admitted.[38]

So the Southerners were caught in a basically unsatisfactory situation: the commanding officer was away at the time of attack, and the number two officer was unwilling to take what should have been an obvious step without orders.

The Northerners didn't have such a problem of indecisiveness: Foote, Smith, and McClernand took direct orders from Grant, who was omnipresent.

It was still pouring at 5:00 p.m. when the Sons of Erin finally reached the south bank of Panther Creek. Pairs of eyes peered out from behind trees on the opposite bank. The arriving Irishmen were warmly greeted by Milner's cavalrymen, alone in the wilderness. It was at this time that Captain Milner told Lieutenant Colonel McGavock that one of his (Milner's) men had been wounded by a Yankee sniper. The men from the northwestern waters were close at hand—too close.

While the two were talking, random shooting started up on both sides of the creek. Visibility was bad, so McGavock put a halt to the waste of ammunition, rounded up his best marksmen, and gave them the best muskets. A double line of eight lads in each line was formed in a wooded area along the creek. Each line alternated four quick volleys, which drove the Boys-in-Blue out of sight.[39]

It could be pretty clearly seen that one of the Federal troopers was knocked off his horse. This was confirmed by their staff to be a single casualty.[40] At that time the "hit" was important to the Sons of Erin, because it represented a first, definite success against the enemy. A debate would rage for years about which skirmisher should have been given the credit for the shot which hit the mark.

50

The five leading candidates were Captain John G. "Gentleman Johnny" O'Neill of A Company, First Lieutenant William F. "Beets" Beatty of C Company, Sergeant "Irish John" Ames of A Company, Sergeant John L. Prendergast, the Clarksville Sharpshooter of D Company, and Corporal Thomas "Long Tom" Connor of H Company, who was favored by most of the lads. Ames and Beatty got into a heated exchange about the origins of that fateful shot and McGavock did his best to settle the issue the next morning at roll call by citing all sixteen marksmen for something called "gallantry under fire."[41]

While the Sons of Erin were excitedly talking about this "second victory" of the day, one of Milner's scouts arrived with the disturbing report of Union infantry transports landing at Bailey's Ferry in full strength on both sides of the river.

That bad news was all that McGavock needed to hear. He started marching the regiment back to the fort, sending R. G. Southall ahead on horseback with the message for Heiman, leaving Milner's men behind in the woods.

Meanwhile, Colonel Heiman was sending his fourth message of the day, with an escort, to General Tilghman, warning him about the unwelcome arrival of the Northerners and advising him to return with an even bigger escort. As water approached the second level of the fort, the "Old German Buzzard" continued to curse in his native tongue.[42]

While the Sons of Erin trudged back in the muck, the Boys-in-Blue seemed to be serenading them with appropriate marching music, the sound of their brass band clearly drifting south up the Tennessee. The lads were regaled with such favorites as "Hail Columbia" and the "Star Spangled Banner." After such a glorious and victorious day, they were especially appreciative of "St. Patrick's Day In The Morning." Amazingly, some of the Tennessee lads believed the tune to be for their benefit. As a matter of fact, several members of the Union band were Irish themselves.[43]

The tired but satisfied Irish regiment made it back to their bivouac shortly after 11:00 p.m., followed shortly by General Tilghman, Major J. F. Gilmer, and three companies of cavalry, who arrived just in time to hear their own Irish regiment sing a loud and stirring rendition of "Yankee Doodle."[44]

Surprisingly, the day's work was still unfinished for some of the lads. At midnight Colonel Heiman ordered F Company under Captain Saint Clair Morgan, and H Company (McGavock's original crew) under Captain William Ford, back out into the storm. Their mission was to do picket duty at the river landing on the Dover road. In the early hours of Wednesday, February 5, the totally exhausted troops returned to report that the blue-clads were moving inland, east and west, thereby blocking any Confederate escape routes north of the fort.

At 5:00 a.m. General Tilghman brought over the Alabama and Arkansas regiments from across the river. Next he transferred First Lieutenants Lafayette McConnico and John W. McLaughlin from Heiman's staff to his own. (As it turns out, McLaughlin would never again serve with the Irish regiment, but McConnico would return briefly between December of 1863 and February of 1864 as adjutant.) The rifle pits north of the fort were assigned to the Tenth Tennessee, with the south entrenchments occupied by the Fourth Mississippi and the other four regiments in between.[45]

By 10:00 a.m. all the Confederate cavalry had been sent out to reinforce Milner's company in an effort to probe the Union advance. A cavalry skirmish was reported around 11:00 at Iron Mountain Furnace, Tennessee, northeast of Fort Henry. Both sides reported one cavalryman killed. Tilghman over-reacted to this news by sending McGavock, with eight of his companies, to reinforce the cavalry, allowing F and H companies to sleep. Colonel Joe Drake soon tagged along with some of his Mississippians. All of this marching proved to be yet another wild goose chase in the mud and fog and rain: the cavalry left before the infantry arrived, and all remained quiet on the wooded front.[46]

More grumbling than before could be heard as the Confederate infantry filed into camp around 4:00 p.m. By this time it was obvious that the U.S. Navy had taken the day off. It was also obvious that the time had come for the Sons of Erin to catch up on the recreation they enjoyed and seemed to use to survive: some serious card playing and whiskey drinking.

That afternoon aboard the *Essex*, Grant and Foote were examining one of Heiman's torpedoes with interest. When it began to hiss, both ran for cover. Meanwhile, in the camp of the Irish Rebels, the card game and whiskey drinking entered a new phase. Four of the lads, Eddie Byrnes and Patrick Hurley of D Company, Tim Flaherty of K Company and Mo Fitzgerald (without his brother) of G Company were engaged in a spirited game of poker for buttons, and the proceedings were being viewed by a good many spectators.[47]

During the contest a heated exchange took place between Hurley and Flaherty over the use of cards not in the original deck. As the growing debate became quite animated and included some of the onlookers, Mo decided to punch Byrnes in the side of the head. A wild melee ensued, with many of the onlookers choosing sides and participating.

Lads must be lads, as McGavock said, and the pressure had been intense in the last forty-eight hours. "Beets" Beatty, however, didn't see the situation that way. The drillmaster threatened to start shooting the drunken Irishmen at random if the fight continued, and the look on his face showed he meant what he said.

In fact there were bumps and bruises all over his face, the result of a sound licking he himself had taken from "Irish John" Ames in that argument over who had shot the skirmisher. Apparently Beatty was in no mood for any more fighting. The brawl ground to a halt.[48]

General Tilghman Versus the United State Navy

That night the rain finally stopped, the temperature was mild, and the Boys-in-Gray enjoyed a decent night's sleep. As the Sons of Erin slept, some nursing swollen eyes or serious bruises, there was a council of war going on inside the fort, featuring Tilghman, Heiman, Drake, and the captains of the gun crews. At that time the seemingly endless stream of Union transports landing at Bailey's Ferry was well known to the whole staff. Tilghman needed to make an intelligent decision, and he did so with imagination, even inspiration.

Tilghman's plans did not call for a surrender in the traditional sense of the word, but an evacuation, an escape, if you will. "Dutch" himself, like the captain of a ship, would remain behind in the fort with a fifty-four-man battery, consisting of B Company, First Tennessee Heavy Artillery, while the infantry and cavalry made the twelve-mile hike east to Fort Donelson, where they would be able to fight another day.[49]

The escape would not be made over the Dover road, a mile or so north of the fort, as the Federals expected, but over the Charlotte road, a mile south of the fort. The general laid out his plan and asked for comments. Given the odds of 17,500 to 2,659, all agreed. However, Colonel Heiman pointed out that there would be serious tactical difficulties that needed to be worked out.

First, the Charlotte road was more narrow than the Dover road, so real organizational skills would have to be used to get 2,600 men in place and moving. Heiman was a good organizer; Tilghman assigned him to be commanding officer en route. It was determined to bring up the rear of the columns with the two formally-trained regiments, the Fourth Mississippi second to last, and the Tenth Tennessee last. This was in the event of a Federal assault from the west, following the fall of Fort Henry.

Union scouts were also said to be everywhere, and troops would need to be seen in the rifle pits early in the next morning to fool the enemy. While the men were marching away, the skeleton crew of artillery defenders would have to hold out for an hour while Heiman put distance between himself and the Yankees, a most difficult task under the circumstances. Of course, the Southern plan depended on their own efficiency, plus the time schedule of the Northerners. Communication was the key, because McGavock, the Sons of Erin,

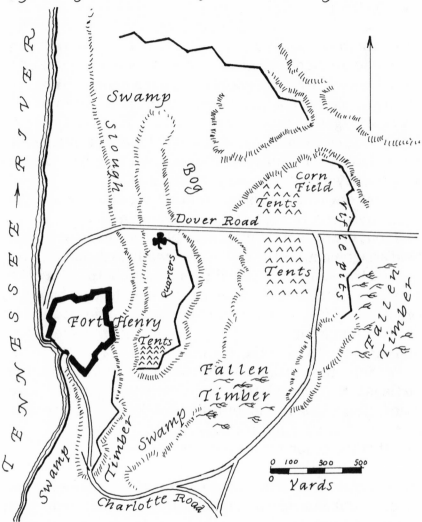

Fort Henry, February 6, 1862
Infantry Position of the Sons of Erin

TENNESSEE RIVER

Swamp

Slough

Bog

Corn Field

Tents

Dover Road

Tents

rifle pits

Fallen Timber

Fort Henry

Quarters

Tents

Fallen Timber

Timber

Swamp

Swamp

Charlotte Road

0 100   300   500
0   Yards

and all the others wouldn't know about the plan until they woke in the morning.[50]

At the same time that the Confederate escape plan was being hatched, over at the Union camp, Grant was awake and uncharacteristically restless. The victory which seemed to lie before his eyes was too easy. His combined army-navy forces would have a numerical advantage of seven to one, going up against only eleven enemy guns, most of them smoothbores. Something was wrong. He could smell it, but he couldn't put his finger on it. In the meantime, he kept his scouts busy all night, looking for clues.[51]

At dawn on Thursday, February 6, Confederate engineers were still trying to get the columbiad back in action. The Sons of Erin, uninformed of the plan, moved into the same field assignments as the day before, ready to do battle, while Federal transports continued to empty on both sides of the river. One of the Boys-in-Blue to get off on the east bank was Grant himself, astride his short-distance horse, Jack.[52] Not trusting McClernand, the Union commander wanted to be himself in the thick of the action.

Sometime around 10:00 a.m. a Southern scout told McGavock that the Northerners were massing on the Dover road. The lieutenant colonel, riding Tenth Legion, relayed the message through Southall to Heiman to Tilghman, who realized that the Union scouts had seen enough.

By 10:30 Colonel Heiman was getting his units in place on the Charlotte road, the Fifteenth Arkansas and the Twenty-Seventh Alabama up front, followed by the Forty-Eighth and Fifty-First Tennessee regiments, then the cavalry, then the Fourth Mississippi, and finally the Tenth Tennessee. That morning the weather had broken warm and sunny, and by early afternoon, it was actually getting hot.[53] Both the Dover and Charlotte roads were quagmires, but at least neither side would be rained on that day. While Heiman was organizing his retreat, Foote had assumed the position of two days before, only this time with the Cincinnati serving as flagship. The seven gunboats approached in a 4-3 formation, and this time they meant real business.[54] When the battle started, the Sons of Erin were just moving into line on the Charlotte road.

At 11:45 a.m. the boats closed to within 1,200 yards of Fort Henry and let go with everything they had. Inside the fort water was about one-third of the way up to the top, but what looked for the Northerners like a situation of shooting sitting ducks with monumental ease took a different turn. With General Tilghman himself serving as gunner of the rifled cannon in the disabled fort, an upset was in the making. The *Essex* and the *Cincinnati* were badly damaged, and the three wooden tubs were knocked out of the fight, all in the first half hour.

By 12:35 thirty-one shots had struck and disabled the *Cincinnati*, killing one and wounding nine. The *Essex* took twenty-two direct hits, one of which passed right through the ship, opening one of the boilers, disabling twenty-eight of the crew, and taking off the head of one unfortunate sailor.[55]

It was at that point, however, that in the space of just a few minutes, a series of disasters struck the Confederate gunners. First to go was the rifle, which burst in firing, disabling not only its own crew, but also those of the flanking smoothbores. Tilghman barely avoided death. Almost immediately the hastily repaired columbiad became spiked with its own priming wire and couldn't be repaired, because its crew was under such heavy fire. Two of the thirty-two pounder smoothbores had already been blown off the walls.

After 1:00 p.m. the battle came down to two ironclads, the *St. Louis* and the *Carondelet,* against six smoothbores, four of which were small twenty-four pounders. If that wasn't bad enough, those last four smoothbores were only a few feet above water![56]

Also at 1:00, after some delay, the Southern escape was under way. Heiman personally reported to the fort with the news that he was finally departing. Already blackened with soot and suffering from minor burns, Tilghman would have to hold out for another hour without his two big guns. To accomplish this he had about thirty-five healthy gunners left to put up against the 17,500 blue-clads. The two German-Americans shook hands. Twenty minutes later "Uncle Dolph" Heiman came galloping up to the rear of the retreat, to the cheers of the Sons of Erin.[57]

The *St. Louis* and the *Carondelet* had taken thirteen direct hits between them. After nearly two hours of artillery bombardment, the two-and-a-half inch metal plates of the ironclads were coming unhinged. But in the fort, one of the thirty-two pounders was blown away around 2:00 p.m., killing the entire crew, while the other one had to be abandoned for lack of thirty-two-pound ammunition. Then two of the twenty-four pounders were taken out by Federal shells, leaving Tilghman to defend the fort with two small smoothbores.

Meanwhile, General C. F. Smith beat General McClernand to the draw and occupied the unfinished and unmanned Fort Heiman with his division of 6,000 infantry soldiers, all of whom had ringside seats for the river battle. It was a classic case of overkill.[58]

At the same time that Commodore Foote was keeping his two gunboats afloat, and General Tilghman was holding out with his two smoothbores, and General C.F. Smith was entering Fort Heiman, twenty infantrymen from the Fifteenth Arkansas were cut off at a crossroads called McCuthens, Tennessee, and were captured by Union troopers, who ran into them completely by accident. Until then the Yankees had no idea that the Rebels were on the Charlotte road. The cat was out of the bag.

Some of the Federal scouts took the prisoners back to the Dover road, while others briefly probed the Confederate rear, only to be easily driven off by skirmishers of the Sons of Erin. Patrick Griffin in his often-read memoir insisted that it was at this point, in this small skirmish, that the regiment received its nickname "Bloody Tenth."

> It is a sure Irishman who will have the first blood
> in a fight. At the evacuation of Fort Henry, when
> the Yankees were pressing us closely, we rose up
> and won the sobriquet of "Bloody Tinth."[59]

It was the first step in the making of a myth and like many myths, the story was founded on inaccuracy. The Irishmen performed their duties very well, but there were no casualties on either side of that brief skirmish.

Meanwhile, back at the Tennessee River, Fort Henry had become a rubble of singed rock, and the last two smoothbores were submerged. The only resistance still coming from inside the fort was from a man in a rowboat with a squirrel gun.

Actually, General Tilghman had been trying to surrender for several minutes by waving the white flag himself from the top of the walls, but there was so much smoke that Commodore Foote couldn't see it. At 2:40 the flag was spotted and recognized. Tilghman's gun crews had held out for three hours, the last hour and a half after Heiman's march began. It was an unheralded stand for the Southerners in that early part of the Western war.

The Union Navy sustained eleven killed and sixty-two wounded. The Confederate batteries sustained five killed and sixteen wounded. Both sides lost one cavalryman, and neither side suffered any infantry casualties.[60]

When General Grant received the unpleasant surprise about the Rebel escape, he sent a courier to General McClernand. Grant's orders to McClernand were to turn right on the Dover road, proceed the two or three miles south through the woods, and attack the heavily outnumbered Southerners on the Charlotte road. It was a simple plan, but McClernand didn't do it. Later he claimed that he never received the message. In any case the Boys-in-Gray marched merrily through the mud, and the relationship between Grant and McClernand became even frostier than before.[61]

By 3:00 p.m. Fort Henry had become an extension of the Tennessee River, and the cutter bearing Foote to receive the formal surrender pulled right in through the sally port, where Tilghman was waiting for him. Tilghman earned Foote's respect by his courage and dignity. "Determined gallantry" was the way Foote described Tilghman's defense of February 6.

General Tilghman wasn't quite as cooperative with the newspapermen who always traveled with the Northerners. A Chicago reporter asked about the spelling of his name. "You will oblige me, sir, by not giving my name in any newspaper connection whatever," was the answer he received.[62]

By the time that Grant arrived with McClernand's division, the surrender was over, and the Stars and Stripes were already flying over Fort Henry.

The commanding general knew then what he didn't know the night before. The problem was himself. First of all, he didn't have any way of taking weather conditions into account. As a result, he wasn't even close to correctly timing the naval bombardment with the troop landings, thereby rendering the army's role as useless. Then he assumed that the Southerners would act in an expected way, by using the Dover road, and they hadn't. Finally, because of the superior numbers that Halleck had given to the First division, Grant had assigned his most important infantry position to his weakest subordinate, who let the gray-clads get away. It probably didn't matter in the long run. At any rate he was a man to learn from his mistakes.

By 6:00 p.m. the Confederate advance was near Peytonia Furnace, Tennessee, only about half way between the river forts, six miles to the good and six miles to go. Already strange things were happening. Captain George Gantt's company of cavalry came down with a bad case of the panics, and ran off, apparently thinking that the enemy was about to attack. They were supposed to be guarding the supply wagons, and McGavock described the flight as "disgraceful and most shameful."[63]

As a result of the summer-like heat, Northerners and Southerners were discarding their jackets, leaving both muddy roads carpeted. Aware that cold weather would resume, McGavock ordered his lads to pick up everything no matter how heavy the equipment was, or how tired and hot they were.

The Sons of Erin made a sort of sport out of it. Dick McAnany of D Company gathered up six coats and eight hats, while Jack Quinn of A Company hauled in five flintlocks. When washed, the coats and hats came in handy. The muskets proved useless, because they couldn't fire, which was probably why the other Southern soldiers dropped them in the first place.[64]

Finally the Confederate march came to a halt in a river bottom that was full of mud and water. The artillery horses floundered and fell, and the wheels went down over the hubs in the muck. The horses were all rescued, but one of the guns had to be left behind. If the Yankees wanted it, let them pull it out!

George and Herm, the regimental mules, were especially uncooperative with Mess Sergeant Barney McCabe, who pulled them out, swearing every oath in the Irish profanity lexicon. The exhausted lads of the "Bloody Tinth" finally dragged themselves into Fort Donelson around midnight.[65]

McGavock still found time and energy to write in his journal.

> *It is fortunate that we took the Charlotte road, for if we had gone over the regular Dover road, we would have been cut to pieces.... Before closing this day's sad work, I must bear testimony that the Tenth Tennessee never broke their lines during the long march,*

was what he proudly recorded.[66]

He found space to praise Tilghman and Heiman, but really blasted General Polk for his neglect of Fort Henry.

General Grant had, of course, obtained a substantial prize which had nothing to do with the heaps of stone rubble the Rebels had hoped to make forts of. He had brought the Tennessee River under Northern control. The very next day Foote's reserve gunboats steamed south up the river, destroying the railroad bridge of the Memphis and Ohio before it could be rescued by General Sidney Johnston. All in all the flotilla covered 150 miles, capturing six Confederate steamboats, including a fast 280-footer that had been converted into an ironclad. The long U.S. Navy thrust, all the way down past the state of Mississippi into Alabama, was dramatic proof that the Federals intended to put their new river to good use.[67]

The Illinois general, however, already had his sights set on Fort Donelson. On that same Friday that the boats went south, he sent a message over a wire headed northwest, destination St. Louis. "Fort Henry is ours. I will take and destroy Fort Donelson on the 8th [the next day] and return to Fort Henry," was what a confident Grant informed Halleck.[68]

The "return to Fort Henry" reference had to be included, because Grant had been given authority to take Fort Henry only. He had no authority to take Donelson.

General Grant need not have been concerned about the reaction of his commander. General Halleck was delighted by the good news, and, of course, used it for his own purposes.."Fort Henry is ours. The flag of the Union is re-established on the soil of Tennessee. It will never be removed," was what he immediately wired to Washington City, taking full credit for Grant's operation, which was really Foote's operation.[69] Grant would get no flack from St. Louis, as long as he kept winning in the name of General Henry Halleck.

Before being hauled off to Federal prison camp, General Lloyd Tilghman sent his official report to General Samuel Cooper, the Confederate Adjutant-General in the Richmond war department.

I feel that it is my duty to commend Colonel A. Heiman, Lieutenant Colonel R. W. McGavock, and the officers and men of the 10th Tennessee regiment (Irish). I hereby give testimony of my high appreciation. I place them second to no regiment I have seen in the army.[70]

Of course Tilghman hadn't seen too many other regiments in the Confederate Army. The praise wasn't really given for a few volleys fired at the Panther Creek and on the Charlotte road. Like McGavock, the commanding general was paying homage to the spirit, hard work and discipline of the Irishmen. Still, the real Confederate hero of Fort Henry will always be remembered as Tilghman himself.

Chapter Three
The Legend of Erin Hollow

Friday, February 7 to Tuesday, February 11, 1862

The weary Irishmen were given the opportunity to sleep in to the late hour of 5:00 a.m., when the bugle sounded roll-call for Friday, February 7, 1862. With his usual tongue-in-cheek humor, McGavock that morning cited George and Herm for "distinguished service" during the march. Even Sergeant Barney McCabe was caught up in the regimental spirit of the occasion, and joined the lads in saluting the pair of heroes with hurrahs. Soon, however, McCabe himself had to lead the obstinate beasts over to the fort to pick up morning rations.[1]

With the better than 2,500 escapees from Fort Henry, the garrison at Fort Donelson was back in strength to about 5,600 men. With General Lloyd Tilghman on his way to Federal prison, Colonel Adolphus Heiman was again in command, a situation which lasted only one day, to Heiman's relief.

Heiman, as original commanding officer of the Irish regiment, was partial to the Sons of Erin, even though they frequently drove him to distraction, and so he granted McGavock and the Tenth Tennessee at least two favors. Nearly ready-made rifle pits were assigned to them, eliminating the need for a lot more digging, and an advantageous bivouac was provided just beyond the cemetery, west of the town, a mere stroll away from the downtown area, including the Dover Tavern.[2] Lieutenant Colonel McGavock checked into the Brandon Hotel, declaring it to be his "headquarters." "It is very much crowded, but I managed to get something to eat and a place to sleep," he said.[3] The enlisted lads were also managing to get something to eat. Sergeant McCabe "borrowed" real pots and pans from the stockade, and there was hot "Irish" stew for supper.[4]

At the same time that the Sons of Erin were pitching their tents near the Dover cemetery, Confederate commander Sidney Johnston was still looking for General Carlos Buell and his 50,000 Federals, whom he believed to be the threat to Middle Tennessee.

Immersed in an old and inflexible military mindset that lumped commanders and commands according to the geographical location of their headquarters, Johnston missed the fact that Halleck's man Grant was directly threatening Nashville through Fort Donelson. That's because he didn't understand that the real menace was from land and not from the river.

At the same time that the Sons of Erin were paying their respects to the keeper of the Dover Tavern, a handsome, dapper little man got off the train at Bowling Green impeccably dressed in the uniform of a full Confederate Army general. P.G.T. Beauregard, one of the South's great heroes of the war's first year after the Battle of Manassas (Bull Run), had been transferred to the Western theatre by President Davis, who was foolishly trying to get rid of him.

Pierre Gustave Toutant Beauregard, 43, of New Orleans, was the highest ranking Catholic army officer in American history. The only quality about him that matched his raw courage in battle was his enormous ego and over-bearing temperament, which caused him considerable difficulty in relating to people, especially Jefferson Davis.

General Albert Sidney Johnston, who had a penchant for holding meetings, asked for a conference with Generals Beauregard and Hardee in Beauregard's Covington Hotel room.

The little Creole's perfectly correct English, enunciated with a slight French Quarter accent, was raspy from a recent bout with fever, but he could still make himself understood.[5]

Beauregard suggested a concentration of all Southern forces at Fort Donelson, where a realistic defensive stand could be made. The idea was that once Halleck (Grant) had been beaten back, the reinforced Confederate command on the Cumberland could then turn north and drive the slow-moving, elusive Buell back to the Ohio River. Hardee liked the plan; Johnston showed his disapproval by a slight shake of his head.[6]

Johnston's counter-plan had its strong points, too. It called for Hardee to evacuate his army corps of 14,000 (including Johnston himself) from Bowling Green, march directly to Nashville, and "commence the rapid building of fortifications" around the state capital, something that J. F. Gilmer was supposed to have done many months before.

While all of this was going on, Johnston said, Beauregard would take over at Columbus, Kentucky, for the immobilized Polk. The key was still Fort Donelson. The Confederates on the Cumberland would have to stall the Federals long enough to allow Hardee to strengthen the defenses at Nashville, while Beauregard was updating the fortifications along the Mississippi. But even if the plan worked, Fort Donelson was eventually going to fall, because of the lack of troop commitment. It would have to be forfeit to the Southern cause; that the generals would accept.

Beauregard and Hardee agreed with their commander's plan and it was undertaken. Johnston gloomily wired Richmond that Fort Henry had fallen and Fort Donelson was about to fall. His next step was to send some Clarksville District troops into Fort Donelson, and he began looking for a brigadier to implement the Dover part of his strategy.

Four of his brigadiers were in the area somewhere, but, amazingly, General Johnston didn't know where they were. His scouts had lost track of even his own army! He sent a vaguely worded message to Brigadier General John B. Floyd, 55, a former governor of Virginia, that Floyd was to command "the entire force."[7] Floyd received the telegram at Russellville, Kentucky, where he was waiting to do something with his five regiments, four from Virginia, one from Mississippi. He prepared to assume some form of command. The problem was that he did not understand that his commanding general was passing down to him control of the entire Clarksville District, including Fort Donelson, and that Fort

Division Commanders of The Sons of Erin

(Top Left) Brigadier General Lloyd Tilghman of Kentucky.
(Top Right) Major General W.H.T. Walker of Georgia.
(Center) Major General Bushrod R. Johnson of Tennessee.
(Bottom Left) Major General William B. Bate of Tennessee.
(Bottom Right) Major General John Calvin Brown of Tennesssee.

Donelson was going to need immediate attention. No one except Sidney Johnston knew Floyd was in charge, including Floyd.

Back at Fort Donelson the uncertainties of the immediate situation were beginning to tell. Command was shifting, with several different "commanders for the day" taking their turn. Colonel Heiman, of course, had come in immediately after the fall of Fort Henry. Then, on Saturday, February 8, Brigadier General Bushrod Rust Johnson, 44, of Tennessee, arrived, taking Heiman's and Drake's two brigades under his command to form essentially the same two-brigade division that Tilghman had at Fort Henry.[8] General Johnson, an Ohio-born Quaker, had been a West Pointer, a college instructor and an army engineer with a distinguished Mexican War record. Quiet, soft-spoken and scholarly, Johnson was an officer any army would have been glad to have. The Sons of Erin called him "The Old Professor."

Unfortunately for the Boys-in-Gray, the Old Professor was on the bottom of the totem pole of the four Confederate brigadiers in the Clarksville District, having received his star just two weeks earlier. He had been sent into Dover from Clarksville by his immediate superior, Brigadier General Gideon Pillow, who was due to arrive the next day himself.

General Pillow, 55, was a pompous fellow from Columbia, Tennessee, one of the few strong pro-slavery regions in the state. As the son of a wealthy plantation owner, he was able to buy his way through law school and secure a brigadier's commission as a paper-pusher on General Winfield Scott's staff in Mexico. He ran afoul of almost everyone who ever dealt with him, with those who sought the truth realizing he was vain, easily offended and completely inept as an officer. To the misfortune of the Confederates, he had the support of Governor Isham Harris, who just happened to be his law partner.[9]

General Sidney Johnston, not knowing what else to do with Pillow, had earlier sent him over to hole up in Columbus as the number two man to Polk, whom he soon alienated. In desperation Johnston shuffled him out of the way–to the Clarksville District. On Sunday, February 9, Johnston ordered Pillow to Fort Donelson, the third consecutive commanding officer for a day.[10]

After making the thirty-mile journey from Clarksville due west to Dover, Pillow had some of the enlisted men hastily assembled for his inaugural address. "The courage and fidelity of the brave officers and men under this command will drive back the ruthless invaders from our soil and again raise the Confederate flag over Fort Henry. Our battle cry will be liberty or death," he said.

Many of the Sons of Erin reported they had trouble keeping a straight face. Instead of talking about practical efforts to defend the still-standing Fort Donelson, the new man was blabbing about retaking the already demolished Fort Henry. Private Willie Fitzgerald muttered that if the new general wished to force a decision on liberty or death, he might be able to oblige with his musket.[11]

At bugle-call the next morning, Pillow made another speech. "I will never surrender this position, and with God's help, I mean to maintain it."[12] Later that same morning of Monday, February 10, without informing any of his subordinates, he decided to move a single infantry company to the artillery batteries—F Company, of the Tenth Tennessee. Not too much time elapsed before Captain Saint Clair Morgan had to inform Pillow that the Irishmen refused to go.

None of the Sons of Erin had any previous artillery experience and knew nothing about it, Morgan insisted. Besides that, they were stubborn when they could not support the action they were ordered to do and clannish, unwilling to separate themselves from their brethren.

General Pillow decided to exhort the recalcitrant Irishmen to do their sworn duty. Riding out to the regimental encampment near the cemetery, he ordered all the lads drawn up into line, once again without checking with division commanding officer Johnson or brigade commanding officer Heiman, or regimental commanding officer McGavock, or company commanding officer Morgan. All were baffled, or outraged by the behavior, which had no respect for the chain-of-command. McGavock reported the speech in full, and the emphasis is his.

> *You are Irishmen and I know that you will prove true to your adopted South. I have come here to drive the Hessians from this neck of land between the rivers, and to replant the stars and bars upon the battlements of Fort Henry. I will never surrender! The word is not in my vocabulary! I had Irishmen with me in the Mexican War, and at Belmont, where they proved themselves equal to any of our soldiery. Many of you know me* personally, *certainly all of you by* reputation, *and I want you to go now when I command you.*[13]

The pronouncement was greeted by utter amazement and dead silence. After a few awkward moments, Private "Crazy Tom" Feeney raised his hand like a child in a country schoolhouse. "General," he asked, "what's a Hessian?" Pillow turned and left without answering the question.

A steaming McGavock ordered the lads to fall out. Jimmy Doyle took Tom Feeney aside and informed him that a Hessian was a German mercenary, a soldier who fights all over the world for pay. (The misconception that Union-German-American soldiers were foreign mercenaries was actually common among the Southerners.)

"And all along if I wasn't but thinking us to be fighting the Yankees, and [now] if it isn't but Germans all over the whole planet earth we'll be in for," "Crazy Tom" responded.[14]

The officers of the Sons of Erin shook their heads in disbelief. No one could ever remember a general as stupid as Pillow. Still, an order was an order and it had best be obeyed. Johnson quietly talked to Heiman. Heiman quietly talked to McGavock. McGavock quietly talked to Morgan. Morgan quietly talked to his lads, and F Company moved out to their new assignment.[15]

Two hours later F Company was transferred back to infantry, and were greeted at the cemetery like long-lost cousins. The Irishmen had proven good at passive resistance.

On Tuesday, February 11, another general arrived. He was Brigadier General Simon B. Buckner, 39, of Kentucky, a West Point classmate and close personal friend of opposing general Sam Grant. In spite of prematurely gray hair, General Buckner was a strikingly handsome man, a likable and highly competent professional, who had recently been a real estate construction superintendent in Chicago.

In 1860 his home state called him back home to reorganize the state militia. When war came, he worked hard for state neutrality, not wanting to see Kentuckians fighting Kentuckians. Buckner was forced to make a choice. Respectfully he declined President Lincoln's offer of a commission as a brigadier general in the Union Army. On September 14, 1861, five months into the war, Buckner accepted the same commission from President Davis in the Confederate Army.

General Buckner ranked ahead of General Johnson but behind General Pillow, whom, from previous experience in the Mexican War he despised as much as other people did. Like Johnson and unlike Pillow, he had been a decorated hero of that conflict.

Lieutenant Colonel Randal McGavock was pleased to see Buckner's Kentuckians come in on the evening of Sunday, February 9, even though "Buck" himself wouldn't arrive for two more days.[16]

Actually, Buckner's "division" had only two completely intact regiments, the Second and the Eighth Kentucky regiments, plus a hodge-podge of small detachments. On Thursday, February 13, some of General Floyd's Virginians were added to Buckner's brigade-size division.

Buckner was frustrated about the small numbers rationed to him by Sidney Johnston. The Kentuckian had been given only one (the Second) of the five outstanding "Orphan" regiments of Brigadier General John C. Breckinridge's First Kentucky brigade. (The Eighth Kentucky was not part of the Orphan brigade consisting of the Second, Fourth, Fifth, Sixth and Ninth regiments.) Most irritating to Buckner was the fact that he hadn't been given any of Captain John Hunt Morgan's Kentucky cavalrymen.[17]

The boys of the Second Kentucky Orphans had a good deal in common with the lads of the Tenth Tennessee Sons of Erin; both regiments contained a large number of hard-drinking, rowdy outcasts. Not surprisingly the Orphans had quite a few Irishmen, lads like Ed Keene, Ollie Steele, and Ed Spears. On February 9 the Orphans were given a campsite well west of the Sons of Erin, but this did not prevent the Irishmen from finding each other like magnets.

The Irishmen of the two units hit it off well, so well, in fact, that they soon started hitting each other, Tennessee Irish against the Kentucky Irish. Using their superior numbers to good advantage, the Sons of Erin soon got the best of it.[18]

The Fighting Fitzgeralds were in the thick of the battle. McGavock, as always, dismissed the latest brawl as "lads must be lads." As usual, Heiman protested the behavior strongly, and to keep the peace with "Uncle Dolph," McGavock sent Mo and Willie Fitzgerald to Father Henry Vincent Browne for "counseling."

Chaplain Browne spoke calmly but sternly to the twins, seeking an explanation for their frequent overly aggressive behavior.

The brothers protested that their feelings had been injured; "Be sure and we win't be fitin' Fi-her, if 'em weren't be sying we tick finny," was what Mo answered. "You dint think we tick finny, do ye, Fi-her?" Willie wanted to know.[19] Browne consoled them without getting a firm promise that they would stop the fighting. Father Henry Vincent Browne was later overheard telling McGavock, in a lighthearted manner, that the twins' souls were as dark as General Bushrod Johnson's horse.

That same evening Lieutenant Colonel McGavock assigned picket duty. The chosen lads included Morris and William Fitzgerald of G Company. The next morning at roll-call, the Fighting Fitzgeralds were cited by McGavock for "commendable regimental spirit."[20]

On the evening of February 10, before Buckner and Floyd arrived, General Pillow had an unexpected surprise. It seems that General Johnston was being uncharacteristically generous. He then had with him at Bowling Green two small units of cavalry, one from Kentucky, the other from Tennessee.

The Western Confederate commander gave the small Kentucky outfit under Captain John Hunt Morgan to Hardee as advance guards for the march to Nashville. He gave the Tennessee "brigade" of eight-hundred men to the garrison at Fort Donelson. These cavalrymen made it to Dover that same Monday night. When the Tennessee horse soldiers reached the fort, their commanding officer, Nathan Bedford Forrest, presented himself to General Pillow at his headquarters in the Dover Inn.

The general greeted his fellow Tennessean warmly and offered him room and board at the inn.[21] Forrest, however, still an unheralded lieutenant colonel of cavalry, politely declined, declaring that he ate and slept only with his own men. The big trooper got down to business, suggesting a battle plan that Pillow expressed much interest in. The

Federals, with their large numbers, were moving slowly through the mud, because of the flooded creeks, ravines, and underbrush. All in all it was the perfect setting for an ambush.

According to the bold plan, the job of the cavalry would be to find the weakest point along the Union line. Cavalry and infantry would then join together and hammer a wedge through that particular spot, turning both Union flanks into the woods.[22] Once the line had been broken, it would be easier for the Confederates to do it again and again. It was a simple, yet brilliant plan which, if implemented, could have altered the course of the war in the West.

General Pillow liked the suggestion, because with his subordinates making all the plans and doing all the work, he could easily pick up the accolades himself.

Forrest, 40, of Memphis, an ex-slave trader and planter, the son of an Irish-American blacksmith, was an untutored military genius, a man with superior physical and mental skills. Equally outstanding in both regular and irregular cavalry operations, he soon became public enemy number one to the Union army. General William T. Sherman later placed a bounty on the head of the ferocious Rebel cavalryman, offering cash and promotion for any soldier who could assassinate him. "That devil Forrest was down about Johnsonville, making havoc among the gunboats and transports.... He must be hunted down and killed if it costs 10,000 lives and bankrupts the Federal treasury," was what Sherman dispatched to Grant in 1864.[23]

On February 11, General Floyd received a second wire from General Johnston, this one in clarification, telling him that he was, indeed, to command all troops at Fort Donelson.

Like Pillow, John Floyd was a political appointee. Not only had he been governor of Virginia, but he had also been the controversial Secretary of War in the cabinet of President Buchanan. The controversy was created when Floyd, anticipating the outbreak of war, moved army supplies and materials down south. His usefulness to the Southern cause ceased when he was commissioned as brigadier general in the Confederate Army.[24]

When General Floyd received the second telegraph from General Johnston, he himself wired General Pillow at Dover to meet him at Cumberland City, midway between Clarksville and Dover. On Wednesday, February 12, the two generals met for the first time.

Pillow laid out Forrest's plan: a flank assault on the Dover road. Floyd liked it for the same reason Pillow had. His subordinates would also make all the plans and do all the work and he could receive the praise. However, when Pillow discovered that Floyd was personally intending to lead the operation, Pillow abruptly abandoned the plan that he himself had just introduced. He could not let Floyd get ahead that way. Floyd for his part, sensing Pillow's retreat from the plan, and wishing to avoid a first meeting confrontation, decided to change directions and agreed that the plan lacked "clarification."[25] In short, the two generals decided to let the Federals keep right on coming.

The two left for Fort Donelson separately, first Pillow, then Floyd. The Virginian had to take care of some "unfinished business" and wouldn't make it until after the battle had begun.[26] Between the two of them, there was no real plan to save the fort. There was not even a clue as to what was going on. Disaster, or at least defeat, loomed.

Meanwhile, on the Union side, on Thursday, February 6, the very day that General Tilghman surrendered to Commodore Foote at Fort Henry, General Grant had met reporters. From his vantage point, it looked like taking forts was going to be a snap. As the newspapermen started to bid the general farewell, he gave them a warning. "You had better wait a day or two. I am going over to capture Fort Donelson tomorrow," was what he boldly predicted.

This startling news interested the journalist from Horace Greeley's *New York Tribune.* It sounded like a real scoop. "How strong is it?" he asked, to which Grant replied: "We have not been able to ascertain exactly, but I think we can take it."[27] Going strictly on a hunch, the reporter decided not to wait. Instead of hanging around, he made the long trip by river and rail back to New York, and filed his story about the fall of Fort Donelson.

When that same reporter made the reverse trip all the way back to North Middle Tennessee, he found himself another real scoop. The Confederates still held Fort Donelson!

Once again Grant had underestimated the strength and tenacity of the Southerners. Part of this was due to the relatively easy success at Fort Henry. Another part was that he had heard, through the scouting grapevine, that Gideon Pillow was the Rebel in charge. His opinion of Pillow was not high. "You can safely walk right up to any position commanded by Pillow and not expect a shot to be fired," was how he evaluated the Tennessean's military abilities.[28] Like Scott, Buckner, Heiman, McGavock, Saint Clair Morgan, and so many others, Grant's low esteem for Pillow was based on his own experience.

Practical conditions, however, got in the way of an immediate assault. It was taking a painfully long time for the Federal infantryman to march over the muddy Dover road. Then too, Commodore Foote's gunboats were back at Cairo under repair. On February 9 Halleck gave Grant an excellent reason for delay. Reinforcements were on the way. "I will send everything I can rake and scrape together from Missouri," was the way he put it.[29]

Actually, Grant's new Third division would be some 10,000 men, which was, in the Western theatre, more of an army corps in itself than a division.

The reinforcements were Westerners from Illinois, Indiana, Missouri, and Kentucky, to be commanded by Brigadier General Lewis Wallace, 34, of Indiana. A brilliant lawyer, writer, and politician, Lew Wallace had accepted his commission as brigadier only after seeking advice from his hero, General C.F. Smith.

General Halleck's plan to move the Third division of General Grant's corps called for eight transports to sail twelve miles south up the Ohio River and then forty miles south up the Cumberland River to Dover. There were 2,500 Boys-in-Blue in reserve at Fort Henry, 15,000 marching over the Dover road, plus the additional 10,000 expected to arrive from Paducah. That would make about 27,500 Union foot soldiers available for Grant to use at Fort Donelson.[30]

However, just as in everything else involving Halleck, there was a problem with the reinforcements. Grant was so confident that he decided to march his 15,000 immediately to the Confederate positions without waiting for Wallace's big division. And that proved to be his next mistake in the campaign.

On Tuesday, February 11, a Union council of war took place aboard the *New Uncle Sam*. Present were Generals Uncle Sam Grant, McClernand, and C. F. Smith, along with Commodore Foote–a Fort Henry reunion of sorts. Grant made sure that his subordinates were ready to go, but told them almost nothing. Later that same day they received a vague written order, stating only that a troop movement would begin the next day at Dover. It indicated no starting time and nothing that even resembled a battle plan. "The force of the enemy being so variously reported, the necessary orders will be given in the field," was the hit-or-miss way the instructions ended.[31]

And so, the coming struggle would pit one over-aggressive, over-confident competent general against two under-aggressive, under-confident incompetent generals. It was for reasons such as these that Civil War soldiers, like the Sons of Erin, drank.

Wednesday, February 12, 1862

Fort Donelson was not Fort Henry. The fort proper was a stockade of log huts that housed artillery gunners. On the Cumberland River, the Confederates didn't have to fight from or for a building, so there wasn't anything to be washed out by rain.

Fort Donelson did have one thing in common with Fort Henry on the Tennessee: it was located at a bend in a river. The Cumberland River flows south up through Paducah. If one follows the river on a map north to south, it crosses Kentucky into Tennessee and then turns east at Dover and runs east to Clarksville before heading south again to Nashville.

After the bend to the east, the banks along the river run north-south instead of east-west. The Confederate garrison was built at an angle, looking south just after that point where the river swings east, like the base of a hook. There were elevated heights all along that section of the river, making it an ideal location for natural defenses.

Confederate batteries were located in two different places. In front of the stockade, there was a one-hundred foot bluff. At the top the Confederates had a large 128-pounder rifled cannon, flanked by two thirty-two pounder smoothbores. Two-thirds of the way down, a ten-inch columbiad and two more thirty-two pounder smoothbores were dug into the bluff at its steepest point. All six of the guns looked out onto the river and were protected by logworks. Just to the left of the bluff, on a low ridge, were the "water Batteries," with more logworks. It was here that the Southerners planted six more thirty-two pounder smoothbores.

All in all there were twelve cannon on the Cumberland, in much better positions than the eleven had been on the Tennessee.[32] Just at face value alone, Fort Donelson would be a much tougher nut for the Federals to crack than Fort Henry.

The Confederate defenses, river and land, ran along a three-mile line. Looking north, from left (west) to right (east) was Hickman Creek, the water batteries, the bluff and the stockade, Indian Creek, the town of Dover, and Lick Creek. The two outside creeks, swollen in February, served as natural buffers for the defenders. Coming out of Dover headed east was the critical Wynn Ferry road to Clarksville, a direct land-link south to Nashville.

Looking out the front gate of the stockade, an observer would have been positioned at a northwest left angle toward Kentucky. Looking out the back gate, he or she would have been facing the hills, woods, and valleys of North Middle Tennessee. The Southerners' infantry rifle pits began a mile south of that back gate.

Directly south of the fort proper was the Confederate right flank in the Hickman Creek Valley, about 250 yards wide. This became the position of General Buckner's division. To the east of that valley was Indian Creek and the Confederate center, which was occupied by General Bushrod Johnson's division, including the Sons of Erin. Over on the far eastern end of the field, directly south of Dover, was the left flank in the Lick Creek Valley, about five-hundred yards wide. This would become the position of General Floyd's division.[33]

Facing south, General Johnson's left brigade was Colonel Drake's and his right brigade was Colonel Heiman's. The last regiment on the extreme right of Heiman was the Tenth Tennessee, which put the Irishmen in the center of the Confederate line. The rifle pits of the Sons of Erin were about two miles southwest of Dover and about two miles southeast of the fort. In their limited accounts, the lads wrote in terms of the Battle of Dover, not the Battle of Fort Donelson.

When Lieutenant Colonel Randal W. McGavock checked out his assigned rifle pits on February 8, he discovered that he had been given an excellent position. Again, with the Confederates pointed south, the Irishmen's trenches were dug into the top right (west) side of a detached V-shaped ridge, soon to be called Heiman's Hill, near the highest point on the three-mile Confederate line. The pits were five feet deep and two feet wide, with a five foot high log-parapet wall in front that had the interesting feature of thorns and prickly branches stuck out onto the far side.[34]

In front (south) of Heiman's Hill was a ravine sloping down a barren plain at a steep angle for about one-hundred yards until it came to a heavily wooded area, where there was another log-wall, about three feet high. Beyond the woods to the left of the ridge was a declivity appropriately called Erin Hollow Creek. (Local residents referred to the area as Erin Hollow.) Beyond the woods to the right end (Irish side) of the ridge was a small stream coming east out of Indian Creek. South of the creek and stream was Indian Creek Valley, the smallest of the three south valleys, mostly an exposed area with few trees.

Because of the outside creeks, there was no possible way for the Boys-in-Blue to get between the gray-clad gunners on the river and the gray-clad foot soldiers on the hills. As was the case with all of the Confederate infantry positions, the combat stations of the Tenth Tennessee were facing away from the river and toward the valleys. Any Northerners wanting to overrun the Sons of Erin would have to march across the open valley to the accompaniment of artillery fire, wade the stream, hike through the woods, climb over the three-foot log-wall, run down and then up the incline to the base of the hill, scale the hill, slide up and over the thorn-wall, take the position in hand-to-hand combat, then hold the position against Southerners coming down the line from Heiman's left, all the while dodging minié balls from Drake's sharpshooters, posted on a hill to the left of Heiman.[35]

McGavock believed no commander in his right mind would attempt that kind of a movement, which would surely necessitate a ten-to-one advantage in troops. Unfortunately for the Federals, not all of their commanders seemed to be in their right minds.

While his troops filed into position, General Pillow kept himself busy by doling out his own regiments to reinforce

Generals Buckner and Johnson, assuming of course, that General Floyd and his five regiments would soon be in the area.

The Irish regiment formed Heiman's far right wing. To the left of the Sons of Erin was the rest of the brigade, namely the Fifty-Third Tennessee and the Twenty-Seventh Alabama deployed front center at the point of the V, with the Fortieth Tennessee equidistant from the Irish regiment near the top of the ridge's left side.[36] Above the Twenty-Seventh Alabama, on the left side of the V, was the Forty-Eighth Tennessee. Above the Fifty-Third Tennessee, to the right of the V, was Heiman's battery, the gunners of Captain Frank Maney and their four smoothbores. Between the Tenth Tennessee and the Fortieth Tennessee, at the center of the peak, was a reserve regiment from Pillow, the Forty-Second Tennessee, temporarily giving the brigade six infantry units and one artillery unit.

On the hill immediately to the left (east) of Heiman was Bushrod Johnson's other brigade under Colonel Joe Drake.[37] Drake's front line regiments were just as well dug-in and fortified as Heiman's and they both shared the same ravine; but Drake's section of the incline was more wooded and not nearly as steep, making his men slightly more vulnerable to a Union attack than Heiman's.

General Johnson's center settled in first, followed by General Buckner's right wing. On February 12 General Pillow filled in the left with his own remaining regiments, because General Floyd's Virginians hadn't as yet arrived. The following day, after the land battle had already begun, Floyd's division arrived to reinforce the Confederate left.

Federal scouts who surveyed the Confederate position were convinced that the Southerners had skillfully protected their flanks by using the swollen river and outside creeks to keep the Boys-in-Blue out. General Grant, however, did not subscribe to that theory: he thought the Confederates had unwisely closed themselves into a rectangular box, with water on three sides of the box forming a trap from which they could not escape.[38] When it came to military strategy, Grant had the annoying habit of being right.

On the evening of Tuesday, February 11, Grant was at his Hickman Creek Valley headquarters in the home of the Widow Crisp. He told C. F. Smith and McClernand to close up the open side of the Confederate box. Their task in the morning would be to bottle up the gray-clads all along the south perimeter of their defensive line, inside the three valleys from outside creek to outside creek.

McClernand's First division would come off the Dover road and swing to the right in front of the Confederate left, while C.F. Smith's Second division would hold down the Confederate right. When Lew Wallace's Third division arrived, the Federals would have a strong center. As all of this infantry movement was going on, the Yankee gunners would keep the Rebel infantry pinned down in their own trenches.[39]

Early on the morning of Wednesday, February 12, Colonel Adolphus Heiman was awakened by one of General Bushrod Johnson's scouts. The first two pieces of news the scout brought were hardly surprising. A few blue-clad cavalrymen had been spotted on the Wynn Ferry road, and a group of blue-clad infantrymen were reported to be marching across the width of the valleys, *out* of artillery range.

The only unexpected news was that the "villains from the northwestern waters" had apparently been quite busy during the night, placing several batteries in the Indian Creek Valley, *in* artillery range.[40] Suddenly, Heiman wished there had been more time to put some extra logworks in front of Frank Maney's gun crew. As it was, the hardworking Confederate artillery horses were still dragging ordnance up the hill.

The Union batteries coordinated to open fire at 7:00 a.m. The Irishmen ducked their heads. Shortly a big cheer went up along the Confederate line. Irish heads popped up. The lads started to clap their hands and cheered wildly.[41] It seems that the Federals in the valley must have failed the lessons of gunnery school. Their solid shots fell harmlessly on the incline, rolling down to the bottom of the ravine, as if part of a children's game. Colonel Heiman joined in the hilarity himself.

Then a big cheer went up from the Northern gunners in the valley. Southern joy ceased. A boom, then another boom, and a cloud of smoke came out of the wooded area in front of the ravine, as a few loose cannonballs came crashing into Heiman's Hill. Captain Maney's men hit the ground, and Heiman grew red-faced with agitation. The Boys-in-Blue had somehow managed to hide a couple of smoothbores down in the protected part of the ravine.[42] Under the cover of trees, their pieces couldn't be seen.

The Confederates in the rifle pits experienced the strange sensation of being fired on by something invisible below. Maney returned the fire, pointing in the general direction of both the smoke below and the valley beyond. Soon the entire area was blanketed with the clouds of smoke and the smell of gunpowder.

There were several lulls during the day for rest and reloading, but the bombardments continued all down the line until 5:00 p.m. when both sides got tired of the noise. With all the commotion going on, the Sons of Erin had to use a variety of sign languages for their card games in the pits.[43] There were no casualties; two Confederate artillery horses were killed, however, falling off Heiman's Hill.[44]

Later that same evening at the Crisp farmhouse, General Grant was taking stock of the situation. C.F. Smith and McClernand had just left with instructions about their commanding officer's three-part-plan of operation for Thursday, February 13.

Flag Officer Foote was ordered to send out one of his boats to test the range of the enemy river-guns. The commodore had hoped to wait a while longer, so that his flotilla could be properly repaired, but nonetheless promised to sail one of them toward the stockade first thing in the morning.

C. F. Smith's troops were supposed to engage in a re-connaissance-in-force, that is, to engage the Southerners at a certain point on their line. If they found weakness, they were to follow through. If they found strength, they were to pull back. In any case Smith was not to initiate a major battle. (Wallace's division was only about a day away.) Because Grant didn't trust McClernand, he waited until morning to inform Smith about deployment details.

It was obvious to the Union commanding general that he had to do something useful with fellow-Illinoisan Mc Clernand and his all-Illinois division. "Blackbeard," however, clearly needed watching. The impetuous and vain glory-seeking politician would have to be kept on a leash, so that he would not risk manpower before Grant's corps was at full troop strength. The sensible solution was to assign the downstater to more artillery duty, designed to soften up the gray-clads on those high ridges to his right—the job of the Union First division was to keep up the bombardment.[45]

At the same time that General Grant was planning, Lieutenant Colonel McGavock went off to find food in Dover.[46] He came trotting up to the cemetery after a disappointing food-forage. All that could be found in town were sardines and crackers, probably off that same blockade runner from Christmas.

Also loaded aboard Tenth Legion were a few more blankets. Even though the air was still mild for February, McGavock figured it wouldn't last. Wearily rider and horse returned to the Brandon Hotel for a few winks.

Thursday, February 13, 1862

The same dull routine followed on Thursday, February 13. The Sons of Erin were blasted out of sleep by the bugle. Commissary Sergeant Barney McCabe, weary with lack of sleep, was ordered by McGavock to take the mess mules to the stockade for morning rations.

McCabe, George and Herm returned around 7:00 a.m. to a standing ovation from the eagerly awaiting Irishmen— in vain. All the stockade could supply was more sardines and crackers.[47]

About the same time that George and Herm were munching on leftover crackers at the Dover cemetery, Union Flag Officer Andrew Foote chose his probe-boat—the *Carondelet,* returning after its previous engagement at Fort Henry. The ironclad, without Grant and Foote, was piloted by the regular skipper, Captain Henry Walke. Making her way south up the Cumberland, the gunboat reached a heavily wooded part of the river bank, about a mile or so from the stockade, within her range of the bluff. Walke ordered the anchor cast overboard and the crew to battle stations. It was a game of cat and mouse.

High on the bluff the Confederate rifle was manned by the Confederate battery of Captain Rube Ross. Assigned to the columbiad below were the gunners of Captain Joe Dixon. Over in the water batteries was the gun crew of Captain Jake Culbertson. At 9:05, Walke's guns began their belching of fire and smoke with sixty-four and seventy-pounder shells. Nothing happened. The trio of Southern gun-chiefs sat patiently, not taking the bait. Walke ordered a cease-fire.[48] The silence was eerie, and the river defenses appeared deserted. All the same the captain didn't like the looks of it, especially those logworks on the bluff. "Dismal-looking sepulchers cut into the rocky cliffs, like those near Jerusalem, but far more repulsive," was the way he described them.[49] Captain Walke had his boat unplugged and ventured a little bit further south, upstream.

At the same time that the *Carondelet* pulled out from the wooded bank, Captain Rube Ross had powder and shell inserted into his prize long-range piece. The initial shot from the big rifle splashed the water right in front of the Union ironclad. A first question had been answered. The Boys-in-Gray had a range of about one mile.

As the *Carondelet* approached, fire was drawn from every one of the six cannon on the bluff. Running past the ominous-looking logworks, Walke opened up on the water batteries, as Captain Culbertson's gunners returned the compliment. Captain Dixon, as overall Confederate artillery chief, quickly rode over to see the results of the shelling. What he saw he didn't like; Culbertson's solid shots were falling harmlessly into the water in front of the boat.[50] While Joe Dixon supervised the elevation of the six smoothbores, moving from one to the next, a metal fragment from a Union ball struck him full in the temple, killing him instantly.

Right after the gun captain was killed, Captain Henry Walke decided he had seen enough of the water batteries. This was the moment of truth for Walke and his Boys-in-Blue. They had to face those tomb-like structures dug into the bluff, as the *Carondelet* moved back north downstream. Between about 10:00 and 12:00 a very noisy shoot-out took place between the boat and the bluff. The Federals got off 139 rounds and received only two hits in return!

The second hit, however, was memorable. A powerful 128-pounder from Rube Ross' Rebel rifle came crashing through a broadside casement into the engine room, where it caromed and ricocheted, ripping at steam pipes and railings, knocking down a dozen sailors and bounding after the others, as one of the engineers said, "like a wild beast pursuing its prey."[51] Shattering beams and timbers, the ball filled the air with splinters fine as needles, pricking and stabbing at the Northerners through their clothes, though in the grim excitement of it all, they weren't aware of this until they felt the blood running down into their shoes. General Grant's probes were becoming a health hazard to Commodore Foote's personnel and equipment. After firing forty-five more rounds into the bluff, Walke called it quits. The damaged *Carondelet* limped off north down the river. The U.S. Navy probe at Fort Donelson was history. A second question had been answered. The gray-clads had plenty of fire-power.

General Charles F. Smith, meanwhile, had his Union Second division ready to strike the right of the Confederate defensive line. Of course neither Grant nor Smith had any way of knowing what Confederate units held what positions. C.F. Smith was actually headed straight for the two Kentucky regiments of Colonel Roger W. "Old Flintlock" Hanson, 34, of Clark County Kentucky, one of the most pugnacious soldiers on the field.[52]

Oddly enough, Smith gave full authority for the operation to two of his commanders, Colonel Jake Lauman, commander of his First brigade, and Colonel John Cook, who commanded his Second brigade. In an action completely out of character for the veteran Mexican War hero, Smith withdrew from the operation and had no part in it. Lauman and Cook and the Boys-in-Blue of the Union Second division were on their own.

Colonel Lauman's Twenty-Fifth Indiana, supported by skirmishers from the Seventh and Fourteenth Iowa regiments, charged the Confederate hill. As Captain Jasper Dresser of Buckner's battery let loose with a fusillade of rifle shot, buckshot, and grape, and as Hanson opened up fire with his skilled riflemen, the Indiana regiment, with bayonets extended, gave forth a mighty Hoosier yell and ascended the one-hundred-foot, lead-swept ridge. With a great deal of courage, the Hoosiers kept coming but they could not make it to the logworks.

The wounded started rolling down into their own comrades, forcing the First brigade to retire.[53]

After conferring with Lauman, Cook launched the assault of the Second brigade farther to his left, spearheaded by the Seventh Illinois. Several of their company officers fell right away, and the Illinoisans were quickly driven off the hill. Colonels Lauman and Cook fell back to the woods, where they kept up their artillery fire, all the while waiting further instructions from General Smith. Nothing happened.

Since another attack would have been contrary to the nature of a reconnaissance-in-force, as well as downright suicidal, the two colonels brought up a company of specialists to cover their retreat. Birge's U.S. Missouri Sharpshooters kept the Kentucky Rebels busy, while the infantry Boys-in-Blue fled back to their original positions in the Hickman Creek Valley.[54]

A third question had been answered. The Confederates could *not* be expelled from their defensive line without much greater Union numerical superiority and troop coordination. The gallant Hoosiers of the Twenty-Fifth Indiana paid the heaviest price for this bit of army intelligence, with fourteen dead and sixty-one wounded.

There are many misconceptions about that strange and fateful Thursday of February, 13, 1862. Contrary to some accounts the Confederates *did* have an edge in manpower at Dover *that day and that day only.* On Thursday, February 13, when all the army and navy fireworks were going on, General John B. Floyd finally arrived with his mostly-Virginia troops.

Army of Tennessee historians Stanley Horn and T.L. Connelly both put the total number of Southern foot soldiers at 15,000, which is almost exactly what Grant had before he was reinforced by General Lew Wallace.[55] Writer-historian

Shelby Foote used a higher figure of 17,500 Confederate infantrymen, which is probably closer to the truth.[56]

One thing is for certain. When Floyd placed his five regiments to the left of Johnson's two brigades of Drake and Heiman, the number of Confederate infantry regiments along that three-mile defensive line was exactly twenty-six, eleven from Tennessee, five from Mississippi, four from Virginia, two from Alabama, two from Kentucky, and one each from Arkansas and Texas.[57] Even if every regiment was small (about 700) like the Sons of Erin, the total would have been 18,200 men. So it's reasonable to attach the numbers 17,500 to the Southerners and 15,000 to the Notherners for that day only.

Grant was unaware of this. If he had known, he wouldn't have needed to send C.F. Smith's division in against the reinforced Boys-in-Gray. If General Sidney Johnston had sent General Hardee's army corps of 14,000 to Dover instead of directly to Nashville, the Confederates, with an army of five full divisions, would have achieved a numerical superiority of better than two to one for February 13. Grant's two divisions, taking any offensive action at all, might well have been crushed, and the Union cause in the West hampered seriously or even lost.

At any rate, about the same time that Floyd's division was forming the Confederate left in front of the Lick Creek Valley, spontaneous sharpshooters' action broke out all along the line, inevitably. Both sides were looking right at each other through the trees, only about two miles apart. Trigger fingers were itchy, and a few sporadic shots soon turned into a spate of random firing.

The Sons of Erin felt trapped in the desperate firestorm in their own logworks. The safest course of action for the Irishmen would have been to climb down the backside (north end) of Heiman's Hill and retire to their tents at the cemetery. However, they had been ordered to battle stations by Lieutenant Colonel McGavock, who had his orders from Colonel Heiman. That was enough for them. "The balls came whizzing by us thick sometimes as hail stones, and after awhile we cannot even hear the report of the guns," was what McGavock recorded.[58]

Add the minié balls from the muskets to the canister and grape from the batteries, and you wind up with an incredible amount of flying danger. At the same time that Irish heads were ducking, Lieutenant Colonel Nathan Bedford Forrest was with his staff in a wooded area near the Wynn Ferry road. Noticing a cavalryman with a fancy Maryland rifle, he asked him if he could borrow his weapon. With the clear eye and steady aim of a true backwoodsman, Forrest fired somewhere into the distance. About a hundred yards up, an unfortunate Missouri Yankee fell from a tree. Not only had the others not seen the sharpshooter, they hadn't seen the tree.

At 8:30 a.m., on that same confusing Thursday, Colonel Heiman told Captain Frank Maney to greet the newcomers in the valley with a loud, welcoming barrage.

General John McClernand, already irritated by Grant's relegating him to an out-of-the-way place in the action and in a foul mood because of it, seemed to take the artillery barrage as a personal affront and responded with a vengeance.

Still as exposed as the day before, Maney's Confederates began to take a pounding. Heiman reported the deaths of gunner lieutenants Byrnes and Massie in the first hour of the bombardment.[59] Captain Maney suffered a hand injury of some sort, and two of his four pieces were disabled.

Then something happened that was to pour iodine on McClernand's already smarting ego. At 9:30 a fragment from one of the Confederate solid shots knocked a wheel off one of the Federal guns in the valleys.

Responding irrationally to the action, the Southern Illinois general let loose his ire. He decided to disregard orders and send his infantry out to get one captain of artillery and two smoothbores. McClernand had slipped Grant's leash.

There was no plan of battle, just a sudden notion of some wild charge up a hill, no coordination between artillery and infantry, leaving Northern foot soldiers exposed to Southern gunners, skirmishers, and sharpshooters.

No thought was given to the placement of reserve units. Even if the Illinoisans could take Maney's guns, they would have no way of holding them.

Neither were there any scouting reports about enemy troop strength on that hill with the pesky cannon. General McClernand had no idea what brigade he was facing, or how many regiments it had. His 2,400 highly exposed Federals would have to charge a hill defended by about 2,400 heavily dug-in Confederates. The reason for the small number of Illinoisans was that McClernand had chosen his smallest Third brigade to make the attack, instead of all three brigades of his all-Illinois division.[60]

The Third brigade of the First division was the worst selection that could have been made; it had gone through a confusing change in command in the past twenty-four hours. The commanding officer of the brigade was Colonel W.H.L. Wallace. On Wednesday, McClernand placed Wallace on his division staff, replacing him with Colonel William Morrison of the Forty-Ninth Illinois. That Thursday morning, McClernand replaced Morrison with Colonel Isham Haynie of the Forty-Eighth Illinois, the only reason being that he knew Haynie better than he knew Morrison.[61]

Captain John Stewart of General McClernard's staff neglected to inform Colonel Morrison about the switch, so that at the beginning of the assault both Colonels Haynie and Morrison thought they were in charge of the operation. To further add to the confusion, both colonels replaced themselves at the regimental level by advancing their senior majors.

Beyond that, in an odd chance of fate, all four of the Union regimental commanders were named Smith, none of whom were related to General C. F. Smith or Colonel M. L. Smith, a brigade commander in C. F.'s Second division! In the years to come Federal historians would remember the February 13 engagement at Dover as the "Battle of the Smiths."[62]

In other words McGavock's Irish regiment and the other five regiments of Heiman's brigade of Johnson's division of the Floyd/Pillow corps of Johnston's army was about to be set upon by the Smith/Smith/Smith/Smith regiments of the W.H.L. Wallace/Morrison/Haynie brigade of McClernand's division of Grant's corps of Halleck's army.

General McClernand's only stated objective was to silence Captain Frank Maney. By 12:00 noon the Union infantry columns were formed in the Indian Creek Valley. The advance came at an angle from their right to left, Confederate left to right, toward the Fifty-Third Tennessee and Maney's Battery.[63] Strictly by accident, each of the four attacking Illinois regiments of the Third brigade would eventually run into four of the gray-clad regiments on Heiman's Hill.

On Colonel Heiman's far left, the Forty-Eighth Illinois (Lieutenant Colonel Thomas Smith) approached the Fortieth Tennessee. To the immediate Confederate right the Seventeenth Illinois (Major Francis Smith) approached the Twenty-Seventh Alabama, supported by the Thirtieth Tennessee in reserve. Further to the Rebel right the Forty-Ninth Illinois (Major John J. Smith) approached the Fifty-Third Tennessee and Maney's Battery, supported by three companies of the Forty-Second Tennessee in reserve. To the far Confederate right the Forty-Fifth Illinois (Colonel John E. Smith), held in reserve, would later approach the Tenth Tennessee.[64]

At 12:45 p.m., with drummers banging and with flags waving, the Boys-in-Blue from Illinois marched across the valley through the woods to the edge of the ravine. Like the Indiana and Iowa farm boys over on the left end of their line, the Illinois farm boys were confronted with fallen trees, thorn bushes, and enemy logworks.

The Forty-Eighth, Seventeenth and Forty-Ninth Illinois

regiments formed a line of skirmishers in the woods, supported by McClernand's artillery. Fearlessly Colonel Morrison came riding out of the woods to lead an assault force up the ridge, followed by his own Forty-Ninth and then the Seventeenth Illinois, led by Major Smith and Major Smith. When the Forty-Eighth lagged behind, McClernand had Captain Stewart slide the third attack regiment to his left toward the Fifty-Third Tennessee and Captain Maney's gunners.[65]

From a distance it looked like a swarm of blue bees climbing a hive. As soon as the men from Illinois started up, Heiman opened up a heavy fire with Maney's two guns and the two regiments up at the point of the V, the Twenty-Seventh Alabama and the Fifty-Third Tennessee. Morrison's invaders got close to the logworks on their left-center, but Colonel Heiman made an effective adjustment and brought the Forty-Second Tennessee right up to the V to reinforce the Fifty-Third. When the Twenty-Seventh Alabama swung right to reinforce the Tennesseans, it became a case of three Illinois regiments attacking three heavily fortified Confederate regiments.[66]

Gaps widened on Heiman's Hill between the advancing Union companies. When the Seventeenth and Forty-Eighth fell back, Colonel Morrison was forced to withdraw down the hill, up the ravine, and into the woods. Some of the hard noses of the Forty-Ninth clung to the cliffs of the ridge. While all of this was going on, General McClernand sent the Forty-Fifth Illinois into the woods to strengthen his skirmish line.[67]

A big cheer went up from the blue-clads below. Again Morrison came out of the woods, leading a small second wave, other companies of the Seventeenth in support of the men from the Forty-Ninth still on the ridge.[68] During the second ascent, a big cheer went up from the Southerners above. A Northern officer was knocked off his horse, seriously wounded in the right hip. It was Morrison, who was carried off the field in tremendous pain. The loss of the popular colonel was more than the gallant Illinoisans could take.[69]

The men of the Seventeenth fled to the rear. The men

of the Forty-Ninth who had remained on the hill, withdrew in an orderly fashion. All the Federals were back in the woods, continuing their cannon and musket fire. The blue-clad wounded and dead were scattered all over the landscape. Incredibly, General McClernand sent a message to his commanding colonel, Haynie, to launch a third wave![70] Only one regiment on each side had not been engaged in the wild, mad, melee.

Engagement at Erin Hollow
1:25 to 1:40 p.m.
Thursday, February 13, 1862
Tennessee Irishmen Versus Illinois Lead Miners

Skirmishers of the Forty-Fifth Illinois continued to support the retiring of the Forty-Ninth. As the infantrymen of the Seventeenth, Forty-Eighth and Forty-Ninth filed back into the woods, the Forty-Fifth kept getting pushed from the extreme Union right to the center, and then to the left of center.[71]

By the time that Colonel Haynie got the word about a third assault wave, his only fresh regiment was in the woods to the left-front of the V. The target was still Maney, but the Union reserves were positioned at an approach angle to the west (Union left, Confederate right) of the Rebel guns. The situation was that the Forty-Fifth Illinois had to charge the steepest point on Heiman's Hill, exactly where the Sons of Erin were dug in.[72]

Colonel John E. Smith of the Forty-Fifth was a forty-five-year-old, Swiss-born jeweler and watchmaker from Grant's hometown of Galena. The men of his regiment were mostly lead miners from that northwestern area of the state.

The Federals, still with the artillery advantage, continued to pound the Confederate hill from the valleys and from the woods, doing as much as could be done to soften

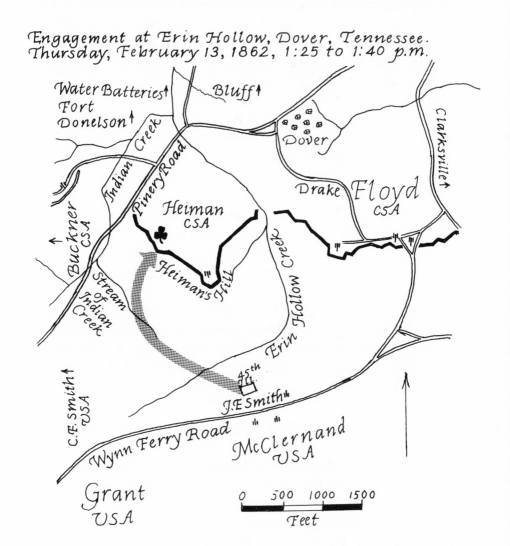

Engagement at Erin Hollow, Dover, Tennessee.
Thursday, February 13, 1862, 1:25 to 1:40 p.m.

Water Batteries↑   Bluff↑
Fort
Donelson↑   Dover

Clarksville↑

Indian Creek

Pinery Road

Heiman
CSA

Drake   Floyd
CSA

Buckner
CSA

Heiman's Hill

Stream
of
Indian
Creek

Erin Hollow Creek

C.F. Smith↑
USA

45th

J.E. Smith

Wynn Ferry Road   McClernand
USA

Grant
USA

0   500   1000   1500

Feet

up the Southerners stationed in the rifle pits. Caught in a crossfire, the V-shaped ridge became a mass of swirling earth and wood. And all the while the bombardment was going on, Haynie's skirmishers behind the trees and Heiman's sharp-shooters behind the logworks kept up their relentless fire. As the smoke began to clear, movement could be seen below.

Drummers of the Forty-Fifth Illinois pounded out the beat of attack, strong and primitive. As the smoke cleared on the crest of the hill, the Sons of Erin could see images of battle in the ravine. A distinguished-looking, middle-aged officer in blue emerged from the woods on a high-spirited battle horse. Then drummer boys and standard-bearers also became visible, all decked out in bright red, white, and blue— the same colors as those on the national flag.[73]

Following the colors of the Forty-Fifth Illinois came the soldiers marching out of the woods onto the edge of the ravine, very much like athletes emerging from a tunnel. Every one of them was dressed in the same dark blue cap, dark blue jacket, and light blue pants lined with dark blue stripes. They advanced in two sets of perfectly-formed columns, twelve across in both sets.

The accounts of the Forty-Fifth document their own excitement at that moment. Their colonel, John E. Smith, rode beside his subordinates firmly but calmly addressing his company commanders, who in turn passed his remarks along to the enlisted men. "Attention, battalion! Fix bayonets; shoulder arms; right shoulder shift, arms. Forward, march," was what he barked out.[74] With half the regiment left on the skirmish line, a detachment of the lead-miners-in-blue slowly began their difficult march down and then up the incline.

When they got to within forty yards of the hill's base, Colonel J. E. Smith called for them to halt. The Illinoisans assumed the firing position, with the front of the columns genuflecting as if in prayer. "Now the time had come for us to show what stuff we were made of; now had come the time to do what we had promised our loved ones at home–to fight gallantly for the dear old flag," was how Private Wilbur F. Crummer of the Forty-Fifth described the moment.[75]

At the same time that Crummer was reflecting, a Union exploding shell crashed into the logworks above, filling the air with earth and branches and leaves and smoke. The lead miners, used to such pollution, closed their eyes to avoid having them seared. When their senses cleared, they looked straight up toward the peak of the hill. They couldn't help but notice a couple of sights standing out like beacons from everything else above.[76]

There was a big, mounted, red-haired officer in a red-and-gold trimmed gray uniform, with a green feather in the red lining of his gray hat, pointing a sword that flashed in the afternoon sun. Above him at a higher point on the hill was a green flag, with white shamrocks, flapping in the Tennessee wind. For many of the youthful lead miners, those were the last two things that they would ever see. For an instant time stood still.

"Fire," was what Colonels McGavock and J. E. Smith yelled as if with one voice. The front lines of the Illinoisans went down like pins in a bowling alley. The Sons of Erin fired and fired again, sending a spray of lead that could only be described as "terrific" down the slope.[77] As if this wasn't bad enough for the Illinois Federals, Frank Maney's two smooth-bores let loose with grape and canister. Crummer described the plight of his comrades: "Presently the balls began to sing about our heads: zip, ping, ping, and as we climbed the hill, we were met by a murderous fire of musketry and canister that the enemy poured into us."[78]

J. E. Smith had his men scramble up onto the lower cliffs to reduce the enemy angle of fire. From this position the Boys-in-Blue were able to return a few volleys of their own. "When we got close enough the order to fire was given, and we boys sent our first lead into the enemy who showed themselves on top of the breastworks," was what Crummer reported.[79]

One of the Irishmen fell back, his face covered in

blood—Private Mo Fitzgerald, who knew how to take a punch or two. Helped to his feet by Willie, he went right back to firing his musket down the hill. As it turned out, the twin's forehead had been merely grazed by a Yankee minié ball.[80] The Fighting Fitzgeralds became fearsome soldiers from that day on.

Private John McElroy of the all-Clarksville company had a slight chunk taken out of a hip, and he recovered from that to become the very best fighting-enlisted lad of them all.[81]

Some of the lead miners remained in the woods as skirmishers. Others remained on the lower cliffs and fired up. Still others continued to ascend Heiman's Hill, veering from their center to left, while McGavock adjusted by turning his right in toward the invaders. The Tennessee Irish commanding officer carefully deployed his best riflemen up high around his perimeter. Captain John G. O'Neill of McEwen, Sergeant John L. Prendergast of Clarksville, and Corporal "Long Tom" Connor of Nashville fired straight down into the oncoming traffic with deadly accuracy.[82]

In spite of the heavy Irish-Rebel fire, a few of the Yankee lead miners made it to the log wall in front of Irish-born Captain Sam Thompson's battalion of five companies. They advanced with fixed bayonets. Irish-born Master Sergeant John Ames, with several weapons tucked inside his belt, fired one of his revolvers point blank into the face of a Yankee on the wall, and the man's head exploded with blood and tissue and bone splinters splattering all over the logworks.[83]

Drummers of the Forty-Fifth Illinois pounded out the beat of retreat, and the Boys-in-Blue hurried off the hill to the woods. Out of a sense of relief, the Sons of Erin began to cheer, until they heard that ominous hum of another incoming shell. An explosion tore a piece of turf out of Heiman's Hill.[84] To Colonel Heiman a continuing artillery cover was a sure sign that the assault wasn't over.

Assisted by his close personal friend, Captain Saint Clair Morgan, McGavock rode up and down the line, warning his Irishmen to have their weapons reloaded.[85] Within a minute the Illinoisans came out of the woods again. This time it was a detachment of the Forty-Fifth reinforced by a detachment of the Forty-Ninth. Still under orders to destroy the artillery position, Colonel John Smith and Major John Smith steered their troops to their far left, Irish right, a poor choice for the advance. Illinois drummers beat the rally.

Major William Grace, 31, of Nashville, number two officer in the Irish regiment was a powerful six feet three-and-a-half-inch giant known for his pugnacious and aggressive leadership style.[86] Colonel Smith and Major Smith ran right into Grace's battalion of five companies. Standing high up on the logworks, as if he didn't have a nerve in his body, "Battling Billie" Grace directed the Irish-Rebel fire right into the heart of the rally, stopping the second wave of the third wave cold. Illinois drummers beat the retreat.

"My regiment behaved nobly and it was as much as I could do to keep them in the pits, they were so anxious to get out and charge them," McGavock reported.[87]

As the Irishmen of the Tenth Tennessee reloaded for the next charge, all four of the Illinois infantry regiments began a withdrawal along their line back out into the Indian Creek Valley. Their gunners hoisted up a flag of truce-cease-fire.

A mighty Irish-Rebel yell went up from the logworks and rifle pits and sharpshooter stations of the Sons of Erin. Then all the Southerners got in on the act, jumping and shouting, as a big Rebel battle flag was waved back and forth. The cheers from the Boys-in-Gray grew to a crescendo when "Uncle Dolph" Heiman rode up and down the line, excitedly waving his hat.[88]

In front of the celebration, the blue-clad dead and wounded lay around the logworks, on the hill, on the incline, in the stream, and in the woods. General John A. Mc Clernand had sent in an infantry brigade to dislodge one artillery commander with two guns and had failed miserably, in spite of the gallantry of his troops. Captain Frank Maney still stood on Heiman's Hill, his tightly bandaged hands held high in triumph.[89]

Excluding preliminary skirmishing, McClernand's folly lasted fifty-five minutes, ending in a crushing defeat. The Sons of Erin were in mortal combat for the last fifteen of those minutes. During the assault, officers and lads acted calmly, coolly and solidly, most notably Randal McGavock, William Grace, and John Ames. However, given their near impregnable position, the defensive efforts of the Irishmen were in no way extraordinary, except in the account of Private Patrick M. Griffin, who continued to unfold the myth of the "Bloody Tinth."

Griffin had a strong sense of ethnic pride and a tremendous regimental spirit mixed in with a wee bit of blarney. The reader sometimes gets the impression from the enthusiastic lad that the American Civil War was fought between the Union Army and the Tenth Tennessee. Although it is contradictory to all existing evidence, Private Griffin suggested that Colonel Heiman's other five regiments were nearly out of ammunition, only to be saved from destruction by the Irish regiment.

> *The Yankees were pressing us closely, and when two of our regiments threw down their guns, the fighting ability of the Tinth carried the day,*

he wrote.[90]

The real horror at Erin Hollow was yet to come. After 2:00 p.m., when the Union stretcher-bearers rapidly approached the battle area, a truly terrible thing happened. Because of all those exploding shells and the warm weather, the woods caught on fire. Cries of panic and pain rose up from the ravine, soon to be replaced by coughing and choking. The wounded were in grave danger.[91] An emergency field hospital was hastily set up near Erin Hollow Creek, and all the Federal troops took part in the rescue mission.

Colonel Adolphus Heiman showed the consistent sense of honor and high-principled leadership that marked his performance as an officer. Without hesitation he assembled volunteers for the rescue operation, and there was a frantic rush of Rebels running down the hill to save the Yankees they had just shot.

American soldiers from Illinois, Tennessee, and Alabama worked together, risking their own lives, to pull the stricken out of that inferno. At least two Illinoisans were rescued by an all-Tennessee team of workers. Victims of both gun shots and burns were sped to the field hospital, where General Grant's own personal staff surgeon, Dr. John Brinton, was already busily at work.[92]

Father Henry Vincent Browne, assisted by Private Mike Carney, moved one especially youthful-looking Boy-in-Blue all the way to the hospital and stayed with him until he was attended to. The Confederate chaplain remained with the Union chaplains of all denominations for the rest of that horrible day.[93] Whole sections of the woods were consumed by a roaring fire, so that, after awhile, there was nothing else that could be done for the wounded.

Soldiers on both sides congregated in the valleys and by the creek, discussing the events of that afternoon. The Sons of Erin mingled with the Galena lead miners; they were, after all, not natural enemies. Shortly the young men in blue and gray were ordered back to their own lines, and the cease-fire was lifted. Immediately the sharpshooters were at each other again.

Considering the fact that the engagement at the center of the field involved only one brigade on each side, the casualty figures were grim indeed. Haynie reported 122 killed, about two-hundred wounded, and about one-hundred missing in action.[94] McGavock believed the enemy fatality total to be much higher.[95] He was surely right. All the missing and many of the wounded can be presumed dead in the fire. Including those mortally wounded who died in the next few days, the Federal killed-in-action count may have gone as high as four-hundred, seventeen percent of those engaged, all in less than an hour's fight. Counting the wounded, the Union brigade had a casualty rate of almost forty percent.

The Forty-Ninth Illinois was hit the hardest, with the Forty-Fifth a distant second, reporting sixteen killed and about twice that many wounded, most or all of whom were victims of the Sons of Erin. There were few casualties in the Seventeenth and very few in the Forty-Eighth. Also of note was the fact that about sixty good quality rifled muskets of the fallen were confiscated by the Irishmen.[96]

In his report that following August, Heiman estimated ten of his men killed and about thirty wounded, all of whom were in either Maney's Battery or the Fifty-Third Tennessee. Ed Bearss, the noted National Park Service historian, suggests the Confederate fatality figure to be even lower than that, pointing out that gunnery Second Lieutenant Massie resigned from the army on November 30, 1862, due to ill health, a full nine months after having been pronounced dead by Heiman.[97]

In his journal McGavock notes the death of one of his Irishmen, but the identification of such a deceased lad cannot be made in Army Official Records, national or state military service records, or the cemetery records of the Tenth Tennessee.[98] It may well have been that the Irish lieutenant colonel mistook one of the Fifty-Third Tennessee for one of his own lads. Certainly the "few slightly wounded," like Mo Fitzgerald and John McElroy, couldn't have been mistaken for fatalities.

Copious and comprehensive as he was as a journalist, McGavock was often careless with details anyway. He identified the invaders on his part of Heiman's Hill as the

Forty-Seventh Illinois, a unit that was not even present with Grant's corps at Dover. Diarist Jimmy Doyle, good for details only, correctly identified the lead miners by observing the number "45" on their regimental banner.

The Battle of Erin Hollow, or the Battle of the Smiths, claimed historical importance only at that moment and only for those immediately concerned. In fact, it wasn't really a battle at all, just an unknown skirmish inside a little known land action called Dover inside the river campaign called Fort Donelson.

For the Sons of Erin, the moment of glory came collectively on Thursday, February 13, 1862, 1:25 to 1:40 p.m. Incredibly, Erin Hollow represented the only combat experience that all the lads ever shared together as a full Confederate regiment. Later in the war, the Irishmen would participate in some of the worst fighting on the Western front, but by that time the regiment had been reconstituted as a much smaller unit. Of such things, however, myths are made.

Over at their headquarters in the Dover Inn, Generals Floyd and Pillow were jubilant. Both telegraphed General Johnston with assurances that Fort Donelson could be held. "We have maintained ourselves fully by land and by water," was what Floyd wired, seemingly oblivious to the fact that he himself had just arrived that day.[99] His own troops hadn't done anything more than fill in space.

Suddenly, the weather shifted, causing great distress to Southerners and Northerners alike. At about 4 p.m. rain came, in torrents, and the flames were doused, leaving the wooded area in an ugly state of destruction. There would be no more trees to cover an infantry advance, no more half-insane Union assaults from the center of the field. And there was no hiding from what would happen next. Mother Nature was about to play one of her really cruel tricks.

At dusk a cold wind blew out of the north, turning the rain to sleet and then to snow. Amazingly, the thermometer plunged from sixty degrees to ten degrees above zero! Winter had quickly returned to North Middle Tennessee. Up on Heiman's Hill McGavock's pickets shivered in the rifle pits and behind the logworks, while the rest of the lads huddled in their tents at the cemetery.[100]

Bad as it was for the Irishmen, they, at least, all had coats, putting them in a better condition than many of the other Confederates. Those extra blankets at Christmas and those extra coats picked up on the Charlotte road made McGavock look like a genius. In spite of the foul weather, Colonel Heiman was determined to put some logworks in front of Captain Maney's Battery, just in case of a future invasion. The Irish detachment assigned to the project was supervised by Major Grace, a tireless worker.[101]

The Federals out in the south valleys were truly miserable, cursing the so-called Sunny South and regretting the day they had discarded the coats and blankets on the Dover road. Worse than that, they still had a few wounded men in the woods, whose deaths by fire had been forestalled by the torrents of rain. The wounded were going to undergo deaths by freezing, locked in rigid agony under the ice storm. By nightfall the icy gale gradually became a roaring blizzard. Throughout the storm sharpshooters on both sides continued to fire away in the dark.[102]

Meanwhile back at the Widow Crisp's farmhouse, General Grant was rocking in front of the stone fireplace and unhappily reflecting on the day, which had been unfortunate. One ironclad had been wracked up, and General C.F. Smith's reconaissance-in-force had not demonstrated any Confederate weaknesses, but plenty of Union weaknesses. Then there was the matter of McClernand! The result of his recklessness was a brigade practically destroyed for combat. In his report to the war department in Washington City, Grant didn't pull any punches.

This general, without orders or authority, undertook to capture a battery of the enemy, which was annoying to him. Of course the assault was a failure and the loss on our side was great for the number of men engaged.[103]

The news for Grant wasn't all bad, however. He had just been informed that General Lew Wallace's Third division was arriving and that Flag Officer Foote's flotilla had been repaired.

Lew Wallace had come in with the 10,000 men from Halleck, plus the 2,500 in reserve from Fort Henry, giving Grant an infantry advantage of about 27,500 to 17,500. Counting navy, cavalry, artillery, and infantry personnel, it was then about 34,000 Northerners against some 21,000 Southerners, still less than the ideal for an offensive advance. Knowing nothing about the Confederate numbers, General Grant scheduled no infantry activity for the next day, while Wallace filled in the center of the field. Reluctantly deciding that he had to continue to rely on the Navy and remembering the easy fall of Fort Henry, Grant ordered Commodore Foote to destroy the river defenses.[104]

Friday, February 14, 1862

When dawn arrived luminous and ghostly on Friday, February 14, soldiers emerged from their holes and tents to find a wonderland that seemed inappropriate for fighting. The tree branches and twigs wore icy armor, and the countryside was blanketed with two inches of pure, white fluff. In order to keep the juices flowing, the lads of the Tenth Tennessee participated in an early morning snowball fight with the boys of the Twenty-Seventh Alabama.[105]

The Alabamans weren't all that used to snow and were

gleefully feeling their oats. Because of a surprise attack, the boys from Alabama gained an early advantage, only to be turned back by an Irish rally led by Marty Gibbons, "Crazy Tom" Feeney, and Mo Fitzgerald, who sported an especially ratty-looking bandage across his Erin Hollow red badge of courage.

Willie Fitzgerald amused himself by throwing rocks. The winter recreation was brought to a sudden conclusion by the ominous hum of an incoming shell. The snow-covered Irishmen flung themselves to the ground.[106] Following the explosion things returned to normal, with sharpshooters firing away at everything that wasn't white.

At the same time that the Sons of Erin were warming themselves at the cemetery, Flag Officer Andrew Foote, recalling the stubborn resistance of General Tilghman on the Tennessee River, spent most of that day preparing for battle. Keenly aware of the potential threat of a "cannonball with a mission," he had chains, lumber, and bags of coal laid on the upper decks of the ironclads to prevent another lucky shot from getting through. With preparations completed, the navy commander gave the starting signal at 3:00 p.m., and the Union flotilla moved south up the Cumberland, splashing through cold water and ice between the snowclad hills of Tennessee's winter wonderland.

Spectators assembled for the next main event of the Dover three-ring circus. One was the Confederate commanding general, John B. Floyd, who took one look at the six Yankee boats and declared that the fort was doomed. Another was Halleck's corps commander Grant, astride Jack, who took one look at the twelve Rebel guns and said nothing, while calmly puffing on a cigar butt in the corner of his mouth. Pickets from H Company, Sons of Erin, including Pat Griffin, Jimmy Doyle, Marty Gibbons, Mike Carney, and "Crazy Tom" Feeney, soon to go on guard duty by the logworks on Heiman's Hill, climbed up the backside of the ridge to view the fireworks.[107]

Commodore Foote advanced in a 4-2 formation, the four ironclads out front, followed by two wooden warships. Because of the intelligence data from the probe, Foote knew that he could safely hold fire until his range was closed to a mile, at which point all six gunboats sent screeching tongues of flames into the snow-covered bluff, lighting it up like a flocked Christmas tree.

The Confederate return fire was feeble. From the flagship *St. Louis,* Commodore Foote could see guns being abandoned, and so he aggressively advanced the four ironclads close to the shore and lined them up between the bluff and the water batteries. The old sailor had made the biggest mistake of his long and distinguished career. It was a Rebel trap.[108]

Every river cannon came alive, catching the close-up boats in a deadly crossfire. As the lads of H Company cheered wildly, a solid shot crashed through the superstructure of the *St. Louis,* carrying away the wheel, killing the pilot, and wounding Foote along with everyone else in the pilot house, except the newspaper reporter. Without a helm the flagship drifted with the current north down the river. Alongside her, the *Pittsburgh* had her tiller ropes shot clean away, and she too careened off helpless, taking more hits as she went.

The *Louisville* was the next to go. She was saved from sinking by the fact that her compartments were full of air. Like her two sister ships, she lost her steering gear and limped off north downstream like a floating piece of Swiss cheese. Left alone again, the *Carondelet,* still piloted by Captain Henry Walke, was a sitting duck. When the columbiad took out her smokestack, she too made her run to safety.[109] The river battle of Fort Donelson was history.

The *St. Louis* had taken fifty-seven hits, the other three ironclads almost as many. Forty-three sailors were wounded and eleven were killed. Not a single Southerner gunner was injured. It was one of the most total of defeats ever inflicted on the United States Navy, any time, any place.

H Company went on picket duty. Floyd sent another fulsome message of victory to Sidney Johnston. The inscrutable Sam Grant sent off two wires. "Appearances indicate now that we will have a protracted siege here. I feel greatly confident in ultimately reducing the place," was what he informed Halleck.[110]

The other message went to the quartermaster at Cairo with instructions for supplies and ammunition to be sent south on the double. Even though imperturbable as always, Grant had to be prepared for the situation to get worse.

It was 11:00 p.m. Friday, February 14, 1862. None of the pickets on Heiman's Hill could possibly keep warm, with hands and feet a special problem. The only effective way for the lads of H Company to neutralize the cold in their extremities seemed to be to keep their bodies totally numb. Commissary Sergeant Barney McCabe supplied the Irishmen of H with three of the somewhat large jugs of Kentucky moonshine that he kept in the supply wagons.[111] Soon the lads couldn't feel a thing.

At the same late hour that the jugs were being passed around, Colonel Adolphus Heiman met at the Dover Inn with the four generals, the cavalry commander, and the other brigade commanders.[112] In spite of all the success of the previous two days, Floyd and Pillow somehow found a way to be pessimistic. Their real problem was Western commander Sidney Johnston, who still couldn't find Carlos Buell's 50,000 Federal troops. The Confederate generals had no idea how many Union soldiers were about and where most of them might be, all of which lent credence to rumors about the arrival of Federal reinforcements.

In reality, with General Lew Wallace's Third division in place, General Grant already had all the infantry that he was ever going to get, exactly thirty-three regiments, nineteen from Illinois, six from Indiana, four from Iowa, and two each from Kentucky and Missouri.[113] It was 17,500 to defend against 27,500. This should have been a secure number for the Southerners, except for the fact that Floyd had no more of an idea about Yankee strength than Grant had about Rebel strength. In addition, Johnston had yet to tell Floyd anything about what he was supposed to be doing.

Left to their own devices, Floyd and Pillow were forced to produce a plan of their own. The Virginian came up with a much better way of structuring the forces than had been tried before. According to Floyd's scheme, all Confederate troops were divided into two full-size divisions, each of three brigades, all under the top two *professional* officers, Simon Buckner and Bushrod Johnson. Pillow was the field commander, with Floyd as operational head.

Surprisingly, Pillow suggested a first-rate order of battle. Early in the morning Bushrod Johnson would launch a surprise infantry strike against the weakened McClernand, as Simon Buckner quietly left his position on the Confederate right and swung around Johnson in full support of the attack. While the startled Boys-in-Blue were pushed further back into the valleys, Lieutenant Colonel Forrest would drive them off the Wynn Ferry road, leaving an escape hatch open to Clarksville.[114]

The proposal was reminiscent of General Tilghman's assault-evacuation of Fort Henry, only better, because it called for the use of infantry, cavalry and artillery instead of just river defenses.

The upshot of the plan was for the Dover gray-clads to get to Nashville and join Hardee. Together Generals Hardee and Floyd could assemble an army of four full divisions of 32,000 men in a defensive perimeter around Nashville. With General Beauregard blocking General Halleck on the Mississippi, General Buell would be forced to commit his unused army against the Tennessee capital. Given all the food, water, and supplies in Nashville, the determined Southerners could hold out indefinitely.[115] All the Confederate officers liked the aggressive nature of the plan, all that is, except for

Colonel Heiman.

Five Confederate brigades were to be used in the assault, with one left behind in reserve, namely Heiman's, which drew the assignment of holding down Heiman's Hill in the last-ditch event of a Federal breakthrough. With Buckner and Johnson concentrating to the Confederate left, C. F. Smith, supported by Lew Wallace, could walk right through the vacated Confederate right and attack the center from front and back. All in all, Heiman was to be a Confederate buffer, separating the Union First division from the Union Second and Third divisions.

In a halting German accent, the agitated "Old Buzzard" reasonably pointed out that he couldn't hold his position with six regiments of 2,400 men against two divisions of 16,000. He was a little reassured, however, when Bedford Forrest assured him that there would likely be no ultimate last stand involving his troops; the plan would work, if properly executed. The key word was *if.* Of the utmost importance was the quickness of the early infantry movement, not allowing time for Lew Wallace and C. F. Smith to advance to their right in support of the crippled McClernand's two healthy brigades.[116]

Randal McGavock was skeptical of the idea when he heard about it, too. Perceptive as always, the lieutenant colonel of the Irishmen was quick to grab onto the heart of the problem when it went to the subject of being a rear guard.[117] Heiman's troops were going to be the very last Southerners to go down the escape hatch, with the Tenth Tennessee at the far right end of the line, pulling up the rear, just as on the Charlotte road at Fort Henry. If anything at all went wrong, the Sons of Erin would be left behind at the mercy of the Yankees.

Saturday, February 15, 1862

At the Widow Crisp's farmhouse, the clatter of a

horse's hooves was muffled by newly fallen snow and the whistling wind. A sailor slid from the unfamiliar saddle and was admitted to the cabin; then, an army aide led him to the kitchen and gently awakened General Grant from his feather-bed sleep. It was 4:00 a. m. Saturday, February 15.[118]

The sailor handed the general a wax-sealed message from Flag Officer Foote. Without saying a word Grant broke the seal and read the message. Foote wanted a meeting, but due to his injury he politely requested that the general make the six-mile journey north. Grant wrote out some orders to his three division commanders and was off.

General Grant had just made three mistakes which would have import for the coming events.

First of all, he, the commanding general, was departing from the scene of his command without consulting his department superior, General Henry Halleck.

Then, the instructions he had sent to the division commanders were fixed and inflexible, calling for the three generals to hold their positions without engaging the Rebels, unless attacked. Furthermore, nothing could unlock the orders without a direct command from Grant himself, who was about to become scarce.

The purpose of the strictly limited orders was to contain McClernand. He got contained, all right. The orders guaranteed that McClernand's two remaining intact brigades would be assaulted by five Confederate brigades, without any possibility of being reinforced by either Lew Wallace or C.F. Smith.[119]

Finally, for the second time in ten days, the Union commanding general incorrectly assumed that the Confederates would act in a predictable way. Based on his knowledge of Pillow's behavioral patterns, Grant expected the Boys-in-Gray to stay put in their pits, as they had for the past three days.[120] Ironically, at the same time he left his command with that belief firm in his mind, Pillow was moving his forces into attack formation.

When General Grant arrived at naval headquarters,

he obliged Commodore Foote and inspected the battered boats while considering the commodore's request to send them to Cairo for repairs.

After the inspection more pleasantries were exchanged about the battle readiness of the boats. At 10:00 a.m. the discussions were interrupted by a hard-riding courier from McClernand. The time on the message read 8:30 a.m. McClernand was under heavy attack and wanted Wallace and C. F. Smith freed to support his endangered position.[121]

Grant said nothing, reached for the reins of his mount, Fox, (his long distance horse) and trotted away. He believed that the temperamental Southern Illinois politician he had come to know so well was exaggerating the threat. Sam Grant wanted to inspect the situation for himself. He was, really, in no hurry to return.

H Company of the Sons of Erin had been relieved at 2:00 a.m. by a detachment of the Fortieth Tennessee. Some of the Irishmen were in such high spirits, or had such cold bodies, that they decided to find another jug or two before sleeping.[122] At exactly that same hour that Colonel John W. Head was summoned to the hotel room of General Simon Buckner, informed about the Confederate plan, and given his assignment within it, the Irishmen began to give themselves a strong nightcap.

When Buckner moved out in support of Bushrod Johnson, Head's Thirtieth Tennessee reserve regiment of 450 raw recruits, then deployed behind Heiman's brigade, would occupy Buckner's rifle pits, and pretend to be the right flank, opposite C.F. Smith's Second division of 6,000 blue-clads. Colonel Head was a bit slow moving his men through the heavy snow and bitter winds, causing the surprise attack to begin forty minutes late at 5:40 a.m., all of which gave Pillow a Heiman-like fit of agitation.[123]

At sunrise pickets from the Ninth Illinois heard something coming right toward them. At ten minutes past sunrise, General Bushrod Johnson's Confederates slammed into the First brigade, First division of Colonel Richard Oglesby, sending the Ninth, Twelfth, and Fourteenth Illinois regiments reeling back. By the time that General John McClernand was warned, he was already under attack.

At the same time that Johnson was pushing the Federals south, McClernand sent a courier west to General Wallace for immediate help. Wallace couldn't respond because of Grant's instructions, and the situation grew worse. At 8:00 a.m. the Indiana general, without orders, made a wise move, took the battlefield initiative, and brought up a single brigade of his Third division in support of the First division.[124]

General Wallace's rescue mission was entrusted to the Hoosiers and Kentuckians of Colonel Charles Cruft, 36, of Terre Haute. When Cruft's four regiments turned right, however, purely by accident, they were blocked by General Buckner's advancing columns of Colonel Hanson's Rebel Kentuckians, temporarily preventing Lew Wallace from reinforcing McClernand.

While Buckner's division pushed Cruft's brigade of Wallace's division back to the center of the field, Johnson's division continued to clobber Oglesby's brigade of McClernand's division.[125] The Federals were desperate for a hero, and such a man was about to show himself on the scene.

As the battle raged, the Fighting Fitzgeralds were engaged in one of their endless scuffles behind the Irish logworks on Heiman's Hill.[126] The latest brawl was interrupted by that ominous hum of an incoming shell, which put a big, black, ugly hole in the beautiful white landscape. When the smoke cleared, Mo and Willie Fitzgerald and the rest of the lads picked themselves off the frozen turf. Artillery fire was something that the Irishmen had reluctantly grown accustomed to. The noise didn't much surprise them anymore.

112

The shell, however, had surprised their commanding officer. Lieutenant Colonel McGavock had been receiving reports from his courier, Second Lieutenant R. G. Southall, that the Yankees had been driven off their original positions in the Lick Creek Valley and turned away from the Wynn Ferry road. Where, then, McGavock wondered, had the latest shell come from? Was Heiman's reserve brigade being surrounded by the unattended Union left? Was attack imminent? He had to know, and knowing meant finding the battery.

McGavock saddled up. From the pinnacle of Heiman's Hill, he spotted smoke drifting away from the woods near the Wynn Ferry road. With Tenth Legion moving quietly through the snow, McGavock made his way to the sight of smoke, the smell of gun powder, and the sound of voices, where he discovered four smoothbores with a crew of some fifty or sixty Federal gunners.[127] The escape hatch hadn't been completely opened.

Lieutenant Colonel McGavock passed his intelligence coup on to Colonel Heiman, who passed it on to General Johnson, who passed it on to General Pillow, who passed it on to General Floyd. The message contained a request for McGavock to take one or two of his companies and knock out the battery.[128] After all, wasn't protecting the road the purpose of leaving Heiman's troops back in reserve? Whether or not Floyd ever received the message remains unknown. What is certain is that no message was ever returned and no action was ever taken.

At the same time the Tenth Tennessee remained posted in the rifle pits on Heiman's Hill, the Thirty-First Illinois of the First brigade of McClernand's division swung into action. This was a unit of pro-Union farmers from the Cairo area, led by Colonel John Alexander "Black Jack" Logan, 36, of Southern Illinois, a big, strong, handsome, swarthy-skinned, raw-boned Irish-American with a handle-bar mustache that matched his complexion. He had the reputation of being able to swear, drink, play cards, brawl, and chase women better than anyone else in the Union Army. An outstanding civilian officer, Logan was later described by General Sherman as "perfect in combat."[129]

By 9:30 the Thirty-First Illinois had not yet been engaged, so Colonel Logan formed his regiment into a defensive line center to right. In the next half hour, he reinforced his men by rallying two Illinois regiments of the Second brigade of General McClernand's First division and three of the regiments of Colonel Cruft's First brigade of General Lew Wallace's Third division. The Confederate advance stopped.[130]

At about 10 o'clock a slight gap became visible in Logan's line, exactly the type of opportunity the cavalry unit in the woods looked for. Lieutenant Colonel Nathan Bedford Forrest's men pressed a flank attack, dismounted and carved up a Union battery with razor-sharp swords.

Alone on horseback Colonel Logan led an infantry counter-attack against the dismounted cavalry. Forrest reacted quickly, firing his navy six-shooters with deadly accuracy into the onrushing traffic. Logan was knocked off his horse, seriously wounded, and Forrest had his horse shot out from under him. While Lieutenant Colonel Forrest mounted a second horse and crashed into a weak spot on the enemy line, turning back both flanks, Generals Johnson and Buckner advanced another time. General McClernand fell back again.[131]

Five of the men from H Company, Tenth Tennessee, had been up all night drinking. By mid-morning Pat Griffin got sick and fell asleep leaning against a tree. Jimmy Doyle tried to jot something into his notebook, but broke his pencil. Marty Gibbons did an Irish jig while Mike Carney played the harmonica. And "Crazy Tom" Feeney informed Barney McCabe that he was hungry.[132]

At about the same time that Sergeant McCabe, with the help of Clarksville drummer boy Danny McCarthy, was getting some food into the Irishmen of H Company to help ease their hangovers, Lieutenant Colonel Forrest's Tennessee cavalrymen, assisted by Colonel Hanson's Kentucky infantrymen, were capturing two more Union batteries, along with all of their ordnance. Forrest, in spite of having two more horses shot out from under him, had not a scratch on him.[133]

McClernand was almost out of small arms ammunition, and all three of his brigades had been mauled and his troops disorganized and demoralized in the past forty-eight hours. General Pillow took a lunch break to send General Johnston another wire. "On the honor of a soldier, the day is ours."[134] The campaign for Fort Donelson had turned into a massive Confederate victory. Or so it seemed.

There was one blessing in disguise for the Federal troops. The combined assault of Johnson and Buckner had been so successful that the entire Union right flank had been pushed into its own center. Stampeding McClernand into Wallace meant that Lew Wallace himself was then under attack, freed from Grant's orders and fully into the fight. As a result the whole scenario changed. High Noon, Saturday, February 15, 1862, would prove to be the Confederate high tide of the Fort Donelson campaign. With Wallace's entire Third division thrown into the fray, the blue-clads would not yield another inch. Actually, the Confederate objective of the day had already been accomplished. The Federals on the Confederate left had been moved out, and the escape hatch was wide open. So General Pillow as field commander had to choose from the two options agreed on at the Council of War.

First, as soon as the Wynn Ferry road was open, begin an orderly retirement due east to Clarksville, and then south to Nashville, or second, pursue the defeated enemy with the hopes of crippling the entire army, and then hook up with Hardee at Nashville via Clarksville. In either case, the operation had worked without a flaw and both options were viable.

Incredibly, General Pillow, needlessly concerned about enemy reinforcements from General Buell, exercised neither of the options and ordered a retreat back to the original Confederate positions in the trenches![135] It was almost as if the latest glorious message to Bowling Green had used up his last ounce of energy and hope.

With curiosity, the losers watched the winners withdraw from the battlefield. All of those red blotches in the snow were for naught.

General Bushrod Johnson was dumbfounded, but he complied. Buckner was livid, refused to follow the order, and sought out Floyd, who was back at the stockade, shaving. When Floyd rode out to see the three other generals, he completely agreed with Buckner and started to direct the evacuation. After Pillow had caught his ear, however, Floyd reversed himself and ordered the Confederate infantry back into line along the ridges, as if the events of the day had never happened.

General McClernand proclaimed a personal triumph. General C.F. Smith, still frozen in place by orders in the Hickman Creek Valley, sent out couriers to keep himself informed. The Sons of Erin were still held in reserve on Heiman's Hill, except for the lads of H Company, who were sleeping it off at the cemetery.

All the Northerners pinched themselves. The Southerners were, obviously and for no apparent reason, falling back after winning. Somebody had to take advantage of the situation. General Lew Wallace reacted immediately to the Confederate foul-up and personally led a ferocious counterassault into the rear of the retreating Boys-in-Gray, inflicting heavy casualties.[136] His men had wanted a fight; now they had it.

Meanwhile General Grant arrived on the field and logically assumed that the Rebels had pulled out their right to support their left. He ordered General C.F. Smith to pound the Confederate right, assuring the former commandant of West Point that he would find only "a very thin line to contend with."[137] Then Grant rode out onto the battlefield to have a look for himself.

A thin line, indeed. With the back end of Buckner mixing it up with the front end of Wallace, the Confederate right flank consisted exclusively of the reserve unit, that of Colonel John Head and his 450 primarily teenaged soldiers of the Thirtieth Tennessee. Their job was to hold off the six-thousand Yankees of the Second division until Buckner returned.

This time the fifty-five-year-old West Point hero decided to lead the charge himself. High up on his war horse, with minié balls whizzing around him, General C. F. Smith moved his alignments with a gesture of his sword. "I was nearby, scared to death," was what one Union infantryman said afterwards, "but I saw the old man's white mustache over his shoulder, and went on."[138] Colonel Head and his men, for their parts, put up a real fight.

While C. F. Smith was moving on Head, Grant mingled with some of the enlisted men of his rear guard to get a better understanding of the situation. One young private observed offhandedly that the Boys-in-Gray had plenty to eat. The commanding general asked him how he knew. "We found some Rebel haversacks filled with rations," was what he replied.[139]

That was it! The Southerners were taking as much as they could carry with them. It was like Fort Henry all over again. They were fighting to break out. Amazingly, General Grant then had a better understanding of the Confederate military objective than did Generals Floyd or Pillow.

As the afternoon wore down to dusk, and the rear-guard action wore down with it, the dejected Confederates marched back to their trenches. On the east end of the field the Federal gunners near the road provided a few more fireworks. Pessimists Floyd and Pillow figured this to mean that the blue-clads had brought up thousands of reinforcements from Buell. In their narrow minds the escape hatch was closed forever!

General Buckner had an unpleasant homecoming reception near his former logworks and rifle pits. After several bloody charges against the lone enemy regiment, General C. F. Smith ousted Head and his tough kids of the Thirtieth Tennessee, many of whom had been surrounded and captured. As a result Buckner's division had to bivouac in an exposed position about a mile away. The Confederate right flank had been turned. In fact, it was worse than that. There no longer was a Confederate right flank, hence no defensive line.

C. F. Smith, entrenched on Buckner's Hill, set up his heavy artillery in range of Bushrod Johnson's position, Simon Buckner's new position, and the water batteries.

While Federal gunners pounded away, the *Carondelet* and the *Louisville* made an unexpected return visit and blasted away at the river defenses.[140]

By nightfall everything had returned to normal, as hundreds of sharpshooters fired away in the snow and ice and cold and dark. Colonel Joe Drake briefed Colonel Adolphus Heiman about the events of the day. The colonels speculated that the withdrawal was an extension of option number two, namely that Floyd and Pillow wanted to whip the Yankees again in the morning, before moving out to Clarksville.

Under the circumstances, what else could they think? McGavock had reported that the road was still open except for one battery, so the escape must still be on. The Stars and Bars remained atop the stockade, but just barely. Heiman was concerned but not overly nervous. His brigade had not been left behind.[141]

Before checking into the Brandon Hotel for the evening, Randal McGavock rode Tenth Legion over to the Dover Inn to get some needed information from the generals. What in the name of St. Patrick was going on?

Floyd and Pillow were alone. Floyd was writing and didn't bother to look up. (After all, this lower level officer hadn't been summoned, and Floyd was devoted to protocol.) Pillow sat there staring into space.[142]

After an awkward minute or two, Floyd started to read

his sheet of paper out loud to no one in particular, as Mc-Gavock continued to stand and Pillow continued to sit. It turned out to be another victory message for Sidney Johnston! It was at this time that McGavock mentioned the single battery on the road and his standing offer to take it out. Floyd said that there were heavy reinforcements out there. McGavock said no, there was only the one battery. Pillow spoke for the first time, announcing that if Buckner hadn't been forty minutes late, everything would have gone as planned. Pillow, apparently, had found a scapegoat for his own miserable mistake.

At this point Buckner himself came in, frosty as the air outside, and McGavock was dismissed. The Tenth Tennessee lieutenant colonel went away with the strong impression that the battle would be renewed in the morning.[143]

After McGavock left, a discussion followed, with a lot of disagreement about the enemy's strength, particularly on the Wynn Ferry road. At 9:00 p.m. the three generals decided to settle the matter and sent for Forrest, with instructions to check out the road.

The big cavalryman went out with two trusted scouts, and returned with the startling report that absolutely no Federals were on the road, not even the one battery. (His troopers had driven them off that day.) The escape hatch was still wide open. After reporting to his superiors, Forrest went back to his cavalry den in the woods, and like McGavock, planned to be ready to lick the Yankees again in the morning.[144]

At 10:00 p.m. Bushrod Johnson entered, half asleep, and suggested they all got some sleep before starting a night withdrawal before the Boys-in-Blue rose at sunrise, which the other three agreed was a terrific idea. Floyd and Pillow favored the plan. But the infuriated Buckner could not leave the day's events alone; he stated that they would presently be in Clarksville had it not been for Pillow's blunder and Floyd's weak leadership.

An extremely heated debate ensued between Pillow

and Buckner, with Floyd waffling between the two, agreeing with no one and both at the same time. An exasperated Johnson asked to be excused, and went to bed firmly believing that he would soon be awakened for the trip to Clarksville.[145]

Shortly after Johnson left, Floyd introduced the remarkable suggestion that he should escape while the three other generals and the seventeen-thousand men of his corps would surrender. (The actual term used was "capitulate," a word that Floyd and Pillow would forever be remembered for.) The vote on this interesting proposal went two to one in favor, and it was not Floyd and Pillow against Buckner. It was Floyd and Buckner against Pillow!

Buckner, who was raving only moments before about honor and needless retreat, seems to have given in to the negative streak that sometimes surfaced in his behavior and accepted Floyd's improbably high figure about Federal strength—the fifty-thousand Northern reinforcements. When it was all said and done, Pillow was convinced. He agreed to the "capitulation" only on the condition that he also be allowed to escape with Floyd!

The two senior, ranking officers were planning to decamp, while leaving their command behind. At midnight the perfidious shift of power occurred. "I turn the command over, sir," Floyd told Pillow. "I pass it," Pillow told Buckner. "I assume it," was what Buckner responded.[146] And thus the largest surrender of troops for prison during the war was concluded with strict military protocol.

Sunday, February 16, 1862

General Floyd rationalized his flight by claiming that he, as a former U.S. secretary of war, was a prime catch for the blue-clads and couldn't turn up as a prisoner; Pillow said he had made that vow of liberty or death and couldn't break it, even if it meant sneaking away in the middle of the night. The import was that they would soon be gone and the men who served so loyally under them would be in Federal prison camps and their strength lost to the Southern cause.

Since the two generals needed a cavalry escort for their operation, they again sent for Forrest. The fearsome cavalryman couldn't believe his ears. "I did not come here to surrender my command," he growled and soon walked out the door.[147] He gathered his horse soldiers, mounted, rode off and never looked back. The Tennessee cavalry brigade, joined by about a thousand discontented infantrymen, escaped over the Wynn Ferry road to Clarksville and then down to Nashville, which they reached by the evening of the next day.

Meanwhile, back at the Cumberland River, General Floyd commandeered two steamboats for his getaway, each carrying two of his four Virginia regiments. His Mississippi regiment, posted as guards at the landing, was left behind.

General Pillow wasn't as lucky. He headed south up the Cumberland in a small boat, rowed by chief engineer Major Jeremy F. Gilmer. In a few months both Generals Floyd and Pillow were court-martialled and found guilty of neglect of duty. A year later, John B. Floyd died in disgrace. Gideon Pillow opened a new law practice after the war with former governor Isham Harris.

With his right flank decimated, and with Floyd, Pillow, Forrest, all the cavalry, all the Virginians, and some of the Tennessee infantry gone, General Buckner didn't have much of a choice. "Give me pen, ink, and paper, and send for a bugler," was what the quarrelsome but honorable Kentuckian ordered an aide. While the cease-fire sounded, Buckner's courier rode two hundred yards and gave a message to General C. F. Smith. It called for an armistice and terms of surrender. Smith set out at once for the Crisp farmhouse. "There's something for you to read," he told Grant. "Well, what do you think of it?" Grant wanted to know. "I think, no terms with the traitors, by God!", C. F. answered. General Grant took a sheet of tablet paper and began to write. When he finished, he handed it to General Smith, who read it by firelight. "By God, it couldn't be better."[148]

With the prodding of Smith, Grant had written the most famous dispatch of the American Civil War. Scorning "capitulation," it called for unconditional and immediate surrender and gave new meaning to Grant's initials: U.S.—Unconditional Surrender Grant.

Disappointed with his Academy friend's high-handedness, Buckner sent a formal note of surrender. "The overwhelming forces under your command compel me, notwithstanding the brilliant success of the Confederate arms yesterday, to accept the ungenerous and unchivalrous terms which you propose."[149]

So there it was. The winners surrendered to the losers.

The Confederate rank and file did not know as yet that they had been sold upriver, literally, to Federal prison. They still labored under the belief that they were going out the escape hatch to Clarksville to fight again. Shortly after 1:00 a.m. Heiman, on Johnson's orders, woke McGavock and told him to have the Sons of Erin ready to march by 4:00 a.m.. Both agreed that it was smart to get the breakout going under cover of darkness. After the events of the previous day, Heiman, McGavock and the Irish lads were eager to get out of Dover.

At exactly 4:00 a.m. on Sunday, February 16, 1862, the Tenth Tennessee was ready and waiting, along with the rest of Heiman's brigade and Drake's brigade of Johnson's division. A half an hour later, the Irishmen were getting cold and restless. McGavock "smelled a rat," and asked Heiman about the delay.[150] Heiman knew nothing. The lieutenant colonel sought out Bushrod Johnson. The scholarly Tennessean figured the retreat had to begin before sunrise, but hadn't a clue about operational details. "The general seemed to be profoundly ignorant as to what was going on," McGavock recorded in his journal.[151]

Simon Buckner finally remembered to send his fellow general a message about the surrender. General Johnson, in disbelief, went back to the Dover Inn to hear about it in person, only to discover that the two commanding generals had flown the coop. Quietly he returned to let his commanders in on the bad news. Heiman was agitated. Drake was bitter. McGavock was furious.

Johnson packed his few belongings onto his black mount, saluted his men, passed through the Union lines unrecognized, and rode off, along with Captain John H. Anderson of the Tenth Tennessee, into the woods to join Forrest. Johnson and the Sons of Erin would meet again.

McGavock's notion of escape was the same as Forrest's. Unaware that the road was open and searching for a way to get his command out intact, he searched for some small boats, but none could be found. In a wild moment he considered having his Irishmen swim to freedom; and Marty Gibbons, a good swimmer, volunteered to show the way. The notion was unrealistic and McGavock realized it. The water was icy cold, many of the Irishmen couldn't swim, and the Yankees could "butcher" the whole regiment in the river.[152]

At sunrise their "Randy Mack," as popular and trusted a commanding officer as any unit ever had, informed the Sons of Erin that escape was impossible, and that he personally would not leave without them. It required six-hundred pages to record all his journals. But one entry stands out above all the rest. "In sorrow, humiliation, and anger I marched my regiment back to their quarters."[153]

McGavock always referred to the trials of that day and the day before as the "betrayal" at Donelson. His negative feelings were directed not at the Federals, but at Floyd and Pillow.

General Unconditional Surrender Grant, astride Jack, rode past white flags to the Dover Inn, where he found two soldiers chatting amicably over a breakfast of cornbread and coffee, exchanging the latest jokes from the trenches. They were Union General Lew Wallace and Confederate General Simon Buckner. Grant shared the breakfast and traded quips with his Rebel friend.

At the same time that Buckner, Wallace and Grant were eating, General Albert Sidney Johnston was getting some bad news. After having been the beneficiary of a spate of glorious telegraphs, he got word from Floyd with the stunning non-glorious results. At least this time Johnston didn't have to read the negative report in a newspaper.

McGavock came into town, heading towards the Brandon Hotel one final time to pick up his gear. He went inside, and when he came back out, Tenth Legion was gone! One of the Yankee staff officers had appropriated the faithful beast. Marching immediately to the Dover Inn, the irritated lieutenant colonel of the Tenth Tennessee ran into a short, stumpy man in a rumpled uniform, smoking a cigar.

McGavock strongly protested the dastardly removal of his mount. Grant said that if he found the horse, he would make the offending officer give him up, but the animal would then have to be turned over to the Federal quartermaster. In short, Tenth Legion remained a goner. McGavock grudgingly admired the simple honesty of the man's judgment, and went away with respect for the Illinois Union commander.[154]

McGavock would miss Tenth Legion, a true thoroughbred. George and Herm, the Irish regimental mess mules, were also captured by the Boys-in-Blue.

Heiman gave McGavock a ride back to the cemetery, where yet another felonious act was discovered. All the Irish regimental valuables were missing, including McGavock's Fort Henry journal. "I suppose they will publish my journal, and sell it to help pay the expense of the war," he wrote. Northerners could be seen slinking away loaded down with contraband. Normally in a foul mood anyway, the Fighting Fitzgeralds were especially outraged. They shared the same deep attachment for their jug that McGavock had for his horse.[155]

The Consequences

General Sidney Johnston accompanied General William Hardee with Hardee's army corps on retreat from Bowling Green to Nashville. Cold and sickness devastated the 14,000 Southern soldiers. When they arrived in the capital on February 15, 5,400 sick men had to be hospitalized in temporary shelters.[156] The last of the troops had come in only hours before Floyd's last telegraph was delivered, just ahead of Floyd himself. There was no time to throw up any kind of adequate defense in the home city of the Sons of Erin, an ominous situation. Although Johnston still didn't know where Buell was, he certainly knew where Grant was.

The consequences of not reinforcing the Clarksville District finally began to sink in with Johnston. The Confederates had lost their narrow foothold in Kentucky, which meant that Generals Beauregard and Polk would have to evacuate Columbus. Then too, with the main body of the army in sick bay, the indefensible city of Nashville, with its railroads and munition factories, would also have to be evacuated. As a result the Federals were free to overrun North Middle Tennessee without much opposition. With Hardee in full retreat, the whole Confederate line in the West was in danger of collapsing.[157]

Sidney Johnston knew that he would have to face Buell or Halleck or both somewhere, but exactly where he didn't know. The place turned out to be Pittsburg Landing, Tennessee. Twenty-four hours after entering the Tennessee state capital, Johnston took off again, leaving Floyd and Pillow behind to rescue supplies, a job they predictably botched. Forrest did manage to get some of the ammunition out on time.

Seven weeks after Fort Donelson fell, General Albert Sidney Johnston, a great soldier, but not a great army commander, was mortally wounded in action while personally leading a charge near Shiloh Church.

With Nashville in a state of panic and chaos, General C.F. Smith occupied the town once administered by Randal McGavock on Tuesday, February 25. A puppet military governor was appointed by President Lincoln, and Andrew Johnson, the Rebel-hating U.S. Senator from East Tennessee, reported for duty. Johnson came to Nashville not only as appointed governor, but also as appointed brigadier general with full military powers, all the while maintaining his seat in the U.S. Senate.

Supported by his own personal investigative staff, Governor Johnson exercised the arbitrary authority of a dictator, rounding up and detaining countless numbers of innocent civilians on trumped-up charges of treason. Arrests took place for the slightest of pretenses, in violation of civil rights. Many Nashville fence-sitters were driven into the Confederate camp and stayed there, and people like the senior McGavocks and Seph lived in constant intimidation and fear that they would have property confiscated or be thrown into compounds, where there was miasma in the air and filthy straw on the floors, because they spoke out on behalf of the Southern cause.

In the months that followed the fall of the inland river forts, Rebel raiders Bedford Forrest and John Hunt Morgan cut off Federal supply routes into Nashville. Food supplies ran out, and the Irish community where the Sons of Erin lived was one of the many groups hard hit. Prices soared, and business ground to a halt, causing Andrew Johnson to become even more despotic. Supervision of the local newspapers, even of the religious press, followed. None of the churches were doing very well anyhow. Only about half continued to hold services, and nearly all the congregations were seriously disrupted in some way.

Father Emmeran Bliemel,(pronounced Blee-mel) a native of Germany and parish priest in the small German parish of Assumption, found it increasingly difficult to keep up his duties.[158] His bishop, James Whalen, then known as "Yankee Jim," because he was a native of Ohio, put the parish on part-time status. (Whalen had carelessly given the impression of publicly expressing pro-Union sentiments in occupied Nashville.)

Father Emmeran had been born in Ratsibon, Bavarian Germany, September 29, 1831. As a teenager, he and a friend, Otto Kopf, decided to become missionaries in America, which was then seeing a healthy immigration of German Catholics. The two boys were accepted at the Novitiate of St. Vincent, a Benedictine community in Latrobe, Pennsylvania. After having taken his vows as a monk, and after having been ordained a priest, Bliemel took up a succession of Pennsylvania clerical assignments and picked up skill as an excellent equestrian, a skill which he would later use as a Confederate Army chaplain. After serving in Kentucky, Bliemel responded to the call of Bishop Whalen for priests to come to his state sized diocese, and soon found himself serving in the wartime parish of the Assumption.

Shocked by what he saw as the ruthlessness of the Andrew Johnson administration, the German pastor was convinced that the Union cause was morally wrong, and requested permission to become a Confederate Army chaplain. There was a real shortage of priests on the homefront, and Bishop Whalen denied permission, so Father Bliemel dedicated his priestly ministry to the sick and wounded Union soldiers who were pouring into the temporary military hospitals all over the city.[159] As a man of compassion, Bliemel looked for ways to help the sick and wounded on both sides.

As the Black Market thrived, converts to the Southern cause put together a smuggling operation, designed to send desperately needed medical supplies down south. By this time anaesthesia was running low in several areas and surgeons lacked even the basic tools of their art. Several local citizens soon became experts at bringing morphine and scalpels and amputation saws to the front.

No one was better at this operation than Father Emmeran Bliemel, who served the Southern cause in his own way in the Nashville underground.[160] At some point in the near future he was destined for other, more direct ministry to the South: he would serve as chaplain of the Tenth Tennessee.

Chapter Four
Jailbirds in the Northwestern Waters

Camp Chase

On the very same night of the surrender of Fort Donelson, a Union steamboat took the non-commissioned officers (sergeants and corporals) and the other enlisted men (privates) of the Sons of Erin north down the Cumberland to Paducah and then west to Cairo. Twenty-four hours later the commissioned officers (lieutenants on up) went north by the same route aboard the *Tecumseh.*

The next evening, Tuesday, February 18, all the prison boats were docked in Cairo, but none of the Southerners were ordered to get off. In the morning almost six-thousand prisoners were sent northwest to St. Louis, where they arrived on the 20th. Lodging was in the boats, where they sat for two days.

Early on the morning of Saturday, February 22, the non-coms and privates were separated and marched off to railroad box cars, as described by eyewitness Pat Griffin. The departure was traumatic for hero-worshiping Griffin, an eighteen-year-old at the time. "For the first time since we left Nashville, Lieutenant Colonel McGavock and I were parted," was what he lamented.[1]

McGavock himself completely understood the idea of separation. "The policy of removing officers from men is done in order to break all ties existing between them, and to prevent any future organization," he said.[2]

Amazingly, the Confederate commissioned officers were given "temporary paroles," being allowed to wander where they would during the day as long as they returned to the boats at night. (This relaxed attitude would change dramatically in the later stages of the war.) In any case, Lieutenant Colonel McGavock returned; he had, after all, pledged to follow his lads to prison.

While taking in the sights, he ran into "Dutch" Tilghman, Lafayette McConnico, and John McLaughlin, Fort Henry compatriots. They had been in St. Louis for better than two weeks.

On February 27 the remaining Confederate officer-prisoners were marched off to that same depot, except for McGavock's courier R.G. Southall, who was sick with a high fever in a St. Louis hospital. Soon Henry Southall, his personal slave, came to care for the Scotch-Irish lad and eventually took him home. The second lieutenant returned to the plantation, recovered fully, but never returned to the regiment.[3]

The officers left St. Louis; their train rushed northeast through barren fields of corn stubble and flooding rivers. In Terre Haute, Indiana, the prisoners were allowed to stretch their legs. McGavock was impressed by the charm of the Hoosier town. "The Irish of this place were very kind to us and really do sympathize with us, as they have everywhere we have met them in the north."[4] This was, of course, wishful thinking. Terre Haute, the home of Lew Wallace and four ferocious regiments of Rebel-hating Hoosiers, had little desire to coddle captured Confederates. In the early morning of March 1, the prison train pulled into the depot at Columbus, Ohio. A new and grim phase of regimental history was about to begin.

One hundred and four Confederate officers were greeted by the Union commandant, Granville "The Fighting Parson" Moody. (Moody was also a Methodist minister.) "A haughty, dictatorial, pharisaical, vile, God-forsaken reprobate," was how McGavock described the colonel.[5]

Putting their "packs on their backs," the weary Southern officers were marched "with much pomposity" through the streets of the town. Then it was a four-mile walk through the wilderness west to Camp Chase. All the buildings were constructed of wood planks, without foundations of substance, all on top of a series of creeks and ditches, large and small.

Of the 104 prisoners, fifteen were officers from the Sons of Erin. Captain Boyd Cheatham came in the next day, along with a trainload of Mississippians, making it a final total of sixteen officers from the Tenth Tennessee at Camp Chase.

We were marched into a pen or high enclosure containing some rough and filthy shantys, where vermin and all manner of creeping things infested. The mud was over our shoe tops. Thirty-six men were placed in a room 12 x 24 including the bunks. Three of us occupied a bunk four feet wide and not long enough to straighten our limbs in. The smell from the pit is intolerable, and I predict that if these men are kept here until warm weather, they will die like sheep with the rots. . .

was McGavock's accurate prediction.[6]

The "mess halls" were the same size and in the same condition. There were ten plank tables with no chairs. Each table had ten tin plates and an equal number of tin cups, and that was all. A chunk of bread about the size of a "man's fist" was on each plate. "None of the men wasted any time at the table," was what the camp historian wrote.[7]

Fortunately McGavock had to endure Colonel Moody's hospitality for only three days. On March 4 the final separation took place. The staff and field officers, that is, generals, colonels and majors were ordered to move out. In the case of the Sons of Erin that meant Heiman, McGavock, and Grace. The thirteen company officers, captains and lieutenants, who proudly decided not to leave at St. Louis, were forced to remain behind. At the time of parting, "there was not a dry cheek in the whole party."[8] All thirteen of the Tenth Tennessee's company officers survived, including Captain Saint Clair Morgan, who escaped.

Fort Warren

On the prison train, the staff officers spent the next two days peering out windows at Cleveland, Buffalo, Rochester, Utica and other spots in the Northeast. For the third time in his life, McGavock was headed for Boston. In the early morning of March 6, the Southerners were taken by boat to their final destination—Fort Warren in Boston Harbor. One-hundred-twenty-four prisoners were incarcerated in the fort, all under the care of Colonel Justin Dimick.[9]

McGavock and the other two officers of the Sons of Erin realized they had left the swinish conditions of Columbus far behind; this was an officers' prison. "These gentlemen [guards] were so kind to us that I really forgot that I was a prisoner," McGavock admitted.[10]

Three or four Confederate officers shared spacious, comfortable rooms, each with its own fireplace, and each with an attractive view of the Bunker Hill Monument and the Charlestown Navy Yard. Best of all, each man had his own bed, complete with mattresses, sheets, and blankets.

After unpacking his meager belongings, McGavock headed straight as an arrow to the mess hall, where three Kentucky soldiers beckoned him over to their roomy table. They were General Lloyd Tilghman, General Simon Buckner, and Colonel (soon to be General) Roger Hanson.

Entertainment at Fort Warren was provided by Lafayette McConnico, then a major on Tilghman's staff. Colonel Dimick would listen endlessly to the major's singing and guitar playing.

Lieutenant Colonel McGavock found himself quartered with his commanding officer, Colonel Adolphus Heiman, and with Colonel John Gregg, commanding officer of the Seventh Texas Infantry regiment. The prisoners were allowed to bring in just about anything that they could afford to buy; roommates frequently shared extra food and liquor. On one occasion Heiman was described as "very tight, quite happy, and felicitous in his remarks" and was heard to sing "Ole Tom Cat," while in a state of undress.[11] On another occasion McGavock climbed the wall of the fort and serenaded one of the lovely belles of Boston, who happened to be passing below. There were no escape attempts at Fort Warren.

Randal W. McGavock spent most of his time in the comfortable brig catching up on his reading. In a letter from his mother, he learned of the "personal disloyalty" of a very special family slave. "She states that my Negro man, Martin, has left Nashville and gone with the Federal army."[12] It never seems to have dawned on McGavock that the family's "personal" property might wish freedom.

In fact, the Fort Warren journal provides a great deal of insight into the character of McGavock and his antebellum Southern philosophy of life. Most especially, the Nashville aristocrat considered the war to be a "gentleman's spat" and could never understand why Northerners considered him personally to be the enemy. The following entries show what a gentleman fighting a war from a prison cell experienced:

March 13.
My tailor sent my clothes today, but took care to get Charles Woodbury to guarantee payment, notwithstanding I patronized him for years and always paid my bills promptly. Just because I am a prisoner, he now needs a guarantee before he sends the clothes.[13]

March 17.
This is St. Patrick's Day. Oh! how I wish that I was with my Irish regiment at Chicago [Camp Douglas] to celebrate the day and cheer the lads in their imprisonment. Mrs. Thayer sent a box to Colonel Heiman and myself today, containing fine whiskey, brandy, cigars, cheese, sardines etc. We

*had some of our friends to visit us this evening
and help us enjoy it.*[14]

April 21.

The lieutenant colonel of the Tenth Tennessee heard
false rumors about the disloyalty of some of his lads at Camp
Chase and Camp Douglas. In spite of his initial disappoint-
ment, his attitude was one of understanding and compassion.

> *Letters have been received here in the last day
> or so from Camp Douglas near Chicago and from
> Camp Chase near Columbus, Ohio, to the effect
> that some officers and many men are about to
> take the oath of allegiance [to the Union] and
> return to their homes. I am sorry to hear this be-
> cause we have already enough [Yankee] prison-
> ers for an exchange. I have no doubt that many
> of them prefer the oath to remaining in prisons
> that may endanger their health. Many have fami-
> lies at home who are suffering and who depend
> on them.*[15]

May 31.

McGavock offers a brief but interesting comment on
the quiet, thoughtful nature of Major William Grace.

> *Major Grace remarked this morning that prison
> was the best place in the world to find out about
> human nature—and I believe he is correct.*[16]

June 23.

This entry reflects the old-fashioned sentimentality,
chivalry, and deep sense of Irish loyalty and unity of
McGavock, Grace, Captain Leslie Ellis and Captain James

Kirkman. The young mother they mention was the wife of James McLauflin, D Company of Clarksville.

> *I was very much amused today at a little romance related to me today by Major Grace. The scene was in Dover on Monday previous to the fight at Fort Donelson. Mrs. McLauflin, an Irish woman who was the wife of a private of the Sons of Erin, 10th Regiment Tenn. Vol. who left the camp at Fort Henry a few days before the bombardment and who went to Dover to be confined. When she arrived everybody was making ready for the approaching battle—and had no time to look after her. Two officers, however, of the 10th tendered their services. Captain Ellis got a room for her and some whiskey, which is considered indispensable by an Irish woman on such occasions, and Jimmy Kirkman, two minutes after the little "Son of Erin" made his appearance, had him tied up in a rag and walked up and down the floor with him in his arms until relieved by the woman's husband. I admire the conduct of these two officers on the occasion and would have liked very much to have witnessed the scene.*[17]

The leisure time afforded the officers, and the availability of newspapers, gave McGavock a good deal of time to catch up on the news. Some of it was personally interesting. *The New York Herald* newspaper dated May 14, 1862, reported that the standard (that big green and gold banner with the harp) of the Sons of Erin had been captured by Brigadier General (formerly Colonel) "Black Jack" Logan and delivered by him, as a trophy, with elaborate ceremony and speechmaking to the Irish Sixty-Ninth New York Infantry regiment.

McGavock sat there picturing in his own mind the Yankees poised to invade the South, rallying behind his own regimental battle flag. He began to carefully peruse the news article.

With nothing better to do, he wrote an indignant letter to the editor. "False from beginning to end," was his summary. He was essentially correct. Although without malice, the article was mostly fiction. It was this article that made specific, in print, the myth of the "Bloody Tenth" already begun at Fort Donelson. For decades the blarney-spreading survivors of the Tenth Tennessee would refer to this source for their exaggerated interpretations of the battle record of the regiment.

The piece was written by the Cairo war correspondent of *The Herald,* Frank G. Chapman, who was trying to put together some human interest material about the Fort Donelson campaign. "The greatest liar of all times," was McGavock's somewhat less-than-objective judgment of the man.[19]

The falsehoods in the story had several facets. The yarn began when the New York Irishmen, asked for stories about Donelson, announced that the battle flag of the Irish Rebel Tenth Tennessee was soon going to be used by the famed New York Sixty-Ninth infantry of the Irish Brigade, United State Volunteers.

According to the fiction they either conjured up or had told to them, the flag was on its way from Fort Donelson to the Seven Days Campaign, where the Irish spirit of their captured memento would inspire the Yankee lads to achieve great success.

The fabrication in the article went further. The New Yorkers who then had the standard said the flag of the Rebel Sons of Erin was taken "from Irishmen by Irishmen" after an especially rousing all-Irish battle, supposedly at Dover, February 15. After the Tennessee Irish carried the flag into mortal combat against their Irish brothers from Illinois, it was "taken and retaken three times," before being seized by "Black

Jack" himself. Finally, as the huge all-Irish struggle wore down, the blue-clad Irishmen licked the "Union at Heart" gray-clad Irishmen, due to the great effort of Irish Colonel Morgan L. Smith, who later delivered the "bloody prize" to the New Yorkers in order to further the "Irish cause."[20]

The entire story was patently ridiculous. In the first place, Colonel Logan's Thirty-First Illinois was not an "Irish" regiment. It consisted of farmers from the Cairo area, some of whom actually happened to be of Irish descent. As indicated earlier, the "Bloody Tenth" wasn't even engaged on that day. Logan's men fought bravely but were forced to withdraw by General Bushrod Johnson's command, very few of whom were "Irish."

In point of fact, the beautiful green flag of the Sons of Erin never was in battle on either side. In the hasty evacuation of Fort Henry, the forgetful lads left it behind to be picked up by some Illinois infantrymen, who sent it to New York as an award for a banquet involving the Sixty-Ninth New York State Militia, not the Irishmen of the famous Fighting Sixty-Ninth! The Nashville banner was never captured at Fort Donelson by Logan or M. L. Smith or any of the other Northern soldiers.

The fabled Irishmen of the Sixty-Ninth New York, United States Volunteers, had nothing whatsoever to do with the May 14, 1862, newspaper blarney. In fact, it was a slander against them to even suggest that they needed some other standard not their own to find glory on the battlefield. These New York Irishmen were, after all, part of one of the greatest military units in American history.

Another flag, planted on Heiman's Hill at Erin Hollow by McGavock, was also green but of a darker shade, much smaller, with white shamrocks and white block letters spelling his name. It was never captured or lost.

(The flag which caused so much to-do eventually found its way back home. The New York banner was returned eventually to Tennessee, and today it rests side by side with the "McGavock" flag, both having faded to yellow in the archives of the Tennessee State Museum.)[21]

But the most significant part of the fabrication in *The Herald* newspaper story was that the Sons of Erin suffered heavy casualties at the February 15 battle of Dover, thus showing that they were the "Bloody Tenth," whereas in reality on that date the lads were following orders by remaining in reserve at their stations on Heiman's Hill. Lew Clark and Pat Griffin, when they turned their memories into memoirs in later years, gladly picked up the mythology, which probably sounded more romantic and gallant than descriptions of sloshing through the mud in blinding heat to build Forts Henry and Donelson.

An interesting question centers on why certain members of the New York Irish community would invent such a story. Part of the answer must be the inevitable feeling of expansiveness and easy exaggeration of the newspaper interview environment, then in its infancy. The New York Irish did probably believe a good deal of what they said. Part of the problem surely was the difficulty of properly identifying the various regiments in the chaos at Fort Donelson. Of course reports in the Civil War, made late and inaccurately by careless or ill-informed officers and filtering through several sources before being printed, were often inaccurate themselves.

But the Irish wished to believe the romantic tale of Irishman against Irishman in a fight for glorious honor, because they were part of a particular historical movement larger than themselves. The Irish nationalists of the Fenian Movement were active in the United States at that time, especially in New York. Some of the well-intentioned but overly zealous Fenians, led by one-armed Union Brigadier General Tom Sweeny, invaded Canada in 1866. The idea was to hold the Canadian government hostage, until the British government gave Ireland her independence. The wild affair ended with the U.S. government arresting the "invaders." The Fenians continued to gain strength in Ireland and New York. Interestingly their Irish national spirit had little or no hold on the South.

Most of Nashville's Irish-American community dismissed *The New York Herald* "blarney" as just another outrageous Yankee fib. But myths are hard to contain and the Sons of Erin casualty myth was sustained and enhanced many times over during the course of the next 130 years. The glory of the lost flag expanded until it became almost as glowing a symbol as the harp that once hung on Tara's walls in Thomas More's Irish songs. Finally, the truth was lost even to those who had lived it.

Camp Douglas

The enlisted lads of the Sons of Erin, about whom the myth was being created, were on the south side of Chicago, far from both Fort Warren in Boston and the offices of *The Herald* in New York City. Camp Douglas was a large military base, designed for the instruction of army recruits. It was located on the ground which held the Seventh Annual Fair of the U.S. Agricultural Society in September, 1859, and just opposite the residence and last resting place of Illinois Senator Stephen A. Douglas.

The south end of the site was then the city limits of Chicago, with boundaries that ran from 31st street on the north to almost, but not quite 34th street on the south, and from Forest Avenue (now Indiana Avenue) on the west all the way beyond the swamps of the Cottage Grove area to Graveland Avenue (now Greenwood Avenue) on the east. The main gate was near the east end at 32nd and Ellis Avenue.

The compound consisted of sixty enclosed acres, divided by partitions, west to east, forming Prison Square (twenty acres), Hospital Square (ten acres), Garrison Square (twenty acres), and Whiteoak Square, a supply stockade (ten acres). As is obvious, there was a problem of space, with the prisoners barracks, west to center, having only the same size plot of land as the guards' barracks, east to center. Capacity was supposed to be 5,700 prisoners and 1,600 guards, but the area quickly became a standing-room-only nightmare.

Between the barracks were four hospitals, running in a north-south line, 31st to 33rd streets. All in all six barracks, four hospitals, three warehouses, and a church added up to fourteen buildings inside the compound, connected by 8,600 feet of water and sewerage pipe, like a town within a city.[22]

The last minute conversion of the place into a prisoner of war camp took place in the initial war year of 1861. By late February of the following year the facility was somewhat ready to accommodate the Confederate enlisted men surrendered at Fort Donelson. Making no stops and doing record time, the prison trains pulled into the Loop the evening of the same morning they left St. Louis.

The Union commandant was Colonel James A. Mulligan, the commanding officer of the Twenty-Third Illinois Infantry regiment, sometimes referred to as the "Western Irish Brigade." Mulligan had been the Union hero of the Battle of Lexington, Missouri, and his Chicago lads were then on temporary assignment as prison guards in their own home town.

Not too surprisingly, Colonel Mulligan was partial to the Tennessee Sons of Erin. The Rebel Irishmen, ever alert to the right chance and schooled in street survival techniques, decided to use the commandant's interest in them to buy themselves better conditions in prison.

The right opportunity was supplied by none other than General Henry Halleck, commander of all Federal troops in the West. "Old Brains" had devised a cock-a-mamie scheme involving the prisoners in his command. He believed Rebels should be given the chance to repent their disgraceful cause; a good use for men shut up in compound, costing money to feed and house, would be to have them fight the war—on the right side, of course! On March 19, 1862, Halleck approved a recruitment sign-up plan for both Camp Chase and Camp Douglas. The Sons of Erin had already been pressing this kind of angle with Colonel Mulligan.

"One Tennessee regiment, the Tenth, is composed almost exclusively of Irishmen and they desire to enlist in some of the companies of my regiment. I would willingly and fearlessly trust them," was what he dispatched on February 27, exactly five days after meeting the Southern lads.[23]

Total enlistments from both places at that time was 1,640 men, mostly from Chase, the worst of the two incarceration facilities in 1862. At Douglas five Irishmen from the Tenth Tennessee put their names on the list, not a one of whom ever served.

Private Patrick M. Griffin explained the strategy. "Very few of the lads intended to go over to the other side. Some of our fellows were in pretty bad shape and certainly needed all the help we could get them from Colonel Mulligan."[24] Griffin's account cannot always be trusted. But in this case the low number of Irish names on that Union list backs him up.

Predictably, Halleck ruined his own project by demanding that each "galvanized Yankee" post a $1,000 bond to assure future loyalty to the Union. Naturally, the five Sons of Erin and the other Boys-in-Gray didn't have that kind of U.S. greenbacks, and so they resigned themselves to the drudgery of prison routine with the hope of surviving it. (Later in the war, many Confederate prisoners did, indeed, join the Union army in order to stay alive.)

By May of that year, Camp Douglas was dangerously overcrowded with 8,962 prisoners, 5,717 of whom were from Fort Donelson, mostly Tennesseans, including 430 lads from the Sons of Erin. The 3,245 new arrivals had been captured at Island Number Ten and Shiloh.[25]

On June 19 there was a change in Federal command. Mulligan and his lads were transferred back to active service. The West Side Chicago Irishman later died a hero's death at the Battle of Third Winchester on the Eastern front. His replacement as commandant was Colonel Joseph H. Tucker, who put the Tennessee lads into the "devil's clutches" for the last three months of their extended stay. But even worse than Tucker and the new guards during that summer of 1862 was the disease of scurvy, which proved to be just as deadly as the smallpox.

Three direct accounts from the Tenth Tennessee substantiate the mistreatment at Douglas during that fateful summer.

Lewis R. Clark, Clarksville:
When Mulligan was relieved of his command, we became guarded by home-guards or 30-day wonders (state militia) who, having no chance to punish the enemy in the field, treated us who were in their power with atrocious barbarity in numerous ways, and even to the extent of shooting through the barracks at night, killing and wounding prisoners asleep in their bunks.[26]

Patrick M. Griffin, Nashville:
That Black Hole of a barracks makes me mad even now [1905] just to think about it. We had to fortify our bunks, and did not dare to poke our heads out after nightfall, unless we were willing to have bullets pitched our way. We were offered every inducement to join the Yankee Army. But after meeting Colonel Tucker, I knew that it would be impossible for me to ever become a Yankee. I think those of us who were there found the latter portion of that seven months about the worst part of our existence.[27]

Jimmy Doyle, Nashville:
The guards call this the southwest box. I do not know north from south, east from west . . .. Last count there were 131 of us in here . . . not even enough room to walk from one end to the other . . . has got to be over 100 degrees in here. This is hell and Tucker is Satan. We get mush once a day but nothing to cook it in . . .. Everyone sick. Carried four more to the smallpox hospital today. Then off to the death-house . . .. Johnny Diggons

142

of A Company died right in here last night. Never could get the lad to the hospital.[28]

The situation, of course, was to get immeasurably worse. A history of Camp Douglas as a prisoner of war facility was filed by the Illinois Adjutant General's Office in June, 1865, filled with the hatred and bitterness which by the end of the war dominated the national mood on both sides, and found its meanest spirit in prison camps.

Political dissenters, also incarcerated, were described as "a notorious gang of rebel scribblers and traitorous copperheads, wallowing in the mire of treason and rebellion . . . [the prison was] a stronghold for treason and a rendezvous for the discontented . . . a wicked and cowardly bosom of seduction . . . crushed by the glorious victories of our gallant armies."

Another part of the report stated that when the Confederates had arrived they were "lean, haggard, and starving. When they left their comfortable and warm quarters [in winter] to return to their homes, their appearances, in every case, was changed into one of strength and health."

But in another account, the Southern prisoners, contradictorily, were themselves described as: "Receipts . . . souvenirs . . . trophies of war . . . fat rascals . . . felonious . . . more wretched than Lazarus, and thinner than Pharaoh's lean kine. Of the whole number [of prisoners]—over 30,000—only about 3500 died."[29] (It was exactly 4,039.)

Bad as the camps were for the Tennesseans and others from Fort Donelson, they were a lot worse for the prisoners who followed. The accusations against Tucker were mild compared with those leveled against later commandants. In fact, as the savage fighting increased and respect gave way to contempt, the condition of prison camps on both sides became intolerable. The men of the Tennessee regiments were fortunate to get out when they did in September of 1862.

Of the 430 inmates at Camp Douglas from the Sons of Erin, twenty-two died of disease while in confinement, their bodies buried at the Confederate "Mound" in Chicago's historic Oakwoods Cemetery, with their names inscribed on the four plated walls of the monument.[30]

It is interesting to survey the numbers in the Irish regiment from September, 1861 to September, 1862. At Forts Henry and Donelson, the Sons of Erin had 720 combatants. Of these two resigned, two went on sick furloughs, and two were transferred to other commands, leaving 714 lads still at Fort Donelson on February 16, 1862.

But only 446 of the 714 lads wound up in the three Union prisons, meaning that 268 escaped or deserted either at Dover or in St. Louis. With twenty-two deaths in Chicago, 423 lads remained to be paroled, excluding escapee Morgan, that is, 408 from Camp Douglas, twelve from Camp Chase, and three from Fort Warren.

Only 383 combatants showed up for the reorganization, which meant that some of those paroled did not re-enlist, and that some of those who had escaped came back. The number 383 represented the equivalent of about four regular-sized companies. There were very few new recruits and only about half of the original lads were still in the Confederate Army by summer of 1862. During the months that followed their release from Federal prisons, 129 of the 383 Irishmen either fell out from sickness or deserted before the reorganized regiment was engaged in its first battle.[31]

The Tenth Tennessee grew continually smaller in ranks between September of 1861 and May of 1863. Very little of this diminishing can be attributed to battlefield losses; the Tenth had experienced only fifteen minutes of combat. It can be honestly said that the "Bloody Tenth" was devastated not by any Federals, but by Confederate Generals John B. Floyd and Gideon Pillow. The story of the Sons of Erin as a full regiment ended at Erin Hollow. The unit would still be a proud one with its own identity: it would still march and camp together and have its own officers, but after release from prison, the military history of the regiment was essentially that of a highly competent sharpshooters' detachment. Military duty, of course, is only one part of the history of a regiment like the Sons of Erin.

The officers of the Irish regiment were coming out of prison, too. By late August, 1862, both Union and Confederate war departments needed to strengthen their battlefield leadership and silence the political clamor of back-home citizens who missed their prisoner relatives. The Federals exchanged a high-ranking officer, Lieutenant Colonel R. W. McGavock, to the Confederates for lower ranking Northerners—First Lieutenant W. H. Eldridge, First Lieutenant J. W. Adams, and Second Lieutenant C. H. Hatch, all of whom were from the Fourth New Jersey.

Colonel Adolphus Heiman went from the Federals to the Confederates for Colonel John R. Kenly of the First Maryland; and in another even-up transaction, the Southerners swapped Major A. Von Penehelstein to the Northerners for Major William Grace.[32]

Colonel Heiman, no longer with brigade responsibility, was back where he had started as commanding officer of the Tenth Tennessee. Lieutenant Colonel McGavock was second-in-command, with Major William Grace as the number three officer.

Reorganization

McGavock made his way down to Richmond, where he tried to see President Davis but failed. He then traveled west to the town of Tunnel Hill in northern Georgia, where he was greeted by Seph and her family. After a happy week with his wife and in-laws, he said goodbye again and took the train to Jackson, Mississippi, to await the return of his regiment.[33]

The enlisted men at Camp Chase and Camp Douglas weren't released until the middle of September, at which time they were put together on a steamer at Cairo and arrived at the Mississippi river town of Vicksburg on the 24th. The next day they were taken east by rail to Clinton, Mississippi, to be reorganized.[34]

Randal McGavock dramatically rode into the lads' camp, attired in a new, perfectly tailored gray and red uniform, waving his hat that featured a green ribbon coming out of a red band. "The men were all exceedingly glad to see me," was the pleased notation in the journal.[35]

It took a week for Colonel Heiman to get the paperwork to reconstitute the regiment completed according to army regulations. On October 2 the Sons of Erin were again mustered into regular Confederate service. At Fort Henry 725 lads had registered for one year. This time around it was 383 for three years. Among the few newcomers was McGavock's younger brother, Ed, who had been commissioned as a captain and appointed as adjutant, and Major Sidney W. Franklin, a young and very skillful surgeon, who would save many lives. Also at this time First Lieutenant Clarence C. Malone, formerly of the Fourteenth Mississippi Infantry regiment, at his own request transferred to the Tenth Tennessee, so he could serve with his fellow Irishmen.

At the recommendation of Father Henry Vincent Browne, formerly the regimental chaplain and at that time the Chancellor of the Nashville diocese, Father Emmeran Bliemel was elected as chaplain. Since Bishop James Whalen refused to let Father Emmeran go, the German priest was listed on the muster rolls as "absent."

Many of the original company officers didn't reenlist, and some who did failed to get reelected. After surviving Fort Henry, Fort Donelson, and Federal prison, the Irishmen had a better idea of whom they wanted to lead them. Ironically not a single commissioned officer from McGavock's old Nashville-Irish company returned, except for "Randy Mack" himself.

The small number of lads from Clarksville did well, getting three of their own elected as company commanders. Tom Gibson was promoted from first lieutenant to captain of his own new company. John L. Prendergast was double promoted from second lieutenant to captain of the original all-Clarksville company. And Lew Clark was triple promoted

146

from master sergeant to captain of his own new company.[36]

Youthful "Gentleman Johnny" O'Neill, born in December of 1840, was reelected captain of the all-McEwen and almost exclusively foreign born, Irish-Catholic A Company.[37] O'Neill's country lads and Prendergast's country lads were probably the best fighting units in the regiment. This is not to say that city lads don't make good soldiers. It's just that in this Irish-Rebel regiment (and in many others in both armies, as a matter of fact) farm-lads were strong, disciplined and used to unpleasant tasks.

The ten posted companies were so small that many of the lower line offices were left vacant. In fact the company designations at the reorganization were nearly meaningless. It was really a skeleton crew.

THE TENTH TENNESSEE INFANTRY REGIMENT OF VOLUNTEERS (IRISH) C.S.A.[38]

Staff And Field Officers
Colonel Adolphus Heiman
Lieutenant Colonel Randal W. McGavock
Major William Grace

Appointed Support Staff
Captain Edward Mc Gavock, Adjutant
Captain John B. Johnson, Quartermaster
First Lieutenant Theodore Kelsey, Assistant
Adjutant—Courier
Second Lieutenant Robert Paget Seymour,
Assistant Adjutant
Master Sergeant Morris Griffin, Drillmaster
Master Sergeant Bernard McCabe,
Commissary Officer
Sergeant James Hayes, Standard Bearer

The Four Hometowns of the Regiment

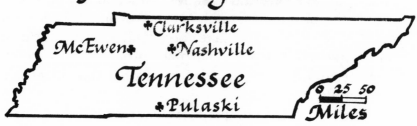

Nashville:
B, C, D, E, F, G, K Companies

Clarksville:
I Company

McEwen:
A Company

Pulaski:
H Company

Non-Combatant Staff
Father Emmeran Bliemel O.S.B., Chaplain (Absent)
Dr. Sidney W. Franklin, Surgeon
Dr. John J. Mallet, Surgeon

Elected Company Officers (Line Officers)
A Company (Same Designation)
Captain John G. O'Neill
First Lieutenant James McMurray
Second Lieutenant Charles H. Stockell

B Company (Formerly K)
Captain Samuel M. Thompson
First Lieutenant John W. Bryan
Second Lieutenant Joseph Evans
Brevet Second Lieutenant Robert Erwin

C Company (Formerly F)
Captain Saint Clair Morgan
First Lieutenant Clarence C. Malone

D Company (Formerly G)
Captain William Sweeney
First Lieutenant Bartley Dorsey

E Company (Formerly B)
Captain Thomas Gibson
First Lieutenant Theodore Kelsey
Second Lieutenant James P. Kirkman

F Company (Formerly H)
Captain Aloysius Berry

G Company (Formerly E)
Captain George A. Diggons
First Lieutenant John D. Winston
Second Lieutenant William W. Foote
Brevet Second Lieutenant William Lanier

H Company (Formerly I)
Captain Joseph Ryan

I Company (Formerly D)
Captain John L. Prendergast
First Lieutenant Lynch B. Donoho
Second Lieutenant James T. Dunlap

K Company (Formerly C)
Captain Lewis R. Clark
First Lieutenant L. P. Hagan
Second Lieutenant James Conroy

At least three of the previous company officers were transferred to service in other units. Captain John H. Anderson, Captain William M. Marr, and Second Lieutenant William Dwyer all switched over to cavalry companies. Dwyer later rode with General John Hunt Morgan and was killed in action.[39]

Chapter Five
The Battle of Snyder's Bluff: Called on Account of Rain

Marching in Mississippi

On October 8 Major William Grace was thrown by his horse and painfully injured.[1] It was the beginning of a back problem that would plague him for the rest of his life. On that same day the Sons of Erin were ordered to Holly Springs, Mississippi, where they were officially registered into the brigade of Brigadier General John Gregg, 34, with Heiman as second in command.

General Lloyd Tilghman had wanted the Tenth Tennessee in his brigade, and he was disappointed to learn that Colonels Heiman and McGavock had requested service with their Fort Warren roommate.

Since his own original regiment, the Seventh Texas, was back in Louisiana, General Gregg was the only non-Tennessean in his own brigade. The Texan was given seven small Tennessee regiments, which he promptly consolidated into three as follows: First/Fiftieth/ Fifty-First, Third/Thirtieth, and Forty-First/Tenth. The Forty-First and the Fifty-First had less than one-hundred soldiers each. All in all there were only about 1,500 Tennesseans in the entire outfit, the size equivalent of one regiment and one battalion.[2] The Irishmen took to Gregg at once. "A magnificent soldier and a splendid man, whom we all dearly loved," was the gushing praise of Lew Clark.[3]

The first order of business for the Gregg brigade was to get reviewed by President Jefferson Davis at a Mississippi town called Water Valley. Then they began to march back and forth among villages so small that some of them were hardly crossroads. During the next few weeks, the Tennesseans went from Water Valley to Tippah Ford back to Holly Springs and then caught the tail end of General Earl Van Dorn's retreat from Corinth to Waterford, Oxford, and Grenada. "One of the severest marches of the war," noted

Pat Griffin.[4]

The Sons of Erin were struck by every illness known to mankind, from head colds to typhoid fever. The problem was the weather—warm and humid with heavy rain from October 16 to 24. "It rained in torrents, and the mud and water were awful."[5] Soon, the bad weather got worse, as rain changed to snow. And this was Mississippi in October!

Between October 28 and November 4, the dry air changed back to unseasonably hot, only to be followed by four days of cold and rain.[6] Not too surprisingly all of this took its toll on the marchers, especially those who had just emerged from half a year of rot in the rat-infested Federal prison holes.

The night before the Sons of Erin reached Grenada, because he was sick and worn out from exposure, Captain Tom Gibson of Clarksville concluded that he would leave camp and go to a nearby abandoned cabin for shelter. After Gibson had gotten a good fire going, in came Irish-born First Lieutenant Lynch Donoho, also of Clarksville, also wet and sick. After drying their clothes and shoes, they went to sleep.

Gibson had made a pillow of his shoes and advised Donoho to do likewise. The lieutenant, however, left his shoes near the fire to completely dry out. While the two were sound asleep, someone entered and took Lynch Donoho's shoes. In the morning the rain was pouring down, the two officers were still sick, the two shoes were still missing, and Donoho was angrily swearing at the shoe-knapper and the war.

Fortunately, Gibson was a good forager and soon hailed a servant of General Sterling Price, who just happened to be passing by the cabin, and who, for a few Confederate dollars, was able to get a pair of shoes for Donoho.[7]

Lynch Donoho was a likable lad when sober. Unfortunately, his drinking meant trouble—for him and others. On New Years Eve of 1862, he requested a "furlough." Permission was denied by McGavock. Donoho went anyhow. On January 3, 1863, he returned and exchanged a few heated words with McGavock, who "court-martialled" him for "disrespect to a superior officer." The whole thing blew over and formal charges were never filed.

On February 1, 1864, Tom Gibson was transferred to the personal staff of Brigadier General John Adams.[8] Adams was later killed at the Battle of Franklin, where Gibson was also wounded.

The death march finally stopped at Grenada, where the Gregg brigade was taken by train to Jackson, the state capital of Mississippi, still firmly in Confederate control. During the last two months of 1862, the whole town became a hospital, not for the wounded, but for the sick. The regular hospital was filled, the smallpox hospital was filled, city hall, the churches, and most places of business were filled with the sick.

The Sons of Erin bivouacked on the state fair grounds, and there was a field hospital out there, too. Just about all of the members of the Tenth Tennessee were sick during this time. Nine of them died, and one of the dead was Colonel Adolphus Heiman.

On October 5 several Southern officers had recommended that Heiman be promoted to the rank of brigadier general. The appointment came through to Jackson confirmed on November 20, four days after he had died. Six days later Tennessee Governor Andrew Johnson confiscated his house.[9]

Since Father Bliemel was absent, McGavock conducted the funeral service. "Uncle Dolph," 53, a much loved father-figure, was mourned by all the members of the Irish regiment who could stand, plus some who couldn't. There was also a large turnout from the Third, Thirtieth and Forty-First Tennessee regiments.[10] No one can state with certainty the exact cause of Heiman's death, as deaths were listed simply as resulting from "fever."

The nameless-faceless fever never slowed down through the rest of November and December. The other eight members of the regiment to die were Master Sergeant Hugh McGuire of D Company, Privates Patrick Conway, Michael Finn, and Michael Donlan of H Company, Private John Murphy of B Company, Private John Cloharty of C Company, Private John Smith of E Company, and Private James McLauflin of I Company.[11] McLauflin was the father of the "little Son of Erin" who, with the help of Captains Ellis and Kirkman had entered the world nine months earlier at Dover.

McGavock was advanced to full colonel and commanding officer of the Tenth/Forty-First Tennessee consolidated regiment, although the official papers from Richmond didn't arrive until the following spring. Within the thinning roster of the Sons of Erin, William Grace moved up to lieutenant colonel, and Sam Thompson was promoted to major.[12]

General Gregg and his staff did their best to prevent the fever from spreading. Captain S. R. Simpson, the quartermaster of the Thirtieth Tennessee, was ordered by his commanding officer, Lieutenant Colonel James J. Turner, to burn the clothing of all the deceased. Commissary Master Sergeant Barney McCabe of the Tenth Tennessee was ordered by his commanding officer, Colonel Randal W. McGavock, to sterilize all the cooking utensils.

McCabe wasn't quite sure he knew the difference between routine washing and sterilizing, so Marty Gibbons and "Crazy Tom" Feeney volunteered to help with the situation. Somehow they came up with the bright idea of burning the poisonous substances right off the tin plates and forks.

Private Feeney got a good fire started, and Private Gibbons pitched the plates and forks into the fire. The plates curled into little black balls and the forks melted and the mess tent caught on fire. After the flames were doused, McCabe noticed a gaping hole in the tent.

The mess sergeant requested a new tent from Captain Simpson, but Simpson didn't have any to give. All that could be done was to patch up the old one up like a patch-work quilt.[13]

The Battle of Chickasaw Bluffs
Monday, December 29, 1862
General Pemberton Versus General Sherman

Lieutenant General John C. Pemberton, 48, of Pennsylvania, had risen rapidly from captain of artillery to high-ranking general in the Confederate Army, with virtually no discernible achievements to justify his promotions. President Davis, a personal friend, gave Pemberton command of the Department of Mississippi, Tennessee, and East Louisiana. The Philadelphia Quaker with the Virginia wife was to be the defender of Vicksburg.

The mighty Rebel garrison on the Mississippi was really all that was left of the Western Confederacy. The Federals controlled everything on the Mississippi River north of the Yazoo River and everything on the Mississippi south of Port Hudson, just above Baton Rouge, Louisiana. If Vicksburg fell, the Mississippi would be completely under Union control all the way from Minnesota to the Gulf of Mexico.

In defending Vicksburg General Pemberton had a lot more going for him than fortifications on the river. His biggest natural asset was an area called the Yazoo Delta. Some thirteen miles above Vicksburg the small Yazoo River meets the big Mississippi, at which point both rivers depart from their logical routes.

The Mississippi curves back north, then west, before zig-zagging back south, all part of the river called Milliken's Bend. The Yazoo cuts severely to the east, then runs northeast about eighty miles, just a little northwest of the town of Greenwood, where it then becomes the Tallahatchie River.

Between the Yazoo and the Mississippi there is a lowland, 170 miles long by fifty miles wide, a bizarre series of sluggish streams, bayous, backwaters, and swamps, all of which flood after every thunderstorm.[14] Nine miles north of Vicksburg, there is a cluster of impassible rocks called the Chickasaw Bluffs. Ten miles inland to the northeast from Vicksburg, there's a smaller but just as impassible cluster of rocks called Snyder's Bluff.

The Yazoo Delta made a good Confederate defensive line. To reach the garrison at Vicksburg from Memphis, the Federals had to go straight and then crooked down the Mississippi by boat, or march down east of the Yazoo and come up to the town of Vicksburg from the rear. Or both.

General Pemberton had his twenty-four thousand Confederate soldiers well deployed. On the river, north to south, gray-clad defenders were at Vicksburg, Port Gibson, and Port Hudson. Inland they were at Grenada, 110 miles northeast of Vicksburg, at Jackson, thirty-five miles due east of Vicksburg, and all along both sets of bluffs.[15] Pemberton's defenses were formidable.

Two days after Pemberton settled into his Jackson headquarters, President Lincoln appointed Major General U.S. Grant to the Department of Western Tennessee, a command that included most of the state of Mississippi and would position him to attack the formidable fortress at Vicksburg which Pemberton was at pains to defend.

At his Memphis headquarters in November, Grant met with Major General William Tecumseh Sherman, 42, the Ohioan who had already been relieved of duty earlier in the war for having "a high strung nature."

Reviewing his scouting reports, Grant decided on a two-pronged plan of assault. The 32,000 Federals at Memphis were divided up into two corps, with Sherman getting three divisions of about 20,000, Grant two divisions of 12,000. In the first phase Grant would march inland down into the state of Mississippi, following the Mississippi Central Railroad, which ran roughly parallel to the Yazoo, and force Pemberton to come out somewhere to meet him. In the second phase Admiral David D. Porter, 49, of Pennsylvania, was to convey Sherman down the Mississippi to the mouth of the Yazoo. With Pemberton under attack from Grant, Sherman was to assault the city defenses of Vicksburg and capture the garrison.[16]

The operation got underway on November 27, as Grant marched out of Tennessee and a week later occupied the northern Mississippi town of Holly Springs, where he established a new supply depot. With no Confederate resistance, he continued to Oxford, Mississippi, arriving on December 20. On that same day Sherman left Memphis on sixty-seven transports, protected by Porter's gunboats.[17]

Meanwhile, Brigadier General Nathan Bedford Forrest, taking a newly recruited detachment with few horses and arms, raided Jackson, Lexington, and Grand Junction in Tennessee, gobbling up one Union supply base after another, seizing enough horses and arms so that the whole outfit could be fully equipped.[18]

On the same day that Sherman was leaving Memphis and Grant was arriving in Oxford and Forrest was laying waste Lincoln's property, Major General Earl Van Dorn and his 3,500 troopers, catching the entire enemy command asleep, raided and fired the Union supply depot at Holly Springs, leaving Grant without a supply line and forcing him to withdraw to Memphis. Because the telegraph lines were cut and communications were confused, Sherman never got a December 23 communique ordering him to abandon the attack.

Thinking that Pemberton was occupied with Grant, Sherman landed on December 26 at Steele's Bayou. From there he marched four miles south through swamps flooded by recent rains to Chickasaw Bluffs, where he found a three-mile-long Confederate line heavily defended by Boys-in-Gray behind rocks.[19] The Union corps commander had to probe the Confederate strength, so on Sunday, December 28, he engaged in a seven-hour, sharpshooter-only skirmish, which showed him that Southern strength was great indeed.

Also on December 26 General John Pemberton sent General John Gregg's brigade, including the Tenth Tennes-

The First Assault Against Vicksburg
November, December 1862
Advance of Grant and Sherman south from Memphis

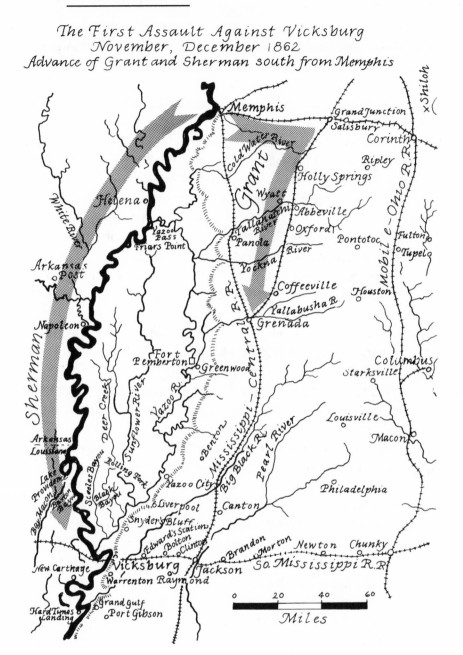

see, from Jackson west to Vicksburg. The next day, after marching thirty-nine miles in twenty-four hours, General Gregg detached the Third/Thirtieth Tennessee consolidated regiment from his brigade and posted it in reserve on the extreme Confederate left (south) flank at Chickasaw.[20] The other two regiments were in for more marching. With the Sons of Erin leading the way, the other two-thirds of the Gregg brigade reached the far Confederate right at Snyder's Bluff much later that same night of the 27th.

> *I do not believe that any man who was there will ever forget that night, even if he were to live a thousand years. Such thunder, rain, and lightning I never saw and heard before or since. We could only take a step when the lightning flashed, and then we moved from one tree to another, clinging to the branches to keep from slipping over the bluff, . . .*

was the way Private Pat Griffin described the lads' new assignment at Snyder's Bluff.[21]

On Monday, December 29, Sherman ignored the strong objections of his division commanders and launched a foolhardy and dangerous series of full frontal assaults against the Confederate infantry posted behind those rocks along the Chickasaw Bluffs. (The Federals called it the Battle of Chickasaw Bayou.) Idly Sherman wondered where Grant was.

"We will lose 5,000 men before we take Vicksburg, and may as well lose them here as anywhere else," Sherman said.[22] His gallant troops made five separate attacks against an immovable object, and were bloodily repulsed each time. In the afternoon, the Third/Thirtieth Tennessee consolidated was moved up to fill a gap between brigadiers John C. Vaughn and Seth M. Barton. The Tennesseans' fire was commended by General Pemberton.

Union casualties on that one day were 1,776 as compared to 187 for the Confederates![23] Incredibly, Sherman wasn't finished. He planned to attack Snyder's Bluff. That

159

same evening General Sherman visited Admiral Porter aboard the flagship to present his latest scheme. The navy commander readily agreed to put his gunboats to maximum use. The plan called for a movement up the Yazoo with 10,000 Federal infantrymen attacking the enemy's far right along Snyder's Bluff. The advance was to take place on New Year's Eve, with the main assault coming the morning of New Year's Day of the new year of 1863. The weather continued to be awful.

At the same time that Porter was transporting half of Sherman's corps, Irish-born First Lieutenant "Long Tom" Connor was amusing the shivering lads by bouncing minié balls off the hulls of distant Yankee gunboats.[24] Colonel McGavock had the Sons of Erin dug in just as well as at Erin Hollow, only this time the Irishmen stuck their heads up from behind rock-works instead of logworks. Southern scouts accurately reported the enemy advance, and Pemberton hurried reinforcements to Snyder's Bluff.

But battle plans proved abortive. "The enemy must have suspected that the Bloody Tinth was waiting to give them a warm reception, for they failed to show up," was Pat Griffin's explanation.[25] What happened was that because of the wind, freezing rain, and fog, Sherman had to postpone operations. Then on January 3 Grant's message of December 23 finally arrived.

That was that. Porter and Sherman packed it in, sailed through the maze of Milliken's Bend and limped back to Memphis.

It was fortunate General Sherman didn't attack the second cluster of rocks. The results would have been the same. In fact, the entire operation represented the worst performance of the war for Sherman. Chickasaw Bluffs, or Chickasaw Bayou, was the most one-sided major Confederate victory in the Western theatre of operations. General Grant himself summed it up best: "The project of a combined movement on Vicksburg, partly by land and partly by river, thus ended in complete failure."[26]

Position of the Sons of Erin
during the Chickasaw Bluffs Campaign
December 27, 1862 to January 3, 1863

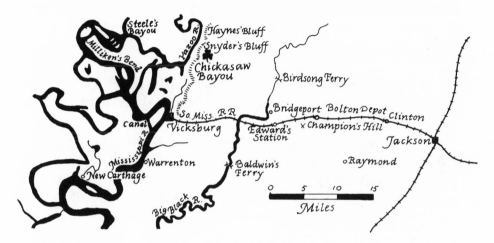

161

As far as the Tenth Tennessee's contribution to this initial battle of the Vicksburg campaign, it is as follows: present but not engaged.

On the day after Sherman fled, Pemberton ordered Gregg down to the southern end of his river line. The Sons of Erin were headed out to cajun country.

The Battle of First Port Hudson
Saturday, Sunday, March 14, 15, 1863
General Gardner Versus Admiral Farragut

The trip down to Port Hudson was the first experience on a Confederate troop boat for the members of the Irish regiment. "Queer things happened on that transport," was the ambiguous declaration of Private Patrick M. Griffin.[27] The lads arrived in Louisiana on January 7, 1863, and it was soon discovered that the boat was missing all of its mirrors, knives, forks, spoons, blankets, and rations.

The captain of the boat reported the matter to McGavock, who ordered his Irishmen to fall into line, spread their knapsacks, open them up, and turn their pockets inside out. The captain of the transport, accompanied by the officers of the Tenth, went from one end of the line to the other; but not one thing could be found that belonged to the boat. Griffin went on:

> *After the search was completed, Colonel McGavock made a speech to the captain of the transport, in which he eulogized his regiment, saying that it was made up of honest and brave lads, and that, as a matter of course, it must have been some other soldiers or thieves that had ransacked the boat. However, Colonel McGavock went to the commissary and drew enough rations to supply the captain and his crew until they got back to Vicksburg.*[28]

Locations of the Sons of Erin
General John Pemberton's Department
1862-1863

The Confederate commander at Port Hudson was Major General Franklin Gardner, 40, of Louisiana, who had been born in New York and appointed to West Point from Iowa. General Gardner and General Gregg had a common friend, the former pro-Union governor of Texas, the legendary Sam Houston.[29]

The Seventh Texas regiment, infantry volunteers, an outfit that had been raised by Gregg himself, was at that time registering recruits at Port Hudson. General Gardner reinforced General Gregg's small brigade by giving back to the Texan his own original regiment.

Gregg divided his seven miniature Tennessee regiments into two Tennessee consolidated units. The First/Forty-First/Fiftieth/Fifty-First was commanded by Lieutenant Colonel T. W. Beaumont, and the Third/Thirtieth/Tenth was commanded by Colonel R. W. McGavock. To make it a full service fighting brigade, Gardner also added a battalion of cavalry, the Ninth Louisiana, and two companies of artillery, the Brookhaven Mississippi Battery and the Bledsoe Missouri Battery.

All in all the Gregg brigade had 215 officers and 2,611 enlisted men, totaling 2,826 effectives, including the Sons of Erin, the size equivalent of three full regiments.[30]

General Gardner had two other brigades with him in January, Brigadier General W. N. R. Beall's and Brigadier General S. B. Maxey's. Gardner deployed his detached division by putting Beall on the left (south), inland from the Mississippi, Maxey in the center closer to the river, and Gregg on the right at the river.[31]

The Sons of Erin were posted on the shore line of the west bank between the water and some water batteries. They were a mile below the port, directly across the river from Ross' Landing on the east bank. Their job was about the same as it had been at Fort Henry, that is, digging out rifle pits and bracing them with logworks. The Irishmen, along with all the other Confederates, were camped a couple of hundred yards inland, up a little incline, an experiment in sanitation. It must have worked, because there was less sickness reported in Louisiana than there had been in Mississippi.

Mess at Port Hudson was better than average. Corn and potatoes were plentiful, and fresh meat was occasionally available. There wasn't much whiskey, but lots of "berry wine," which the Irishmen were able to get their hands on through Captain S.R. Simpson, the quartermaster from the Thirtieth Tennessee. In early February Lieutenant Colonel William Grace and a small detachment of Irish lads borrowed Simpson's supply wagon and "foraged sweet potatoes, corn, seven gray jackets, five pairs of pants, and one odd shoe." [32] McGavock was then Simpson's consolidated regiment commanding officer. One day the two of them drove into Baton Rouge to get special supplies: chickens, eggs, milk, jams, bacon, and molasses.

While in town they received word that some of Union Major General Nate Banks' soldiers had broken into the nearby farmhouse of Mr. and Mrs. Alexander, where they stole "93 bales of cotton and 22 niggers." [33] Captain Simpson reported the Alexanders to be "good secessionists."

General Gregg was a likable gentleman and responded to all requests in a fair manner. Tenth Tennessee Commissary Master Sergeant Barney McCabe got most of what he requisitioned, including seven mess mules from the stockade. He was especially fond of one of the new "recruit" mules, nicknamed "Paddy O'Murphy," whom he allowed his share of the wine jugs.

McGavock once cited the animal for "unusual service," but by spring, the favored beast had become a hopeless alcoholic, unfit for regular duty. At that time another mule died of a heart attack. [34] So far none of the lads of the Irish regiment had suffered either fate.

Rear-Admiral David G. Farragut was the sixty-two-year-old, Tennessee born, Virginia bred Union veteran who commanded the Federal Navy on the Mississippi River.

He had decided on a combined army-navy venture against the Louisiana Rebel garrison of Port Hudson, using his gunboats and the three infantry divisions of General Banks. But on Saturday, March 14, 1863, Admiral Farragut called off the infantrymen, thinking that he could do without them. That was a mistake; in reality, the old Southern Yankee sailor needed the army to help destroy the Rebel gun crews.

Admiral Farragut sailed up from New Orleans with a flotilla that consisted of three ironclads and four heavy-gunned wooden warships—frigates. The most famous of this lot was the frigate *Mississippi,* which had been Commodore Matthew Perry's flagship ten years before, when he steamed into Tokyo Bay and opened Japan to the western world.

At 9:30 p.m. the Union boats came within sight of Port Hudson. The flagship *Hartford,* with Farragut aboard, along with the small ironclad *Albatross*, ran west and north of the port upriver, which meant that the admiral had successfully deployed himself between Port Hudson and Vicksburg.[35] However, the rest of his fleet never made it.

At 11:30 p.m. the Sons of Erin set fire to some pitch-pine knot logs that they had piled up below the port, right opposite of the location where some Confederate boats were anchored, at Ross's Landing. Patrick Griffin explained the purpose of the oversized Irish bonfire: "The pine knots were ablaze instantly, and every movement of the fleet was seen by the gunners at the port."[36] In other words, the Sons of Erin had turned on the lights for the artillery. The *Richmond* and the *Monongahela* were racked up in short order by the Confederate batteries on the eastern bluffs above the port and were forced back down the river.

In several reports, the Sons of Erin were referred to as the "west bank sentinels," who kept adding timber to their oversized bonfire.

When the *Mississippi* appeared, the battery behind the Sons of Erin, known as the "red hot shot battery" opened fire

Position of the Sons of Erin
in front of the Red Hot Shot Battery
March 14, 1863

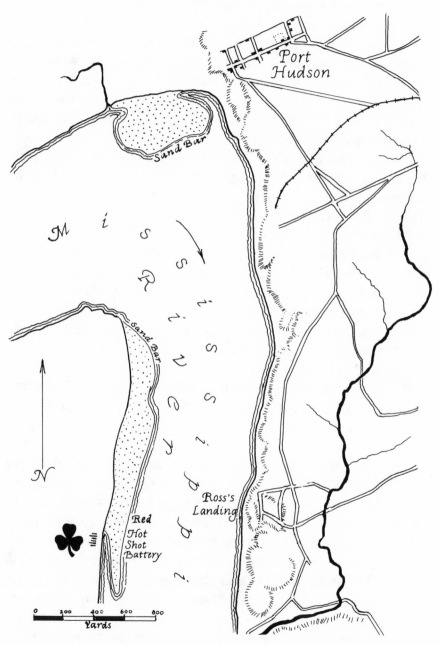

on the historic frigate with flaming solid shots.[37] Meanwhile, with the other two Union warships already trying to get away, the remaining ironclads concentrated their fire at the eastern bluffs, providing shields for the historic old boat.

At 12:30 a.m., March 15, the red hot shot gunners found their target, and the *Mississippi* grounded on the west bank up at the point of the bend. "The machinery of the warship stopped, and she began to swing around and around. Fire reached the ammunition, and shells and cartridges began to explode in a grand fusillade."[38]

At 2:00 a.m. the *Mississippi* began to float helplessly back down the Mississippi past the Sons of Erin. At 5:30 the magazine of the old warship exploded a few miles below the port, and Pat Griffin described the event:

> *It was a wonderful sight to see. Farmers who lived ten miles away told me afterwards that the light was so bright at their places on that night that they could pick up pins on the road. After this disaster, the Yankees decided that it would be best to make an entrance by the back way.*[39]

The dangerous nature of such an explosion is obvious; the Union rescue mission that night was a major operation. On the deck of the Mississippi was a young U.S. navy lieutenant, who saved as many as sixty-four lives by getting most of the crew into the small boats before the whole thing blew. Included among those he rescued was a badly frightened ship's boy hidden under a pile of corpses. The lieutenant jumped into the water just before the massive explosion. "He must have been a pretty good swimmer," testified Griffin, who was known to be a pretty good swimmer himself.[40]

(Thirty-five years later that same Northern sailor, as Fleet Admiral of the United States Navy, destroyed the entire Spanish fleet in the Philippines without suffering a single casualty. He was George Dewey. One of the Southern red hot shot gunners was Lieutenant Edward White, later to become

Chief Justice of the United States Supreme Court.)

There were many Federal casualties at First Port Hudson. Thirty-five were killed and sixty-seven wounded for a total of 102 losses. Surprisingly, there were more navy casualties in that one brief bombardment than there had been in all the bombardments for New Orleans put together.[41] For the Confederate defenders, it was one gunner killed and nineteen wounded or injured, including two Irish foot soldiers from the Sons of Erin, who were treated for minor burns.[42] The Tenth Tennessee was present but not engaged in a second straight one-sided victory. They, and the Confederate Army, were beginning to get a much-needed taste of victory along the Mississippi River.

By April the war seemed far away, and General Gardner's soldiers had settled into the frontier routine of army life. For many of the members of the Tenth Tennessee, Port Hudson was the fondest of memories. The surrounding countryside was friendly and food plentiful, and each of the Irishmen had his turn at foraging.

One bright sunny afternoon the Fighting Fitzgeralds returned to camp, each carrying a freshly acquired chicken which they claimed to have "purchased" from a local farmer. Mo was tired from the hunt and took a nap, while Willie plucked and prepared both birds. Willie also ate both birds, all of them.

Mo woke to the sight of a pile of bones, and a fight began, with several of the lads observing and cheering. Mo got the upper hand, for the simple reason that Willie was too stuffed to fight. "His energy had been spent," was the assessment of Private Jimmy Doyle.[43]

Without regard for peace and quiet, General Sam Grant launched a spring offensive on May 1, 1863, by assaulting Port

Gibson on the Mississippi. The place was above Port Hudson, below Vicksburg and slightly inland from the river. With a numerical advantage of three to one, he ousted the Confederates with ease, causing General John C. Pemberton to become more than a little nervous about the viability of his situation. The Southern commanding general needed to reinforce his most strategic positions.

On the same day that Grant's offensive began, Pemberton wired Gardner to send Gregg back up to Jackson. Gardner, however, couldn't decipher the code and requested the dispatch over again. Finally on May 6 the Gregg brigade, including the Sons of Erin, marched to a small town called Osyka on the Louisiana-Mississippi border. There they met a train to Jackson, which pulled in on May 11.

The townsfolk of the Mississippi capital were pleased to see the Southern reinforcements. In the streets of Jackson, McGavock was able to do another of his political campaign style performances, graciously bowing from his horse, tipping his hat with the green feather, accepting bouquets of flowers and so forth. The Sons of Erin were feeling far from gracious; they were about to do some more marching in Mississippi.[44]

The Second Assault Against Vicksburg
May–July, 1863
Grant's Advance from Memphis, South, East, and West.

Chapter Six
The Great Siege of Jackson That Never Happened

General Grant's Spring Offensive

The date was May 2, 1863. The river town of Grand Gulf, Mississippi, was General Grant's second conquest in two days. This time, however, there was no Confederate resistance. General John C. Pemberton made the decision to abandon the place and safely withdraw his troops. The Philadelphia Rebel firmly believed that he could not afford to lose any men, given the numerical advantage of the Union Army.

General Grant at that time had three full army corps under Major Generals William T. Sherman, John A. McClernand, and James B. McPherson. McClernand had proven hard to remove; he was connected to President Lincoln. McPherson, 34, of Ohio, was a friend of Sherman's and had just been promoted from division to corps command.

Instead of directly striking at Vicksburg with its concentration of Confederate forces, Grant looked east to shut down the Southern Mississippi Railroad, which linked the Rebel garrison with the state capital of Jackson, thirty-five miles away. His purpose was to cut off supplies and materials coming into Vicksburg and also to prevent enemy forces in the area from reinforcing the objective. Logically Grant chose to hit Edwards Station, the first major depot on the Southern Mississippi line coming east out of Vicksburg.

This plan had to be altered almost immediately when the Union commanding general received scouting reports that Confederate General Joseph E. Johnston, 56, of Virginia, was headed to Jackson with an army of unknown quality and quantity. As a result of this latest development, General Mc–Pherson was ordered to bypass Edwards and to keep moving east towards Jackson.[1] The Federal corps moved through Edwards on May 11 that same day that General John Gregg arrived in Jackson.

The move was made on an erroneous assumption. Remarkably, the Union scouts had mistaken Gregg's single brigade of 2,730 effectives for Johnston's army. An entire Union Army corps of 18,000 was coming right at the Texans and Tennesseans of General John Gregg, Colonel Randal Mc-Gavock and the Sons of Erin!

General McPherson's command was divided into three full divisions, each of three full brigades. His divisions were commanded by Scots-born Brigadier General John McArthur, 36, of Chicago, Illinois; by Brigadier General Marcellus M. Crocker, 33, of Des Moines, Iowa; and by Major General John A. Logan.[2] At his own request Logan had been transferred out of McClernand's corps into McPherson's, a move which made General Logan the senior division commander of the Federal Seventeenth corps.

The strength of the Confederate "army" was something that McPherson needed to know. Cautiously he approached from the west. In the early morning of Tuesday, May 12, the Federal columns were a few miles southwest of the tiny hamlet of Raymond, Mississippi, which was twelve miles southwest of Jackson. Northern scouts reported that the Southerners were blocking both roads into Raymond and Jackson. McPherson ordered his artillery to the front to confront the waiting foe.[3]

Colonel McGavock, for his part, was ill and worn out, and so were many others in the Tenth Tennessee. When Colonel Heiman had died, the whole Irish regiment had also been sick. The cold and wet exposure at Snyder's Bluff, followed by construction in the lowlands of Louisiana and marching in fever-laden Mississippi had continued to undermine the health of the regiment. To top it all off, the Dixie springtime was already sizzling hot.[4]

The minute that Gregg got off the train at Jackson, he received a written instruction from Pemberton which said that there were reports of an unspecified number of Yankees around Edwards Station. The ambiguous and contradictory communique said:

*Do not attack the enemy until he engages . . .
Be ready to fall on his rear or flank at any
moment. Do not allow yourself to be flanked
or taken to the rear. Be careful not to lose
your command.*[5]

General John Gregg, then, was given the responsibility of protecting the approaches to Jackson. That same day of May 11 he marched his brigade the twelve miles to Raymond. That same night he bivouacked just south of the village. For deployment purposes, "Texas Jack," adjusted his command structure from one Texas regiment and two Tennessee consolidated regiments to four regiments, one consolidated regiment, and one battalion.

The regiments referred to are the Seventh Texas regiment, and the Third, Forty-First and Fiftieth Tennessee regiments. The First Tennessee was the battalion and the Tenth/Thirtieth was the Tennessee consolidated regiment, commanded by McGavock.[6] The colonel's consolidated Tennesseans consisted of 253 of his own lads, and the 171 boys of Lieutenant Colonel James J. Turner, for total effectives of 424, the size equivalent of a battalion of four companies. Turner was the second ranking officer of the consolidated regiment and Lieutenant Colonel William Grace of the Sons of Erin was the third.

Gregg's artillery consisted of exactly three Missouri cannon. Because there wasn't enough cavalry in the small brigade, General Pemberton assigned a company of state militia troopers to Gregg.[7]

At the same time that Gregg was camping at Raymond, McPherson was camping at Utica, sixteen miles to the southwest. Early the next morning the Mississippi home guard cavalry scouts reported seeing some 2,500 or 3,000 blue-clads coming up the Utica road. What they saw was Logan's advance brigade, which they mistook for the entire enemy force!

Gregg was led to believe that a lone Union brigade was out on a "marauding excursion."[8] Apprehension and in-

adequate scouting were taking their toll on both sides—
McPherson believed Gregg's single brigade to be Joe Johnston's army, while Gregg figured McPherson's corps to be a
single brigade. In reality the only Southerners between
Grant's massive three-corps army and the Mississippi state
capital were Gregg's 2,730 Boys-in-Gray.

Very skillfully General Gregg carved out a small battlefield area which he could control, located between the only
two roads to Raymond, about a mile and a half southwest of
the tiny Mississippi hamlet. On the western end (Union left,
Confederate right) Gregg blocked the Utica road, in front of
McPherson, with Colonel Hiram B. Granbury and the Seventh Texas.[9]

The Texans were deployed on the forward slope of a
wooded hill, just to the left (east) side of the Utica road. About
a thousand yards due east of Granbury was the Gallatin road
(Union right, Confederate left). Lieutenant Colonel Thomas
W. Beaumont and the Fiftieth Tennessee were deployed there
on the crest of low ridge at right angles west of the Gallatin
road.

An insignificant stream called Fourteen-mile Creek
flowed across the Utica road about three-hundred yards to
the front (south) of the Confederate line, offering only a slight
natural buffer against a Union attack. Posted on the highest
hill behind (north of) the infantry was the Missouri Battery
of Captain Hiram M. Bledsoe, supported by Major Stephen
H. Colm's small First Tennessee battalion.

Deployed southwest of Beaumont and the Gallatin
road were McGavock and his consolidated Tennesseans. The
Tenth Tennessee was to the front of the regiment, with the
Thirtieth to the rear. Colonel Robert Farquharson and the
Forty-First Tennessee were inside the village, immediately
to the north of Colonel Calvin H. Walker and the Third Tennessee at the Raymond graveyard just south of the village.

On the hills south of Fourteen-mile Creek and
Granbury's position, the Federals opened up with heavy artillery and sharpshooter fire. It was 10:00 a.m. Tuesday, May
12, 1863.[10]

The Battle of Raymond, Mississippi
Tuesday, May 12, 1863, 10:00 a.m. to 4:00 p.m.
General Gregg Versus General McPherson

Since General McPherson thought he was up against a larger force, he attacked tentatively. Since General Gregg thought he was up against a smaller force, he defended aggressively, and the battle did indeed become a more even match than it logically should have been.

McPherson kept McArthur out of the area to protect his rear, left Crocker in reserve, and advanced with Logan. The three brigades of this Third division of the Seventeenth corps were commanded by Brigadier General Elias S. Dennis, 50, of Illinois, by Brigadier General John D. Stevenson, 41, of Missouri, and by Brigadier General John E. Smith, the Swiss watchmaker from Galena who had led the Forty-Fifth Illinois at the engagement of Erin Hollow.[11]

Captain Stephen DeGoyler of McPherson's Michigan battery covered the Federal infantry movement by blasting away with his six guns at Bledsoe's three. General McPherson blocked the Gallatin road south of Fourteen-mile Creek with General Stevenson and charged Colonel Granbury's position near the Utica road with Generals Dennis and J.E. Smith.

Dennis advanced on the Union far left nearest the Utica road with his four regiments, the Twentieth Ohio in the lead. To his right J.E. Smith's brigade came up with the Twenty-Third Indiana in front. The Boys-in-Blue entered a heavily wooded area that began one-hundred yards south of Fourteen-mile Creek and ended two-hundred yards north of it.[12]

Easily crossing the shallow stream, the Federals marched the remaining two hundred yards to the north edge of the woods. There the Twentieth Ohio and the Twenty-Third Indiana took up positions along a low ridge which served as an observation post. They urgently needed to know how many Southerners were up ahead. Throughout the morning light skirmishing took place.

There were eleven other Union regiments resting in the woods behind the lead two, all with restricted vision when

177

it came to the action. Gregg was able to take advantage of the Federal blind spot with his aggressive tactics, re-deploying his troops westward to his right, north of the wooded creek and east of the Utica road. The new Confederate line, west to east, was: the Seventh Texas strongly supported to the rear by the Forty-First Tennessee, then the Third Tennessee, the Fiftieth Tennessee and finally the Tenth/Thirtieth Tennessee consolidated regiment, still on the east end of the line nearest the Gallatin road.[13]

At high noon, with sword drawn, General "Texas Jack" Gregg charged ahead of his surging, yelling Boys-in-Gray, with the Texans striking the Twentieth Ohio and with the Third Tennesseans striking the Twenty-Third Indiana. The surprised Boys-in-Blue were driven off the ridge into the confusion of the dense woods.[14]

Unaware that only two of Logan's regiments had been engaged, McPherson was then convinced that he was up against at least a gray-clad division. During the confusion in the creek woods, he prematurely sent two of Stevenson's four regiments to the west, the Eighth Illinois in support of Dennis and the Eighty-First Illinois in support of J. E. Smith.

Soon realizing that he had just severely weakened his eastern left flank, General McPherson adjusted by getting General Crocker into the action. Adding to the chaos, McPherson detached two regiments from Colonel John B. Sandborn's brigade of Crocker's division, the Forty-Eighth and Fifty-Ninth Indiana, sending them up to Stevenson to reinforce his two remaining regiments, the Seventh U.S. Missouri and the Thirty-Second Ohio.[15]

While all of this shifting was going on, "Black Jack" Logan, dismayed by the Ohio-Indiana retreat, personally led a counter-assault to the northeast. "Logan dashed up, and with the shriek of an eagle turned the men back to their places. It was the sight of Logan riding up and down the line, firing them with his own enthusiasm that kept the troops firmly in position," was the way a newspaper reporter described the Northern rally.[16] Logan's earnest stand was the

The Battle of Raymond, Mississippi.
Tuesday, May 12, 1863
1:00 PM Positions

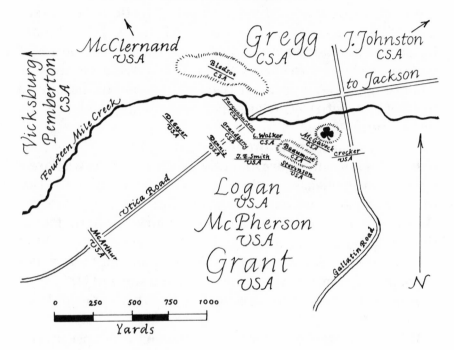

first signal that the Federals might finally be taking advantage of their superior numbers, and Colonels Granbury, Farquharson, and Walker were soon being chased around in the woods by fifteen blue-clad regiments.

At 1:00 p.m. Gregg ordered the Fiftieth Tennessee into the fight, to be followed by the Tenth/Thirtieth Tennessee consolidated after the Fiftieth became engaged. Lieutenant Colonel Beaumont went forward to the hill on the southeast edge of the woods to survey the situation. What he saw was what Gregg had not yet seen: two Union divisions massing in front of him, with DeGoyler's six cannon being reinforced by fifteen more.

Disregarding his orders by taking the battlefield initiative, Beaumont, overprudently as it turns out, withdrew his Fiftieth Tennessee to the rear, away from the battle. Historian Ed Bearss has appropriately described this move as a "bug-out."[17] Even worse, Beaumont's courier tried to deliver the unpleasant news to Gregg and McGavock but couldn't find either one. The upshot of all of this was that there was a four-hundred-yard gap between Farquaharson and McGavock that nobody knew about, except the hastily departed Beaumont.

By 1:30 the Confederate right began to collapse, eventually leaving only a few companies of the Seventh Texas, Third Tennessee and Forty-First Tennessee on the front line. Colonel McGavock, whose vision was blocked by the woods, had no idea that Beaumont and his entire regiment were gone.[18]

Meanwhile McPherson ordered Stevenson's brigade to attack the Confederate left, then reduced to the Tenth/Thirtieth Tennessee consolidated regiment. At that moment the only Rebel-Missouri-rifled cannon burst, leaving Captain Bledsoe with two smoothbores to compete against twenty-one enemy guns.

When General Gregg finally discovered that the Fiftieth Tennessee was not where it was supposed to be, he ordered Colonel McGavock to stop General Stevenson. McGavock trotted up the bare hill near the edge of the woods and saw what Beaumont had seen, a heavy line of Union artillery and infantry coming right at him.[19]

The commanding officer of the Tennessee consolidated regiment had two options. He could decide that wisdom was nine-tenths of valor, disobey orders, take the battlefield initiative, as Beaumont had, and withdraw, saving his fighting unit for another day, but guaranteeing an enemy victory.

Or, like a good soldier he could promptly follow instructions and risk the decimation of his regiment. He chose the latter.

It was 2:00 p.m. Without hesitation Colonel McGavock prepared to attack, deploying his Tenth Tennessee in front of the Thirtieth. The enemy were coming across an open valley at a northeast angle. With his red-lined gray coat thrown over his shoulder with one hand, he turned toward his faithful Irishmen, waving his sword in the other hand as the signal to advance.[20]

The Sons of Erin, with a deafening Irish-Rebel yell, surged into the oncoming traffic. Outflanked through the gap, the consolidated Tennessee advance was stopped by a fearsome artillery bombardment. After making the signal, McGavock turned his head full front to face the blue-clads coming directly at the base of the hill.

At that precise moment a single Yankee minié ball struck him in the heart, knocking him to the ground. Near the spot was the regimental surgeon, Dr. Sidney Franklin, who immediately came to the colonel's assistance. McGavock spoke not a word. His features were relaxed in a soft expression, as if taking a needed rest. Five minutes after having been hit, the beloved "Randy Mack" of the Sons of Erin was dead at the age of thirty-six.[21]

Dr. Franklin took charge of the body. Lieutenant Colonel William Grace led the Irishmen forward. Most of the Sons of Erin, not knowing their colonel was gone, were fighting desperately for their own lives. Union batteries were cutting them up. The Tenth Tennessee was locked into a savage hand-to-hand combat with General Stevenson's lead regiment, the Seventh U.S. Missouri.[22]

In the first minutes of the engagement, Captain George A. Diggons had a knee blown off, disabling him for life. Second Lieutenant John Ames, the hard-nosed drillmaster, was killed after having been wounded several times. A fragment from a Federal shell tore into the thigh of Captain John L. Prendergast. Amazingly, the Clarksville Sharpshooter got to his feet and in spite of a gaping wound, staggered forward, only to be wounded again. Sergeant James Hyde, from McGavock's original company, was killed. Private John McElroy, wounded three times, drew upon some incredible inner strength and stayed on his feet.[23]

After about twenty minutes of this carnage, the Missouri Federals were reinforced by some of the companies of the Thirty-Second Ohio. The Tenth/Thirtieth Tennessee was driven back to the Confederate line behind Beaumont's bald hill. The Third and Forty-First Tennessee regiments of Colonels Walker and Farquharson had really hung tough, but at this point in the brawl were already out of the fight. Two ferocious companies of the Seventh Texas, under Colonel Granbury, clung tenaciously to their positions near the Utica road.[24]

At the other end of the line, closest to the Gallatin road, an orderly retreat was organized by Lieutenant Colonel James J. Turner of the Thirtieth Tennessee, then in command of the Tenth/Thirtieth Tennessee consolidated.

Lieutenant Colonel Turner led his Tennesseans up a wooded ridge known to history as O'Neill's Hill, where he had them "lie down, load, fire, and reload."[25] The skirmishing action slowed down the Seventh U.S. Missouri long enough for the Sons of Erin to catch their breath. Almost immediately one of Turner's pickets excitedly warned him about another enemy unit to his left rear. It was the rest of the Thirty-Second Ohio.

Turner, like many of the Irish lads, must have had visions of Federal prison camp, and made an extremely aggressive on-the-spot decision. In record time he marched the consolidated regiment off the ridge to the rear, where he entered the same dense part of the woods that the Ohioans were using for cover.

Once there and on a moment's notice, Turner organized a surprise attack, ordering his command to charge at a "double quick pace." The Sons of Erin, still at the front of the consolidated regiment, came out of the pine "yelling like savages."

The ambushing Federals of the Thirty-Second Ohio got ambushed. Surprised, they managed to return only one volley before breaking in confusion. As a single company of the Ohioans tried to rally, Grace and the Sons of Erin came right up to thirty steps in front of them, killing their standard bearer and finishing the rout. By this time the Tenth Tennessee knew of McGavock's death. The Fighting Fitzgeralds, filled with rage and with bayonets extended, fought like demons to avenge their colonel's killing.[26]

The Tennesseans chased the Ohioans back until they reached that dense area of the creek woods and pine forest. At this point two or three companies of the Thirty-Second Ohio were reinforced by a few of the companies of the Seventh U.S. Missouri and the Eighty-First Illinois. Realizing that he was outnumbered, J.J. Turner again reacted quickly and wisely, and withdrew back to O'Neill's Hill.

It was here that Captain John G. O'Neill, the twenty-two-year-old native of Ireland, became a hero.

Lieutenant Colonel Turner ordered A Company of the Sons of Erin detached as a sharpshooter unit, adding First Lieutenant "Long Tom" Connor and a few others from Nashville and Clarksville to the company of McEwen farmers, all in all about forty-five Irishmen. As the commanding officer of the detachment, O'Neill deployed his lads at the highest point on the ridge, behind a farm house and some trees.[27] At the lower levels Turner strung out a double line of skirmishers.

By this time the action had degenerated into a series of pitched battles in the wooded areas all over the field. Both commanding generals had lost control of events and there was no coordination of movement. Combat officers had to improvise as best they could without specific instructions, knowledge of enemy troop strength and accurate intelligence data.

Union General John Stevenson, a true and brave soldier, had no idea what was going on. He knew he had a brigade of four regiments. What he didn't know was that the enemy forces in his area totalled less than four-hundred men.[28] With the correct information at his disposal, Stevenson could have encircled Turner's fellows and captured the whole lot of them. Unfortunately for his Boys-in-Blue, that is not what happened.

At 3:00 p.m. a battalion of the Seventh U.S. Missouri and a battalion of the Eighty-First Illinois emerged from the thick woods with their skirmishers advancing at a run to a ravine near the base of O'Neill's Hill. Captain O'Neill's Irishmen were so well deployed, and their fire was so concentrated and accurate, that the Federals had to lie flat for several minutes before attempting to crawl back to the woods, all the while under a murderous crossfire. It was all over in a half hour. Blue-clad bodies covered the open ground in front of the ridge.

The lads at the top of the hill were given a rousing Rebel salute by the boys at the bottom.[29] From that day on the Sons of Erin were used frequently as sharpshooters.

Twelve of the infantry invaders were so pinned down by Captain O'Neill that they were forced to surrender to Lieutenant Colonel Grace. The captured Yankees consisted of seven from the Seventh U.S. Missouri and five from the Eighty-First Illinois. During the half-hour of action around O'Neill's Hill, the Federals suffered in the vicinity of 150 casualties, while the Confederates reported none. Turner credited

O'Neill's detachment with much of the damage.[30] O'Neill's Hill was more of an execution than a military engagement. Randal McGavock had been avenged with a vengeance.

It was about 4:00 p.m. or six hours into the disorganized battle, when General John Gregg came to the inescapable conclusion that the Union force was somewhat bigger than a lone brigade on a "marauding excursion." He withdrew Granbury, Walker, and Bledsoe, with Colms, up the Utica road, sending Farquharson, Turner, Grace and the Sons of Erin up the Gallatin road to join Beaumont.[31]

General James McPherson, still not sure what he had been up against, did not pursue vigorously. Gregg retired through Raymond and bivouacked six miles to the northeast, halfway between the village and the state capital. McPherson occupied Raymond sometime after 5:00 p.m. where he set up camp for the night.[32]

The Battle of Raymond, Mississippi, was over, and like hundreds of small battles, it soon became a footnote in the annals of the Civil War.

General James McPherson, later to become a highly successful corps commander, had made his rookie mistakes. He fought his troops piecemeal throughout the struggle. There was never a coordinated attack. Despite what has been written in some accounts, it wasn't really a corps versus a brigade at any time. It was more like two brigades and a part of one brigade versus one brigade. As it was, about 5,500 Federals ran into 2,730 Confederates, giving the Boys-in-Blue a numerical advantage of about two to one—a numerical advantage that was not properly used.[33]

Gregg's aggressive tactics coupled with the failure of his scouts to assess the Federal strength, should have been the Confederate general's undoing. But against a cautious and hesitant Union commander, Gregg fought successfully until there were just too many Yankees. The Texan must also be given credit for choosing the turf on which the battle would be fought. The woods around Fourteen-mile Creek worked to the advantage of a smaller, concealed force.

The most notable hero on the Union side was General John A. Logan, the division commander, whose tactics really put the Boys-in-Gray on the defensive and kept them there. Certainly one of the heroes on the Confederate side was Lieutenant Colonel James J. Turner, who severely banged up three Union regiments with a command of only four-hundred men, two-thirds of whom were the Irishmen of the Tenth Tennessee.

Southern born and bred, Union General John Stevenson was so impressed by Turner's performance that he reported the Tenth/Thirtieth Tennessee consolidated to be "three Rebel regiments."[34] McPherson was so impressed by Gregg's performance that he reported the brigade to be a "full Rebel division." General U.S. Grant, fooled into thinking that Gregg's brigade was the "vanguard" of a Confederate Army that did not exist, completely set aside his plans for Edwards Station and marched on undefended Jackson with his full force of fifty-four-thousand troops.[35]

Given this strange scenario, the Battle of Raymond can be seen from at least three different viewpoints. First, that it was a Northern tactical victory that opened the front door to the Mississippi state capital. Secondly, that it was a Southern moment to be proud of, the moral victory of a small force holding off a large force for six hours.

Or, seen another way, since there was no high level Confederate commitment to defend Jackson, it was an insane waste of human life, achieving nothing that could not have been achieved without it. All three views are historically correct.

The Tenth Tennessee had performed well at Raymond. On the offensive between 2:00 and 2:30 p.m., they held their own against heavy Union artillery and the Seventh U.S. Missouri. In Turner's surprise attack between 2:30 and 3:00 p.m. they decisively defeated a single company of the Thirty-Second Ohio, without the necessity of being reinforced by the Thirtieth Tennessee. In a defensive deployment between 3:00 and 3:30, their skirmishing and sharpshooting was effective against companies of the Seventh U.S. Missouri and the Eighty-First Illinois.

Raymond was the single best effort of the Sons of Erin in the War Between the States. The leadership of Lieutenant Colonel Turner, who was suddenly thrust into command of the consolidated regiment, was highly unorthodox but near perfect. Turner was a courageous combat officer who would be wounded many times and then finally survive the conflict.

In Army Official Records, Grace, O'Neill and First Lieutenant Theodore Kelsey, the Irish-born regimental courier, were honored for "bravery and gallantry."[36] William Grace was promoted to full colonel in command of the Irish regiment. Samuel Thompson was promoted to lieutenant colonel, moving up to the number two slot. And John G. O'Neill was promoted from company command to the regimental staff, with the rank of major, third in the chain of command.[37]

In the Tenth/Thirtieth Tennessee consolidated, Turner had been the senior ranking lieutenant colonel and thus succeeded McGavock as commanding officer. But for reasons that are not clear, the Richmond war department chose not to promote Turner to full colonel along with Grace, which meant that Grace outranked the commanding officer of his own regiment, causing a military anomaly. Because of this, Gregg was obliged to separate the command of the Tenth Tennessee from that of the Thirtieth Tennessee, leaving both Grace and Turner with independent commands that were the size equivalent of two companies each.[38] The Sons of Erin would not be officially consolidated again for another eighteen months.

187

Following the Battle of Raymond, McPherson reported sixty-six killed, 339 wounded, thirty-seven missing or captured, most in Logan's division, a few in Crocker's division, for total losses of 442 men. In Stevenson's brigade there were eighteen killed, eighty-eight wounded, and twelve captured. Those twelve were the men picked up by Grace in front of O'Neill's Hill. Stevenson's total losses were 115, of which seventy-three alone were in the Seventh U.S. Missouri.[39] Most or all of those casualties were inflicted by the Tennessee consolidated regiment.

General Gregg reported seventy-three killed, 251 wounded, and 190 missing or captured for total losses of 514 men, bringing his brigade strength down to 2,216 effectives. The Third Tennessee was hit the hardest with 187 losses, followed by the Seventh Texas with 158. Third on the list of regimental casualties was the Tenth/Thirtieth Tennessee consolidated with fifteen killed, sixty-three wounded, and ten captured or missing for a total loss of eighty-eight men.

Taken separately the Thirtieth had seven killed, twenty-eight wounded, and one captured or missing, adding up to thirty-six losses. The Tenth suffered eight killed, thirty-five wounded, and nine captured or missing for a total loss of fifty-two Irishmen, or twenty percent of the 254 lads engaged.[40] While Raymond may have been the single best effort of the Irishmen, it was also the costliest in terms of total losses. Besides Colonel McGavock, Second Lieutenant Ames and Sergeant Hyde, the Sons of Erin who gave their lives for the Southern cause on that hot Mississippi battlefield were Privates Richard Eagan of A Company, Thomas Branerly of B Company, Darby Martin of C Company, Michael Levins of D Company and Patrick Barrett of K Company. Captain John L. Prendergast and Private John McElroy, two fighting Irishmen from Clarksville, recovered fully.[41]

The Sons of Erin mourned the leader who had raised the regiment, guided it since the early days of the war, went to prison camp with it and reconstituted it to fight again. Lieutenant Colonel Turner described the death of his commanding officer:

> *Colonel McGavock, in a few seconds after ordering the charge, while gallantly leading his men, fell, mortally wounded, and some five commissioned officers of the Tenth Tennessee were wounded at about the same time. The fire thus continued for about half an hour [2:00 to 2:30] without intermission on either side.*[42]

When General Joe Johnston got the word about McGavock's death, he expressed "much regrets" and included them in his own personal memoirs.

In a bitter irony, the first lad from the Irish regiment to be killed in action was probably Randal McGavock himself. And though the Sons of Erin would go on, fighting to the bitter end, a central light had been extinguished. The Tenth Tennessee would never be quite the same ever again.

The body of the ex-mayor of Nashville was buried in the Raymond, Mississippi, graveyard on Wednesday, May 13, 1863. A few weeks later McGavock's sister Ann and her husband, Judge Henry Dickinson, traveled to Raymond, where they arranged for the body to be brought to their home in Columbus, Mississippi. Funeral services were held on July 29. After the war the remains of the colonel of the Tenth Tennessee were shuffled one last time to the final resting place at Mount Olivet Cemetery, Nashville.

On Sunday afternoon, May 17, Dr. John B. Lindsley read the bad news in *The Louisville Democrat*.[43] Jacob and Louisa McGavock took the news hard but with considerable dignity; Seph McGavock's life was changed forever.

A Tale of Two Rebellious Padres

Two of the nine members of the Tenth Tennessee to be captured at Raymond were Second Lieutenant William W. Foote and Private Patrick M. Griffin. Because of their capture, one of those bizarre sidelights occurred which give such an odd flavor to the doings of the Sons of Erin. Pat Griffin in his lengthy memoirs describes a long and rambling trip back to Nashville—one of the three times he took "French Leave" from the Confederate Army.[44] The lad garrulously alleges that it was to deliver the watch of his beloved late colonel to Mrs. Louisa McGavock in Nashville. This has to be an out-and-out fib, since Dr. Sidney Franklin, as was of course logical, gave both the watch and the journals to Captain Ed McGavock, brother of the colonel.

More likely Griffin set for himself the mission of escaping from Yankee clutches and then heading back to home territory to eat some decent food and drink some decent whiskey and involve himself in some real or fancied intrigues with the very real "Nashville underground." Some of the tale probably did happen.

The strange scenario follows. Second Lieutenant William W. Foote and Private Patrick M. Griffin were marched off to Raymond, where they were placed in the care of the Union captain of the guard, another Irishman named Captain Raymond McGuire. Whether because he liked the joking fellow wearers of the green or whether he thought it best to separate the prisoners from others who were being held, McGuire put the two lads from the Tenth Tennessee in a room by themselves at the local hotel.

Foote and Griffin were not eager to spend more time in some Federal prison, and a way out offered itself in an unusal discovery that Pat made.

I looked around the little old room in which we were confined and found that there was a door leading to another room. This door was locked,

190

but it did not take me long to effect an entrance, and there I found stored away boxes of plug tobacco that reached half-way to the ceiling. Well, that find was equal to a gold mine, for tobacco was very scarce at that time.[45]

At the same time that Griffin found the tobacco, "Tinfoot" Foote learned that the guards would have to keep their prisoners holed up in Raymond for another four or five days.

Bribing McGuire and the other Boys-in-Blue, Griffin secured a pass and a sales permit, and sold out the whole secret room, clearing $500 in U.S. greenbacks.

In a few days Foote, Griffin and the others were marched to the Mississippi River, via Port Gibson, where they were placed on a transport headed back up to Federal prison.

In charge was Captain Elias Neff of the Fifty-First Indiana Infantry regiment, whose destination was Two Mile Island, just above Memphis. Griffin planned his escape. Foote had been injured at Raymond and couldn't swim anyhow; he would have to be left behind. When Griffin boasted to Neff that he was about to escape, the captain laughed and challenged him to a five U.S. dollar bet. The pair shook hands. If Griffin got away, the cash would be passed along through Foote. Actually, the debt was late in being collected, because Foote and Griffin would not see each other for thirty-five years!

As the boat passed Memphis, Griffin, decked out in stolen civilian clothes, jumped and swam to a steamboat, which docked in Memphis.

One must rely, of course, on Griffin's boasting latter-day memoirs for the tale which follows, but the story which he told could have happened in Memphis of the occupation, where Federal commanders changed every few months and the hostile citizenry was practicing every chicanery and guerrilla tactic in the book to thwart the Yankees.

Griffin swore later that when he jumped, not only was

the watch undamaged, but the $500 in U.S. greenbacks and the $900 he carried on himself in Confederate currency didn't even get wet.

Before making his way to freedom, the young Irishman had been told by a Southern spy on the boat that he could find shelter in the home of a certain state militia colonel. Unfortunately, the wife of the colonel had no idea what the young lad at her door wanted and sent him away. Undaunted, escapee Griffin decided to see Memphis by cab.

> *The hackman was waiting for me at the gate [of the colonel's house]. I asked him the amount of his bill, and he said 'one dollar.' Of course he did not know but what I was a millionaire; so I told him to take me to the Gayoso House Hotel, and make it two dollars. On the way, I slipped out of the hack and the poor Jehu found himself minus his fare.*[46]

His next stop was Maggie's Saloon, a cheap waterfront inn, where thugs could get a room for a few cents. While Maggie was showing Pat to his quarters, he cased the cupboard. Later that night he cleaned out the china and left without paying his bill.

In order to unload his sack of hot plates, Pat went down to the waterfront and "mingled with the roustabouts," as he said.[47] The fellow who purchased the goods was a tough in a brown leather jacket. Another roustabout, who had been twice arrested for expressing "rebellious sentiments" in occupied Memphis took compassion on the young Irishman and offered him assistance. This kindly underground Rebel was Father Francis Xavier Ryan, whose special ministry was converting Confederate currency into U.S. greenbacks to serve the Southern cause.[48]

Griffin's $900 would be in good hands. Later that same night, Father Ryan and Griffin, both wearing disguising coats and hats although it was the middle of the summer, groped their way to an abandoned warehouse where the money was finally exchanged. Then the Catholic priest gave Griffin the name and address of a Memphis family who could get the young Irish lad safely to Nashville.

The McCoombs had a pretty young daughter by the name of Molly who invited the Southern soldier to stay a while. Others in the "underground" offered more money and clothing, and Griffin eventually made his way to Nashville so he could supposedly complete his "mission of mercy."

Ryan was not the only Catholic priest in Tennessee known to be flouting the Federal occupation force. Father Emmeran Bliemel, pastor of the Assumption parish, was arrested in Nashville for sending morphine south to ease the horrible pain of Confederate amputees.

But it was not only Confederates he helped. On the last day of 1862 and the first two days of 1863, a bloody engagement called the Battle of Stones River had taken place at Murfreesborough, Tennessee. In Nashville the number of wounded Union soldiers rose to crisis proportions. Throughout his smuggling operation, designed to aid Southern soldiers, Father Emmeran continued to minister to wounded Northern soldiers, too.

The German-born priest was anti-slavery and pro-Union, but also pro-southern. He explained his stand:

> *I have never taken an active part in this rebellion. I am a conservative Union man. I would prefer the old Union as it was, but believe that the South has been deprived of rights, which justify this rebellion.*[49]

Father Bliemel, who as had been said, had already been named chaplain of the Tenth Tennessee, continued to be eager to get to the front to join the troops. His bishop, James

Whalen, continued to refuse to allow him to go—and there were other problems.[50]

Major General William S. Rosecrans, 43, of Ohio, the commanding general of the Union Army of the Cumberland and the replacement for Major General Don Carlos Buell, had set up headquarters at Nashville in late October, 1862, prior to his advance to Stones River. Rosecrans, a devout Catholic, had a brother in the priesthood, who was later to be the Bishop of Cincinnati. The future Bishop Rosecrans was a close personal friend of Bishop Whalen of Nashville.

Although he had hesitated at first to question Father Bliemel, General Rosecrans instructed his military police, commanded by Colonel William Truesdale, to investigate the activities of the priest. Convinced that Bliemel was indeed smuggling to Confederate troops, Rosecrans wrote to the Benedictine abbot in Pennsylvania, asking him to recall the obstinate clergyman. There is no record of the letter even having been answered, and Bliemel remained in Nashville.

With his own parish church building being used as a Federal military hospital, Father Emmeran was placed under virtual house arrest at St. Mary's Cathedral. He continued to yearn to actively take up his chaplaincy in the field with the Sons of Erin.

About the same time that Bliemel was pressuring Whalen and being pressured by Truesdale, Griffin was on the loose in the civilian world, still ostensibly delivering a watch to the grieving mother of the late Randal W. McGavock, of blessed memory, which, as has been said, he could not possibly have had. After a series of wild adventures, the lad managed to elude the "secret police" of the Yankee occupiers of both Memphis and Nashville (who in the account, written in 1905 seem for some reason to have shown a deep interest in the activities of an AWOL eighteen-year-old Irish ditch-digger).[51]

During his "furlough" in Nashville, Griffin courted the "little auburn-hair girl" he would later wed. After having stolen the black mount of a Union officer, Private Patrick M. Griffin headed south, laden with dozens of socks, long bundles of underclothing, sundry letters and several sacks of chewing tobacco that were sewn into the saddle blanket.

During the fall of 1863 the youthful Irishman made his way down the line of the Western and Atlantic Railroad, where he found the Sons of Erin on the East Tennessee-Georgia border. He sold the hot horse to "Gentleman Johnny" O'Neill for $250 U.S. greenbacks and disposed of the other items in a short time. Pat Griffin's "mission of mercy" had been successful.

The Fall of Vicksburg

Late in the evening of Tuesday, May 12, 1863, General John Gregg was reinforced by a "brigade" of about a thousand men brought in from South Carolina, under the command of Brigadier General William Henry Talbot Walker, 46, of Georgia. The combined Confederate forces of Gregg and Walker were the equivalent size of two regiments and two battalions.

General Joe Johnston finally arrived in Jackson on the evening of the 13th with an "army" of 3,000 men borrowed from General Braxton Bragg's Army of Tennessee. Altogether Johnston, Gregg, and Walker had about 6,200 Southerners between them, in size the equivalent of a single Union division, or about one-ninth of Grant's army, which was soon to be reinforced.

Johnston got a troubled night's sleep at the Bowman House Hotel, dispirited by the double bad news of General Stonewall Jackson's death at Chancellorsville, Virginia, and General Earl Van Dorn's assassination at Spring Hill, Tennessee. The next morning, after getting reports about Grant's advance, Johnston withdrew to the north, leaving behind a few hundred cavalry scouts and infantry pickets to slow the Federals down.[52]

General Grant's plan of attack against Jackson called for General McPherson's Seventeenth corps to go nine miles northwest from Raymond to the town of Clinton and then follow the Southern Mississippi another nine miles southeast into Jackson, which meant that McPherson would approach the state capital from the north. The Boys-in-Blue of the Seventeenth corps advanced all day May 13, tearing up the tracks behind them.

General Sherman's Fifteenth corps, bivouacked in Dillon, twenty miles southwest of Jackson, was ordered northeast through Raymond for the purpose of striking the state capital from the south. General McClernand's Thirteenth corps was given the task of occupying the Bolton Depot, eight miles west of Clinton, midway between Vicksburg and the state capital.[53] This was Grant's way of preventing Pemberton from reinforcing Johnston at Jackson.

At 10:00 a.m. on Thursday, May 14, General Sherman's corps and General Crocker's division of General McPherson's corps advanced on Jackson. Johnston posted pickets from W. H. T. Walker's brigade in front of Clinton to harass Crocker; and he posted pickets from Gregg's brigade in front of Raymond to harass Sherman.

Gregg's troops consisted of a few companies of the Seventh Texas. Very few of the brigade's Tennesseans were used to defend Jackson, and none at all from the Sons of Erin, who were held in reserve north of the state capital, along with most of the men in the small Confederate command.[54]

Walker and Crocker skirmished in the pouring rain around the Jackson depot before 11:00 a.m.; after that time the rain stopped. Crocker advanced, and Walker withdrew along the Canton road and out of Jackson. As the slowly moving vanguard of Sherman's corps reached Jackson at 1:00 p.m. Gregg also evacuated his skirmishers along the Canton road and out of Jackson to join with Johnston, Walker and the rest of his brigade, including the Sons of Erin.[55]

And that was the Battle of Jackson, an engagement

that some historians have referred to as the "siege of Jackson."[56] In reality, the fight for the Mississippi state capital had taken place two days earlier at Raymond.

General W.T. Sherman excelled at two things. He fought extremely well, and he destroyed people, places and things extremely well. On the morning of Friday, May 15th, General Grant instructed General Sherman to destroy the "military installations" of Jackson. Included on Sherman's list of "military" targets were foundries, stores, machine shops, warehouses, factories, stores, churches, farms, and homes.[57]

The town was burned to the ground. From ten miles away the Sons of Erin could see the skies over Jackson covered with black smoke.[58]

Landmarks such as the beautiful Catholic church were razed, along with most public buildings. In the residential district solitary chimneys rose above the rubble. These lone-standing columns of stone were known as "Sherman's Sentinels," giving the Mississippi city the temporary nickname of "Chimneyville."

Following Raymond a new command structure for the Tenth Tennessee regimental staff was in place:

-Colonel William Grace, Commanding the regiment.
-Lieutenant Colonel Samuel M. Thompson, Commander, A Battalion Infantry.
-Major John G. O'Neill, Commander, Sharpshooters.
-Captain Saint Clair Morgan, Commander, B Battalion Infantry.
-First Lieutenant Theodore Kelsey, Adjutant/Courier.[59]

Individual lads would retain their old company designations, but because of the diminished size of the Irish regiment, companies could be longer be deployed. Grace divided his command into three logical components. His three ranking staff officers, Thompson, O'Neill and Morgan, each commanded one of the platoon-sized components of about seventy Irishmen.[60]

The commands of Gregg and Walker were combined at first into a single brigade, still detached from the main body of the Confederate Mississippi army. On May 23 Walker was promoted to the rank of major general at the insistence of General Johnston, who, bypassing Gregg, pronounced Walker to be the only present officer fit to lead a division. Between Walker and Gregg there were slightly fewer than three thousand men present for duty; still, on the 26th Johnston declared this assortment to be Walker's division.

Johnston ordered Walker west toward Vicksburg through Clinton and Canton to a final destination at Yazoo City, some forty-one miles northeast of the Confederate garrison. It was a long and bizarre three-day march that covered some thirty miles per day.[61] The state of Mississippi held plenty of food and water, especially in the fertile Yazoo Delta, but the area was as rotten with disease as one of the above-ground burial houses the men saw on the march.

The small division reached Yazoo City on Monday, June 1, after covering the last thirty-two miles the previous day. One of the Sons of Erin didn't make it. Private John Keaton collapsed in the sun and died a few days later of an unknown sickness.[62] He was one of McGavock's original ninety-two recruits.

Having possession of Jackson and the railroad, General Grant could then focus his attention exclusively on General Pemberton. The Southern commanding general from the North faced a real dilemma of conflicting orders. President Jefferson Davis told him to hold Vicksburg "at all costs." General Joseph E. Johnston, commanding the Mississippi theatre of operations, told him to march eastward and meet the

Federals near Clinton. Unfortunately for the Southern cause, Pemberton tried to do both.

To comply with Davis' instructions, Pemberton kept the smaller part of his army at Vicksburg. To comply with Johnston's instructions, he moved out on May 15 through rain and high water with a view to striking Grant's supply line. Grant, however, was living off the rich Mississippi countryside and didn't need a supply line.

The next day, at Champion's Hill or Baker's Creek, General Pemberton's forces were badly defeated by the Union Seventeenth and Thirteenth corps, commanded by Generals McPherson and McClernand. General Lloyd Tilghman, serving as the Confederate artillery commander, was killed when a shell fragment struck him in the chest and passed completely through his body.[63] The Fort Henry commanding general the Sons of Erin had respected had survived Colonel Heiman by six months and Colonel McGavock by four days.

On May 17 the Boys-in-Gray fell back and were again defeated in a series of engagements along the Big Black River. The Northerners crossed the river over pontoon bridges on the 18th, while the Southerners scrambled back to Vicksburg. General Grant assaulted the Rebel stronghold on the 19th, but was driven back. On May 22 Admiral David Porter's gunboats bombarded from the riverside, while Grant sent his reinforced infantry of seventy-one-thousand in from the land side.

During the six-week siege that followed, Johnston raised an army of almost thirty-thousand green recruits, including two more brigades for W.H.T. Walker's division, hoping to join Pemberton's thirty-thousand defenders. Grant, however, skillfully kept the Confederate commands apart.

During the siege of Vicksburg, the Sons of Erin, deployed as a guard detachment, were doing picket duty three miles south of Yazoo City, where absolutely nothing was going on.[64] They listened for news of the drama which was unfolding elsewhere—in the city of Vicksburg.

Running low on food and supplies, and with the citizens suffering, Pemberton surrendered Vicksburg on July 4,

199

Corps Commanders of The Sons of Erin

(Top Left) Major General John C. Breckinridge of Kentucky.
(Top Right) Lieutenant General William J. Hardee of Georgia.
(Center) Lieutenant General James Longstreet of Georgia.
(Bottom Left) Lieutenant General Stephen D. Lee of South Carolina.
(Bottom Right) Major General B. Franklin Cheatham of Tennessee

200

the very day after General R.E. Lee's defeat at Gettysburg. The Southern cause was staggered. While Lee retreated north to south, the Confederacy had been cut in half west and east, with the Mississippi River completely in Federal control.

On July 13 Johnston sent Walker, Gregg, Grace and the Sons of Erin back to Jackson, or whatever was left of it. The Confederates were force-marched east thirty-one miles on the first day, resulting in more exhaustion and sickness and weakness of the intestinal variety. After halting a few days in the Jackson area, the march continued via Brandon, Morton, and Forest City to Meridian. At the town of Morton, Captain S.R. Simpson of the Thirtieth Tennessee, in Gregg's brigade along with the Sons of Erin, recorded that he observed "a lot of Yankee prisoners, some niggers, a few Indians, and two deserters."[65]

There were many more than two deserters during those awful Mississippi marches of the summer of 1863. In fact in the Sons of Erin, Privates Marty Gibbons, "Crazy Tom" Feeney, and the Fighting Fitzgeralds all vanished at this time.[66]

For the Irishmen of the Tenth Tennessee it was the worst march of the war. Captain Lew Clark commented on the conditions:

> *This summer's campaign was excessively trying to the men. Continuous marching over hot, dry, dusty roads, under the piercing rays of a relentless sun, made the scarcity of water severely felt.*[67]

From Meridian General Walker went to a crossroads called Enterprise, Mississippi, then to the Chickaseeha River, where his weary troops packed it in for six weeks of rest. The Tenth Tennessee was reduced to 190 lads present for duty. On Monday, September 7, the Irishmen were pleased to catch a train ride to Mobile, Alabama, where they transferred to another train, traveling through Montgomery, Auburn, and finally Atlanta, Georgia. The Sons of Erin had been assigned to the Army of Tennessee.

The trip north from Atlanta was marked by a head-on crash that killed about a hundred soldiers, mostly from the First and Fiftieth Tennessee regiments of Gregg, but none from the Tenth.[68] W. H. T. Walker's division reached its destination at Ringgold, Georgia on the evening of September 17, 1863.

The brigade of General John Gregg, including the Tenth Tennessee, was detached from Walker and attached to the division of General Bushrod Rust Johnson.[69] The Sons of Erin were glad to see the "Old Professor" again. He had last been spotted headed east along the Wynn Ferry road out of Dover and away from Fort Donelson. After having been wounded at Shiloh at about the same time that General Albert Sidney Johnston was receiving his mortal wound, the Ohio-born Nashville Quaker was back in action.

Johnson bivouacked Gregg's brigade in northern Georgia, just about nine miles southwest of Chattanooga, and just to the east of the low, winding West Chickamauga Creek, an Indian name that means "River of Death," or literally "River of Blood."

Theatre of Operations
Western Armies
1863 - 1865

Chapter Seven
River of Blood

The Chickamauga Campaign
Thursday, September 17, 1863
General Bragg Versus General Rosecrans

The Army of Tennessee was the main fighting force of the Western Confederacy, just as the Army of Northern Virginia was the main fighting force of the Eastern Confederacy. The Army of the Cumberland was the main fighting force of the Western Federal Union, just as the Army of the Potomac was the main fighting force of the Eastern Federal Union. Commanding the Army of Tennessee in 1863 was General Braxton Bragg, 46, of North Carolina. Commanding the Army of the Cumberland in 1863 was Major General William S. Rosecrans, the Ohioan who had been investigating the activities of Father Emmeran Bliemel in Nashville.

Between June 23, 1863, at Tullahoma, Tennessee, and September 7 of that same year at Chattanooga, Tennessee, General Bragg managed to accomplish one of the most amazing feats in American military history. He retreated the Confederate Western army out of the critical town of Chattanooga and completely out of the state of Tennessee with hardly a shot being fired in anger.[1] This remarkable deed was due in part to General Rosecrans' successful tactics; Rosecrans was, in fact, considered a master strategist by even his worst enemies. However, the main cause for the Confederate crisis in East Tennessee was Bragg's ineptitude as a field commander. For Southerners, the good news about Braxton Bragg was the low number of casualties in his army; the bad news was his refusal to do battle with the enemy.

Northerners considered Chattanooga to be the all-important entrance ramp to Dixie. The town is just a few miles above the Tennessee-Georgia border, the very last Confederate stronghold in the Volunteer State, or at least it was before General Bragg's untimely evacuation. Without Chattanooga, not only was Tennessee gone from the South, but so, eventually was Georgia.[2] The Western and Atlanta railroad line ran directly north-south between the hills of Chattanooga and the plains of Atlanta. The importance and convenience of the route had already been demonstrated to the Sons of Erin when they had taken the train north from Atlanta to the town of Ringgold, Georgia, a mere fifteen miles south of Chattanooga.

Chattanooga was, then, the key to Atlanta, which was at the very heart of the Confederacy. The Georgia capital was a vital production center, just as Nashville and New Orleans had been. With Chattanooga and its railroad system firmly under Federal control, the highly organized General Rosecrans could march into central Georgia and rip the heart out of the Confederacy.[3] With Vicksburg and the entire length of the Mississippi River once again in the hands of Abraham Lincoln, and with General Robert E. Lee's army withdrawing back to Virginia after Gettysburg, the Confederate government in Richmond could not have long survived the loss of Atlanta. But to secure Atlanta, the Southerners had to reoccupy Chattanooga.

General Bragg was gone and General Rosecrans was exultant. On September 8 he occupied Chattanooga unchallenged. The next day he sent a telegram to the Washington City war department. "Chattanooga is ours without a struggle and East Tennessee is free."[4] "Old Rosy" never even thought about stopping, and he advanced his army down into North Georgia to the town of Lafayette, twenty miles south of the border town of Rossville, Georgia. Not content with just Chattanooga, Rosecrans wanted Bragg and his army.

Rosecrans set a trap with himself as bait, figuring that even the unaggressive Bragg would have to come out somewhere and fight. If his troops could neutralize the Army of Tennessee, Atlanta would come as easily as Tullahoma and

Chattanooga. With this end in mind, Rosecrans formed a line along the Lafayette road that led to Chattanooga, extending it from the town of Lafayette on the south fourteen miles north to Lee and Gordon's Mills, a granary compound.[5]

The Army of the Cumberland was divided into four corps of eleven divisions. The northern left flank was the Fourteenth corps of four divisions, commanded by Major General George H. "Old Pap" Thomas. The center of the line was held down by the Twenty-First corps of three divisions, commanded by Major General T. L. Crittenden, 44, of Kentucky, the younger brother of G. B. Crittenden, the Confederate general who had been defeated by Thomas at the Battle of Mill Springs in the Cumberland Gap.

The southern right flank was the Twentieth corps of three divisions, commanded by Major General Alexander McDowell McCook, 32, of Ohio, one of the many "Fighting McCooks" in the Union Army.

The Reserve corps was stationed up on the border near Rossville to block the Lafayette road into Chattanooga, while protecting the rear of the army. It was a single division of three brigades, commanded by Major General Gordon Granger, 42, of New York.[6]

This long Union defensive line was thrown up west of the Lafayette road facing east, bold as day. Between September 10 and 17, the Northerners sought out and skirmished here and there with the Southerners. The next move was up to Bragg.

The Confederate Western army commanding general had lost his top subordinate. Lieutenant General William J. Hardee had been transferred to General Joe Johnston on the Mississippi front because of the personal differences Hardee had with Bragg. This move proved to be unfortunate for the Southerners. Replacing Hardee (who was number one corps commander) would be the number two corps commander—a man almost as incapable in his job as Bragg was—Lieutenant General-Bishop Leonidas Polk.

The Richmond war department, then, had to find another number two corps commander for the Army of Tennessee and seized upon one of General Lee's many capable Eastern division commanders and sent him west. He was Lieutenant General Daniel Harvey Hill, 42, of North Carolina, known to history as D.H. Hill, although no one ever called him that.

From the moment they met, fellow-North Carolinians Bragg and Hill did not get along. "My interview with General Bragg at Chattanooga was not satisfactory," was what General Harvey Hill reported.[7] As the result of all of this, the Confederate forces in East Tennessee and North Georgia had one incapable army commander, Bragg, one incapable corps commander, Polk, and one inexperienced corps commander, Hill, who openly disliked both Bragg and Polk. The situation did not auger well for what looked to be crucial battles ahead.

After a series of political rumblings in Richmond, the Confederate adjutant general wired General Bragg with a question: "If we reinforce you, can you attack the enemy?" "Yes," Bragg wired back, "if we can fight on equal terms."[8] Major General Simon Buckner's corps was sent down from Knoxville to General Bragg. Nothing happened.

President Davis then made one of his wiser military moves, transferring troops from the Virginia front. Two thirds of Lee's famed First corps, two divisions, nine brigades of battle-hardened Eastern front troops were sent to reinforce the Western army. They were commanded by the senior lieutenant general of the Confederate Army, the great battlefield technician James "Peter" Longstreet, 42, of Georgia.[9]

There was, however, a logistical problem in moving General Longstreet's troops. When General Buckner moved out to join General Bragg's forces, Union Major General Ambrose E. Burnside, 39, of Rhode Island, occupied Knoxville with his Army of the Ohio, effectively blocking the railroads between Southwest Virginia and North Georgia. As a result, Longstreet's corps had to go down through the Carolinas and across Georgia, a distance of 965 miles, using the tracks of sixteen different lines![10]

By the time that Colonel William Grace and the Sons

of Erin arrived at Ringgold on the evening of September 17, with Generals W. H. T. Walker and John Gregg, only one of Longstreet's brigades, the legendary Texas brigade, then under the command of Brigadier General Jerome Robertson, had arrived. In spite of that, however, the normally indecisive Bragg inexplicably decided to attack on the morning of the 18th, without the rest of his reinforcements from the east. The Confederate objective for Friday, September 18, was to advance west and cross the West Chickamauga Creek in front of the Union line along the Lafayette road. (There are actually three Chickamauga creeks: West, East, and South.) General Bragg at that moment had four corps of nine divisions, with eight more brigades on the way.

General Gregg's command, including the Sons of Erin, formed one of the four brigades of General Bushrod Johnson's division. Johnson's other three outfits were commanded by Robertson of Texas, Brigadier General Evander McNair of Arkansas, and Colonel John S. Fulton of Tennessee. Robertson had four regiments, three from Texas and one from Arkansas. McNair had five regiments, four from Arkansas and one from North Carolina. Fulton had four regiments, all from Tennessee, all originally commanded by Bushrod Johnson himself.[11]

General Gregg consolidated the tiny First Tennessee battalion with the Fiftieth Tennessee under Colonel Cyrus A. Sugg, giving him six small infantry regiments, five Tennessee and one Texas. In addition to the First\Fiftieth Tennessee consolidated, there were still the Seventh Texas under Colonel Hiram B. Granbury, the Third Tennessee under Colonel Calvin H. Walker, the Thirtieth Tennessee under Lieutenant Colonel James J. Turner, the Forty-First Tennessee under Colonel Robert Farquharson, and the Tenth Tennessee under Colonel William Grace.[12]

Colonel Grace continued to deploy his 190 Irishmen in three company-sized battalions, two infantry and one sharpshooters'. The infantry units continued to be commanded by Lieutenant Colonel Sam Thompson and by Captain Saint

Clair Morgan. The Sharpshooters detachment was led by Major John G. O'Neill.[13] None of these officers or the lads serving under them could have imagined the demands the next few days would place on them.

The Lafayette road, running parallel to the railroad in a north-south direction, was the key to Chattanooga and the coming battle. The Federals held the town and the road; the Confederates wanted both town and road back. Prior to September 18 Lee and Gordon's Mills was the furthest northern position of both armies. But because of some odd circumstances, all of the fighting on September 18 to 20 took place on a five-mile line extending from Lee and Gordon's Mills on the south to the Snodgrass family farmhouse on the north.

Distinctive mountains rise out of North Georgia into Southeast Tennessee in that area. To the west of where both armies were bivouacked there are two huge round mountains: Sand Mountain to the south and Raccoon Mountain to the north. The northern extremity of Raccoon lies just across the Tennessee border and ends in front of the south bank of the Tennessee River, west of Chattanooga.

To the immediate east of Sand-Raccoon is a long, narrow range called Lookout Mountain, broken in the middle by a single gap. Lookout runs forty-five miles south to north, the last four of those miles inside the state of Tennessee, ending six miles southwest of Chattanooga. Directly east of Lookout is a short, narrow range called Missionary Ridge, separated by four gaps, extending further north than Lookout into Tennessee, running just east of Chattanooga and ending a little northeast of the town.

At the northern end of the Chickamauga military line was the Snodgrass farm, a mile and a half east of Missionary Ridge, a little west of the Lafayette road, and three miles west of Reed's Bridge on the West Chickamauga Creek. In the cen-

The Battle of Chickamauga
September 18-20, 1863

The Positions of the Sons of Erin
on 3 straight days

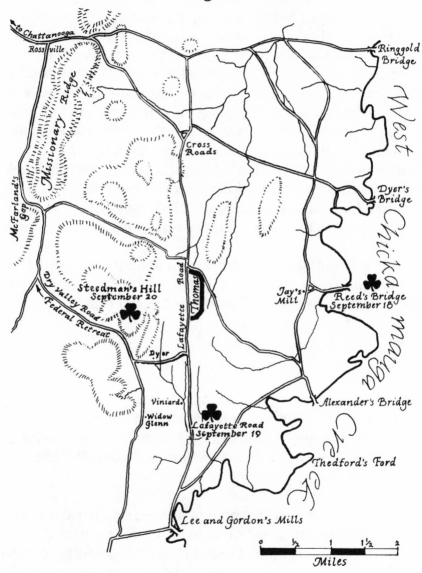

ter of the battlefield was the Brotherton family farmhouse, two miles east of Missionary Ridge, right on the Lafayette road, and two miles west of Alexander's Bridge on the West Chickamauga. At the southern end of the line, the road and the creek met at Lee and Gordon's Mills.

On Friday, September 18, according to the most reliable nineteenth century sources, the battlefield dimensions were four miles long (N-S) by one mile wide (W-E), entirely east of the road from Reed's in the northeast sector down to Lee and Gordon's on the south. On Saturday, September 19, the dimensions were three miles long by two-and-a-half miles wide, extending from the Widow Glenn's farmhouse, two miles above Lee and Gordon's, on the southwest back up to Reed's on the northeast. On Sunday, September 20, the battlefield was two-and-a-half miles long by one-and-a-half miles wide, entirely west of the road, from the Widow Glenn's on the southwest straight up to just above Snodgrass' on the northwest.[14]

Incredibly, this small area would hold 124,548 soldiers during the battle.[15] In the middle, in the thick of it on all three days were the 190 lads of the Sons of Erin.

The Chickamauga Campaign
Friday, September 18, 1863
Pea Vine Ridge, Reed's Bridge, Lee and Gordon's Mills
General Bushrod Johnson Versus Colonel Wilder

At 5:00 a.m. on Friday, September 18, General Johnson was given the wrong set of orders by General Bragg's courier. After his division had marched six miles south, the correct instructions arrived, so he turned around and marched back the same six miles before heading west on the Reed's Bridge road to the West Chickamauga Creek. During all of this marching, Colonel Grace and the Sons of Erin were assigned by Gregg to protect the First Missouri Confederate Battery.

Johnson's division was the Confederate right (north) flank. The center was W. H. T. Walker's division-size corps, which was supposed to cross the creek at Alexander's Bridge after Johnson's crossing at Reed's. The left (south) flank was Simon Buckner's division-size corps, assigned to cross at Thedford's Ford, down by Lee and Gordon's, after Walker's crossing.

This coordinated advance was designed by General Bragg to concentrate his troops in front of the blue-clads' northernmost position.[16] Bragg, however, had failed to inform his three commanders of the objective—the occupation of the road that led to Chattanooga. The strategy was vital: if the road was blocked anywhere north of the Federals' position, they wouldn't be able to get back in and control the East Tennessee town.

Bragg's written instructions called for marching, crossing and concentrating, but nothing about capturing the Lafayette road, a mere two miles west of the creek.[17] In other words Johnson, Walker, and Buckner had absolutely no idea why they were doing what they were doing.

Not that it made much difference. Most of the Confederate infantrymen never made it across the creek that day. Held up by the harassing delay tactics of the "Lightning Boys"—Colonel John Wilder of the Second Cavalry division—Walker and Buckner couldn't cross the creek.

John S. Wilder, a superb soldier who was the commander of the Seventy-Second Indiana Dismounted Cavalry regiment, was at that moment in charge of a scratch division composed of one brigade and one battalion known as the Lightning Brigade—a tribute to the quickness of the unit's movements.

When General Rosecrans received word that General Bragg's infantry was moving west, he sent Colonel Wilder's cavalry to slow them down.

Wilder, in turn, detached slightly more than half his

force, consisting of four dismounted cavalry regiments, over to Alexander's Bridge. This was the temporary command of Colonel Abram O. Miller, the Seventeenth and Seventy-Second Indiana, the Ninety-Eighth and One-Hundred-Twenty-Third Illinois.[18] Colonel Miller's men pulled all the planks out of the bridge before General Walker arrived.[19] Since Walker couldn't cross, General Buckner to his south was also frozen in place by his orders.

Colonel Wilder rushed up his other three dismounted cavalry regiments to do havoc with Reed's Bridge. These regiments were under the command of another outstanding Union cavalry officer, Irish-born Colonel Robert H. G. Minty, the Fourth United States, the Seventh Pennsylvania and the Fourth Michigan. Minty's "demi-brigade" had a total of only 973 Federals.[20] To the harassed Confederates, it seemed like many more.

Due to the early morning mix-up, General Bushrod Johnson's four infantry brigades didn't arrive near Reed's until almost noon. By that time Colonel Minty's men had already dismounted, deployed an artillery battery, and dug out trenches around Pea Vine Ridge, a hill about five hundred yards east of the bridge.

General Johnson deployed General McNair on his far right (north) with General Robertson on the center right. Colonel Fulton was in the center at a right angle, blocking the road to the east, and General Gregg formed the left, south of the road. When Minty opened up his artillery on Pea Vine Ridge to the right of the road, Johnson responded with Gregg's First Missouri Confederate Battery, then commanded by First Lieutenant L.R. Wood.[21]

The Sons of Erin were still detached from Gregg's brigade as infantry support for the Missouri guns. Colonel Grace sent Major O'Neill up front with his sharpshooters' battalion on both flanks of Wood's four cannon. This unit, having made a reputation for itself on O'Neill's Hill at Raymond, then consisted of about seventy lads, mostly Irish-born farmers from McEwen and Clarksville. The three top officers of the sharpshooters, who had long since established themselves as expert riflemen, were Major John G. O'Neill of McEwen, Captain John L. Prendergast of Clarksville and First Lieutenant Thomas "Long Tom" Connor of Nashville.

The two infantry battalions of the Tenth Tennessee were deployed by Colonel Grace as rear guards for Wood's battery. During the artillery bombardment, Grace's riflemen sent a heavy fire of repeated volleys into the position held by the Federal gunners.[22] The front regiments of the two Confederate brigades on the right advanced from the east, while Fulton slid to the right and faced the Union position from the south. During the advance, McNair wound up a little to the north, turned left, and faced the Boys-in-Blue from the northeast. Bushrod Johnson proceeded to assault the Pea Vine area from three directions, with the Seventeenth and Twenty-Third Tennessee regiments of Fulton's brigade opening the action.[23]

It was because of such maneuvers that Johnson was so highly regarded by the Southern high command. His on-the-spot battlefield judgments were nearly always perfect. The offensive movement against Pea Vine Ridge would probably have gone right into some military textbook, except for the fact that it didn't work. Some of the toughest hard-noses in the Army of the Cumberland could be found among John Wilder's "Lightning Boys." At 2:00 p.m. the dismounted Union cavalrymen still held the hill.

At that moment a slight gap became visible in Minty's line. With his usual sense of timeliness Brigadier General Nathan Bedford Forrest dashed out of the woods and onto the scene. "That Devil" Forrest, of course, knew a thing or two about dismounted cavalry operations. With only 240 of General John Hunt Morgan's Kentucky troopers he slashed away at the Yankee battery and left flank. Seeing the hand-to-hand combat in progress around the hill, Robertson's Texas brigade surged forward.[24] The combination of gray-clad cavalry and infantry finally drove the Federals back.

Colonel Minty retired in orderly fashion, down the hill,

across the road, and over the bridge, pulling his artillery back, all the while pursued by the vanguard of General Johnson's division. The gunners of the Missouri battery moved their equipment forward to the east bank, protected by Colonel Grace and the Sons of Erin.

Unfortunately for the Southerners, Minty prevented a crossing by setting up shop on the west end of the bridge, with gunners and skirmishers.[25] Unfortunately for the Northerners, the fire from the Tenth Tennessee and other enemy regiments made it impossible to pull the planks out of the rickety and narrow bridge as they had intended.

All around the Missouri gun crew, O'Neill, Prendergast, Connor and the Irish Rebel sharpshooters of the Tenth poured lead across the creek, taking some of the thunder out of the Lightning Boys.[26] At 3:30, however, not a single Confederate infantryman anywhere along the line from Reed's Bridge to Thedford's Ford had crossed the West Chickamauga Creek. The on-paper perfect attack hadn't worked.

Shortly before 4:00 p.m. the Confederate fire slackened. Something was happening. A swirl of dust could be seen coming west on the Reed's Bridge road. A huge cheer went up from the veterans of the Texas Brigade. The Northerners couldn't figure out what was going on. The Southerners of the other three brigades turned to see for themselves. The rider was clearly visible. The lads of the Sons of Erin had never seen the man before, but instantly they knew who he was. A useless arm hanging in a sling, the result of a wound from Gettysburg, gave him away. Then all of the Boys-in-Gray started shouting for joy, waving their hats, and jumping up and down.

Major General John Bell Hood, 32, of Texas, one of General Lee's most fearsome combat officers, had arrived from the Eastern front. Three Union cavalry regiments were about to be confronted by John Bell Hood, Nathan Bedford Forrest, Bushrod Rust Johnson, the Texas brigade, three other Rebel brigades and—the Sons of Erin.

General Hood, a big raw-boned Texan with the sad eyes

216

of a basset hound, was the ranking Confederate officer on the field, and in that capacity he declared Johnson's division to be Hood's corps. With a calm manner that was reassuring to his new staff, Hood listened to Johnson's description of the situation. He then issued the only order he ever used in battle—full frontal assault.[27]

Hood, whose lack of concern for his own safety bordered on madness, rode up and down the east bank of the creek, giving orders in his own reserved way, boosting the morale of the troops, all the while ignoring the Yankee balls buzzing around him like bees.

"Charge!" Hood led the Southerners racing across the bridge, yelling like demons.[28] Overwhelmed by the numbers and the ferocity of the attack, Minty was forced to retreat without destroying his objective, withdrawing west and then south. Between 4:30 and 6:00, the four Confederate brigades crossed the West Chickamauga. In an hour and a half Hood had accomplished what neither of the other two corps commanders could do all day.

Never slowing down, Hood took a left turn and headed south after Minty and toward Lee and Gordon's Mills.[29] He selected the brigade of fellow-Texan John Gregg to lead the advance, and Gregg selected his own original Seventh Texas regiment as the front line of the brigade, followed by the Missouri gunners with the Sons of Erin and then the other four Tennessee regiments of Gregg.[30]

As Colonel Minty continued to withdraw in front of General Hood's lead brigade, he sent a request for reinforcements to Colonel Wilder. "Lightning Johnny" detached the Seventy-Second Indiana and the One-Hundred-Twenty-Third Illinois from Miller at Alexander's Bridge. Leading the detachment himself, Miller pressed ahead, allowing Minty's exhausted men to fall back. The terrain was heavily wooded and by then it was getting dark. Both Northerners and Southerners were groping around, and at about 9:00 p.m. they groped into each other.

The only forces involved in the evening fracas were the six regiments of Gregg's brigade and the two dismounted cavalry regiments of Miller's detachment. Lines of skirmishers were formed but visibility was almost nil. The job of courier, dangerous in the best of conditions, was even more so in the dark. First Lieutenant Ted Kelsey, the popular courier of the Sons of Erin cited for gallantry after Raymond, was killed by a Yankee sharpshooter while relaying a message from Grace to Gregg and then back to Grace.[31] He was replaced as courier by First Lieutenant Robert Paget Seymour, one of only three members of the Tenth Tennessee to have seen service in a previous war.

Because of the aggressiveness of Hood, Johnson and Gregg, the Federal cavalrymen, outnumbered and in pitch darkness by now, were forced back down to their original position at Lee and Gordon's Mills. Of the three Confederate commands, only Bushrod Johnson's had achieved the mission, with Generals Walker and Buckner still on the east bank of the West Chickamauga Creek.

General Hood's left bivouacked almost on top of the Federals, along the west bank of the West Chickamauga, a couple of hundred yards east of Lee and Gordon's Mills. Oddly, the Confederate right was then left of the Confederate left.

It was time to take stock of the situation in individual units. Just as at Erin Hollow and O'Neill's Hill, the Irishmen of the Tenth Tennessee suffered no casualties at Pea Vine Ridge and Reed's Bridge, while at the same time inflicting a number of casualties on the enemy. The first Irish lad killed at Chickamauga was First Lieutenant Kelsey, lost in the evening skirmish near Lee and Gordon's Mills.

The new Northern Irish courier, who replaced Kelsey, was referred to by the other lads as "Sir Robert," a nickname that was used in all sincerity, without the slightest trace of sarcasm. Captain Lew Clark explained the reason:

> *Robert Paget Seymour was of a distinguished Irish*
> *family, a godson of the Earl of Clanricarde, and*
> *had belonged to the Royal Household troops. He*
> *served through the Crimean War as Adjutant of*
> *the Sixth Dragoon Guards. A braver spirit and a*
> *tenderer heart never animated the form of man.*
> *He was a soldier, every atom of him.*[32]

Private Jimmy Doyle, the son of immigrants from the seven counties, concurred with the assessment of Captain Clark. "Sir Robert is an Irish warrior right out of the pages of an old book."[33] It is important to understand that Clark, Doyle, and the Sons of Erin considered Seymour, an Episcopal native of Northern Ireland and a veteran of the British Army, to be an Irishman just as they were.

That night, with the death of Ted Kelsey, Sir Robert needed all the respect he could get as he made his way on horseback amidst a furnace of sharpshooters' fire.

General Rosecrans received Colonel Wilder's report that the enemy had come across the creek up at Reed's Bridge. He then moved his advance troops up four miles to the Snodgrass farm/Reed's Bridge area to avoid being flanked by the Rebels. Confederate Commanding General Braxton Bragg didn't know this, but he himself had ordered his own advance troops to march four miles down to the Thedford Ford/Lee and Gordon's Mills area so the Yankees wouldn't outflank him. Rosecrans wasn't aware of this move either.

In other words, Rosecrans was where he thought Bragg was, and Bragg was where he thought Rosecrans was. Saturday, September 19, 1863, would prove to be one of the most chaotic battlefield days in American history.[34]

The Battle of Chickamauga, First Official Day
Saturday, September 19, 1863
The Lafayette Road and the Widow Glenn's Farm
General Hood Versus General Wood

In the morning the Confederates were still crossing the West Chickamauga at a ford between Alexander's and Thedford's. Since Bragg believed that the Union line extended only as far north as Lee and Gordon's, he jammed all his forces together just north of that area, with one inflexible order of battle. He would advance west to the Lafayette road, block the road to the north, and turn the far Union left in toward the south—a flank attack.

Because the Union left was further up, however, Bragg's Southerners would march directly into the path of a moving Union left, transforming the planned flank action into a pointless series of frontal assaults.[35] The tactics never fit the plan, but Bragg never wavered from them, continuing to move his units around piece by piece, without any real central coordination.

The Army of Tennessee then had five corps of ten divisions under Generals Polk, Hill, Buckner, Walker, and Hood. Two more of General Pete Longstreet's brigades, those commanded by Brigadier General Henry L. Benning and Colonel James L. Sheffield, had come in during the night. The remaining six Eastern brigades were still off somewhere on a train. Hood took Robertson from Johnson and added him to Benning and Sheffield, giving him an all Eastern front, three-brigade division under the command of Brigadier General Evander M. Law, 27, of Alabama. Hood's other division was Johnson's, cut down to the three brigades of Gregg, McNair, and Fulton. The Sons of Erin, no longer attached to the Missouri Battery, were back on regular duty in Gregg's brigade.[36]

It is difficult to comprehend Confederate flanking movements in this battle, since the Southerners were clustered together. On September 19th General Bragg used two advance corps, with General Buckner's right at Alexander's standing next to General Hood's left at Thedford's.[37] General Rosecrans for his part still believed that Bragg would strike first up near Reed's Bridge.

The Federal left was General Thomas' corps, in the process of moving up to the Snodgrass farm. The center, around the Widow Glenn's farm, was General Crittenden's corps. (The widow's house served as Rosecrans' headquarters.) The right, General McCook's corps, was still south of Lee and Gordon's. "The army is simply a mob. There appears to be neither organization nor discipline," was what Union Brigadier General John Beatty reported about his own Boys-in-Blue.[38] He was, as a matter of fact, accurately describing the conditions on both sides.

At 9:00 a.m. the Confederates of General Walker's corps were finishing their creek crossing, while the general himself was finishing his breakfast to the rear (east) of Buckner's corps. While awaiting a message to attack, he was attacked by two of Thomas' divisions commanded by Generals John M. Brannan and Absalom Baird. The Federals were badly beaten off until they were reinforced by Brigadier General Richard W. Johnson's division, which in turn was pushed back by Nashville General Frank Cheatham's division.[39] The mad-as-a-hatter contest for the Lafayette road was in full swing.

At 2:30 p.m. Confederate Major General Alexander Peter Stewart, 41, of Tennessee, went directly to Bragg for instructions. The army commander didn't wish to confer with subordinates during battle and curtly refused. In disgust, Stewart took the initiative and charged the road, east to west, his division routing the Union division of Brigadier General Horatio P. VanCleve.

Continuing his westward movement, A. P. Stewart's Confederates came screaming up to the hill in front of the Widow Glenn's, almost capturing Rosecrans himself. The Northern commander was spared this humiliation because Stewart's besieging troops were battered back east of the road by divisions under Union Major Generals Joseph J. Reynolds and James S. Negley.[40]

221

While all of this was going on, Hood, along with Bush–rod Johnson, Gregg, Grace and the Sons of Erin awaited some kind of an order. Nothing happened. Like Harvey Hill, Hood was experiencing the difference in command style between Lee and Bragg. He sat on his horse with a sad, hurt look on his face, like a child about to burst into tears, but he was really fiercely annoyed.

By 4:00 p.m. General Hood's remarkable patience was all used up, and, on his own initiative, just like A.P. Stewart, he decided to attack the Federal position on the Lafayette road, some six or seven hundred yards in front of him to the west. When General Gregg went forward to reconnoiter the road with some of his staff officers, he found the First division of McCook's Twentieth corps, under the command of a Union brigadier with the improbable name of Jefferson C. Davis.

On the way back, General John Gregg was shot in the neck and fell from his horse seriously wounded, while his aides rushed him to the rear for the medical assistance which saved his life. [41] The timing of General Gregg's removal from the battlefield couldn't have been worse. Gregg had been with his brigade for nearly a year. On that Saturday afternoon his men would have to go into battle under a man who had been on the job for five minutes—Cyrus A. Sugg of the First/Fiftieth Tennessee consolidated regiment, the senior colonel of the brigade. [42]

It would seem that the Sons of Erin were unaware that brigade command had passed from Gregg to Sugg, not unusual, of course, for a small unit in a big battle. [43] In any case the Irishmen were ready for combat, knowing full well the reputation of John Bell Hood.

General Hood formed an assault wedge of four brigades to the front and two brigades to the rear. Law's division of Benning and Sheffield was the right (north) flank, with Robertson in reserve. Bushrod Johnson's division of McNair and Sugg was the left (south) flank, with Fulton in reserve. Sugg was the extreme far left of the line. His right, next to

McNair's left, consisted of the Third and First/Fiftieth Tennessee regiments and the Seventh Texas. Sugg's left, and the far Confederate left, consisted of the Tenth and Forty-First Tennessee regiments, with Turner's Thirtieth in reserve. The senior commander of Sugg's left wing was Colonel "Battling Billie" Grace of the Sons of Erin.[44]

Hood's corps slashed another big hole in the Union center by blasting its way through J. C. Davis' Federals. The only part of the Confederate line not to get through was Sugg's left flank, consisting of Grace's three regiments, which was pinned down two-hundred yards west of the road in a wooded area. Fulton moved up one of his four regiments, the Seventeenth Tennessee, in support of Grace.[45] Hood surged westward then, pouring General Jerome Robertson's four regiments and Colonel John Fulton's other three regiments into the fight.

The Widow Glenn's farm was about two-thirds of a mile west of the Lafayette road, with its farmhouse standing atop the hill. For the second time in two hours, Rosecrans looked down from the hill to see shouting Rebels running right at him. He never bolted. Rosecrans was well known for his courage in the heat of battle, but at Chickamauga, he seemed almost oblivious to mortal danger. This time he was saved from death or capture totally by accident.

The division of Brigadier General Thomas J. Wood, a Kentucky Yankee from General Crittenden's Twenty-First corps, came marching by at exactly that time. Wood kept Hood busy, giving Rosecrans time to adjust.

The Union commanding general moved in two other close-by divisions, one of which was General Brannan's. The other was commanded by one of the most famous major generals of the war, Irish-American Philip H. Sheridan, 32, of New York. Gradually Rosecrans' Federals, with superior numbers, began to push the gray-clads back eastward toward the road.[46]

Meanwhile, Colonel William Grace was commanding an on-the-spot scratch brigade of four Tennessee regiments—the Tenth, Seventeenth, Thirtieth and Forty-First.[47] Grace, still stuck in the woods just west of the Lafayette road, was engaged in a real donnybrook with the right flank of General J.C. Davis. It was here that Captain William Sweeney of the Sons of Erin was killed by fire from a Yankee skirmisher.[48]

About the same time that Irish-American Sweeney fell, the other six regiments of Fulton and Sugg were withdrawing, west to east, from Wood into the rear of Davis. While Irish-Americans Brannan and Sheridan, along with Wood, surged toward the road, and just before Bushrod Johnson's division ran into Davis' division for the second time, Irish-American Grace received a message from the courier of the Forty-First Tennessee.[49] More blue-clads were headed north up the road!

The four Tennessee regiments of Colonel Grace's makeshift brigade clung tenaciously to their wooded position on the west side of the road. From the sound of the cannonade, it was certain that heavy enemy reinforcements were coming from the west. If other Federals were coming up from the south, Grace's Tennessee regiments would be trapped between the woods, west of the Lafayette road and the road itself. Visions of the Fort Donelson fiasco and prison rot must have come into Grace's head. He had to get his lads out of the trap.

Unfortunately for the Confederates, the scouting report about an enemy advance up the road was completely false, though Grace had no way of knowing it. He ordered the Sons of Erin to fall back east across the road, and the Thirtieth and Forty-First regiments followed.

Sir Robert Paget Seymour was galloping all over the place, ducking Union lead, trying to deliver Colonel Grace's instructions about an orderly retiring. The royal Irishman located Lieutenant Colonel James D. Tillman and Lieutenant Colonel James J. Turner, but he couldn't find Lieutenant Colonel Watt W. Floyd, commanding the Seventeenth Tennessee.[50]

Because the area was so heavily wooded, W. W. Floyd couldn't see the withdrawal. With no message from Colonel Grace and in the confusion of the random troop movements, the Seventeenth Tennessee got left behind. However, Lieutenant Colonel Floyd and his men were saved by the appearance of the other six regiments of Fulton/Sugg, still withdrawing from Wood's advancing troops.

General McNair's brigade of General Bushrod Johnson's division drove off the last regiment of General J.C. Davis' left flank from the south end of the field, but General Wood was approaching rapidly from the west. The rest of Johnson's division then consisted of the seven available regiments of Colonels Fulton, Sugg and Floyd, namely the Seventh Texas regiment and the Third, Seventeenth, Twenty-Third, Twenty-Fifth and Forty-Fourth Tennessee regiments, plus the First/Fiftieth Tennessee consolidated.

General Bushrod Johnson rallied his left flank as his seven regiments dug in to defend against the next enemy onslaught. However, the far left of Hood, Johnson and Sugg was still east of the road and temporarily out of the fight; that is, the three Tennessee regiments still with Grace—the Tenth, Thirtieth and Forty-First.[51]

John Bell Hood formed a five-brigade defensive line west of the Lafayette road, from left to right, with Sugg/Fulton, McNair, Robertson, Sheffield, and Benning. He was soon set upon by the divisions of Wood, Davis, Sheridan, and Brannan.

At the same time that Rosecrans was counter-attacking and Hood was defending, Bragg was over at Thedford's Ford, doing nothing. Twice the Confederates, without any direction from their commanding general, had sliced a big hole in the Union center, and twice had been turned back for lack of reinforcements. All day long General Harvey Hill's entire corps and Major General Tom Hindman's division of Buckner's corps were in readiness nearby. Bragg refused to let them go. "The sparring of the amateur boxer, not the crushing blows of the trained pugilist" was the way the disgruntled Hill described Bragg's performance in battle.[52]

At the same time that General Bragg was being consummately passive, General Wood's far right brigade came charging through a clearing right in front of the First/Fiftieth Tennessee. This was the command of Colonel Charles G. Harker, 27, of Ohio. Harker was a remarkably courageous and skillful combat officer, soon to become the youngest general in the Union Army. His two first-line regiments, the Third U.S. Kentucky and the Sixty-Fifth Ohio, broke through the Sugg/Fulton line.[53]

General Bushrod Johnson swung two of McNair's regiments, the Twenty-Fifth Arkansas and the Thirty-Ninth North Carolina, to the left. At that moment a tremendous slugfest took place right on top of the Lafayette road.

Lieutenant Colonel Thomas W. Beaumont, the man who had evacuated the Fiftieth Tennessee prior to Colonel McGavock's death at Raymond, had been accused of acting with timidity during that battle. Actually, Beaumont's problem at Raymond was insufficient competency, not courage. When Colonel Sugg moved up from regimental to brigade command, he was again replaced by Lieutenant Colonel Beaumont. During the desperate brawl on the Lafayette road, Beaumont, commanding the First/Fiftieth Tennessee consolidated, held his ground but was killed in action. That regiment then had its third commanding officer of the day, Major C. W. Robertson. Colonel Calvin H. Walker of the Third Tennessee, another veteran of the Raymond, Mississippi battlefield, was also killed.[54]

About the same time that T.W. Beaumont and C. H. Walker fell, Commissary Master Sergeant Barney McCabe was fording the West Chickamauga Creek with a pack of mess mules. The supply train of the Gregg/Sugg brigade had arrived the previous day at Alexander's Bridge only to find that the bridge had been destroyed by the Lightning Boys. Consequently, the lads and the rations were on opposite sides of the creek. Ordnance officers like Quartermaster Captain S. R. Simpson of the Thirtieth Tennessee lent the commissary fellows a helping hand, spending most of the day preparing rations.

Instead of pulling everything up to Reed's Bridge,

Simpson and McCabe found a ford south of Alexander's. All the noncombatants took turns loading, crossing, and unloading.[55] They couldn't help but hear all the fireworks to the west and knew that the men would be hungry after a hard day's fight. So it was that Barney McCabe crossed the creek and headed up to the encampment of the Sons of Erin.

About the same time that McCabe was cursing out the mules, Hood moved Jerome Robertson's four regiments over to the left in support of C.W. Robertson and Johnson's other weary Southerners. Harker countered with his second line regiments, the Sixty-Fourth and One-Hundred-Twenty-Fifth Ohio. On the south end of the line the Confederates held a numerical advantage, but Harker's assertiveness with his rested troops was gaining the upper hand. On the north end of the line, Law was being chewed up by Wood's battery of Captain Eli Lilly of Indiana, who just after the war would found one of the largest drug firms in the world.

Back in the woods, Colonel Grace and the Sons of Erin crept up to a clearing in front of the Lafayette road. The Forty-First Tennessee, then commanded by Lieutenant Colonel James D. Tillman, came up behind the Irishmen.[56] Tillman had replaced the wounded Colonel Robert Farquharson the previous day; otherwise, the senior colonel commanding the scratch brigade would have been Farquharson, not Grace. Major John G. O'Neill hung out a line of sharpshooters to the front of Colonel Grace's forward regiment, the Tenth Tennessee, at that moment commanded by Lieutenant Colonel Samuel M. Thompson.[57]

Later Lieutenant Colonel W.W. Floyd of the Seventeenth Tennessee was critical of Grace and Tillman for not jumping back into the action sooner. However, at the time he didn't know about the fire that O'Neill was throwing up in his support. About the same time that Captain John L. Prendergast and First Lieutenant "Long Tom" Connor fired away, Barney McCabe, who was unloading the commissary mules, somehow managed to get himself shot in the head. Out of nowhere, Yankee lead struck him in the forehead, and the blood ran down his face into his shirt like a faucet. Stunned and shaken, the wounded lad lowered himself under the shade of a tree. A devout Catholic from the "Old Sod," he began to pray for intercession to the Blessed Virgin and all the saints in heaven.

A few minutes later his curiosity got the best of him, as he began to wonder why, with a head wound, he didn't feel a lot worse than he did. He had the wound examined and discovered it was from a spent ball which had come over a mile, and the wound was slight.[58] For the rest of his life, the jovial Irishman never let anyone forget about the day his hard head had stopped a Yankee ball in North Georgia.

About the time that Sergeant McCabe was washing his head in the creek, Major O'Neill climbed a tree and fired away at the right flank of the One-Hundred-Twenty-Fifth Ohio.[59] By the time that Colonels Grace, Thompson, Tillman, and Turner advanced to the road, Colonel Sugg's troops were retreating from the charge of Colonel Harker's brigade, causing Colonel Grace's troops to be pushed back to the same woods east of the road. The strong effort of the Tenth Tennessee sharpshooters' battalion was too little, too late.

With his left flank nearly collapsed, Hood was forced to withdraw both his divisions to the east of the Lafayette road. All up and down the road the two armed mobs had been going at each other for over nine hours. It was 6:30 p.m., Saturday, September 19, 1863. Exhaustion had set in. Both sides fell back to their original positions.[60] The Southerners were still west of the creek but east of the road. The Northerners still held the road. Nothing in that regard had changed.

The bodies of the dead and wounded littered the battlefield.

Colonel William Grace had led a brigade of four small regiments for slightly better than two hours.[61] A false scouting report had been his undoing. Probably as the result of his premature withdrawing of the troops, the capable Irish-American was never again assigned to brigade command.

That night the regiments of the wounded General John Gregg were reunited under the command of Colonel Cyrus A. Sugg. For the historical record, the command structure of the temporary Tennessee brigade had been:

> Colonel William Grace, Commanding Provisional Brigade.
> Lieutenant Colonel Samuel M. Thompson, Commanding Tenth Tennessee.
> Lieutenant Colonel Watt W. Floyd, Commanding Seventeenth Tennessee.
> Lieutenant Colonel James J. Turner, Commanding Thirtieth Tennessee.
> Lieutenant Colonel James D. Tillman, Commanding Forty-First Tennessee.

At the northern (left) end of the Federal line General George Thomas continued to direct his Fourteenth corps. The divisions of Generals Richard Johnson and Absalom Baird were on battle alert, protecting the Lafayette road.

Major General Patrick R. Cleburne, described by historian Bruce Catton as "a tremendous soldier with pugnacious Irish eyes" prepared to play his part in the unfolding military drama. Like First Lieutenant Robert Paget Seymour, General Cleburne had been raised in the Episcopal Church of Ireland. Like Colonels Adolphus Heiman and Randal McGavock, General Cleburne was a member of the Masons. Unlike Seymour, Heiman, and McGavock, Cleburne had been born in County Cork on St. Patrick's Day. Like Charles Stewart Parnell after him, Pat Cleburne was then, and is now, one of the most famous non-Catholic heroes of the Catholic Irish.

Under the cover of darkness, General Cleburne's division advanced from the west bank of West Chickamauga Creek, passing through the reclining men of General W.H.T. Walker's corps, and then moving through a forest that opened up in front of Generals Richard Johnson and Baird.

The assault of the Rebel Irishman would demonstrate the power of terrorism on a field of battle. If Thomas had not prepared his troops for such a possibility, as he certainly had done, the Union left flank would have been destroyed. Peering intensely ahead through the darkness, General Pat Cleburne charged on horseback at the front of his yelling foot soldiers, their muzzle-fire glowing in the dark.

The rapid loading, firing, and reloading action of Cleburne's division was considered the best of any unit on either side of the war.[62] When Cheatham's men reinforced Cleburne's, the Federals were driven a mile west. Three-hundred prisoners were taken from the Seventy-Seventh Pennsylvania Infantry regiment alone. The Boys-in-Gray kept yodeling the Rebel yell through the eerie darkness continuously during the attack and even for a while after the withdrawal. The Boys-in-Blue were shot up and intimidated. Those who survived that night would never forget the gun flashes and the yelling in the dark.[63]

The Sons of Erin had been worn out ever since Raymond. On this first official night of Chickamauga, they slept right on the ground, wherever they were.[64] Some made it back to their camp on the west bank of the creek, just south of Alexander's former bridge. Thanks to the mighty efforts of Barney McCabe, the lads had some cooked rations; but many of them were too tired to eat.

To make matters even worse, the air was unseasonably cold that night, and with the front lines so close to each
other, bonfires weren't possible. The lads shivered and listened to the horrible moans and pleas of the wounded. Litter-bearers and medical staffs on both sides worked
feverishly all night long. The early days in which jovial Irish
comrades had played cards and drunk whiskey in the rifle
pits near Ft. Henry seemed far away. Bad as that Saturday
was, the next day would be even worse for the Sons of Erin
and all those American soldiers caught up in the living nightmare of Chickamauga.

The Battle of Chickamauga, Second Official Day
Sunday, September 20, 1863, 11:30 a.m. to 3:30 p.m.
Brotheron's Farm and Dyer's Farm
Colonel Sugg Versus First Lieutenant Schueler

On that same day that Generals A.P. Stewart and J.B.
Hood broke through the Union cener at the Widow Glenn's
farm, Lieutenant General Peter Longstreet finally arrived by
train from the Eastern front. Since General Bragg did not see
fit to provide an escort, Longstreet and his staff had to wander through woods over unfamiliar roads and didn't reach
the Western commanding general's headquarters until ll:00
p.m. When the Eastern corps commander met with Bragg,
he made an astonishing discovery. Earlier that evening, in
the middle of one of the bloodiest battles in American history, Bragg had completely reorganized his army! He had
done so without telling anyone except General Leonidas Polk.
Longstreet listened incredulously. He was to lead half
of Bragg's entire army at sunrise without having had a chance
to meet his new division commanders and without ever having seen the battlefield.

There were two army wings, under Generals Polk and Longstreet. Polk's wing had two corps of five divisions, under Generals Harvey Hill and Walker. Longstreet's wing had two corps of six divisions, under Generals Buckner and Hood. In spite of the previous success against the Union center, Bragg held fast to his only plan of battle. He would assail the northern end of the Federal line and then turn their left flank to the south. Longstreet's wing would be the Confederate left (south) held in reserve, while Polk's wing would assault the Northerners up around the Snodgrass farm. Again the tactics didn't fit the plan.

The best Southern commander, Longstreet, with the strongest part of the army, would have to wait around, while the worst Southern commander, Polk, with the weakest part of the army, would attack the best enemy commander, Thomas, with the strongest part of their army. So tired he couldn't think, Longstreet found the closest tree, pulled off some branches, and immediately went to sleep atop his branch-bed.[65]

After a few fitful winks, the Sons of Erin rose at 4:00 Sunday morning to find themselves in Grace's regiment of Sugg's brigade of Johnson's division of Hood's corps of Longstreet's wing of Bragg's army. Given all that aggressiveness below the army level, the Irishmen all stood a good chance of getting themselves killed.

During the night two other brigades arrived from the Virginia theatre; one of soldiers from South Carolina, the other of troops from Mississippi. These brigades comprised the division of Brigadier General Joseph B. Kershaw, 41, of South Carolina, a citizen-soldier who was one of General Lee's most distinguished combat veterans. The other four brigades of Major General Lafayette McLaws' division as well as Longstreet's entire artillery never made it in until the battle was over.[66]

General Hood's corps then had three divisions of eight brigades, commanded by Generals Bushrod Johnson, Evander Law, and Joe Kershaw. The last two of these divisions and five brigades consisted exclusively of Eastern front veterans. The Sons of Erin, down to about 170 able-bodied Irish lads, were part of what had to have been the best Confederate fighting unit on the field. The field, however, in this circumstance was not the safest place to be.

On Sunday, September 20, General William S. Rosecrans had four infantry corps of eleven divisions of thirty-one brigades of 124 regiments and five battalions, plus one artillery division of three brigades of ten battalions of thirty-two batteries, plus one cavalry corps of two divisions of five brigades of eighteen regiments for a total of about fifty-two-thousand effectives.[67]

General Bragg had two wings of four infantry corps of ten divisions of thirty-one brigades of 103 regiments (including the Tenth Tennessee) and fourteen battalions, plus seven sharpshooters' battalions, plus one artillery division of ten battalions of thirty-two batteries, plus two cavalry corps of four divisions of nine brigades of thirty-two regiments and six battalions for a total of about 58,000 effectives.[68] Remarkably, the infantry brigades (thirty-one) and the artillery batteries (thirty-two) were exactly even, but the Confederates held an important edge in cavalry and sharpshooters.

General Braxton Bragg had given General Leonidas Polk the task of communicating with the various commands in the army about operations for the day, but Polk mismanaged the courier assignments, and the advance, scheduled for 5:30 a.m. (sunrise) began four hours later than it should have. At 9:30 General Harvey Hill's division under Major General John C. Breckinridge assaulted the position of General Thomas.

When Breckinridge advanced, Rosecrans shifted Crittenden's center corps north in support of Thomas. After Breckinridge moved out, Hill quickly sent in Cleburne's division, just to the south of Breckinridge. While the two infantry divisions of Breckinridge and Cleburne savagely slammed into General Thomas' reinforced corps, General Bedford Forrest's cavalry swept in from the north in support of General Harvey Hill's corps.

Stubbornly General Thomas held his position around the Snodgrass farm, as General Rosecrans kept sending up more and more units from his center and right. As a result, Generals Crittenden and McCook were attending to their positions with skeleton crews.

By 9:45 Rosecrans became impatient with his slow-moving support units. He rode right up to General Wood and lambasted the Kentucky officer in front of his own staff. "What is the meaning of this sir? You have disobeyed my specific orders," he roared. "By your damnable negligence, you are endangering the safety of the entire army, and by God, I will not tolerate it! Move your division at once, as I have instructed, or the consequences will not be pleasant for yourself!"[69] General Tom Wood, a West Point professional soldier, choked back his resentment, spoke not a word, saluted and hurried his three brigades along.

Earlier that morning, General Bushrod Johnson had given General Longstreet a tour of the battlefield. The two officers had just met for the first time. Longstreet was impressed by Johnson's obvious intelligence and understanding of the situation and decided to use the Tennessean's division to spearhead one of his famous "clenched fist" assaults.

On his far right, General Longstreet lined up General Hood's corps. Bushrod Johnson, with the Sons of Erin and the rest, was the far right flank and in the lead position.[70] General Law was south and east of Johnson, and General Kershaw was south and east of Law. On the left of Longstreet's wing were two divisions of General Buckner's corps, with General Hindman in front, backed up to the south and east by Brigadier General William Preston of Kentucky.

At 10:00 a.m. Federal scouts told General Rosecrans that General Negley's division had vanished. Rosecrans, considering the situation, assumed that Negley had moved up on his own in support of General Thomas. The assumption was incorrect, because the scouting report was incorrect. Negley's division was right where he was supposed to be, but hidden away in a dense forest. Frantically, Rosecrans sent a message to Wood, ordering him to move up and occupy Negley's vacated spot.

General Wood knew for certain that there wasn't a gap in the Union line, because he could see what Rosecrans' scouts couldn't see, that Negley's division was sitting right next to his in the woods.

Reynolds' division was posted on the left of Brannan's division, which in turn was on the left of the position I was just quitting. I had consequently to pass my command in the rear of Brannan's division to close up on and go into the support of Reynolds, . . .

he later wrote.[71]

If Reynolds' division was posted on the left of Brannan's division, then there was no gap and no place for Wood to place his division as ordered, and he knew it. But Wood had already been reprimanded publicly earlier in the day by his superior; he didn't want to have the experience again, so he spent the next hour moving his division around Irish-American Major General John M. Brannan and alongside Irish-American Major General Joseph J. Reynolds, in accord with Rosecrans' orders.

In attempting to fill a gap that did not exist, Rosecrans created one, a hole, in fact, that was big enough to drive an entire army corps through.[72] At the same time that Wood was moving out, Longstreet had just finished putting his divisions in place. Hindman was ready to advance across the Lafayette road and strike the south-center of McCook while Bushrod Johnson's three brigades of McNair, Fulton, and Sugg, with the Sons of Erin, were set to charge the north-center of Crittenden.[73]

Like Eastern front veterans Harvey Hill and John Bell Hood before him, Longstreet became impatient with Bragg. On his own initiative General Pete Longstreet ordered an all-go with his clenched-fist assault. It was 11:30 a.m. Sunday, September 20, 1863. Strictly by accident and good luck, it was precisely the same moment when the last of Wood's men had cleared the field.

It was also precisely the same moment when the Boys-in-Blue almost lost the Civil War in the West.

At the vanguard of Longstreet's charge, General Bushrod Johnson's division roared west to the Lafayette road, gaining six-hundred yards in record time, yelling their lungs out all the way. It was a cool, clear day and the quick-step march gave the Boys-in-Gray a feeling of exultation. The Sons of Erin never felt so proud nor patriotic in all their lives.[74]

General Evander McNair was on the right, with Colonel John Fulton on the left, and Colonel Cyrus Sugg temporarily in reserve behind McNair. As the Southerners surged over the road, their rear was fired on by Northerners around the Brotherton farmhouse. The Federal unit was a single company of dismounted cavalry. The First/Fiftieth Tennessee of Sugg's brigade was heavily fired on and had to be moved to the front. The Tenth Tennessee was not yet engaged.

Thanks to Rosecrans' untimely move, there were no Federals anywhere to the front. In fact, Wood's abandoned rifle pits were just west of the Brotherton place. In an open field, 220 yards long, south of the farm, the Union skirmishers had formed a line behind some trees at the west end of the field. Bushrod Johnson's troops easily encircled the outnumbered blue-clads and captured the whole lot of them, animals, weapons, and all.[75]

Eight-hundred yards to the south of Johnson's division, Hindman's division advanced directly to the Widow Glenn's farm with virtually no opposition. General Rosecrans was perched atop his horse on the house-hill. A few yards away Assistant Secretary of War Charles A. Dana, who happened to be visiting the front and was an unwelcome guest of Rosecrans, was sleeping under the shade of a tree. For the third time in two days, a swarm of yelling Rebels came running up to the unprotected commander of all Yankees! Only this time there was not a thing he could do about it.

All the commotion startled Dana out of his cat-nap. When he opened his eyes, he saw something alarming. Rosecrans, the devout Catholic, was repeatedly making the Sign of the Cross. This meant only one thing. The Boys-in-Blue were in big trouble. What happened next terrified him. Rosecrans turned slowly toward him in the calmest of manners and spoke in a controlled and icy cool voice. "If you care to live any longer, get away from here."[76] No politician ever moved any faster.

General Longstreet would later become equally as Catholic as General Rosecrans, but on this Chickamauga Sunday morning he had no need to cross himself. Many of the Federal officers reacted in panic, as if knocked unconscious by Longstreet's punch. Generals McCook and Crittenden and the remnant of their corps not already with General Thomas, fled back up to Chattanooga. They were followed in quick order by the newspapermen, merchants, politicians, and other do-gooders who hung out around Union headquarters. Dana, chief spy of Secretary of War Edwin M. Stanton, was one of the first to arrive.[77]

Still Rosecrans did not bolt, riding north to look for Thomas, with no intention of stopping the fight. As he moved through heavy fire at the rear of J. C. Davis' division, he tried to puzzle out what had gone wrong but couldn't. One thing was absolutely certain in his mind, namely his military career and his reputation were finished. The balls continued to fly all around him. Hundreds of Confederate riflemen shot at him that day. They all missed. "Old Rosy" would live another thirty-five years.

Equally Catholic as Rosecrans and Longstreet, Colonel William Grace, mounted, with sword drawn, led the Sons of Erin further west. The lads were on an emotional high, screaming their Irish-Rebel lungs out, like madmen escaped from some institution. Two hundred yards west of Brotherton's farm, they entered a forest. Upon exiting, they were greeted by the ominous hiss of incoming shells. The Irishmen hit the ground.[78]

General Phil Sheridan's division had just withdrawn from the center of the battlefield. The rear guard of the division was the four regiments (two Illinois, two Missouri) of Colonel Bernard Laiboldt's German Brigade. Laiboldt posted his First U.S. Missouri Battery of nine cannon, under First Lieutenant Gustavus Schueler, behind his infantry to slow down the rapidly advancing Southerners.

Detached in support of Schueler were two companies of Lieutenant Colonel Arnold Beck's Second U.S. Missouri Infantry regiment.[79] First Lieutenant Schueler deployed five of his guns with very little infantry support at the southwest end of a wheat field. Colonel "Battling Billy" Grace of the Tenth Tennessee never hesitated; his Irish lads overran the exposed position, capturing all men and equipment.[80]

West of the wheat field was the Dyer family farmhouse in front of a small open field, in front of yet another wooded area. The other half of the First U.S. Missouri Battery with four guns and most of the infantry support was posted on a wooded ridge in the northwest corner of the field in a better position.

General Bushrod Johnson deployed the small brigades of Colonels Sugg and Fulton around the farm with Fulton on the right, Sugg on the left. Sugg advanced with two lines, the Seventh Texas, the Third and First/Fiftieth Tennessee regiments in front, the Thirtieth, Forty-First and Tenth Tennessee regiments coming up in support.[81]

Since the Sons of Erin formed the far Confederate right to the north, Colonel Grace was able to enter the woods by the back door. His Irishmen sprang out from behind some trees, climbed Schueler's Hill and engaged in a hand-to-hand combat with First Lieutenant Schueler's gun crew, supported by Lieutenant Colonel Beck's infantrymen.[82]

238

The German Yankees were surrounded by Colonel Sugg's men on all sides and were forced to surrender. General Bushrod Johnson captured all the gunners, thousands of rounds of ammunition, thirteen cannon, sixteen horses, four mules, five ordnance wagons with four wheels, one ordnance wagon with three wheels, and one ambulance.

The First Confederate Missouri Battery of First Lieutenant L.R. Wood was presented a trophy by Colonel Sugg. Actually, it was four trophies—those last four guns of the First U.S. Missouri Battery, all prized three-inch rifles.

The fight for Dyer's farm was costly. Colonel Hiram Granbury of the Seventh Texas was seriously wounded, and Major C. W. Robertson of the First/Fiftieth Tennessee was mortally wounded. The unfortunate men of the First/Fiftieth then had their fourth commanding officer in two days, First Lieutenant Fletcher Beaumont, the younger brother of the colonel who had been killed the day before. By the end of the day, that regiment would have forty-one men left out of 192.[83] The largest of Sugg's six regiments was the Forty-First Tennessee, which was also hit hard by the German-American defenders.

The action around Schueler's Hill left Colonel Grace and the Tenth Tennessee with a seriously depleted command situation. Captain John L. Prendergast was wounded in the left hand, and First Lieutenant "Long Tom" Connor was wounded in the left leg.[84] Amazingly, both pugnacious lads continued to fight with the regiment for the rest of the day.

Lieutenant Colonel Sam Thompson was wounded in both feet, and the right one had to be amputated by Dr. Franklin, leaving him permanently disabled. Captain Saint Clair Morgan, a gentleman twice elected to company command, was killed in action and replaced on the spot by First Lieutenant Clarence C. Malone, the Irishman who had transferred from the Fourteenth Mississippi.[85]

Thompson and Morgan were Grace's two infantry battalion commanders, the top combat officers of the Sons of Erin. Their losses, coming at the same time, represented a staggering blow to the battle viability of the Rebel Irishmen.

During the mop-up at Dyer's farm, General John Bell Hood caught up with General Bushrod Johnson. "Go ahead, and keep ahead of everything," was what the corps commander ordered.[86]

The three Eastern front brigades of Evander Law's division came up in Longstreet's line just to the south of Bushrod Johnson's division, but Law wasn't as fortunate as Johnson. At the same time that Johnson, Fulton, Sugg, Grace and the Sons of Erin advanced west of Dyer's, Law's Texas brigade under Jerome Robertson was surprised by an ambush from the four regiments of Charles Harker's brigade of Tom Wood's division. Just as fiercely active as on the previous day, Harker had come back to the sounds of battle at Dyer's farm. Amazingly he routed Robertson, causing the fabled Texans from Lee's army to flee in panic to the rear, running past their flabbergasted original commander.

Tall in the saddle, and without a shred of fright in his body, Hood rode among the rapidly disbursing Texans, exhorting them to turn and fight. It was here, in the middle of the Chickamauga battlefield, that a Yankee ball struck him high up on his right thigh. Falling into the arms of his fellow Texans, he muttered the same thing that he had just told Johnson: "Go ahead, and keep ahead of everything."[87]

As the big Texan was carried off the field in tremendous pain, he was informed that General Kershaw's division of two Eastern front brigades had moved up in support of General Law to drive the Federals off the field. At the medical examinations, the doctors discovered the General Hood's leg bone was shattered. The resulting amputation left him barely enough of a stump to accommodate an artificial leg.

At the same time that Hood was carried off and Harker was driven off, Longstreet, Preston, Hindman, Kershaw, Law, Bushrod Johnson, McNair, Fulton, Sugg, Grace, and the Sons of Erin continued their westward advance another two hun-

Army Commanders of The Sons of Erin

(Top Left) General Albert Sidney Johnston of Texas.
(Top Right) Lieutenant General John C. Pemberton of Pennsylvania.
(Center) General Joseph E. Johnston of Virginia.
(Bottom Left) General Braxton Bragg of North Carolina.
(Bottom Right) General John Bell Hood of Texas.

dred yards to a point where they came to the base of a large hill, which was actually one of the spurs of Missionary Ridge. It was here that Johnson's Confederates captured some very surprised Union officers from the staffs of Rosecrans and Van Cleve, who were wandering around.[88]

After sending the prisoners to the rear, Johnson made a right turn and marched his men north along the western side of the spur, a distance of about one thousand yards. His lead two brigades of Sugg and Fulton occupied the far north end of the spur unopposed.

In front of them, on the spur known as Vittetoe's Hill, the Sons of Erin could see a fertile valley extending another thousand yards or so to the north. To the west was the Vittetoe family farmhouse. Straight ahead to the north end of the valley was the Snodgrass family farmhouse, surrounded by six knobs that formed a horseshoe, with the open end of the horseshoe pointed northwest through McFarland's Gap of Missionary Ridge, an escape hatch to Chattanooga. Known to history as Horseshoe Ridge or Snodgrass Hill, this was the position of the last Federals still on the field, the reinforced Fourteenth corps of General George H. Thomas.[89]

The Battle of Chickamauga, Second Official Day
Sunday, September 20, 1863, 3:30 to 9:00 p.m.
Colonel Grace Versus Lieutenant Colonel Warner

At 2:30 p.m. General Longstreet attacked General Thomas. The Sons of Erin advanced from Vittetoe's Hill to the southern end of a low ridge just west of the southernmost knob of Horseshoe Ridge, known to history as Steedman's Hill. Colonel Sugg's brigade, including the Irish regiment, was held in reserve there for about an hour.[90]

When Johnson, Fulton, Sugg, Grace, and the Sons of Erin advanced from Vittetoe's Hill to Steedman's Hill, farmer Vittetoe peered out from the cracks in his house, while his wife and three daughters continued to hide under floor boards in the kitchen, as they had for the past few days "to shield themselves from the insults and dangers of the vandal foe." The Yankees had commandeered the farm for a supply center and, according to the Vittetoe family, had committed "many outrages" before retiring to Horseshoe Ridge.

As the Confederates marched by the farmhouse, farmer Vittetoe shouted, "the Rebels have taken the field; the Rebels have taken the field." Mrs. Vittetoe and her three daughters rushed out of the house and ran right up to the Boys-in-Gray, waving handkerchiefs and shouting for joy, causing the front columns to pause. With tears in their eyes the Southern soldiers, including the Sons of Erin, made reassuring comments like, "we will save you or die." Surprisingly, this non-military event was recorded in the midst of three separate Confederate battle reports in Army Official Records. Lieutenant Colonel Watt W. Floyd of the Seventeen Tennessee regiment explained the reason. It seems that the liberated family included "four very nice looking ladies."[91]

General Bushrod Johnson assumed command of General Longstreet's left flank and charged the position of General John Brannan's division on Horsehoe Ridge with four assaulting brigades. From left (west) to right the Confederate forces consisted of Colonel Fulton's brigade, both of General Kershaw's brigades, and one of General Law's brigades.

On the far right end of his line, General Brannan deployed a single large regiment, the Twenty-First Ohio, to block the advance of Colonel Fulton's four small Tennessee regiments. In spite of General Bushrod Johnson's efforts to turn the Union right with Fulton's forces, the lone Twenty-First Ohio held. In the center of the Horseshoe Ridge battlefield, General Joe Kershaw came to as close as forty paces in front of the Yankee logworks. The pugnacious South Carolinian struck, again and again, under sustained and heavy fire, but not one of his Rebels reached the crest of Snodgrass Hill, whose slopes were covered with dead and wounded.

Johnson, Fulton, Kershaw and Law dug in as best they

could, their troops out of breath, panting like "dogs tired in a chase," while Colonel Sugg's brigade, with the Sons of Erin, remained in reserve at the south end of Steedman's Hill.[92]

Back up at the Tennessee-Georgia border near Rossville, Major General Gordon Granger, commanding the Union Reserve corps, was getting impatient. He could hear the sounds of battle coming from Horseshoe Ridge, but he hadn't received orders from Rosecrans to support Thomas. His chief-of-staff warned that he could get court-martialled if he acted impulsively. Still Granger took that risk, keeping one of his brigades behind to block the Lafayette road into Chattanooga, while leading the other two south towards the scene of the action.[93] It was one of the best pieces of battle-field initiative in the entire War Between the States.

An elated Longstreet took a lunch break of bacon and Georgia sweet potatoes. The meal was interrupted by that ominous hum of an incoming shell that exploded in some trees nearby. A second bombshell followed. General Bragg wanted to see General Longstreet. The Confederate commander was near the Sons of Erin encampment on the west bank of the West Chickamauga Creek between Alexander's and Thedford's, awaiting a progress report. Longstreet excitedly told him, accurately, that the Union Army south of Thomas had been crushed and that many of the Federals were running back up to Chattanooga.

It was at this time that General Braxton Bragg announced that his army was in the process of being defeated! Bragg was angered because *his* plan against the enemy left hadn't worked; if *his* plan was a failure, then the battle was a failure.[94] Bragg rode up to Reed's Bridge to await further reports and, utterly mystified, Longstreet returned to do battle with Thomas.

The early response from the Northern defenders to General Kershaw's ferocious assault had been slow, because the Confederate Eastern front veterans were wearing new blue uniforms, a gift from a Richmond politician. When more blue-clad troops were spotted coming in from the north, General Thomas had Old Glory hoisted high up on the ridge. The national flag wasn't shot at.[95] The troops approaching from the north were the two brigades of General Gordon Granger.

Thomas was never so glad to see reinforcements. Grizzled U.S. Army veterans Thomas and Granger shook hands atop Horseshoe Ridge. It was 3:30 p.m. Just then more columns could be seen moving towards them from the south. There was no mistaking these troops. They were wearing gray and butternut brown.

"Those men must be driven back," was what Granger said to Thomas. The Union commander agreed. "Can you do it?" he asked. Granger nodded grimly. "Yes," he said. "My men are fresh, and they are just the fellows for that work. They are raw recruits and they don't know any better than to charge over there."[96]

As the two Union generals made plans to defend their position, the Confederate reinforcements continued to advance north from the rear to the front end of Steedman's Hill. They were the six regiments of Colonel Cyrus Sugg's brigade, including Colonel William Grace and the Sons of Erin.[97]

The field commander of Granger's two brigades was Brigadier General James B. Steedman, 46, of Ohio, an excellent combat officer. Before he went into battle that afternoon, he told his chief-of-staff to be sure that his name was spelled correctly in the newspapers, in case he was killed. General Steedman's brigade commanders were Colonels Walter C. Whitaker and John G. Mitchell. Whitaker advanced on the Federal left, with Mitchell on the right.

At the same time that Colonel Mitchell was coming down from the south end of Snodgrass Hill, Colonel Grace and the Sons of Erin were coming down the north end of Steedman's Hill.[98] It was 4:00 p.m. A mounted General Bushrod Johnson, with sword drawn, rode north exhorting Colonel

Sugg's men to support Colonel Fulton's men. A mounted General Steedman with sword drawn rode south exhorting Colonel Whitaker's men and Colonel Mitchell's men to push the Southerners back.

Steedman's horse was shot out from under him. "Brave, bluff old Steedman, with a regimental staff in his hand, led the way on foot."[99] The Boys-in-Blue surged forward, stampeding Bushrod Johnson's Boys-in-Gray back up the north end of Steedman's Hill.

In the chaos atop the low ridge, Whitaker's six regiments, reinforced by two of Mitchell's advance regiments, the Ninety-Eighth and the One-Hundred-Twenty-First Ohio, crashed into the four beleaguered Tennessee regiments of Colonel Fulton's brigade. At the crest of Steedman's Hill, Colonel Mitchell's other two regiments, the Seventy-Eighth Illinois and the One-Hundred Thirteenth Ohio, swung to the right and surprised the right (east) flank of Colonel Sugg's brigade.

Commanding the Seventy-Eighth Illinois, 353 men, was Lieutenant Colonel Carter Van Vleck, while the commanding officer of the One-Hundred-Thirteenth Ohio, 355 men, was Lieutenant Colonel Darius Warner.[100] Van Vleck and his Illinoisans charged Sugg's four advance regiments, the Seventh Texas, and the Third, Forty-first, and First/Fiftieth Tennessee regiments. Darius Warner and his Ohioans accidently came across Sugg's two second-line regiments, the Tenth and Thirtieth Tennessee, giving Warner a slight numerical advantage.[101]

Colonel Grace, Lieutenant Colonel Turner, and Major O'Neill were thrown together again, just as they had been at Raymond, only this time Grace was the ranking officer. Grace withdrew his two regiments to their original reserve positions along the south end of Steedman's Hill, where he formed a defensive line.[102]

When Lieutenant Colonel Warner charged with the front line companies of the One-Hundred-Thirteenth Ohio, Major O'Neill's sharpshooters repulsed the attack. The second wave of the Ohioans was, however, much stronger and better coordinated, and Grace, Turner and the Tennesseans were driven off Steedman's Hill. While the Sons of Erin prepared to counter-attack, the One-Hundred-Thirteenth Ohio dug into their vacated positions. The engagement at the western end of the ridge was over in twenty minutes.

Even worse, the four regiments of Fulton and the other four regiments of Sugg had already been routed and were fleeing south in confusion, as a result of the successful attack by Steedman, Whitaker, Mitchell and Van Vleck. Grace had no choice and ordered a general retirement of the Tenth and Thirtieth Tennessee through the cover of some trees all the way back to Vittetoe's Hill.

Still mounted, "Battling Billie" Grace made sure that his Irishmen were properly evacuated in an orderly fashion. In the early stages of the Confederate withdrawal, Colonel Grace's horse was shot out from under him.[103] He was apparently injured worse than Steedman had been in his fall. Already afflicted with a back injury from that fall eleven months earlier in Mississippi, the Irish commanding officer was in terrific pain and couldn't get to his feet. The One-Hundred-Thirteenth Ohio did not pursue, but their skirmishers from Steedman's Hill fired away at the colonel.[104]

Major O'Neill's sharpshooters turned around, knelt, and fired in an attempt to shield the immobilized Colonel Grace. It was at this time that First Lieutenant Robert Paget Seymour saved his colonel's life. The royal Irish courier came galloping across the valley and dragged Grace up onto his mount. Sir Robert sped to the rear to the shouts of the Sons of Erin.[105] On that bloody Sunday afternoon, it was about the only thing that the Irishmen had to cheer about.

The fight for Steedman's Hill was the last engagement at Chickamauga for the Tenth Tennessee, but the horrific battle was far from over. Back on Vittetoe's Hill, licking their wounds, the Sons of Erin watched as General Longstreet continued to pour all his troops in from the south, while General Polk's two corps of Generals Harvey Hill and Walker struck again and again from the east.

A tremendous defensive commander, General George

H. Thomas held. It was here that the Union Virginian earned his well-deserved nickname, "The Rock of Chickamauga." If Thomas was the rock, then certainly Granger, Steedman, Wilder, Minty, Harker, Wood, Brannan, Whitaker, Mitchell, Van Vleck, and Darius Warner were his support stones in the bulwark of that memorable stand.

At the same time that the battle was raging around General Thomas, General Rosecrans was still wandering the field, in the later words of President Lincoln, "like a duck who had just been hit over the head."[106] Rosecrans didn't find Thomas, but he did find his own chief-of-staff, Brigadier General James A. Garfield, 31, also of Ohio, who was later to serve as President of the United States for four months. Rosecrans wanted to get a message through to Thomas for a withdrawal. Garfield had talked Rosecrans into returning to Chattanooga, where he could organize the defenses, but although Thomas received the message from Garfield, he refused to quit.

It was only fitting that the straw that finally broke the camel's back would come from a Northern Rebel. Two officers from Alabama were brigade commanders in Preston's division of Buckner's corps of Longstreet's wing. They were both superb soldiers and both Irish-American. Brigadier General Archibald Gracie Jr., 30, was born and raised in New York City. Baby-faced Colonel John H. Kelly, 23, would soon become the youngest general in the Confederate Army.

Irish-Americans Gracie and Kelly launched a bloody assault against Horseshoe Ridge that lasted for nearly two hours. They were assisted by Irishman Pat Cleburne, who moved his artillery to within a short distance and blasted away, and by Irish-American Bedford Forrest whose cavalrymen were everywhere, dismounting, loading, firing, and mounting.[107] The Irishmen of the Tenth Tennessee, in reserve on Vittetoe's Hill, viewed the frenzied action.

Low on ammunition, Thomas had no choice but to withdraw his defenders through McFarland's Gap, back toward Chattanooga. The Southerners chased after Thomas' rear guard, blazing away in anger, frustration and revenge.

By 9:00 p.m. the last of the Federals were leaving the field, and in the next couple of hours, most of them were pushed completely out of the state of Georgia. In sheer relief and nervous exhaustion, the Confederates celebrated for hours by yelling and yelling and yelling some more. The Northerners would remember that humiliating sound all of their lives. They had left behind them better than 4,000 prisoners, fifty-one cannon, 2,381 cannonballs, 23,281 muskets, about 135,000 rounds of small arms ammunition, and countless numbers of horses and wagons.[108]

Chickamauga was the greatest Confederate triumph in the West, a dramatic reversal of the back-to-back disasters at Gettysburg and Vicksburg. But because of the stand made by General George H. Thomas, the Army of the Cumberland was crippled but not destroyed, and the town of Chattanooga was not lost. Ironically, on the Northern side General William S. Rosecrans refused to accept responsibility for the defeat, while on the Southern side General Braxton Bragg took full credit for the triumph.

Lew Clark and Stanley Horn
The Myth of the Bloody Tenth

The engagement of the Sons of Erin on Steedman's Hill lasted only twenty minutes, not much longer than the action at Erin Hollow. However, it was the regiment's worst twenty minutes of the war. The defeat was total, and the carnage was appalling. First Lieutenant Thomas Connor had his right thumb blown off and his left arm shot up. The arm had to be amputated, leaving him disabled for life. "Long Tom," the very best of his kind, would never fire a rifle again. Captain John L. Prendergast was shot in the right arm, his fourth wounding in two battles. Again the news was good about him. The Clarksville Sharpshooter would recover fully and soon

249

return to duty. The rest of the bad news was truly terrible. First Lieutenant John D. Winston of G Company and four of the lads from E Company were all killed in the action around the hill, while many others were wounded.[109]

Colonel William Grace's back injury has never been medically described, but the pain was severe enough to keep him on the sidelines until the following spring. In the meantime, he kept busy by assigning himself the duties of adjutant, assisted by Sir Robert and Lew Clark.

The three-day toll for the Irish regiment was eleven killed or mortally wounded, and thirty-seven wounded, two of whom were captured, for a combined forty-eight losses out of 190, twenty-five percent of those engaged.[110] In just an hour-and-a-half at Raymond, the losses had been fifty-two, including the death of Colonel Randal McGavock. But the destruction at Chickamauga was worse, because the regimental command structure was shot to pieces. Grace was out of commission for several months, and Thompson was disabled for life. Morgan and Kelsey were both killed. The only member of Grace's staff left standing on Sunday evening was sharpshooter detachment commanding officer Major John G. O'Neill, two months shy of his twenty-third birthday, who immediately took over as acting regimental commander.[111]

A complete list of the lads who gave their lives for the Sons of Erin and the Southern cause in North Georgia is as follows:

Captain Saint Clair Morgan of C Company, Captain William Sweeney of D Company, First Lieutenant Theodore Kelsey of E Company, First Lieutenant John D. Winston of G Company, Private James Flowers of C Company, Private Patrick McGettighn of H Company, Private James Murray of A Company, and Privates James Kelly, Jeremiah Harrington, James Mahon, and Thomas Murphy, all of E Company.[112]

The overall casualty figures were horrendous. The Federals had 58,222 men engaged on both days, of whom 1,657 were killed, 9,756 were wounded, and 4,757 were captured or missing for total losses of 16,170 or twenty-eight percent of those engaged.

The Confederates had 66,326 men engaged on both days, of whom 2,312 were killed, 14,674 were wounded, and 1,468 were captured or missing for total losses of 18,454 or the exact same twenty-eight percent of those engaged that the Federals experienced.[113] Gettysburg was the bloodiest three days of the war. Sharpsburg or Antietam was the bloodiest single day. Taking only Saturday and Sunday into account, Chickamauga surpassed Shiloh as the bloodiest two days.

The numbers were even more grim in Bushrod Johnson's division. The Gregg/Sugg brigade had 1,337 men engaged to 1,207 for McNair and 869 for Fulton, a total of 3,413 effectives. Gregg/Sugg had 109 killed, 474 wounded, and eighteen captured or missing for 601 losses. McNair had fifty-one killed, 336 wounded, and sixty-four captured or missing for a total of 451 losses. Fulton had twenty-eight killed, 271 wounded, and ninety-eight captured or missing for 397 losses. Total losses for the division were 1,449 out of 3,413 or forty-two percent!

At the regimental level the 1,337 men engaged in the Gregg/Sugg brigade can be broken down as follows: Forty-First Tennessee (325), Third Tennessee (274), First/Fiftieth Tennessee consolidated (192), Tenth Tennessee (190), Thirtieth Tennessee (185), and Seventh Texas (177). The 601 brigade losses out of 1,337 represents forty-five percent![114] There is no individual breakdown by regiment for casualties in Army Official Records, except for the First/Fiftieth. General Johnson mentioned that figure of 151 losses out of 192 for an incredible seventy-nine percent, a statistic not corroborated in any other source.

The losses for the Sons of Erin, forty-eight out of 190 for twenty-five percent, is horrible by any sane standard. Yet it was slightly lower than overall losses (twenty-eight percent) and much lower than the losses of some of the other regiments in the same division (between forty-two and forty-five percent).

Early on, however, a story began to surface that the Sons of Erin had the highest casualty rate of all the hundreds of units that fought in North Georgia. The "Bloody

Tinth" myth had already been created earlier, as has been shown, by the exaggerated bragging after Erin Hollow and with the 1862 New York newspaper article. The false assertions in the New York paper which McGavock repudiated at that time had also been reprinted in an Atlanta newspaper article.

Just after Chickamauga the myth grew again, like an expanding balloon, and it continued after the Southern cause became the "Lost Cause." In this case the balloon was fed on hot air.

In 1886, twenty-one years after the end of the war, Captain Lewis R. Clark of the Tenth Tennessee and Clarksville wrote his article "Tenth Tennessee Infantry" for Doctor Lindsley's serial *Military Annals of Tennessee:Confederate*. In this periodical, Lew Clark made a startling announcement to the historical community.

> *Tennyson immortalized Cardigan's Light Brigade for the famous charge made by them at Balaklava. Their loss, in killed, wounded and prisoners was less than the two-thirds of the number that went into the charge. We [the Sons of Erin] carried three·hundred and twenty-eight men into action at Chickamauga, and lost two-hundred-and twenty-four killed and wounded —more than two-thirds.[115]*

Not only is comparing the Tenth Tennessee with the Light Brigade a little too much to comprehend, but Clark's figures don't make any sense, no matter how they are analyzed. If he erred and considered his Irishmen to be still consolidated with the Thirtieth Tennessee, the total engaged would have been 375, not 328. Adding any other regiment from the brigade to the Sons of Erin does not add up to a total of 328.

The 190 engaged is an absolute. It appears in four separate government documents.[116] It is, obviously, not possible for 224 lads to be lost out a total of 190 present for duty. The

252

figure of forty-eight losses also comes from a variety of sources.

In 1940 the myth created by Lewis R. Clark and Patrick M. Griffin was carved in granite by the distinguished historian Stanley Horn in his account of the Army of Tennessee. The Sons of Erin are cited in that work for having the heaviest losses in the entire army: "Among the Confederate regiments, the percentage of loss ran amazingly high—for example, 10th Tennessee, 68%."[117]

It's easy to understand where the figure of sixty-eight percent came from. It is precisely 224 from 328. Horn's source was Lew Clark or someone quoting Lew Clark. Exactly a quarter of a century later, in 1965, however, Stanley Horn corrected himself in the scholarly first volume of *Tennesseans in the Civil War:*

> *At Chickamauga, General Gregg's brigade was in General Bushrod Johnson's division. The 10th (Tennessee) reported 190 men engaged. The brigade captured a Federal battery of nine guns.*[118]

Unfortunately, *Army of Tennessee* has been read much more than *Tennesseans in the Civil War.* Even though very little has ever been written about the Sons of Erin, nearly every reference about them contains the theme of the "Bloody Tenth," the Irish regiment that sustained heavy casualties. An example is the excellent article written by Father Peter Meaney about Father Emmeran Bliemel: "The Valiant Chaplain of the Bloody Tenth." Fortunately for the Tennessee Irishmen and their families, there never was a real "Bloody Tenth" which sustained staggering casualties.

In spite of that, the regimental reputation can stand on its own. Though they were not anywhere near the top regiment in terms of battlefield losses, the Sons of Erin earned their own portion of glory at the Battle of Chickamauga. The Irishmen were in the thick of the fight on all three days. Their best performance was at Dyer's farm, where they played a major role in capturing the First U.S. Missouri Battery. The effort at Steedman's Hill was futile but heroic.

It isn't clear, anyhow, if getting an entire regiment killed in a battle is a clear-cut sign of battlefield success. Fighting valorously and surviving to fight again may be just as good an indicator. At Raymond and Chickamauga, the Irish regiment had suffered nineteen killed and eighty-one wounded or captured. That is probably enough to rank them in anyone's honest tabulation for honorable fighting records.

The Federals were in disarray, and the Confederate Army was eager and willing to go after them. On Monday, September 21, General Nathan Bedford Forrest chased the rear of the retreating Yankees. He used the dismounted brigade of Brigadier General Frank Armstrong, 27, who came from Boston, was a graduate of Holy Cross College, had fought at First Manassas as a first lieutenant of volunteers in the Union infantry, and then switched sides and rose to the rank of general in the Confederate cavalry.

From Missionary Ridge Forrest and Armstrong could see wagons moving around Chattanooga in obvious disorder. General Forrest sent a dispatch to General Bragg, assuming with a good many of the other Southerners that the army would soon be receiving instructions to push the blue-clads back up to Knoxville or beyond. Nothing happened.[119] Bragg was again immobilized; he sat in North Georgia waiting for the Northern troops to evacuate the town of their own free will! The delay, of course, gave Rosecrans the chance he desperately needed to strengthen his defenses and receive reinforcements.

History's assessment is that Bragg let the Federals off the hook by not pursuing. His only accomplishment was occupying the north ends of Lookout Mountain and Missionary Ridge, allowing a beaten enemy to come to him. Chickamauga was a tactical victory turned into a strategic defeat. It was about this time that Bedford Forrest marched into his commanding general's tent, thrust his left index finger into his commander's face and said:

> *You have played the part of a damn scoundrel, and are a coward, and if you were any part of a man, I would slap your jaws and force you to resent it. You may as well not issue any more orders to me, for I will not obey them. You have threatened to arrest me for acting without your orders. I dare you to do it. And I say to you that if you ever again try to interfere with me or cross my path, it will be at the peril of your life.[120]*

General Bragg said not a word, moved not a muscle, and never reported the incident. At his own request, General Forrest was transferred to an independent command in Tennessee and Mississippi. This is how it came about that in its most critical moment, the Army of Tennessee lost its greatest cavalry commander.

Just about every Confederate general in the Western army was outraged by Bragg's ineptness and worked to have him removed. President Davis, however, stood behind his appointee and allowed Bragg to avenge himself against those who had opposed him. What resulted was a process of demotions and transfers and shifts that decimated the command structure of the Army of Tennessee. Generals Longstreet, Harvey Hill and Buckner were moved back out of the Western theatre. At his own request, General Leonidas Polk was switched back to General Joe Johnston's command in exchange for General William J. Hardee.

Meanwhile back in East Tennessee, President Abraham Lincoln fired Generals Rosecrans, Crittenden, and McCook. Rewarding both Generals Sherman and Thomas for services rendered, past and present, Lincoln presented each with his own army. Appropriately, George H. Thomas was moved up to command the Army of the Cumberland, while William T. Sherman was appointed commanding general of the Army of the Tennessee, named after the river, not the state.[121]

While Jefferson Davis was allowing Braxton Bragg to dismantle the Army of Tennessee in North Georgia, Abraham Lincoln was assembling a mighty juggernaut in Chattanooga. To coordinate the two Union Western armies, the President brought in a short, plain-looking man who was already well known to the Sons of Erin—General "Unconditional Surrender" Grant.

Chapter Eight
Fighting for Clouds

The Battles for Chattanooga
General Bragg Versus General Grant

The reduction of General Bragg's army from 48,000 to 36,000 cannot be entirely explained away by transfers and purges. Some of the Boys-in-Gray simply left the war, letting their feet register their dissatisfaction. Their frustration with the Southern cause is understandable after the horrific fighting at Chickamauga and the subsequent lack of confidence in leadership. All of the Confederate regiments were affected in some way, including the Sons of Erin. Between September 21 and November 12, 1863, the ranks of the Tenth Tennessee evaporated from 142 to 104, because of desertions.[1]

When Pat Griffin returned from his "mission of mercy," he viewed the North Georgia scenery, got "slightly wounded," and headed right back out again. It does explain why Griffin had nothing more to add to his narrative after Raymond. Surprisingly, the indefatigable lad returned to the regiment again in January of 1864, only to formally resign from the Confederate Army on April 12 of that same year.[2]

From the point of view of the historian, the most significant loss occurred when the loyal and amusing Jimmy Doyle disappeared, leaving the Sons of Erin with only one eyewitness—Captain Lew Clark.[3] If the Irishmen were still playing cards and drinking whiskey through the hell that was the last days of the war in the West, there was nobody left to record it.

The Sons of Erin got shuffled around during the reorganization, going from Grace's regiment of the Gregg/Sugg brigade of Johnson's division of Hood's corps of Longstreet's wing of Bragg's army to O'Neill's regiment of Tyler's brigade of Bate's division of Breckinridge's corps of Bragg's army.[4] All of the transfer was accomplished on paper and the Irishmen remained at their same encampment along the eastern foot of Missionary Ridge. Many probably didn't know there had been a switch.

General John Gregg, recovered from his neck wound, replaced General Jerome Robertson as commander of the Texas brigade, and was sent to the Eastern front, where he was killed in action at the Wilderness at the age of 35. Colonel Cyrus Sugg was put back in command of the First/Fiftieth Tennessee regiment, and was killed in action at Missionary Ridge at the age of 34.

Major General John C. Breckinridge, 42, of Kentucky, the former vice president of the United States, moved up to corps command to fill one of the vacancies created by the departure of Hill and Buckner. (Hardee filled the other one.) Major General William B. "Old Grits" Bate, 37, of Tennessee, was promoted from brigade to division command when Breckinridge moved up from division to corps command.

Bate was given three brigades. The Orphans of Brigadier General Joseph H. Lewis, 39, had five regiments, all infantry, all Kentucky. "The Sunshine Boys" of Brigadier General Jesse Finley, 51, had four infantry regiments and one dismounted cavalry regiment, all Florida. (There were only three other Florida regiments in the entire Confederate Army.) The Tennessee-Texas brigade of Gregg/Sugg was broken up, and part of it was given to Colonel Robert C. Tyler, 30, of Tennessee, who had been promoted from command of the Fifteenth Tennessee to brigade command when General Bate moved up the ladder.

Colonel Tyler's Tennessee-Georgia brigade consisted of five miniature infantry regiments, one infantry battalion, and one sharpshooters' battalion. There was the Thirty-Seventh Georgia (Colonel A. F. Rudler), the Tenth Tennessee (Major John G. O'Neill), the Fifteenth/Thirty-Seventh Tennessee consolidated (Lieutenant Colonel R. Dudley Frayser), the Twentieth Tennessee (Major William W. Shy), the Thirtieth Tennessee (Lieutenant Colonel James J. Turner), the First Tennessee Battalion (Major Stephen H. Colms), and the Fourth Georgia Battalion Sharpshooters (First Lieutenant Joel Towers).[5]

Major O'Neill's riflemen had done considerable damage to the Federals at Erin Hollow, O'Neill's Hill, Pea Vine Ridge, Reed's Bridge and Dyer's farm. On November 12, the entire Irish regiment wasn't much larger than O'Neill's original A Company. The smaller they became, the more the Sons of Erin came to be deployed as a sharpshooters' detachment in itself. Given his skill with a musket, "Gentleman Johnny" O'Neill was the right lad to lead the remaining Irishmen up a mountain.

General Bragg held the north end of Lookout Mountain, a mile south and a little west of Chattanooga, as well as Orchard Knob, two miles east of the south end of town, and a mile west of Missionary Ridge. Also in his possession was the length of the Tennessee end of Missionary Ridge, that is, from Rossville on the south to the far northern knob of the ridge, called Tunnel Hill, which was three and a half miles northeast of the town.

General Grant, already in control of Chattanooga and East Tennessee, planned to drive the Confederates off Lookout Mountain, Orchard Knob, Tunnel Hill and Missionary Ridge in anticipation of an all-out assault against Atlanta. The Union commanding general deployed General Thomas' Army of the Cumberland southeast of Chattanooga (Federal right), with General Sherman's Army of the Tennessee forming the Federal left northeast of town.

With eight-thousand of his troops, Sherman crossed the Tennessee River over a pontoon bridge at Brown's Ferry, a process that took all morning of November 23, and then marched to the knob at the very northern end of Missionary Ridge. It was here that he experienced his first surprise. The area contained no Southerners. Soon to follow was his second surprise, which wasn't as pleasant. The Rebels had occupied Tunnel Hill, an ugly and foreboding piece of rock just to the east of the unoccupied knob.[6] This was the Confederate right, General Cleburne's crack division of General Hardee's corps. Sherman spent the afternoon deploying his troops in front of the hill and bivouacked there for the night.[7]

Meanwhile the Sons of Erin were moving into position in Colonel Tyler's brigade of General Bate's division of General Breckinridge's corps on the Confederate center—a position which was, in fact, at the top of Missionary Ridge.[8]

At the same time that Sherman was preparing to attack Cleburne, Grant ordered Thomas to seize Orchard Knob. "The Rock of Chickamauga" used two divisions of Gordon Granger's corps commanded by Tom Wood and Phil Sheridan. All the Federals found at the top were some of Bragg's pickets, who were easily driven off. The elevation on Orchard afforded a perfect view of the length of Missionary Ridge, so Grant established his headquarters there.

One of the most publicized battles of the war took place on Tuesday, November 24, the day the Sons of Erin set up their logworks along the center crest of Missionary Ridge. This time Grant detached three divisions of Thomas' army, the Twelfth corps, under Major General Joseph Hooker, 48, of Massachusetts, who had been demoted from Eastern army command and sent west after a humiliating defeat by General Lee at Chancellorsville.

Because Lookout Mountain rises 1,100 feet above the Tennessee River, the engagement there was known as the "Battle Above The Clouds." It was in actuality about the same kind of mop-up operation as Orchard Knob. When the Federals scaled Lookout, which was no easy trick, they discovered two small Confederate brigades at a location called Craven's farm.

At about noon the gray-clads fell back some four hundred yards and both sides were reinforced. The three Union divisions skirmished with the Confederate brigades in a heavy fog until midnight. There were no major attacks, and the thoroughly outnumbered Boys-in-Gray evacuated in orderly fashion. Next morning Hooker had the Stars and Stripes hoisted dramatically for all to see.[9]

At the same time that the Southerners were coming down Lookout Mountain, and while General Hooker was waving the flag, General Sherman charged General Hardee's magnificent defenses and was stopped cold by General Cleburne.[10]

As a result of this, a protracted stalemate was then

possible. Grant's department of two armies consisted of three infantry corps of thirteen divisions of thirty-five brigades of 202 regiments and seven battalions, plus one artillery division of three brigades of ten battalions of thirty-four batteries. Bragg's lone army consisted of two infantry corps of seven divisions of twenty-six brigades of 106 regiments (including the Tenth Tennessee) and two battalions, plus seven sharpshooters' battalions and one artillery division of two brigades of six battalions of twenty-three batteries. Neither side employed cavalry on the mountainous ground.

The problem for the Confederates was that Bragg's defensive line could not be described as balanced. On the Confederate right (north), Hardee had four divisions of about eighteen-thousand men, all bunched up around Cleburne at Tunnel Hill. To the left of Cleburne's division were the divisions of Generals W.H.T. Walker and Frank Cheatham with a reserve division to the rear under Brigadier General Carter L. Stevenson. Way down on the Confederate left at Rossville, there was the lone Alabama brigade of Brigadier General Henry D. Clayton from General A. P. Stewart's division. The Confederate center, including the Sons of Erin, was commanded by General Breckinridge and stretched four miles long, and covered two-thirds of the line.[11]

The former vice president was expected to hold this position with fragments of three divisions of seven brigades of fewer than fourteen-thousand men against Thomas' army of twenty-three-thousand camped a mile in front of him. Complicating the matter was the fact that the Confederate center consisted of two separate lines. One was at the western foot of Missionary Ridge, with 3,500 men in rifle pits, the second was up at the crest with the other 10,500 men behind logworks. Forming Breckinridge's corps left (south) to right were the forces of Stewart, Bate and Brigadier General J. Patten Anderson.

Of A.P. Stewart's division, Clayton was detached to Rossville and the brigade of Brigadier General Daniel W. Adams was on temporary loan to Patten Anderson, leaving Stewart with the two brigades of Brigadier Generals M.A.

Stovall and Otho F. Strahl. Anderson's makeshift division consisted of the three brigades of Adams, Brigadier General A.W. Reynolds, and Colonel William F. Tucker.[12]

General Bragg's crowning piece of juggling occurred in the afternoon. He sent General Hindman's division and General Joe Lewis' Kentucky Orphans of General Bate's division away from General Breckinridge's center up to General Hardee's right, thereby taking the heart out of the Missionary Ridge defenses.

Anderson deployed the brigade of A.W. Reynolds down in the rifle pits. To the left of Reynolds, Bate added one regiment from Colonel Tyler, the Fifteenth/Thirty-Seventh Tennessee consolidated, and two regiments from General Finley's brigade, the First Florida and the Fourth/Sixth Florida consolidated.[13] All of this shifting left Breckinridge with four small brigades and a scattering of regiments from Bate's two remaining brigades, including Major O'Neill and his 103 Irishmen, to post along his four mile crest line.

O'Neill divided his lads into three platoons—the sharpshooters' detachment, which he himself commanded and two infantry detachments, commanded by Captain John L. Prendergast, the Clarksville Sharpshooter, and Captain Clarence C. Malone, the Fighting Irishman from Mississippi.[14] Major O'Neill and the Sons of Erin were all dug in behind logworks atop the center of Missionary Ridge.

The defending Confederate units along the top of the ridge were, south to north: Stovall's brigade, Strahl's brigade, the Third Florida regiment, the Seventh Florida regiment, the Tenth Tennessee regiment; the Thirtieth Tennessee regiment; the First/Twentieth Tennessee consolidated regiment; the Thirty-Seventh Georgia regiment; an open space where Reynold's brigade used to be, Adam's brigade, and Tucker's brigade.[15]

Reasonably, Bate shifted the line to the right so that Tyler's regiments rested next to Adams' regiments. Breckinridge, on orders from Bragg, shifted the line back to the left, reopening the brigade-size hole between Tyler and Adams. The reasoning was vintage Bragg. A reserved space had to be provided in case A. W. Reynolds needed to retreat up the hill. The Confederate commanding general virtually insured that the Southerners in the pits would be forced to retreat. If attacked, they were ordered to fire one volley and retire to the top. Unfortunately, Breckinridge fouled up Bate's communications and not all of the Boys-in-Gray got the message.[16]

Since Sherman's Union left couldn't turn Hardee's Confederate right, Grant instructed Hooker to take the southern end of the line by pushing Clayton out of the Rossville Gap. The Union commanding general then ordered Thomas to advance Granger's corps to Breckinridge's rifle pits at the base of Missionary Ridge and await further instructions.

Brigadier General Richard W. Johnson's division was detached from Major General John M. Palmer's corps to Granger's, giving Granger four attack divisions of eleven brigades. It was 3:00 p.m.

Grant wanted to bag the enemy rifle pits before the winter sky turned dark.[17] However, Granger decided to fire the six-shot cannon starting signal himself, so that the advance didn't get underway until 3:40.

As soon as the Federals moved forward across the plain, the Confederate guns opened up from the top of Missionary Ridge. The Boys-in-Blue roared away with an equally deafening noise from the top of Orchard Knob. Granger's columns moved forward from their left (north) to right with the divisions of Absalom Baird, Tom Wood, Phil Sheridan and Richard Johnson, with Sheridan serving as field commander.

The Southerners at the foot of the ridge held their fire until the Northerners closed to within two-hundred yards. As instructed, the Southerners at the lower level fired one volley and scampered up the hill to the utter amazement of the Northerners. All withdrew except for those Southerners who never got the message. While most of the rifle pits were being abandoned, Bate's four *lower level* regiments continued to blast away right into the three oncoming brigades of Sheridan's division.[18]

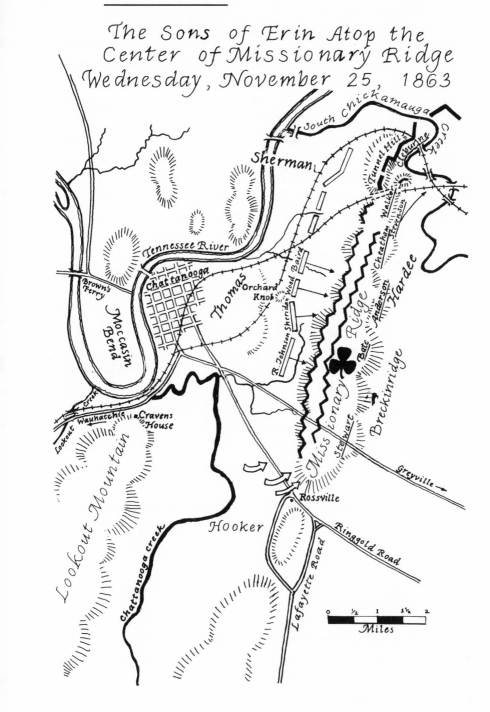

The Sons of Erin Atop the
Center of Missionary Ridge
Wednesday, November 25, 1863

The Battle of Missionary Ridge
Wednesday, November 25, 1863, 4:00 to 9:00 p.m.
Major O'Neill Versus Captain Keegan

At the same time the Union infantry was assaulting the Confederate skirmishers in the rifle pits at the base of Missionary Ridge, General Bate, at the center of General Breckinridge's line, moved his men on the crest out from behind their logworks to the very edge of the ridge. On his far right Colonel Tyler deployed the Fourth Georgia Battalion Sharpshooters, and on his far left Major O'Neill and the Sons of Erin.The Georgians and the Irishmen fired straight down into General Sheridan's division in the valley, shooting Sheridan's horse out from under him.[19]

The charging blue-clads came on fiercely with a second wave, killing, wounding, or capturing the remaining few valiant gray-clads in the pits. The men of General A. W. Reynolds' brigade fired their lone volley and went flying up the ridge at a right angle and reached the crest on the Crutchfield road in front of General A. P. Stewart's division, about a mile south of their original position. General Bragg's parking space was still empty.

The Federals had a problem. They had already achieved their objective, cleaning up the rifle pits, and they were awaiting further orders from General Grant. But they couldn't survive in the place where they stood, because the Sons of Erin and the other Confederates at the top were cutting them to shreds. It was a trap, and there was only one place for them to go and find shelter from their tormentors. Missionary Ridge rose above the plain anywhere from six-hundred to eight-hundred feet along the various locations on the Confederate line. With no orders from any officers, the Northern enlisted men charged the hill!

At the crest of the hill, the lads of the Tenth Tennessee watched in absolute amazement. Their reaction was nothing compared to that of Grant, watching from Orchard Knob. He lit into Thomas and Granger. "Thomas, who ordered those men up the ridge?" "I don't know. I did not," was the impassive response. "Did you order them up, Granger?" "No, they started without orders. When those fellows get started, all hell can't stop them," was what he answered. Grant considered calling them back but that was impossible. "Someone's going to pay for this," was what he muttered, clenching his teeth down on his cigar.[20]

Meanwhile back in the rifle pits, Sheridan knew only too well that the reckless charge was against orders. But with hundreds of his men already on the hill, there wasn't time for a debate, so he assumed an aggressive stance.

Sheridan borrowed a silver flask from one of his staff officers. Raising the flask toward the Rebels on the crest, he shouted: "Here's to you." This tribute, naturally enough, drew attention from above. Two rounds burst near Sheridan, kicking up dust onto his freshly-laundered blue dress uniform. Casually brushing the dirt from himself, he yelled up, "That was very ungenerous. Just for that I'll take those guns away from you."[21]

With that "Little Phil" Sheridan, on foot, charged up the hill right behind the enlisted men waving his hat in one hand and his sword in the other, yelling exhortations all the way.

In Sheridan's division the brigade of Brigadier General George D. Warner veered to the Union left, while in General Wood's division the brigade of Colonel Charles G. Harker charged straight up the center. To the right of Harker, with Sheridan himself, was the brigade of Colonel Francis T. Sherman, no relation to the general. There was understandable confusion in the Federal ranks, as Warner's regiments charged up, stopped, went back down, and charged up again!

Just to the north of George Warner, the rest of Wood's men were the first to reach the top.[22] The two Confederate brigades of General Patten Anderson's division turned and fled across the summit and down the east slope of the ridge. Bate tried to rally the remnant of Anderson's left, but F. Sherman came through Bragg's "vacant parking lot," causing Tyler to turn his right regiments at a right angle and fire volley after volley.[23]

In Francis Sherman's brigade, three men of the Twenty-Fourth Wisconsin Infantry regiment were killed charging the Confederate logworks. The regimental colors they carried were in danger of being lost until First Lieutenant Arthur MacArthur, Jr., 18, of Milwaukee, grabbed the flag pole and waved it, shouting, "On Wisconsin." The youthful MacArthur led Sheridan and Francis Sherman through the gap on the crest, routing the last of Anderson, and turning back Bate's right flank.[24] Colonel Sherman's right regiments came storming up and blew away General Bate's center position. Colonel Tyler, in an attempt to hold his Georgians and Tennesseans on the line, was seriously wounded, and Colonel A. F. Rudler of the Thirty-Seventh Georgia took command of the brigade. The Fourth/Thirty-Seventh Georgia and the First/Twentieth Tennessee fell back but refused to leave the ridge. Rudler set up a new defensive line on the summit some 1,500 yards to the rear of the logworks.[25]

When Francis Sherman's intermingled regiments made it to the top, O'Neill, Prendergast and Malone made a half-right turn and fired in a northwesterly direction into the frenzied Yankees. That exchange didn't last very long, because other units of Boys-in-Blue were coming straight up the hill at the Sons of Erin. The Irishmen turned back due west and fired down from their logworks.[26] The unwelcome new arrivals were the left wing of General Richard W. Johnson's division.

R.W. Johnson had three brigades, but one of them had been kept in reserve at Chattanooga, so he advanced up the ridge with his First brigade on his right, commanded by Brigadier General William P. Carlin. The Second brigade was divided into two "demi-brigades," with Colonel William L. Stroughton commanding R. W. Johnson's center and Colonel Marshall F. Moore commanding his left.[27] Because the Union charge up the ridge was so fluid, it was difficult to tell who ran into whom.

Certain facts are known. Richard Johnson's brigades of Carlin and Stoughton defeated A. P. Stewart's brigades of Stovall and Strahl, chasing them off the ridge.[28] After Bate's center had been overrun by F. Sherman's right, Moore's three regiments contested the position of the last four regiments of Breckinridge's corps still left in the logworks. The Confederate units left to right were the Seventh Florida, the Tenth Tennessee, the Thirtieth Tennessee, and a small remnant of the Twentieth Tennessee.[29]

Colonel Moore attacked with the Nineteenth Illinois on his right, and captured some of the Floridians.[30] The Sixty-Ninth Ohio, on his left, made it to the crest first, overwhelming and capturing the undersized Twentieth Tennessee, while planting their banner in the logworks.[31] The Eleventh Michigan, in the middle of Moore, didn't do nearly as well by a long shot. Repulsed by the fire of the Tenth Tennessee and Thirtieth Tennessee, the Michigan regiment was forced back about halfway down the slope in a state of disorder.[32]

An Irishman by the name of Captain Patrick H. Keegan was in command of the small Eleventh Michigan. He had 255 men, only slightly more than the combined total of the tiny two remaining Tennessee regiments, not good numbers for a frontal assault. With Turner and O'Neill still behind the logworks, Moore's three regiments attacked from the south (Nineteenth Illinois), the north (Sixty-Ninth Ohio), and the west (Eleventh Michigan).[33]

To their lasting credit, the Tennesseans of the Tenth and Thirtieth held, but the situation all along Missionary Ridge was hopeless. Bate ordered the Seventh Florida to fall back to Rudler's new position, but in the confusion, Turner and O'Neill never got the message.[34] With both flanks exposed to all the Northerners on the hill, the last of the Southerners were in danger of being captured *en toto*. On his own, James J. Turner withdrew, while John G. O'Neill's sharpshooters covered the withdrawal.[35]

As a result of being deployed as rear guards, the Sons of Erin were the last unit on the Confederate center to leave their position.[36] It is an irony that with all the blarney about the "Bloody Tinth," this remarkable truth has been overlooked.

In spite of being bloodied by multiple wounds to back

and side, Captain Clarence C. Malone, the Fighting Irishman from Mississippi, removed himself from the battlefield, thereby avoiding capture. Because of the lateness of their retiring, seventeen other Irishmen, not as fortunate as Malone were, indeed, captured.[37] Between O'Neill's rear and the rest of the Tyler brigade with Rudler, a few stray Yankees were captured. As at Raymond, the Sons of Erin were both capturers and captured, all in the same battle.

By the time that Major O'Neill joined Lieutenant Colonel Turner with the remnant of the Tyler/Rudler brigade, Colonel Rudler himself was seriously wounded and Lieutenant Colonel James J. Turner, the next ranking officer, became the third brigade commander of the Sons of Erin in little more than an hour. At 5:30 p.m. Bate ordered the brigades of Finley and Turner to fall back in a southeast direction down the opposite side of Missionary Ridge along the road to the South Chickamauga Creek.[38]

General Hardee was shocked to discover that General Breckinridge's center had collapsed. As a result, his flanks were just as exposed as John G. O'Neill's had been, so he had no other choice but to withdraw his corps from the north ridge. The last Southern troops off the line were Cleburne's Boys-in-Gray from Tunnel Hill, who were then assigned to cover the rear of the army. The last Confederate commanding officer off the center had been O'Neill. Two men born in Ireland were among the last to retire in the battle for Missionary Ridge, though they probably hadn't met.

The triumphant Federals hoisted about sixty of their regimental banners all along the length of Missionary Ridge and the staff officers on Orchard Knob shouted excitedly in relief and joy. On the ridge the enlisted men and their commanders went wild in what has to have been the ultimate "soldiers' battle" of the Civil War. Phil Sheridan gave Arthur MacArthur a bear hug, as officers and men yelled and yelled and yelled some more.[39] Chickamauga had been reversed.

But the battle wasn't quite over. General Sheridan sent Colonel Francis Sherman's brigade down the east side of the ridge and after the rear of General Bate's two brigades. Bate,

Others Who Served the Southern Cause

(Top Left) General P.G.T. Beauregard of Louisiana.
(Top Right) Lieutenant General Nathan Bedford Forrest of Tennessee.
(Center) Major General Patrick R. Cleburne of Arkansas.
(Bottom Left) Father Emmeran Bliemel of Tennessee.
(Bottom Right) Private Patrick M. Griffin of Tennessee.

who had made a splendid effort, withdrew in an orderly fashion to the west bank of the South Chickamauga in two lines, with Finley's Floridians closest to the creek, and with Turner's Tennesseans and Georgians, including the Sons of Erin, forming the second line out front. While Turner moved in front of Finley's columns and crossed the railroad bridge, Finley's skirmishers kept the pursuing Sheridan busy for about an hour, 7:00 to 8:00 p.m.[40]

During the crossing one of the Florida fellows fired the last shot of the Battle of Missionary Ridge. Colonel Sherman's men were exhausted and didn't pursue. At 9:00 p.m. General Cleburne crossed the creek and burnt the bridge behind him.The next day was Thanksgiving, and the Northerners had a lot more blessings to count than did the Southerners.

Grant sent Hooker's corps south in the hopes of finishing off Bragg's army and earlier in the morning of Friday, November 27, Cleburne ambushed Hooker at Ringgold Gap and drove him back, thereby securing the Confederate rear.[41] The next day the Army of Tennessee settled into winter quarters at Dalton, Georgia.

Dejected and humiliated, Bragg sent a letter of resignation to the Southern high command dated November 30, which was quickly accepted. General Joseph E. Johnston was assigned command of the Western army with a task that was more than formidable. Chattanooga was lost and the front door to Atlanta was wide open.

General Bate's division was kept together with the same three small brigades, as was the Tyler/Rudler/Turner brigade with the same five small regiments. Colonel Robert Charles Tyler lost a leg in the battle and was promoted to brigadier, one of a small number of soldiers on both sides to rise all of the way from private to general. Because of his handicap, he was assigned to fort duty for the duration. Ten days before the surrender of the Western army, General Tyler was killed by a Yankee sharpshooter. He was thirty-two years old.[42]

The new commander of the brigade and the old commanding officer of the Twentieth Tennessee was Colonel Thomas Benton Smith, 25, of Tennessee. The Sons of Erin referred to him simply as Tom, but others called him Benton.[43]

Including the Kentucky Orphans, who had been detached from the division, the three brigades of General Bate suffered a composite forty-three killed, 224 wounded and 590 captured for total losses of 857, about one-third of those engaged. The Tenth Tennessee suffered four killed, one wounded but not captured (Malone), ten wounded and captured, and seventeen captured but not wounded for total losses of thirty-two out of 104, which like Bate's division, represented nearly one-third of those engaged.[44] Youthful Captain Clarence C. Malone spent several months in an Atlanta hospital before being released to the Invalid corps.[45]

The four Sons of Erin who gave their lives for the Southern cause at Missionary Ridge were Second Lieutenant John McCullough of C Company, Sergeant Patrick Kennedy, and Private Patrick Delaney of G Company, and Private Philip McDermott of H Company. Like General Stonewall Jackson before him, Sergeant Kennedy was fatally wounded by "friendly fire," the only Irish regimental death described as such during the war.[46] It may well have occurred during the bridge crossing at night.

While camped in Dalton, Major John G. O'Neill submitted a battle report to army headquarters. Unfortunately it has been lost, but some of his statistics have been preserved. After Missionary Ridge the Sons of Erin had sixty-nine combatants, eleven non-combatants, and forty-four muskets, leaving twenty-five of the Irishmen seemingly unarmed.

Because of O'Neill's integrity, the exact number of regimental desertions is known. By that late date in the war, 221 of the lads had already deserted, one of the higher totals in the army.[47] The Sons of Erin, however, reported no more desertions for the rest of the war. Apparently, only Irish hard noses were left.

During the first two years of the Civil War, the Sons of Erin had gone through their experiences almost without a scratch. But in the six months between May 12 and November 25 of 1863, the lads participated in three battles that left them with twenty-three killed and 109 wounded, captured or a combination of both. Not too surprisingly the Irishmen celebrated the end of that year wearily.

On December 31, 1863, Confederate army headquarters submitted a list of active regiments. A familiar name headed the top of the Tenth Tennessee. Colonel William Grace was back.[48]

Chapter Nine
I Never Knew His Name

Confederate Benedictine Monk

In late September of 1863 word reached Nashville that a great battle had been fought south of Chattanooga along a winding creek called the Chickamauga. Hearing the news, Father Emmeran Bliemel again put pressure on Bishop James Whalen to let him go to the front to join the Irish-Catholic regiment that had elected him their chaplain nearly a year before. Whalen, himself distracted with other matters centering around the occupation, continued to refuse. Finally, with his state-size diocese in ruin from the war, Whalen resigned his post in October and devoted himself to caring for his elderly mother.[1]

Father Bliemel wasted no time in getting permission from the Benedictine community to locate the Sons of Erin. Permission was also gladly granted by the Vicar General and acting bishop of Nashville—Father Henry Vincent Browne, the Northern convert to Catholicism and Rebellion who had been the lads' spiritual head at the river forts. Father Browne gave his German friend a written transfer to the Catholic community of Humphries County as a cover. Emmeran needed the identification in case he happened to be stopped by a Federal patrol.

Passenger service from the two railroads out of Nashville had been suspended, and with the ever-increasing military traffic in the area, travel south on the main roads was forbidden. But his early Pennsylvania days in the saddle really came in handy for the future Confederate chaplain. Wisely he first traveled west to McEwen, the Humphries County Irish settlement that was the hometown of John G. O'Neill and the other Irish-born farmers of A Company. There the priest received a much better mount and supplies for his adventure to Georgia.[2]

Later that month a lone rider trotted into the camp of the Tenth Tennessee at the foot of Missionary Ridge, to a warm welcome. Colonel Grace, nursing his bad back, was a devout Catholic, a convert. Major O'Neill, a cradle Catholic, carried rosary beads somewhere in his saddlebags.[3] Grace, O'Neill and all the Irishmen were glad to see any priest. Then, safely inside Confederate lines, Emmeran traveled south to Savannah, where he presented his credentials to Bishop Augustine Verot, diocese of Georgia and Florida, who was pleased to grant him permission to serve in the area.

After the battle of Missionary Ridge, Father Bliemel found the Sons of Erin in their winter quarters at Dalton. Colonel Grace was then doing some of the regimental busy work himself and sent a request for an official chaplain commission to Richmond. The request was a mere formality and didn't prevent Emmeran from eagerly getting into his new duties. The commission was dated February 10, 1864, and arrived March 3. It was official indeed. Nearly three years into the war Father Emmeran Bliemel, a Benedictine monk and priest became a Confederate Army chaplain.[4]

It was there in Georgia that Father Bliemel (Bleimel or Blemmel or Blemil or Bluemel were also spellings) received his regimental nickname of Emery. The largely uneducated and odd-speaking Irishmen had never been able to say "Adolphus Heiman," and for them, Emery was a short-cut like "Uncle Dolph." Odd name or not, the man known only as Father Emery became one of the most liked and respected chaplains in the Army of Tennessee.

Being a Catholic chaplain in the largely Protestant Confederate Army was clearly being odd man out. No one understood that better than Father Emery himself, who served every man within his range just the same, regardless of denomination, or lack of it. Even though he was officially chaplain of the Sons of Erin, others soon claimed him as their own, especially the predominantly Baptist, Methodist, and Presbyterian Fourth Kentucky Orphans, who also had two companies of Irish-Catholics.[5]

The new chaplain took his mess with the medical staff

and other chaplains of Colonel Benton Smith's brigade. Many years after the war, Dr. Deering J. Roberts, a member of the Masons, still had fond memories of his "messmate."

How crisp but never sharp his joke; how bright but never painful his repartee; how kindly was the gleam in his blue eyes; how choice the many anecdotes around the campfire; how interesting his memories of scenes from the Old Country; how deep and profound the learning; how earnest and devoted to his spiritual charge,

he wrote.[6]

There was no doubt that Father Emmeran Bliemel was singularly loved in the camp situation in which he found himself.

There were at least two other Catholic chaplains associated with the Army of Tennessee at that time. Father Emery knew Father Darius Hébert of the First Louisiana regulars during the Atlanta campaign. The other priest was the much better known Father Abram J. Ryan, who did the Lord's work at Missionary Ridge with his musket. Although he is most often remembered as the middle-aged Southern patriot who wrote poems about General Lee, Ryan was an outspoken Yankee hater during the war. His brother, David, a trooper with K Company of the Eighth Kentucky Cavalry regiment in Brigadier General John Hunt Morgan's brigade, had been killed earlier that year at Monticello, Kentucky.[7] Bliemel's mission was in obvious contrast to that of Ryan's; the chaplain of the Tenth Tennessee had no personal vendetta against the enemy and seemed to have no desire to participate in combat.

However there was at least one habit the German Benedictine had in common with the Irish-American Vincentian. Both went into battle with the troops. In the case of Father Emery, he prayed over the wounded, assisted the medical staff, and volunteered his services as a litter-bearer. Most chaplains tended to the wounded only after the shooting stopped, and the presence of the monk-priest in the middle of the melee was one of the reasons he was so popular with the fiercely competitive Kentucky Orphans.

During that winter of 1863-64, one of Father Emmeran Bliemel's most frequent companions was First Lieutenant Robert Paget Seymour. Scholarly Emery and learned Sir Robert were avid students of European history, so there was much to discuss.[8]

The Great Siege of Dalton

On Tuesday, March 22, 1864, what has to have been the largest recorded snowball fight in the war took place in Dalton, Georgia. The previous night a foot of snow came down on the Confederate camp, obviously unusual for Georgia at that time of year. Winter wonderland was a novel sight for the boys from the deep South, except for those who had already been in on the weather change at Fort Donelson.

At about 1:00 p.m. skirmishing broke out between some of the Georgians of General W.H.T. Walker and some of the Tennesseans of General Frank Cheatham. The frolicking was contagious and before long a major engagement ensued. The line of battle extended for more than a mile along the Western and Atlanta Railroad. Not too surprisingly the Thirty-Seventh/Fourth Georgia of General Bate's Tennessee division seceded from Colonel Benton Smith's brigade to join their fellow Georgians defending home soil. Very surprisingly the Kentucky Orphans betrayed Bate's trust and also sided with the Georgians.[9]

Sometime before 2:00 p.m. with drummer boys banging and standard bearers waving, the two divisions advanced and crashed into each other, with generals, colonels, and other officers directing the movements. At least 5,000 troops were engaged, with hundreds of civilian spectators watching from surrounding hills. Unfortunately, the Tennesseans' right (south) flank was exposed and the Georgians began to turn it back. A hero was needed.

Colonel (later General) George W. Gordon of the Eleventh Tennessee was ordered by Cheatham to lead a rally. Gordon recalled that the "air was white with whizzing and bursting balls; my men were tripped up, knocked down, covered with snow, or run over."[10] Fearlessly mounting his warhorse and seizing the Tennessee colors (a disreputable bandana handkerchief), Gordon led a ferocious counter-assault against the heavily fortified Georgia position. A tremendous roaring Rebel yell went up from the Tennessee regiments when Gordon took the field, even though he and his horse were pelted with hundreds of snowballs.

Major John G. O'Neill deployed his lads skillfully and the Sons of Erin routed the inexperienced "Sunshine Boys" of General Jesse Finley's Florida brigade who had allied themselves with Walker's Georgians.[11] With several gaps in their line, the Georgia columns were forced to fall back though their own camp. In his "official report" Cheatham described the Georgia retreat as a movement made in "great confusion."[12] The victorious Tennesseans plundered the Georgia tents of the spoils of war, namely food recently arrived from home.

The soldiers from the Volunteer State were unable to pursue the defeated foe because, after four hours of battle, ammunition was running low. Casualties were staggering. Although no exact figures are available from Livermore, hundreds of men reported blackened eyes and running noses. And, as always, the Irishmen of the Tenth Tennessee sustained fewer losses themselves than they inflicted on the enemy.

The Six Battles of the Sons of Erin during the Atlanta Campaign

Rocky Face Ridge, May 5-9

Resaca, May 14-15

New Hope Church, May 23-27

Decatur, July 22

Utoy Creek, August 6

Jonesborough, August 31

The Battles *for* Atlanta
Rocky Face Ridge, Resaca, New Hope Church
General Joe Johnston Versus General Sherman

In the spring of 1864 President Abraham Lincoln appointed Lieutenant General U.S. Grant to command all Federal armies in the field. General Grant assigned himself to the Eastern front to take on General Robert E. Lee with the huge Army of the Potomac under Major General George G. Meade and the Army of the James under Major General Benjamin F. Butler. At the same time he assigned Major General William T. Sherman as head of all Western armies. Sherman's objective was to march down from Chattanooga along the Western and Atlanta railroad line through Atlanta and to penetrate as far south as possible. To accomplish this task the Union Western commander had at his disposal three armies of 98,757 infantrymen.

The Army of the Cumberland, three corps of nine divisions of twenty-seven brigades of seventy regiments of 60,733 men under Major General George H. Thomas, was the Union center around the railroad station at Ringgold. Sherman's old command, the Army of the Tennessee, three corps of seven divisions of twenty brigades, eighty-four regiments of 24,465 men under Major General James B. McPherson, was the Union right (west), coming over from North Alabama to North Georgia. The Army of the Ohio, one cavalry division and one infantry corps of three divisions of nine brigades of thirty-eight regiments of 13,559 men under Major General John A. Schofield, 32, of Wisconsin, was the Union left (east) coming down the East Tennessee and Georgia railroad line, which joined the Western and Atlanta at Dalton.[13]

Sherman also had a full cavalry corps under Major General George Stoneman, 41, of New York, and an artillery corps of two divisions of four brigades of sixteen battalions of fifty-eight batteries, bringing his total number of effectives up to 110,123 men. Sherman advanced south on May 5, the exact day that Grant launched his offensive into Northern Virginia. The Confederacy was under siege.

General Joe Johnston's lone Army of Tennessee had three infantry corps of ten divisions of thirty-six brigades of one-hundred seventy-two regiments (including the Tenth Tennessee) under Generals Hardee, Polk, and Hood, plus one cavalry corps of four divisions of twelve brigades under Major General Joseph Wheeler, 28, of Alabama, plus one artillery division of three brigades of ten batteries for total effectives of 66,089 men.

General Polk's corps was coming over from Mississippi piece by piece, as General Longstreet's Virginia corps had come to Chickamauga. General Hood, possessed at that time of but one useful arm and one leg, had to be strapped to his horse. In spite of that he was still ready to roar, his ire and determination seemingly intensified each time an extremity was lost. Johnston's objective was easy to understand, hard to do. Stop Sherman.

Between May 5 and July 17 Sherman and Johnston played a game of chess in which both players moved their pieces round the board brilliantly. Sherman, an expert with offensive tactics, attacked. Johnston, quite skilled when it came to defense, defended. Every time Sherman assaulted the Confederate positions, Johnston held fast until he was in danger of being encircled (militarily, enveloped.) Then he withdrew, burning bridges and pulling up tracks behind him.

General Bate's division of General Hardee's corps was engaged in all of the battles between Sherman and Johnston. Bate consistently advanced with the same formation, the Kentucky and Florida brigades in front, the Tennessee-Georgia brigade held back in reserve. Because of this deployment, General Joe Lewis' Orphans were engaged in every action, General Jesse Finley's Floridians were engaged in most actions, and Colonel Benton Smith's Tennesseans and Georgians were engaged in some actions.[14]

Thomas Benton Smith consistently deployed the Tenth Tennessee Infantry regiment and the Fourth Georgia

Battalion Sharpshooters as rear guards for the brigade. Consequently, the Sons of Erin were slightly engaged in only three actions.[15]

Apparently Colonel Grace's back wasn't one hundred percent healed, because Major John G. O'Neill was still acting field commander of the Tenth Tennessee. In addition to his self-imposed duties as adjutant, Grace was then assisting Bate's division staff.[16]

As soon as Sherman moved down from Chattanooga, Johnston came up from Dalton to greet him at the railroad town of Rocky Face. (The battle was called Rocky Face Ridge, Buzzard's Roost, Mill Creek, Dug Gap, and Snake Creek Gap, among other designations.) On May 8 General Schofield attacked the position of General Hood's corps on a ridge at Rocky Face, but was repulsed by the Alabama brigade of Brigadier General Edmund Pettus and the Tennessee brigade of Brigadier General John Calvin Brown.[17]

Between the 5th and the 12th, Bate's division was posted in the Mill Creek Gap, where there was some skirmishing, mostly by the Ninth Kentucky regiment, some by the Fourth Georgia Battalion Sharpshooters and the Sons of Erin. Casualties in the division were light, and none at all were reported in Colonel Benton Smith's brigade, which included the Tenth Tennessee. When McPherson moved south to go around the Confederate Army, Joe Johnston fell back further south through Rocky Face and Dalton to the railroad town of Resaca, where he deployed a defensive line on May 13. Bate's division was posted to the rear of Hardee's corps, with Finley on the left, with Lewis on the right, and with Benton Smith, John G. O'Neill and the Sons of Erin in reserve.[18]

Shortly after 12:00 noon on Saturday, May 14, Sherman attacked the Resaca defenses with General John Palmer's corps of General John Schofield's army against positions held by General Thomas Hindman's division of Hood's corps and by General Jesse Finley's brigade of Bate's division of Hardee's corps.

The Kentucky Orphans also got into the fight, as three

waves of Union assaults failed to break the Confederate line. On the next day all of General Bate's troops were involved in sharpshooting and skirmishing action, including the Tenth Tennessee.[19]

When Sherman threatened another envelopment from the west with McPherson's army, Johnston was forced to fall back again. Bate moved out of his position at 10:00 p.m. that night with three detachments assigned to protect the rear of the division's retiring. They were the Fourth Georgia Battalion Sharpshooters, a single company of the Kentucky Orphans, and the Sons of Erin.[20]

It was during this rear guard action that Major John G. O'Neill was shot in the chest, the ball penetrating both lungs.[21] At first he was thought to be dead, but due to a quick Irish rescue operation, he survived, barely. Irish-born Captain John L. Prendergast and his lads were able to move him back along with the detachment. If O'Neill had been captured, he certainly wouldn't have received prompt medical attention and would have died. At Resaca as at Missionary Ridge, the Clarksville Sharpshooter was the second ranking officer of the Tenth Tennessee and withdrew his Irishmen in orderly fashion.[22]

Private John McElroy was the aggressive, native Hibernian from Clarksville who was slightly wounded at Erin Hollow. McElroy had also been wounded at Raymond and Chickamauga. At Resaca he suffered multiple wounds to the groin, jaw, and right eye, and spent the last months of the war in the Reserve corps. Captain Prendergast described Private McElroy as "a good, brave and true soldier."[23] (John McElroy, a Clarksville farmer, survived the conflict by nearly half a century. On July 9, 1902, he received a veteran's pension from the state of Tennessee.)[24]

During the Battle of Resaca, General Bate's division of General Hardee's corps suffered twenty-one killed and 121 wounded. The Sons of Erin had one lad killed, Private Patrick Flaherty of A Company, an Irish-born farmer from McEwen, and six wounded, including O'Neill and McElroy.[25] O'Neill was laid up in an Atlanta military hospital for several months and missed the rest of the Atlanta campaign. In spite of his bad back, Colonel Grace again took command of the remnant of the Irish regiment.[26] Johnston continued his retreat down through the railroad towns of Calhoun, Adairsville, Kingston, and Cassville, with some skirmishing at each place.

On May 20 the Confederate Army crossed the Etowah River and set up a defensive perimeter around the mountainous railroad town of Allatoona Pass. Knowing that Allatoona was one of the strongest defensive positions on the Western and Atlanta, Sherman wisely took a pass on the Pass and took his flank movements elsewhere. This time he marched all three of his armies to the south and west in an effort to turn in Johnston's left flank.

The Federal destination was the small village of Dallas, Georgia, fifteen miles southwest of Allatoona Pass and the railroad. Four miles northeast of the village was a Methodist meeting house called New Hope Church. (The battle which followed has been variously called New Hope Church, Dallas, Pickett's Mill, Burnt Hickory, Pumpkin Vine Creek, Allatoona Hills, or a combination of some or all of the above.)

As a result of a quick and accurate scouting report, Johnston's Southerners arrived at Dallas before Sherman's Northerners. At 2:00 in the afternoon of May 23 General Bate took up a line of march in the rear of General W.H.T. Walker's division, also of Hardee's corps, and there went into bivouac on the Dallas and Allatoona road.

Just before midnight General Bate received orders from General Hardee to move up to the Pumpkin Vine Creek behind the New Hope Church.[27] At 2:00 a.m. on May 24, Colonel Grace deployed the Sons of Erin as sharpshooters between the creek and the church. Once again the lads served as rear guards, while the rest of Hardee's corps marched wearily into Dallas.[28]

Later that same morning Bate's division was broken up. Hardee instructed Lewis to block the Burnt Hickory road with his Kentucky brigade. At the same time he kept Finley's

Florida brigade at New Hope Church, and detached Colonel Benton Smith's brigade to support the Confederate cavalry below Dallas. During the day the Irishmen of the Tenth Tennessee were engaged in light skirmishing with Union troopers.[29]

On Friday morning, the 27th of May, Sherman sent the Fourth corps of McPherson's army, under one-armed Major General Oliver Otis Howard, 33, of Maine, to Pickett's Mill, about two miles northeast of New Hope Church. It was there that Howard's corps, along with General J.C. Davis' division of Palmer's corps of Schofield's army, was promptly whipped by General Pat Cleburne's division of Hardee's corps.

The Second and Fifth Kentucky Orphan regiments of Lewis' brigade and the Fifteenth/Thirty-Seventh Tennessee consolidated regiment of Benton Smith's brigade got caught up in the fight.

The next day Johnston ordered Hardee to probe the defenses of McPherson's army south of Dallas. Things went well for the Boys-in-Gray early on, until Major General John A. Logan's Fifteenth corps rallied to victory late in the day, an action which washed out the Confederate success at Pickett's Mill. In Bate's division Thomas Benton Smith's Tennessee and Georgia brigade, including the Sons of Erin, weren't engaged in the Dallas brawl with "Black Jack" Logan, but the Kentucky and Florida brigades were badly cut up, the Orphans alone losing twenty killed and 177 wounded.

Still bivouacked south of the village but out of the way of the main event, the Sons of Erin were again used in skirmishing action against enemy cavalrymen for most of Sunday, May 29.[30] On Monday General Bate attached Colonel Benton Smith's infantrymen, including the Sons of Erin, to the cavalry of General Frank Armstrong for the purpose of dislodging some dismounted Yankees on a wooded hill in front of Dallas. Armstrong ordered an infantry assault, but by the time that Grace and the other regimental commanders got to the top, the Boys-in-Blue were gone.[31]

In fact a disgruntled General Sherman, increasingly

impatient with his own flanking movements, was withdrawing through the Dallas area back east to the railroad. On that same day of May 30, the Sons of Erin, with the Benton Smith brigade, reoccupied Dallas and captured a few straggling Federals.

The Irishmen, though, were truly not prepared for the horror story that unfolded. Wounded Confederate prisoners had been uncared for the past two days. Some thirty of them had undressed wounds in which insects had found lodging. The hospital was filled with amputees and there was no medicine anywhere.[32] Fortunately, a few heroic Union doctors had volunteered to stay behind. Assisted by non-medical volunteers like Father Emery, Dr. Deering J. Roberts and other members of the Confederate medical staff worked frantically with the Union surgeons to save as many men as possible. The Sons of Erin would never forget the sights and sounds and smells of that day.[33]

While all of this was going on, Sherman occupied the abandoned Confederate positions at Allatoona Pass and prepared for a massive assault to the south. It was the first time in the campaign that the Union Western commanding general had altered his flank strategy, and it would prove to be his only major mistake. At the same time that Sherman was getting ready to unload his offensive fire-power, Johnston was digging in on defense down at Kennesaw Mountain, just above the railroad town of Marietta. Kennesaw Mountain would prove to be the toughest Rebel rock of them all.

In June the Tenth Tennessee, along with the rest of General Bate's division was assigned to Pine Mountain, the far Confederate left flank, slightly west of Kennesaw Mountain and about five miles west of the railroad.[34] When Sherman tried to turn the Confederate left flank in, there was some skirmishing on the fourteenth of the month.

It was here that General Leonidas Polk was killed by a freak artillery shot coming from six-hundred or seven-hundred yards away. Polk was a fine gentleman, a good bishop, but an unsuccessful military leader. He was replaced at corps command by General A.P. Stewart, a vastly superior soldier.

The next day Johnston ordered Bate to fall back toward Kennesaw, no easy task due to the particularly rainy weather that June. Kennesaw Mountain was northwest of the railroad station at Marietta. Actually, there are two Kennesaw Mountains, separated by a single gap. The northern piece of rock is Big Kennesaw, seven-hundred feet at its highest peak. The southern ridge is Little Kennesaw, four-hundred feet at its highest peak. Sherman's three armies advanced from the west, as Johnston's army defended from the east, facing west.

Starting out at 8:30 a.m. on June 27, some 13,000 Union infantrymen assaulted the Confederate line. To the north at Big Kennesaw, Brigadier General Morgan L. Smith's division of General McPherson's Army of the Tennessee charged one division and one brigade under Major General W.H.T Walker and Brigadier General Samuel French, 45, of New Jersey, a Northern Rebel.[35]

To the south at Little Kennesaw, Thomas ordered Hooker's divisions of Brigadier Generals J.C. Davis and John Newton, 41, of Virginia, a Southern Yankee, to attack Hardee's divisions of Cheatham and Cleburne, who bloodily repulsed the invaders. Sherman instructed Thomas to charge twice more with some negative results, as Cheatham and Cleburne held fast to a salient known as the Dead Angle.[36]

During the battle, Hardee had placed Bate, Benton Smith, Grace, and the Sons of Erin in the gap between the Kennesaws, not engaged, except for some light skirmishing involving the Kentucky Orphans.[37] Kennesaw was just the victory the Confederates desperately needed to take the wind out of the Union offensive. General Sherman learned his lesson, regrouped around Marietta, and resumed his flanking movements, pushing General Johnston back over the Chattahoochee River, July 4 to 9.

Peachtree Creek flows out of the Chattahoochee a mere twelve miles north of Atlanta. By July 17 the Boys-in-Blue had reached that point, only to find the Confederates dug in all along the creek. Sherman, in no mood for any more frontal assaults, went around the creek and advanced toward

Atlanta from the northeast. It was one of the most critical moments of the Civil War in the West.

Remarkably, President Jefferson Davis sent General Johnston a telegram on that same day: Davis had lost confidence in his commanding general and replaced him with General John Bell Hood.

> *That as you have failed to arrest the advance of the enemy to the vicinity of Georgia, and express no confidence that you can defeat or repel him, you are hereby relieved from command of the Army and Department of Tennessee, which you will immediately turn over to General Hood.*[38]

The message represented a huge error in judgment. Johnston had used his defensive skills aggressively at New Hope Church and Kennesaw Mountain, but Davis and his cronies in Richmond believed all defensive movements to be unaggressive in themselves. They chose a man who was crippled in body and in spirit, one the common soldier did not trust.

"The Confederate government has rendered us a most valuable service," was the comment of General William T. Sherman. He was right. Sherman himself, a brilliant commander, was personally flawed too; the fires of human compassion burned low in him. "I regard the death and mangling of a couple thousand men as a small affair, a kind of morning dash," was what he admitted in a letter to his wife in a particularly trying time in the war.[39] Because of his own battle wounds, General Hood completely associated valor with casualty figures. Success or failure was to be determined by one standard—whether or not sufficient blood had been shed. These tendencies were described by historian T. L. Connelly as "psychotic."[40] Sherman against Hood was an American calamity waiting to happen.

Some minor reorganization took place when Hood replaced Joe Johnston as commanding general of the Army of Tennessee. Promoted to corps command to replace Hood

Opponents of The Sons of Erin

(Top Left) Major General William T. Sherman of Ohio.
(Top Right) Major General Philip H. Sheridan of New York.
(Center) Lieutenant General U.S. Grant of Illinois.
(Bottom Left) Major General William S. Rosecrans of Ohio.
(Bottom Right) Major General George H. Thomas of Virginia.

was Lieutenant General Stephen D. Lee, 30, of South Carolina, no relation to the Lees of Virginia.

S.D. Lee was an outstanding officer who would soon be compared to corps commanders like Longstreet and Hardee. At that point the Confederate Western army, with Hardee, Stewart, and Lee, had three excellent top subordinates to go along with one wild and overly aggressive army commander, namely John Bell Hood.

The Battles *of* Atlanta
Decatur, Utoy Creek, Jonesborough
General Hood Versus General Sherman

General Schofield, a West Point classmate of General Hood's, warned General Sherman that an attack was imminent. Sherman didn't need to be told and put all his commanders on battle alert. He also didn't need to wait long. At 3:00 p.m. on the very next day, July 20, the fearsome Texan struck the Union line on Peachtree Creek, the first of four full frontal assaults known as "Hood's Sorties."

Early that morning General Thomas had established a bridgehead across the creek, while Generals McPherson and Schofield were enveloping Atlanta from the east, leaving a gap of nearly two miles between Thomas and Schofield. Hood hit the gap first with Hardee and then with Stewart but Thomas' army again held fast.

In the Battle of Peachtree Creek, the Florida and Kentucky brigades of General Bate's division were fully engaged, while most of the Tennessee-Georgia brigade, including the Sons of Erin, was held in reserve.[41] The only thing that John Bell Hood had accomplished was the loss of about 2,500 men killed, wounded, and captured. Meanwhile McPherson, with some trouble from General Wheeler's Confederate cavalry, had occupied the town of Decatur, six miles directly east of

Atlanta.

When McPherson advanced to the outskirts of the Georgia "Gate City of The South" on July 22, Hood came out to meet him in the critical Battle of Atlanta, or "Hood's Second Sortie." The big Texan's plan was to have the divisions of Generals W.H.T. Walker and Bate strike the blue-clads in the Decatur area, while the divisions of Generals Cheatham and Cleburne struck them in the Atlanta area.[42] As the Southerners marched south to block the Northerners at the eastern end of the city, the fight came down to the corps of Generals Hardee and Wheeler against the armies of Generals McPherson and Schofield. Bate was Hardee's far right (east) flank and Colonel Benton Smith and the Sons of Erin were Bate's far right flank, the Confederates closest to Decatur.[43]

Major General Grenville Dodge's corps of McPherson's army consisted of the two divisions of English-born Brigadier General John W. Fuller and Irish-born, one-armed Brigadier General Thomas W. Sweeny, who despised each other. Strictly by accident these fresh troops advanced in front of the positions held by the divisions of Walker and Bate.

To the left (west) of Bate's division was Walker's division, minus Walker himself, who had been killed by a Union sharpshooter an hour and a half before. Brigadier General Hugh W. Mercer, 55, of Georgia, commanding Walker's men and General Bate attacked Generals Sweeny and Fuller at 12:15 p.m.

The Irish Yankee deployed his line along Sugar Creek, and the Irish Rebels of the Tenth Tennessee had to go through heavy undergrowth to get at him. As was his custom, Bate advanced with Generals Joseph Lewis and Jesse Finley up front, and Colonels Thomas Benton Smith and William Grace forming a second line.[44]

The Kentuckians, Floridians, Tennesseans, Georgians and Irishmen of General Bate's division became heavily engaged with General Sweeny's First brigade of Brigadier General Elliott Rice, and experienced some initial success, until Mercer was driven back by Sweeny's Second brigade under

German-born Colonel August Mersy.[45]

Hardee rested the Kentucky and Florida brigades and attacked Dodge at 3:00 p.m. with Cleburne's division on his right and Cheatham's division on his left. Also, Hardee detached Colonel Benton Smith's brigade from General Bate's division and sent the Tennesseans, Georgians, and Irishmen further east toward Decatur to join General Wheeler's cavalrymen, who were engaged with the enemy cavalrymen of Colonel John W. Sprague.[46]

Father Emery and most of the Sons of Erin assisted Wheeler's wounded in Decatur, while ducking Sprague's lead.[47]

At the same time that Bate and Mercer withdrew from the field, McPherson was killed by a Rebel sharpshooter and replaced on the spot as army commander by General John A. "Black Jack" Logan, who handled himself brilliantly. It was Logan and Schofield who drove off Hardee's divisions of Cleburne, Cheatham, Mercer and Bate and forced Hood to retire all along his line. General Sherman held the northern and eastern sections of the city. The Battle of Atlanta was over.

Casualties were mind-boggling. Union losses were just under two-thousand, while Confederate losses were just under eight-thousand, or about thirty percent of the infantry that had been engaged! In two days, July 20 and 22, Hood lost more men than Johnston did in his whole campaign.[48]

In the Tenth Tennessee Private Patrick Conry of C Company was killed, Private William A. Mentiss of A Company was mortally wounded, and seven other Irishmen were wounded.[49] Due to the fact that the Tenth spent most of the day in and around the town of Decatur, Colonel Grace listed the action of July 22 as the Battle of Decatur.[50] During the Confederate retreat into southwestern Atlanta, the Sons of Erin counted fifty-three able-bodied lads.[51]

Sherman moved to cut Hood's line of communication to the south by circling north of the city down to the southwest, where Logan met S.D. Lee at Ezra Church, or "Hood's

Third Sortie," July 28. Hood lost another five thousand Boys-in-Gray to the Federals' six-hundred, but somehow managed to hold onto the far southern end of Atlanta. In a single week the big Texan's total of killed, wounded, and captured was better than eighteen-thousand men, or one-third of the army he had inherited from Joe Johnston.

Not too surprisingly, the loss of so many officers and enlisted men necessitated more change in the structure of the dwindling Army of Tennessee. The brigade of Brigadier General Henry R. Jackson was transferred from General Mercer's division to General Bate's, giving Bate four battalion-sized brigades. Jackson had four regiments, an infantry battalion and a sharpshooters battalion, all from Georgia.[52]

The Second Tennessee Infantry regiment, originally organized by Bate and then under Colonel William D. Robinson, was transferred from Brigadier General Lucius Polk's brigade to Colonel Thomas Benton Smith's brigade, giving Smith six tiny infantry regiments, plus one microscopic sharpshooters' battalion, namely the Second, Tenth, Twentieth and Thirtieth Tennessee regiments, the Fifteenth/Thirty-Seventh Tennessee consolidated regiment, the Thirty-Seventh Georgia regiment, and the Fourth Georgia Battalion Sharpshooters.[53]

The E Company of the Second Tennessee consisted of the Memphis Fire Department, mostly Irishmen.[54] It can be safely assumed that the hook-and-ladder-lads quickly located the Sons of Erin.

The reinforcements for Bate's division reported on July 31, just in time for a lull in the storm. Henry Jackson's brigade increased Bate's number of effectives to 2,771, while W. D. Robinson's regiment increased Benton Smith's numerical strength to something close to 450 men, not all of whom were armed.[55]

To ease the pressure around Ezra Church, General

Hood detached General Bate's division from General Hardee's corps and attached it to General S. D. Lee's corps. On August 4 Lee detached Benton Smith's brigade from Bate's division and posted the brigade slightly less than five miles south–west of Ezra Church, along the east bank of the north tributary of Utoy Creek, where General Schofield was planning a crossing, prior to attacking the Macon and Western Railroad. Arriving that same evening and working through the next day, the Sons of Erin and the other members of the brigade established a skirmish line on the east side of the creek and constructed some logworks one-hundred yards east of the creek on a wooded hill.[56]

Thomas Benton Smith, promoted the week before from colonel to brigadier, was in high spirits, glad to be removed from the main body of the army. The new general deployed his six regiments from left to right, south to north: the Thirty-Seventh/Fourth Georgia, the Fifteenth/Thirty-Seventh Tennessee, the Twentieth Tennessee, the Thirtieth Tennessee, the Second Tennessee, and the Tenth Tennessee.[57]

General Schofield didn't know the Rebel strength ahead, or even if there was any Rebel strength. Due to the fact that General Benton Smith had only about 450 Boys-in-Gray, the Union scouts reported no new Confederate movement in the area.

Schofield directed his Third division under Brigadier General Jacob D. Cox to make a reconnaissance-in-force. General Cox passed the command down to lawyer-soldier-Irish-American Brigadier General James W. Reilly, 36, of Ohio, the commanding officer of his First brigade, all the while keeping Colonel John S. Casement's Second brigade in reserve. General Reilly had seven regiments: the Eighth U.S. Tennessee, the One-Hundred-Twelfth-Illinois, the One-Hundredth and One-Hundred-Fourth Ohio, and the Eleventh, Twelfth, and Sixteenth U.S. Kentucky.[58]

Early in the morning on Saturday, August 6, General Benton Smith sent the Fourth Georgia Battalion Sharpshooters down from the logworks to the skirmish line on the bank, while Colonel Grace sent about half the Sons of Erin under Captain John L. Prendergast from the north end of the logworks down to join the Georgians. The commanding officer of the skirmish line detachment was Major Theodore D. Caswell of the Fourth Georgia.[59]

Along the west bank General Reilly deployed a skirmish line, with the One-Hundred-Fourth Ohio on his right (south) and the Eleventh U.S. Kentucky on his left (north). These two regiments were commanded by Colonel Oscar W. Sterl and Lieutenant Colonel Erasmus L. Mottley, respectively. At 10:00 a.m. the Eleventh U.S. Kentucky first and the One-Hundred-Fourth Ohio second, crossed Utoy Creek, covered by the Eighth U.S. Tennessee from the west bank.

The wading-through-the-water advance of the two Union outfits drove Caswell and Prendergast and their fifty or sixty riflemen back to the Confederate logworks. Even more importantly, it established a beachhead for the Boys-in-Blue. General Cox ordered General Reilly to chase after the Irishmen and Georgians of the Confederate sharpshooter detachment.

Around 11:00 a.m. Reilly charged the one-hundred yards of cut trees with Colonel Sterl's Ohioans veering to his right, and with Lieutenant Colonel Mottley's Kentuckians veering to his left. The One-Hundred-Fourth Ohio was quickly dispersed by fire from the Thirty-Seventh/Fourth Georgia and the Fifteenth/Thirty-Seventh Tennessee. The attack by the Eleventh U.S. Kentucky lasted longer and penetrated further, but was eventually repulsed by the Sons of Erin and the other Tennesseans on the Confederate right.[60]

In response to Reilly's call for reinforcements, the One-Hundred-Twelfth Illinois, the One-Hundredth Ohio, and the Eighth U.S. Tennessee crossed the creek. At 1:00 p.m. the Yankee-Irish-American unleashed another piecemeal assault against the narrow and heavily defended enemy position, deploying the Illinoisans on his right, the One-Hundredth Ohio on his left, supported by five companies of the One-Hundred-Fourth Ohio, leaving the Eleventh U.S. Kentucky, the Eighth

U.S. Tennessee, and the other half of the One-Hundred-Fourth Ohio on the skirmish line. All along the logworks the Northerners closed to within a few yards of the Southerners, but were again forced to fall back, suffering heavy casualties.[61]

After the second Union wave had run its course, General Bate detached the Second and Fourth regiments of the Kentucky Orphans to the rear of Thomas Benton Smith's brigade, giving the reinforced Southerners a second line. Reilly's third and last charge, made shortly before 3:00 p.m. was a poor idea. His left flank was the Eighth U.S. Tennessee and his right flank was the other five companies of the unfortunate One-Hundred-Fourth Ohio, commanded by Captain J. F. Riddle.[62]

The Eleventh U.S. Kentucky, the One-Hundred-Twelfth Illinois, the One-Hundredth Ohio, and the first half of the One-Hundred-Fourth Ohio were all left on the east-bank skirmish line, while the Twelfth and Sixteenth U.S. Kentucky were still on the west bank skirmish line in reserve. The Union East Tennessee regiment had only 223 men left, so the third wave of Reilly's reconaissance-in-force consisted of no more than four-hundred Boys-in-Blue making a full frontal assault against Smith's reinforced position of about six-hundred Boys-in-Gray.[63]

While bringing up the two Kentucky regiments to support his front line brigade, William B. Bate suffered a leg wound near the knee, which forced him to retire to the rear, and put him out of the rest of the fight. The damage had been inflicted by a Yankee sharpshooter.[64]

Colonel William Grace of the Sons of Erin was the second highest ranking officer in the Benton Smith brigade, next in line after Smith himself. Smith commanded the troops on his left and rear, the Thirty-Seventh/Fourth Georgia, the Fifteenth/Thirty-Seventh Tennessee, and the Second/Fourth Kentucky. "Battling Billie" Grace, commanding Smith's right,

Successful Counter-Assault Along Utoy Creek
Saturday, August 6, 1864, 3:30 P.M.

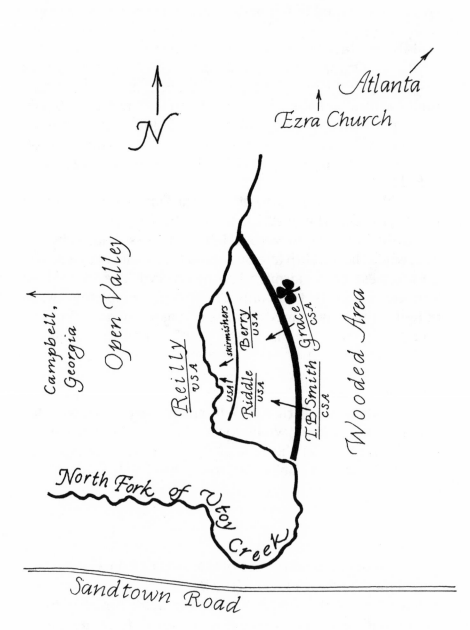

Atlanta

Ezra Church

N

Campbell, Georgia

Open Valley

Wooded Area

Reilly
USA

skirmishers

USA

Berry
USA

Riddle
USA

T.B.Smith
CSA

Grace
CSA

North Fork of Utoy Creek

Sandtown Road

consolidated his four regiments of about 250 effectives into one unit—the Twentieth/Thirtieth/Second/Tenth Tennessee consolidated.[65]

The upshot of all of this was that the third brawl on the Union left/Confederate right would be fought exclusively by Tennessee soldiers against Tennessee soldiers.

Captain Riddle's overworked, undersized, and weary Ohioans were blasted away by Benton Smith's Georgians, Tennesseans, and Kentuckians. However, Captain James W. Berry's East Tennesseans fought ferociously against Colonel Grace's Middle and West Tennesseans, until Smith swung the two Irish companies of the Fourth Kentucky over to support the Sons of Erin and the Memphis Fire Department at the right end of the Confederate line.[66]

When Berry wavered, Smith ordered a counter-assault all along his front.[67] After Reilly saw what was happening, he ordered a withdrawal of his entire east-bank skirmish line back across Utoy Creek, covered by the fire of his Twelfth and Sixteenth U.S. Kentucky regiments, still posted on the west-bank skirmish line.[68]

Grace, on horseback, led the two Irish companies of the Fourth Kentucky, the E Company of the Second Tennessee, and the Sons of Erin over the cut trees and after the retreating Yankees, followed by the rest of his yelling, surg–ing Rebels.[69] Reilly's retiring was made in considerable haste. It was Tennesseans chasing Tennesseans and Kentuckians chasing Kentuckians.

The engagement at Utoy Creek ended around 4:00 p.m. some six hours, three assaults, and one counter-assault after it had begun. The Confederates still held a narrow position on the east bank of the small creek in front of Atlanta, so Schofield couldn't cross at that point. Although an obscure minor engagement between a Confederate brigade and part of a Union brigade, the August 6 event was nonetheless an emotionally-charged victory for the remnant of the Sons of Erin.

Captain Lew Clark of the Tenth Tennessee had vivid memories of what he referred to as the "Battle of Utah Creek."

*We were vigorously assaulted in our half-en-
trenched position; repeated charges were made
in the most determined manner, but we repulsed
them in every instance. Occasionally some of the
enemy pressed into our very lines, only to find
themselves prisoners. Finally we ourselves made
a charge and captured a good many more prisoners.*[70]

Surprisingly, the engagement along Utoy Creek would
prove to be the very last decisive *infantry* victory for the Army
of Tennessee.

The conduct of the Tenth was commended by both
Benton Smith and Grace. The Irish lads, led by Prendergast,
were given the honor of escorting the Federal prisoners to
the rear. The next day corps commander S. D. Lee sent a
dispatch to Richmond praising the efforts of the Benton Smith
brigade. "Soldiers who fight with the coolness and determination that these men did will always be victorious over any
reasonable number."[71] Unfortunately for the Confederates,
the numbers would no longer be reasonable.

Five regiments of James Reilly's First brigade of Jacob
Cox's Third division of the Twenty-Third corps, temporarily
commanded by John Palmer of John Schofield's Army of the
Ohio of William Sherman's department, were the only Northern units in combat at Utoy Creek on August 6. It was a poor
performance by Reilly, otherwise a distinguished officer. The
Federals reported seventy-six killed, 199 wounded, and thirty-
one captured for total losses of 306 out of less than a thousand, or about thirty percent of those engaged. The Eighth
U.S. Tennessee was hit the hardest with thirty-one killed or
mortally wounded, thirty-six wounded, and sixteen captured
for total losses of eighty-three or thirty-seven percent of the
223 engaged.[72] The East Tennesseans also lost nearly thirty
good muskets, which the Southerners desperately needed,
plus two battle flags.

The Confederates reported "between 15 to 20 casualties" out of about six-hundred engaged, and none at all for the Sons of Erin.[73] As is obvious, the myth of the "Bloody Tenth" couldn't be further from reality here. The troops who made the mad dashes against the Irishmen were the ones who got bloodied.

On Heiman's Hill at Dover, on O'Neill's Hill at Raymond, at Reed's Bridge at Chickamauga, and at Utoy Creek the Sons of Erin had inflicted as many as two hundred casualties in total against the Federals, while sustaining zero casualties themselves in those four engagements. The twenty minutes at Steedman's Hill at Chickamauga was the only possible time during the war when the Sons of Erin could have come out in worse shape than their Union foes.

General Bate, whose leg wound kept him out of action for six weeks, was replaced as division commander by Major General John Calvin Brown, 37, of Tennessee, the original commanding officer of the Third Tennessee regiment, and, like Bate, a future governor of the Volunteer State.

Utoy Creek was a minor inconvenience for Generals Sherman, Schofield, Palmer, Cox and Reilly, who simply went around the Confederate position, and crossed the creek at another point, which was all they had to do in the first place to avoid 306 casualties. Sherman planned to envelop Hood by moving his forces below Atlanta, thereby striking up from the south and cutting off the city's last supply line, the Macon and Western Railroad.

General Hood deployed his army west of Atlanta, north to south, blocking any approach from west to east. This simplistic strategy almost dictated General Sherman's decision to march north to south and then strike up from the south, but Hood never did make the proper adjustment.[74]

At the same time that the Sons of Erin were doing picket duty for three weeks along Utoy Creek, Sherman was advancing his Boys-in-Blue west of Hood's troops, on his way down to Jonesborough, a town on the Macon and Western line fifteen miles south of Atlanta.

By August 27th Sherman was amassing his troops around Jonesborough, with the armies of Thomas and Schofield coming down the railroad line from the north, and with McPherson's army, then under the command of General O.O. Howard, coming in from the west. On August 30 Hood found out about Howard, but not about Thomas or Schofield.

On that same evening the Confederate commander sent Hardee and S.D. Lee down to attack O.O Howard's army, leaving A.P. Stewart's corps behind in Atlanta. This would prove to be another Hood mistake. When Hardee and S.D. Lee arrived in Jonesborough the next morning, they found Sherman waiting for them. It was "Hood's Fourth Sortie" of the Atlanta campaign and Hood's last sortie of the Atlanta campaign.

During that month of August, all four of Bate's brigades then commanded by Calvin Brown had been detached for various odds and ends. On the 29th Hardee put them all back together again. Early that next morning the Sons of Erin, in Thomas Benton Smith's brigade of John Calvin Brown's division of William Joseph Hardee's corps of John Bell Hood's army, moved out from Utoy Creek for a long march south to Jonesborough, arriving twenty-four hours later, Wednesday, August 31, 1864.[75]

Later that same day the two Confederate corps of Hardee and S.D. Lee, 24,000 men, were deployed on the western edge of town, while the Federals were posted to the north on a high wooded ridge, facing the town. These were the troops of the Fifteenth and Sixteenth corps of O.O. Howard's army, commanded by "Black Jack" Logan and Brigadier General Thomas E. Ransom, 29, of Illinois, replacing the wounded Grenville Dodge. General Howard kept his other unit in reserve—the Seventeenth corps of Major General Frank Blair. The Southerners were along the Macon and Western

Railroad, the Northerners in front of Flint Creek.

The Boys-in-Gray were tired of the Atlanta campaign in general and from the long night march in particular. But Hood insisted on throwing them up against another set of protected Federal logworks. Hardee put General Pat Cleburne in field command of his corps, while Brigadier General Mark Lowrey, 35, of Mississippi, an Irish-American Baptist preacher, moved up to command Cleburne's division. The Union defenses ran north-south, with their right flank bent westward at nearly ninety degrees.

Hardee's plan called for Cleburne to launch an assault from the left of his line at 3:00 p.m. in an attempt to turn Howard's southern flank. S. D. Lee on the right was to attack Howard's front as soon as he heard the gunfire signifying that Cleburne was hotly engaged on the left.[76]

Cleburne had Lowrey's division on his left and Calvin Brown's division on his right, both backed up on a second line by the division of Brigadier General George E. Maney, 38, of Tennessee. Brown's division had Henry Jackson's Georgia brigade on the left, supported by Benton Smith's Tennessee-Georgia brigade, including the Sons of Erin, with the Kentucky brigade on the right and the Florida brigade in reserve.[77]

Everything went wrong for the Confederates. At 2:20 p.m. S.D. Lee mistook the sounds of heavy skirmishing on his left for Cleburne's attack, advancing prematurely into Logan's Fifteenth corps, deploying the divisions of Generals Carter Stevenson on his left and Patten Anderson on his right. When Pat Cleburne heard the fighting on his right, he took the battlefield initiative before his troops were ready and assaulted Ransom's Sixteenth corps, also before the scheduled starting point of 3:00.[78]

The Kentucky Orphans of Calvin Brown's division stormed the exact point on the Union line that separated Logan from Ransom, being bloodily repulsed by Ransom's Second division under Brigadier General John M. Corse, 29, of Pennsylvania. Colonel Grace of the Tenth Tennessee and

Lieutenant Colonel James J. Turner of the Thirtieth Tennessee were two of several officers who tried to rally Brown's Southerners around Corse's logworks. The rally failed, as it did all up and down the line, with the Confederates getting mauled.[79]

While all of this mayhem was going on, Father Emery Bliemel was working with the litter-bearers of the Fourth Kentucky, praying with the wounded, and making a frantic effort to get them to the rear, all the while dodging enemy minié balls. Around 4:30, as Hardee was ordering a withdrawal Father Emery was making one of his trips forward. In the confusion of the Confederate retreat, the Catholic chaplain was informed that one of the soldiers of the Sons of Erin lay dying in front of the Union works. It was Colonel William Grace.[80]

Grace had been shot in the gut, part of his lower intestines blown away, a wound that was always fatal. When Father Emery and the stretcher-bearers found him, they helped the huge man to his feet and moved him toward the rear, all the time under heavy skirmishing fire. The Kentuckians put the colonel down close to the Baptist Church, near the Jonesborough Depot.

Grace was in tremendous pain as Father Emery knelt to hear his confession. While the priest was administering the sacrament of Extreme Unction, he noticed a flash of light out of the corner of his eye. It was the very last thing he saw in his life. The Yankee cannonball took Father Emery's head cleanly off his shoulders. He was dead before his headless body was violently flung on top of Grace.[81] Father Emery was thirty-two years old, a Confederate Army chaplain for five months, his destiny complete.

Reverend Emmeran Bliemel O.S.B. was the first American Catholic military chaplain killed in action on a battlefield in the history of the United States, and the only Catholic chaplain on either side to give his life in the Civil War.[82] Colonel William Grace was carried off the field, spattered in the blood of his chaplain-friend. Knowing that he was about to die, he volunteered to be left behind, regretting only the death of Father Emery and the fact that he would no longer be able to serve the Confederacy. "Do not move me. I am suffering and cannot live long. Let me die here," he told the others.[83]

In the early morning of Thursday, September 1, exactly six days after having been recommended for promotion to brigade command, with the corresponding rank of brigadier general, "Battling Billie" Grace of the Sons of Erin died at the age of thirty-three.[84]

After the Battle of Jonesborough General John Bell Hood apologized to the Confederate high command for the lack of casualties in his army—not enough men had been willing to fearlessly die for their country. Total Federals killed and wounded were 179. Total Confederates killed and wounded were 1,725.

Sergeant James Hayes, the color-bearer of the Sons of Erin since day one at Fort Henry, was killed in front of the Union entrenchments. Captain John L. Prendergast, number two officer of the regiment, was struck by a piece of metal from an exploding shell, which opened up the old hip wound he had received at Raymond.[85] The Clarksville Sharpshooter survived again, but was forced out of the war, disabled, leaving Captain Lewis R. Clark, also of Clarksville, as temporary commanding officer.[86] (Private John Connelly of B Company was struck in the back of the head by a similar shell fragment and was awarded a disability pension thirty-five years later.) [87]

At Jonesborough the Tenth Tennessee suffered three killed: Grace, Bliemel, Hayes, eight wounded, and seven captured for total losses of eighteen. The Atlanta campaign was over. All told, from Rocky Face Ridge to Jonesborough, the Irish regiment had six killed, twenty-one wounded, and seven captured for total losses of thirty-four, or a little less than half of the sixty-nine Irishmen engaged. Seven-hundred and twenty-five lads had started out with Heiman and McGavock at the river forts. On September 1, 1864, thirty-five were left in the Confederate Western army.[88]

After having nearly destroyed his own Army of Tennessee, Hood evacuated all of Atlanta as Sherman took possession. It was 5 p.m. September 1.

Earlier that same day the bodies of Colonel William Grace and Father Emmeran Bliemel were hastily but tenderly buried by a small detachment of the fleeing Sons of Erin near a clump of trees about a hundred yards southeast of the old stone depot.[89] The burial detail was led by First Lieutenant Robert Paget Seymour.[90] Father Darius Hébert of the First Louisiana regulars officiated at the hasty service and then marked the graves and fenced them in, as Sir Robert and his lads rejoined their retreating regiment.

The fate of the graves of William Grace and Father Emmeran Bliemel is worth pausing to note. There was only one Catholic family living in Jonesborough in those days, the Hollidays, who took on the responsibility of caring for the graves.[91] Without those good samaritans the location would probably have been lost forever.

After the war the Daughters of the Confederacy had the bodies transferred to the Patrick Cleburne Cemetery, where they were given another religious burial by Father Thomas O'Reilly of Atlanta. Later the remains of Colonel William Grace were removed to the Mount Olivet Episcopal Cemetery in Nashville, where the bones of the Catholic soldier rest today, along with those of Lutheran Colonel Adolphus Heiman and Presbyterian Colonel Randal McGavock, all three commanding officers of an Irish regiment that fought in the U.S. against the U.S.[92]

Word about the death of Father Bliemel never found its way back to the Assumption parish in Nashville or the Benedictine Abbey in Pennsylvania. For the next quarter of a century the German-born priest was listed as missing.[93]

In the nineteenth century, there were several tributes paid to the life and death of Emmeran Bliemel, all from non-Catholic Southern sources.

Another gallant soldier from Nashville killed at the Battle of Joneboro was Colonel Gracey of the Irish l0th Tennessee, the Bloody Tinth. There was a devoted Catholic priest attached to the l0th who was killed at the same time, I think. His name, as I recall it, was Father Blemuel. Dr. Roberts of the 20th Tennessee remembers him.[94]

Rev. Father Blieml was killed while administering the sacrament of extreme unction to the dying on the field of battle. He was a gallant soldier of Christ, who feared death in no form while doing the work of his Lord and master.[95]

True to a sense of duty, and shrinking from no danger, he always went with his regiment into battle, endearing him to the soldiers of his charge, both Protestant and Catholic . . .. Father Blemill knelt beside Captain Gracie. At that time a cannon ball from one of the enemy's guns carried away the head of the heroic priest. He had evidently perceived that Gracie was wounded unto death, and halted to supplicate Heaven for the repose of his soul.[96]

Father J. Emerson Blimeol was mortally wounded while ministering to a Catholic soldier during the Battle of Jonesboro, Georgia.[97]

Father Blemil, chaplain of the Fourth Kentucky, was killed while praying for a mortally wounded soldier. He was ours; no other shall claim him. There will be trouble if the Bloody Tinth Tennessee doesn't give up claim to the gallant, glorious, martyred priest-chaplain of the 4th Kentucky.[98]

The veteran Tenth mourned the loss of Colonel William Grace, mortally wounded. The chaplain of his regiment, Father Bleiml, was killed while giving the Last Rites.[99]

The heathen old 4th Kentucky, who discouraged so many parsons in this war, had another one with them in their advance. This man of God the Orphans respected for he went into the fight with them, and though a Catholic, he made no distinction in his ministrations with the largely Protestant Kentuckians. As [General] Lewis rode to the rear observing his broken lines, he saw Father Blemill bending over a wounded man. He lifted his hands in prayer for the dying soldier, and at once a cannon ball carried away the priest's head. The poor 4th Kentucky just could not keep a preacher. "He was with us such a short time," said Captain John Weller, "that I never knew his name."[100]

In October the Sons of Erin were reinforced by exactly one Irishman, bringing their roster total up to thirty-six lads. Newly promoted Lieutenant Colonel John G. O'Neill was back.[101]

Chapter Ten
Four Lads

A Footnote to History

Meanwhile, in the disease-infested Confederate prisoner of war camp at Andersonville, Georgia, Federal prisoners, mostly from the Nineteenth Massachusetts, got released by enlisting in a unit designated as the Tenth Tennessee Infantry Regiment of Volunteers (Irish) C.S.A.

Not one of the Massachusetts Sons of Erin ever spent a minute with the Tennessee Sons of Erin, who never even knew they existed. Because the Richmond war department failed to locate John G. O'Neill and his thirty-five lads, the Irish Yankee-Rebels were sent over to the Trans-Mississippi theatre, where they surrendered at a place identified as Egypt Station, Mississippi, on December 28, 1864. At this point they proceeded to re-enlist in their original army, thus becoming Yankee-Rebel-Yankees.[1]

The "Boys in Blue-Gray-Blue" are technically listed among the Army of Tennessee rosters, with a "Tenth Tennessee" regimental designation, but without company designations, which they never had. The outcome of all this was that those additional 253 names caused considerable confusion to future historians. It was first believed that those Irishmen without company designations were Tennessee soldiers who had gone over to the Union army at Camp Douglas. And so, the myth grew another strange branch, one that couldn't be further from the truth: the Sons of Erin were supposed to have transferred to three companies of the Union army. The reality: three companies of the Union army transferred to the Sons of Erin.

On January 24, 1865, O'Neill was authorized to enlist 192 other Irish-Yankees from Andersonville, but the war ended before the red tape could be processed.[2] The record shows that none of the Sons of Erin ever served with the

Yankees, and that none of the Yankees ever served with the Sons of Erin.

Many years after the war, some of the members of the Nineteenth Massachusetts applied for and received pension checks from both the state of Massachusetts and the state of Tennessee, both of which they were legally entitled to.

The Confederate Counter Offensive Into Tennessee
Franklin, Third Murfreesborough, Nashville
Lieutenant Colonel Shy Versus Colonel McMillen

Instead of retreating down to block the Union penetration into the Deep South, General Hood retreated over to the town of Palmeto, twenty-five miles southwest of Atlanta. In the next few weeks he marched north of the Georgia capital along the Western and Atlanta line, making Joe Johnston's retreat in reverse, for the purpose of destroying Sherman's lines of communication with Atlanta, forcing Sherman to abandon the city. It didn't work. General Sherman, fearing a rear guard action from the gray-clads, sent General Thomas up in pursuit, frustrating General Hood's plans against the railroad.

By November 1 Sherman had repaired all the tracks between Chattanooga and Atlanta. The Union trains moved a constant stream of supplies and materials down to Dixie. Sherman moved Thomas' Army of the Cumberland further north to protect Tennessee, reinforced by Schofield's Army of the Ohio.

After evacuating all old men, women and children by November 15, Sherman burnt Atlanta to the ground. Scarlett O'Hara and Melanie notwithstanding, none of the ladies were forced to escape the flames. Using the Army of the Tennessee, Sherman headed southeast along the Macon and Western Railroad toward Savannah on the Atlantic coast, a campaign known to history as the infamous "March to the Sea."

While the Union Army of the Tennessee destroyed South Georgia virtually unopposed, the Confederate Army of Tennessee was up in North Alabama. Hood had left Dalton in mid-October and marched his army west over a hundred miles to the town of Tuscumbia in the extreme northeastern tip of the state of Alabama. Arriving on Halloween, he talked President Jefferson Davis into allowing him to chase after Schofield, who was then in camp above the Alabama border at the South Middle Tennessee town of Pulaski on the Nashville and Decatur (Alabama) Railroad, home of H Company, Sons of Erin.

In early November the Confederate Army of Tennessee advanced into Tennessee with John Bell Hood's half-crazed invasion of Federally occupied Tennessee. The thirty-six Irishmen of the Sons of Erin were still in that army.[3]

When General Frank Cheatham of Nashville was promoted from division to corps command replacing Hardee at Hood's request, General John Calvin Brown was transferred over to the command of Cheatham's old division. Command of the Bate/Brown division was given back to General Bate himself, who had recovered from his latest wound.[4] General Benton Smith's brigade remained in Bate's division, then in Cheatham's corps, along with General Jesse Finley's Florida brigade and General Henry Jackson's Georgia brigade, minus the Kentucky Orphans, who were reorganized as a dismounted calvary battalion. In fact, Benton Smith had a unit that wasn't much bigger than three companies of one regiment.[5]

While General Thomas fortified Nashville with his thirty-thousand troops, General Schofield reached the town of Franklin, about fourteen miles south and a little west of the capital, with General Hood in hot pursuit. The Federals had been building defenses around Franklin since March of 1862, so the Second and Third divisions of Schofield's Twenty-Third corps piled into the waiting trenches.

The Three Battles of the Sons of Erin
General Hood's Invasion of Tennessee
November, December 1864

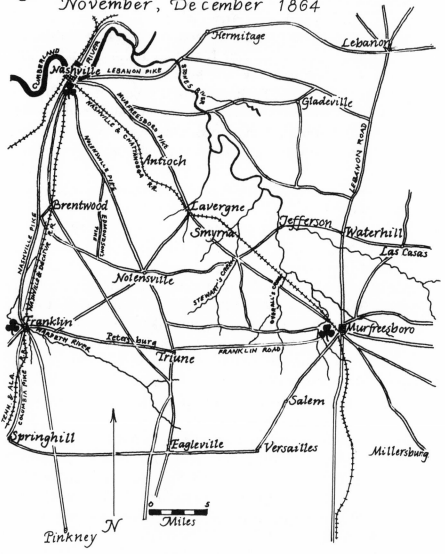

With increasingly sophisticated engineers involved in their design, and with examples from the Eastern theatre as models, these fortifications were no ordinary logworks. They were constructed of deep outside ditches, headlogs atop dirt parapets, with a menacing array of booby-traps.

Franklin obviously wasn't an ideal location for another reckless series of frontal assaults. Unfortunately, this was precisely what Hood, whose aberrational mind was locked somewhere back in time of the first Indian wars, had in mind. With the misguided approval of Jefferson Davis, John Bell Hood was resolved to draw Union military attention away from the Deep South, which meant that Confederate Tennesseans who had previously defended home soil would then be attempting to liberate home soil.

Arriving shortly after Schofield on Wednesday, November 30, Hood advanced toward the town with Cheatham on his left(west), A.P. Stewart in the center, and S.D. Lee on his right. Cheatham's corps had three divisions, which were commanded by Patrick R. Cleburne, John Calvin Brown, and William B. Bate.[6]

Bate's was the infantry division on Cheatham's far left, approaching the town from the southwest toward the heart of the Union entrenchments. A half an hour later, at 4:00 p.m., with drums beating and flags waving, the first assault began.

General Bate charged with the Georgians and Floridians in front and with General Thomas Benton Smith's troops, including the Sons of Erin, forming a thin second line.[7]

The regimental-sized Confederate division of Bate ran into the rifle pits of Schofield's First division under Brigadier General Thomas H. Ruger, 31, of Wisconsin. Before Lieutenant Colonel John G. O'Neill even had a chance to deploy a skirmish line, Ruger's counterattack overran Bate, Benton Smith and the Sons of Erin, chasing the Southerners to the rear, capturing many of them in the process.[8]

Bate's poor field position and lack of reserve strength kept him out of the rest of the battle, but other assaults were made until Hood finally ended the attack around 9:00 p.m. In the madness that was the Battle of Franklin, Federals killed, wounded, or captured totaled 2,326. The Confederate tally was 10,052, almost 1,800 of whom were killed, including six generals!

One of them was Hiram B. Grandbury, from the Seventh Texas, who had been promoted to brigade command. Another was Patrick R. Cleburne, who was felled by a single shot through the heart at the age of thirty-six.[9] Cleburne died in exactly the same way and at the same age as Randal McGavock.

Private Martin Fleming of E Company, Sons of Erin, was killed. One of the Irishmen was wounded but not captured, another was captured but not wounded, and nine others were both wounded and captured for total losses of twelve or precisely one-third of the thirty-six lads engaged.[10]

The wounded and captured group included drummer boy Danny McCarthy of Clarksville, then seventeen and an officially registered private in the Confederate Army. Private McCarthy, the youngest of the Sons of Erin, had been shot in the chest. As he later recalled, he was carried off by the Union litter-bearers.[11] His only sensation was the cold winter wind whipping across the battlefield. He tried to speak but nothing came out. The wind howled and howled. And then there was nothing but darkness.

Danny McCarthy's "nothing but darkness" is an apt description of that sad period in American history, when the South's cause was collapsing in dreary defeat, taking with it all the resources, human and economic, that had propped it up. It is astounding that the Southern soldiers in general, and the Sons of Erin in particular, did not bolt from the army.

General Schofield retired with two of his three divisions north to Nashville, reinforcing General Thomas, but giving General Hood a chance to retreat south without pursuit. The insanity continued, as the big Texan followed in Schofield's path. This time Hood was after Thomas; no human logic can possibly explain it. As the rag-tag remnant of the once proud Army of Tennessee marched north, the Nashville area became covered with ice and snow. Many of the men were barefoot.

The marching continued, little balls of cornmeal and rancid bacon were consumed if any could be found, camp was made and broken.

At the end of any war shreds of honor and hope, outlandish rumors, paranoia and almost suicidal last-ditch attempts fuel the low-burning fires of the spirit that make the losers fight on when the cause is about to die. They may be all that keeps the defeated soldier on his feet.

In the case of the Sons of Erin, the case differs only slightly. The Tenth Tennessee had been founded by Randal McGavock on the principle of Irish pride. The fierce sense of loyalty to Irish-America had never wavered though the leaders had changed: the torch was passed from McGavock to William Grace to John G. O'Neill. The very last of the Tennessee Irish warriors had to keep fighting, had to keep the tiny regiment viable because of an idea those brave leaders had shown them: that Irishmen in America had a right to their pride and the chance to show their strength.

Then there was also Irish common sense. To youthful John G. O'Neill and his twenty-three Irishmen, the war was already lost, and they were already killed, wounded or captured. This fatalistic attitude, coupled with a sense of enduring honor, allowed them to tolerate the desperate conduct of a badly crippled commanding general in a floundering war effort.

Every history that has ever been written about the Irish in America has neglected to mention the existence of those last twenty-four lads who proudly called themselves the Sons of Erin. It must be noted, however, that the horrible winter of 1864-65 was the finest hour of the Tenth Tennessee Infantry Regiment of Volunteers(Irish)C.S.A. The Tennessee Irish had won the right to be called Southern American patriots.

The Position of the the Sons of Erin at Franklin Wednesday, November 30, 1864

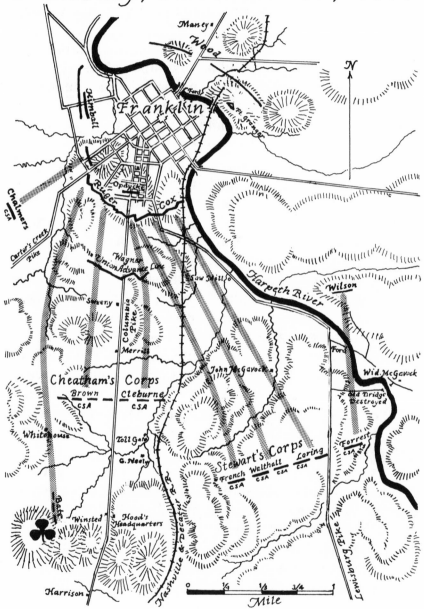

Meanwhile Hood detached Bate, Benton Smith, O'Neill and the Sons of Erin from Cheatham and sent them thirty miles southeast of Nashville to the war-torn town of Mur–freesborough, with instructions to destroy the bridges, there-by preventing Thomas from being reinforced. Hood was apparently the only army commanding general of the war who could be bleeding to death, cornered on all four sides, and worrying about the enemy getting away from him, all at the same time.

In addition to the three brigades of Generals Jesse Finley, Henry Jackson and Benton Smith, including the Sons of Erin, General Bate's detachment was given two other units—a Tennessee brigade from General S. D. Lee's corps and a Mississippi brigade from General A. P. Stewart's corps.

According to the latest Confederate scouting report, the Federals had evacuated the town. The report was wrong.[12] After some skirmishing along Overall Creek, the Sons of Erin arrived in Murfreesborough on the morning of December 4, right behind two Confederate cavalry divisions commanded by Major General Nathan Bedford Forrest.[13] The Confeder-ates found the place fortified by seven-thousand Federals, an infantry division detached from Thomas under Major Gen-eral Lovell H. Rousseau and a federalized militia division of East Tennessee cavalrymen under Major General Robert H. Milroy.

That same evening Bate probed the Union line with his Georgia/Florida/Mississippi/Tennessee infantry, sustaining fifteen killed and fifty-nine wounded. During the probe Benton Smith deployed a line of skirmishers that was a combination of the Fourth Georgia Battalion Sharpshooters and the twen-ty-four Irishmen of the Tenth Tennessee.[14] The skirmishing continued for the next two days, all the while with the South-erners outside the town and the Northerners inside.

The battle of Wednesday, December 7, involved both sides launching a reconnaissance-in-force at the same time. Forrest charged with his troopers and some of Bate's front line veterans, while Rousseau charged with one of Milroy's brigades leading the way. Suffering from fatigue and battle-

shock, most of Bate's regulars fled to the rear in panic, leav–
ing Forrest with infantry support from only Benton Smith's
troops, numbering less than two hundred effectives. Bate
tried to rally his front line but failed. Lieutenant Colonel
O'Neill and the Sons of Erin hung tough as sharpshooters,
their fire covering the cavalry probe. It was for this strong
effort that youthful Benton Smith praised youthful John G.
O'Neill for "gallantry."[15] This engagement at Murfreesborough
was indecisive, leaving both sides in the same position.
However, at that stage of the conflict, a draw was really a
Union victory.

    While the Sons of Erin were on detached duty, John
Bell Hood continued to push the exhausted remnant of his
army up to Nashville—fifteen-thousand half-frozen and half-
starved infantrymen. They were supposed to conduct a
"siege" against some seventy-thousand Boys-In-Blue from
two army groups, commanded by the "Rock of Chickamauga,"
dug in behind two miles of logworks, inside of what was perhaps the most strongly fortified town in America.

    Needing all the help he could get, General Hood or-
dered General Bate back up toward the main body of the
army. On December 9 Bate's boys-in-rags began their freezing
thirty-mile trek northwest, with the Fourth Georgia Battalion
Sharpshooters and the Tenth Tennessee serving as rear
guards for the detached division.[16] They arrived on December 15, just in time to see other Southerners retreating in front
of them during the first day of the Battle of Nashville.

    By this time practical necessity forced General Tho-
mas Benton Smith to divide his "brigade" into two consolidated regiments that were each the size of one company. The
two Georgia units were combined into the Thirty-Seventh/
Fourth Georgia consolidated regiment, and all the Tennesseans, including the Sons of Erin, were combined into the

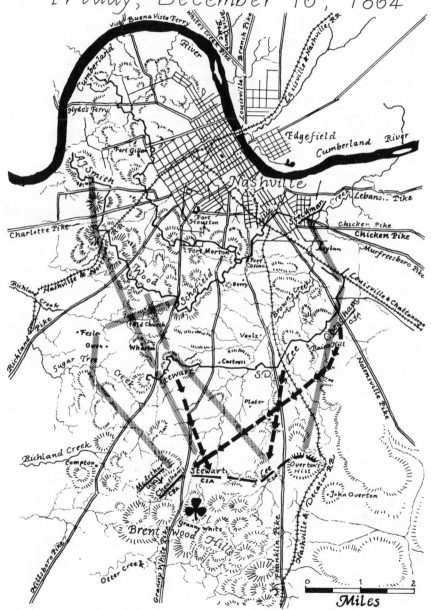

The Position of the Sons of Erin at Nashville Friday, December 16, 1864

Second/Tenth/Fifteenth/Twentieth/Thirtieth/Thirty-Seventh Tennessee consolidated regiment commanded by Lieutenant Colonel William W. Shy of the Twentieth Tennessee instead of the wounded Lieutenant Colonel James J. Turner of the Thirtieth Tennessee.

W.W. Shy had a few days' seniority on Lieutenant Colonel John G. O'Neill of the Tenth Tennessee, who was the second ranking healthy officer in the Tennessee consolidated regiment.[17] The consolidated Tennesseans of Benton Smith had fewer than one-hundred men, and Smith's consolidated Georgians had fewer than that.

Brigadier General John McArthur, the Scottish Chicagoan from the Vicksburg campaign, commanded a division in Major General Andrew Jackson Smith's Sixteenth corps of General Thomas' army. At 9 a.m. on December 16, McArthur assaulted the position assigned to General Bate along the Brentwood Hills with the five regiments of his First brigade under Colonel William L. McMillen, an Ohioan who suffered from acute alcoholism and nervous tension.

After a heavy bombardment from his artillery, Colonel McMillen attacked and surrounded the section of the ridge held by the Tennessee consolidated regiment. Lieutenant Colonel Shy was killed defending the hill that bears his name and Lieutenant Colonel O'Neill, ably assisted by First Lieutenant Lynch Donoho, took command of the Tennesseans and Irishmen still on Shy's hill.[18] Generals Thomas Benton Smith and Henry Jackson organized a withdrawal down the right rear slope of the hill but were captured, along with most of their men, by McMillen's original command, the Ninety-Fifth Ohio Infantry regiment.

While being conducted to the rear as an unarmed prisoner of war, Benton Smith, 26, was savagely and repeatedly struck over the head with a blunt sword by McMillen. At the field hospital it was found that Smith's brain was exposed and his death was expected imminently. It didn't happen. Only his mind died. Thomas Benton Smith spent the last forty-seven years of his life as a vegetable in the Tennessee State

Asylum at Nashville.[19]

This kind of brutality toward prisoners became all too common on both sides during the last several months of that horrible war of attrition.

General William Bate escaped and in spite of having six horses shot out from under him to go along with three battle wounds, survived to become one of Tennessee's most beloved favorite sons, twice being elected governor and twice being elected to the United States Senate. Sixty-four of the men from his three brigades also escaped, separately as individuals, mostly officers on horseback.[20]

During the December 15-16 Battle of Nashville, the Federals had 387 men killed and 2,562 wounded for total losses of 2,949, while General Hood reported Confederate losses to be "very small." Confederates killed and wounded probably totaled 1,500. One thing was certain in General Thomas' report: the number of Confederates captured was 4,462.[21] Most of the Southerners who didn't get killed at Franklin got captured at Nashville. The Army of Tennessee was decimated.

General John Bell Hood, deeply distraught, resigned his army command. (After the war he married and had eleven children in ten years, before being killed by yellow fever, something that the Yankees could never accomplish.) In spite of his horrendous performance at the top, the big Texan is still considered one of America's best combat officers at the brigade level.

The Sons of Erin lost twenty captured out of twenty-four, including two who were also wounded. One of those captured was Corporal Mike Carney, the harmonica player, who was one of McGavock's precinct captains in the St. Patrick's Club.[22] Three escaped on horseback and one Irishman wasn't present with the regiment on December 16.

Of the thirty-one lads captured at Franklin and Nashville, twenty-nine survived imprisonment and the war. Private Patrick O'Donnell of K Company, captured at Nashville, died in Camp Chase on January 17, 1865. Private James

Haggerty of I Company, captured at Franklin, died in Camp Chase on February 3, 1865. Haggerty had been wounded, but O'Donnell had not.[23] The final toll of prison deaths for the Tenth Tennessee was twenty-six.

Surrender in North Carolina

The remnant of the Army of Tennessee fell back into Mississippi and regrouped at Tupelo in January of 1865. The two consolidated regiments from General Benton Smith's brigade were combined into a single unit officially identified as the Thirty-Seventh/FourthGeorgia/Second/Tenth/Fifteenth/Twentieth/Thiritieth/Thirty-Seventh Tennessee consolidated regiment, commanded by Colonel Anderson Searcy of Brigadier General Joseph Palmer's brigade. This command had sixty-five soldiers, including the four lads remaining in the Sons of Erin.[24]

The Confederate Western army was reinforced from the Trans-Mississippi, and by February was up to some 21,000 men. On February 22, General Joseph E. Johnston was again assigned to lead the Army of Tennessee. Johnston marched east to try his luck a second time with General William T. Sherman.

Tennessean Joseph Palmer's brigade, including the four Irish Tennesseans, was assigned to Tennessean Frank Cheatham's corps, but the two corps of Generals Cheatham and A.P. Stewart were so small that they were deployed as a single brigade, commanded by Stewart, another Tennessean.[25] The last-ditch Confederate effort to locate and turn back Sherman had no hope of success.

Johnston did give Sherman's left wing a hard fight at Bentonville, North Carolina, on March 19, only to be battered back with 195 killed, 1,313 wounded, and 610 captured for total losses of 2,118. Three of the four lads from the Sons of Erin were engaged and captured in this last battle. They were Lieutenant Colonel John G. O'Neill, Captain Lewis R. Clark, and First Lieutenant Robert Paget Seymour.[26]

322

The Last Stand of the Sons of Erin
Bentonville, North Carolina
Sunday, March 19, 1865

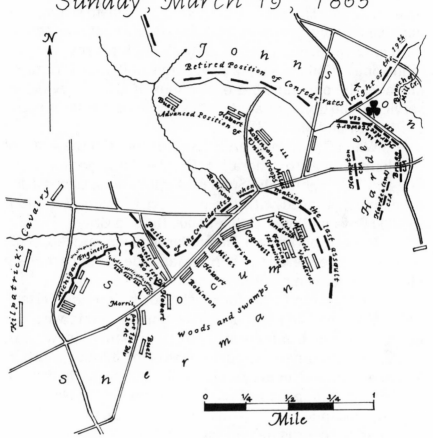

Of the 725 lads who started out at Fort Henry, exactly one was still on duty in the Confederate Army.

After the battle of Bentonville, the largest original unit remaining in Colonel Searcy's Tennessee consolidated regiment was the Fifteenth Tennessee, nine men strong and commanded by youthful Irish-American First Lieutenant Patrick Lavin. Lavin needed an Irish cook for his men. He found one in Commissary Master Sergeant Bernard "Barney" McCabe, the only member of the Sons of Erin to see active service in the Confederate Army every day between September 1, 1861 and May 1, 1865.[27]

When General Robert E. Lee surrendered the Army of Northern Virginia to General U.S. Grant at Appomattox Courthouse, Virginia, on Palm Sunday, April 9, 1865, General Joe Johnston was faced with the prospect of taking on about 250,000 Boys-in-Blue with his 18,000 Boys-in-Gray.

Outside of Durham, North Carolina, on April 26, 1865, Johnston surrendered to Sherman, and the worst part of the ultimate American nightmare was over.

On May 1 at Greensborough, North Carolina, O'Neill, Clark, Seymour, and McCabe were paroled along with the other Western Confederates.[28] Clark made his way to Clarksville, where he fostered the myth of the "Bloody Tenth."[29] McCabe returned home to Nashville, where he became a prominent and prosperous businessman.[30] O'Neill and Seymour disappeared from history, leaving no post-war Federal or state records behind them.

The fighting on the battlefields was history. But for the Sons of Erin, and many like them, the real fight lay ahead. It was the fight for survival in the harsh, post-war world of the Reconstructed South.

The Last Toll

All of the Irish lads were captured or escaped at Fort Donelson. Several of them were captured again, and 221 of them deserted, all of whom had previously been captured or escaped. So the total number of Irishmen captured, escaped, or deserted greatly exceeds the total number of Irishmen, rendering such numbers as meaningless. On top of this there were no casualties in the regiment for the first two years of the war.

All of the battlefield losses came after the tour of duty at Port Hudson, involving only 254 of the original 720 combatants. The losses resulted exclusively from service in the Western armies of Pemberton, Bragg, Joe Johnston, and Hood.

Discounting the meaningless numbers of captured, escaped and deserted, the Tenth Tennessee suffered thirty killed and ninety-one seriously wounded for total losses of 121 or seventeen percent of the original 720 combatants. However, the numbers can be looked at it in another way. Considering only the second half of the war, there were 121 casualties out of 254 lads or forty-eight percent of the effectives!

In reality the number 720 represents the total combatants present for duty at Forts Henry and Donelson only. The actual fighting regiment of McGavock, Grace, and O'Neill was represented by the 254 Irishmen who participated in three battles—Raymond, Chickamauga, Missionary Ridge and two campaigns—J. Johnston/Hood/Atlanta and Hood/Tennessee.

In any case, by any modern military standard, 121 casualties out of anything less than a thousand is considered catastrophic. In Confederate regimental terms, the number 121 was relatively low. This is why the sobriquet "Bloody Tenth" ("Bloody Tinth") doesn't really apply to the Sons of Erin, except in the sense that all Civil War regiments were the bloody something. Of course, no figures were kept, or even known, about the number of casualties inflicted on the enemy by the Sons of Erin. Certainly, though, those numbers are much higher than 121.

In addition to the thirty lads killed or mortally wounded in battle, there were the twenty-six who died in confinement, plus the ten who died of disease in Mississippi. Sixty-six is the total number of lads who gave their lives for the Southern cause, a significant contribution, indeed.

It is well to recall that the Tenth Tennessee was a small unit of Irish laborers, whose job it was to construct the two inland river forts. They were hired on and regarded as engineers more than they were thought of as infantrymen. Considering the sense of betrayal they felt, the fact that they came back at all after a half year in Federal prison camp was a tribute to the spirit of McGavock and the Sons of Erin.

In the Army of Tennessee, the Irishmen consistently did well as skirmishers and sharpshooters from a defensive deployment. Their true record was an honorable one; the myth never served them well. Like so may other American soldiers, before and after, who did their job and did it well, they deserve to be remembered.

Postscript

Last Will and Testament

Toward the end of that same year of 1865, the Nashville home of Colonel Adolphus Heiman, which had been confiscated by a harsh and vengeful Governor Andrew Johnson, was returned to its rightful estate. The property was sold for $11,000. According to the last will and testament, the money was sent to the colonel's brother, Louis, and his sister, Henrietta, both still living in Prussia.[1]

The bitterness that had been fostered by the Union governor of Tennessee and others like him was at least partly undone by one honest and courageous public servant in Washington City who later rejected the harsher measures of Reconstruction and did his best to reunite the people of North and South. It was he who presided over policies which returned Heiman's home. In the process he risked his own political career. He was Andrew Johnson, one of the most pleasant surprises of the American presidency.

Home to Nashville

Appropriately it was St. Patrick's Day of 1866. Nearly three years after his death, the body of Randal W. McGavock was transferred from the Columbus, Mississippi Dickerson family graveyard to be re-interred at Mount Olivet Cemetery, Nashville. The notice had appeared the previous day in *The Nashville Dispatch*, with a lengthy story, describing the colonel's exploits from City Hall to the Vicksburg campaign.

"The friends of Mr. and Mrs. Jacob McGavock are requested to meet on Saturday, the 17th, at 11:00 at their residence to convey the remains of their son, the late colonel, to the family vault," the newspaper instructed. The burial was handled with dignified pomp and ceremony by the Phoenix Lodge, Order of Free Masons. A large crowd assembled, including most of the city's Irish, most especially the veterans of the Sons of Erin. The lads bid farewell to "God's own gentle-

327

man."

Seph, still beautiful at age thirty-one, continued to live with Jacob and Louisa, devoting her time to the Robertson Association and the cause of the poor. In 1868 she married an older man by the name of Judge Connally F. Trigg, a pro-Union Knoxville East Tennessean. The second marriage, like the first, was childless. Trigg died in 1880.[2]

The Bloody Tenth

Colonel McGavock's brother-in-law, Dr. John B. Lindsley, put together his military history of Tennessee in 1886. It was a serial for subscribers only, and included the seven-page text of Captain Lewis R. Clark of the Tenth Tennessee and Clarksville.

The account includes poetry, including one snippet about Colonel Heiman's death that describes the expiring colonel: "Like one that wraps the drapery of his couch about him, and lies down to pleasant dreams," all of which was about as enlightening as the casualty figures Lew quoted.[3] Captain Clark's text, devoid of Irish dialect was straight-forward. Its two most quoted words were "Bloody Tenth."

Missing No Longer

Benedictine Father Otto Kopf had been looking for the whereabouts of his friend for twenty-five years. In 1889 the Benedictines were invited to Alabama for the purpose of founding a new mission parish at Tuscumbia. Not long after he arrived, a local ex-Confederate told Father Otto that another German priest by the name of "Father Bluemel" had been killed in action at Jonesborough.

Father Otto traveled down to Georgia, where he was well received by some ex-Confederates at the cemetery. They gladly allowed him to take the remains back home. What was re-interred at St. Mary's parish cemetery in Tuscumbia was a small black box of headless bones.

Well into the twentieth century, in magazines and in

newspapers, the survivors of both the Tenth Tennessee and the Fourth Kentucky proclaimed Father Emmeran Bliemel to be their champion. Today a large stone cross marks the grave of the priest of St. Benedict, who was known only as Father Emery to the Sons of Erin.[4]

The Death of a Soldier

State of Tennessee Veterans Pension Application No. 153 was granted at Nashville on June 4 of 1891. The recipient had been totally disabled for the previous sixteen years, a proud Irish lad who had no job, no income, and no visible means of support. The examining physician had been alarmed at the condition of the old soldier, and duly noted that he was missing a left arm and a right thumb; in addition his left leg was paralyzed, and he could barely see.

The Confederate veteran, born in Ireland fifty-one years earlier, died the following spring, alone and forgotten, never to benefit from his $300 per year army pension.[5] If a unit history accomplishes nothing else it may give the tip of the fatigue hat to a few people who don't deserve to be forgotten. From this day on, almost exactly one-hundred years after his passing, First Lieutenant "Long Tom" Connor will always be remembered as the very best rifleman of the Sons of Erin.

Port Hudson Reunion
Thirty-Fifth Anniversary

In 1898 Patrick M. Griffin and the little auburn-haired girl that he had married were vacationing in San Francisco, watching Admiral George Dewey's fleet come home, when an old friend, William Foote of the Sons of Erin just happened to stroll by. The two lads hadn't seen each other in thirty-five years, since Pat escaped to Memphis, leaving "Tinfoot" behind on the steamer.

As they watched Dewey's ships come into the bay,

they laughed and slapped each other on their backs, remembering that time at Port Hudson when their Rebel gunners had blown that same Yankee sailor out of the water. Pat never gave a sucker an even break. It was here that Griffin collected from Foote the five dollar bet from another Yankee on a boat, Captain Elias Neff of the Fifty-First Indiana.[6]

Fort Donelson Reunion
Fortieth Anniversary

The General Frank Cheatham Camp of the United Confederate Veterans was active in the Nashville area, sponsoring many events that were celebrated in a downtown hotel. At the beginning of 1902, the officers of the camp organized a reunion for the Confederate survivors of Fort Donelson.

The former Rebels were decked out in new gray uniforms that were covered with citations and medals, some of which were self-awarded. Men who had never risen above the rank of private were now captains, majors, and even colonels. Most had kept their period beards, which were long since out of vogue. Long white facial hair covered the faces of the former soldiers, mostly in their sixties and seventies, many with crutches or in wheelchairs.

Some 150 veterans turned out, a few of them representing the Sons of Erin. Present and accounted for were Sam Thompson, without a foot, Tom Gibson, the shoe-forager, Pat Griffin, the story-teller, and Mike Carney, the harmonica-player. Surprisingly the host, the owner of the hotel where the reunion was held, was also a former member of the Tenth Tennessee. At the age of sixty-eight, Commissary Master Sergeant Barney McCabe was still providing rations for the lads. As he did on all such occasions at McCabe's Hotel, the jovial old Irishman went from table to table, reminding the Boys-in-Gray about the time when his hard head stopped a Yankee ball in North Georgia.[7]

The Bloody Tinth

In 1905, compatriot S.A. Cunningham, a veteran of the Forty-First Tennessee, was the editor of the *Confederate Veteran Magazine*. Featured in the December issue was a prominent article about a close personal friend of his, "Captain" Patrick M. Griffin of the Tenth Tennessee.

The Irishman had presented his paper at one of the regular meetings of the General Frank Cheatham Camp.[8] The magazine preserved the lengthy presentation word for word. "The Famous Tenth" was the title; the "Bloody Tinth" was the best remembered expression. Pat Griffin's published account has made a remarkable contribution to American history. It left future researchers in a state of total confusion as to the true history of the Sons of Erin.

Widows

In the 1890s many Confederate and Union Tennessee veterans were beginning to receive regular pension checks. When they passed away, their widows, a few of whom had married the Sons of Erin, were able to apply for the funds.

By 1909 the following widows were receiving army pensions: Mrs. John L. Prendergast, Mrs. Thomas Gibson, Mrs. William Foote, Mrs. Morris Fitzgerald, Mrs. William Fitzgerald, and Mrs. James Doyle.

Mrs. Doyle, as it turned out, had not been married to diarist Jimmy Doyle, but to a lad from the Nineteenth Massachusetts![9]

The Diamond Lady

President Woodrow Wilson and the U.S. Government had become entangled in the Great European War. In 1917 Mrs. Augustus Pettibone, 82, stood on the steps of Mrs. J. D.

331

Waller's boarding house on Seventh Avenue and watched the volunteer companies from Nashville march to the train station. Men going off to war was a sight she had seen before.

Her husband was Major A. H. Pettibone, also 82, a Union veteran of Steedman's Hill and former congressman, who was then a retired official of the U.S. Department of Agriculture. The two of them were regarded as "local characters." He had a long, white, unkempt beard and spent most of his time in drinking establishments. She was obese and wrinkled, and made herself look even worse by covering the lines in her cheeks with layers of rouge and powder, all topped off with a ridiculous brown wig.

About the only time that Mr. and Mrs. Pettibone were seen together was on Sunday when they strolled arm in arm down the aisle of the First Presbyterian Church. Women in the pews murmured behind their fans that the dresses and silly hats Mrs. Pettibone wore were designed for much younger women. They gawked at her diamonds, which it was said had been a wedding present from her first husband long ago.

None could remember a more pretentious person than old Mrs. Pettibone, putting on airs, demanding special treatment. "She sat up front with me. So I can't say that she was a backseat driver. I *can* say that she was one big pill," was the judgment of auto-rental driver Duncan Dorris.[10] One day Dorris had the distinction of driving a car full of ladies from Nashville out to the Hermitage for an observance of Andrew Jackson's birthday. Mrs. Pettibone was constantly agitated, nervous, and nearly hysterical, accusing him of speeding, churning up dust, and reckless driving all the way there and back.

The old woman was like that all the time—vain, helpless, insufferable, an expert at superficialities. No one seemed to like her, including Major Pettibone, especially Major Pettibone. She insisted on dragging him off to gala balls, where he became drunk and she became the source of much mockery.

As a small child Miss Annie Lindsley Warden begged

her aunt to tell her stories about the Civil War. The usual answer was: "But dear Annie, child, I was too young to remember anything about that war." In the Nashville census of 1910, Mrs. Pettibone listed her age as fifty-eight, instead of seventy-five. This meant that when first married in 1855, as public records proved, she was exactly three years old. (The 1860 census gave her age as twenty-five.)

During that wartime winter of 1917-1918, the old woman was affected with two severe attacks of the grippe and was confined to her room for three months, abandoned by her husband, attended to only by the kindly Mrs. Waller. In January she was not strong enough to attend the Jackson Day Ball, the biggest social event of her declining years.

Old and unloved, a butterfly to the last, she died on March 20, 1918. Obituaries appeared in both *The Nashville Banner* and *The Nashville Tennessean*. The deceased had been married three times, and had borne no children. Her second and third husbands were mentioned, but not her first. Because of her fixation about age, she never talked about him, so very few people even knew about the original marriage.

Since she was so impressed by "social position" that denial was really ironic. The first husband had been Mayor of Nashville and a war hero. But all of that had been so many years before, when Mrs. Pettibone was a stunning beauty, the First Lady of Nashville known as Seraphine Deery McGavock.

The Questionnaire

Private W.S. Lunn was one of the lads who did picket duty at the Paris Landing near Fort Henry on the evening of Friday, January 31, 1862. "Lunny" Lunn kept a low profile for the next sixty years and surfaced again in 1922. Between 1915 and 1922, about 1,600 Tennessee veterans of the Civil War were sent questionnaires as part of a state research project. Historians wanted insights into the routine of antebellum life. W. S. Lunn was the only survivor of the Sons of

Erin to send back a completed form.[11] Here is a sampling of the forty-six questions and his answers.

1) Q. State your full name:
    A. W. S. Lunn.

2) Q. State your present age:
    A. Borne 1840.

4) Q. Were you a Confederate soldier or a Federal soldier?
    A. Yes.

9) Q. State your ancestry:
    A. None.

10) Q. Did you own property at the opening of the war?
    A. None

11) Q. Did your parents own slaves?
    A. None

14) Q. What kind of house did your parents occupy?
    A. Log.

15) Q. As a boy what kind of work did you do?
    A. House.

16) Q. State clearly the kind of work your father did:
    A. Done all kinds.

20) Q. To what extent were there white men in your community leading lives of idleness and having others do their work for them?
    A. All straight and upright.

25)   Q.   Were the opportunities good in your community for a poor young man, honest and industrious, to save up enough to buy a small farm or go in business for himself?

         A.   All stuck to one another.

27)   Q.   What kind of schools did you attend?

         A.   Plaine log.

28)   Q.   About how long did you go to school all together?

         A.   1 year or more.

29)   Q.   How far was it to the nearest school?

         A.   Aboute too miles.

32)   Q.   How many months in the year did it run?

         A.   Too tearmes.

34)   Q.   Was your teacher a man or a woman?

         A.   Both.

35)   Q.   What was your company?

         A.   I company 10 tenn. irish regament.

42)   Q.   What church do you attend?

         A.   Blacksmith.

43)   Q.   What is your occupation?

         A.   Cumberland presbyterian church.

44)   Q.   Give the names of some of the great men you have known in your life:

         A.   ———

46)   Q.   Give the names and addresses of other surviving members of your company:

         A.   All ded I supose.

"Lunny" was wrong about the last question. Not all of the lads were "ded."

Grandpaw

A vegetarian sociopath in Germany was attacking everything that moved, plus a few things that didn't. Because one of her sons was a career army officer, Barbara Ahern was concerned about the possibility of America's getting involved again. Her grandfather had always warned her about what a terrible thing war was.

It was a typical blustery mid-January evening in Boston, Massachusetts during the year of 1940. A very old man lay dying in the home of his oldest granddaughter, then middle-aged herself. George and Barbara had several children, all grown, who had children of their own, who had children of their own. Two other people lived with them in the big wood-frame house.

Erlene Reese was the housekeeper-cook who had been with the family for years. Well up in her years, "Miz Reez" as Barbara called her, was no longer able to do much work, but was still considered a member of the family. Barbara's grandfather referred to the aging domestic as "That old colored lady," even though he was about ten years older than she was.

The fourth member of the household was the old man himself—*Granpaw*—as he pronounced it. There was a lyrical, almost magical quality to his voice, a wee bit of a brogue mixed in with a faint Southern drawl. In fact the old lad had an excellent singing voice. He had been a small time song-and-dance man whose career paralleled almost exactly the era of vaudeville.

The aged Irishman had lived in Philadelphia, New York and Boston, but mostly had been on the road, with his wife and children at his side. Unlike Irish-Americans George M. Cohan and Eddie Foy, he hadn't used them in his act. Also unlike Irish-Americans George M. Cohan and Eddie Foy, he wasn't rich and famous. Near eighty when he retired in the mid-1920s, he never gave up his active life, though.

Everyone called him "Grandpaw," and some had forgotten what his name really was. Not an Irish soul could remember a man as good and kind and generous as Barbara Ahern's grandfather. During the Great Depression he visited children's hospitals, doing his old soft shoe, along with a few card tricks that he had learned at a place called Fort Henry, he said.

Kids loved Grandpaw and he loved them. He had a strange but wonderful custom of giving a new pair of shoes to a different poor child every Christmas.

Grandpaw also visited veterans' hospitals. The misfortunes of those patients moved him a good deal. He was interested in marches, drills, parades and all things quasi-military. There was an organization called the United Veterans of the Grand Old Army that Grandpaw exchanged good-natured barbs with. He had once been a soldier himself, having been wounded in action at one of the bloodiest battles in American history.

Mrs. Reese was Barbara's friend. For hours on end they would talk and knit. Grandpaw was her husband George's friend. The two men would listen to the radio—Red Sox baseball games, Notre Dame football games, "The Shadow," "Jack Benny," "Amos And Andy," "Fibber McGee and Molly." All of this, of course, was before the stroke.

Grandpaw lived a full, happy and healthy life for ninety years, until a serious stroke knocked him for a loop early in 1938. "The never-ending smile was wiped off his face, and the twinkle went out of his sparkling blue eyes." There was never to be a recovery or even a rally. For nearly two years the old man was unaware of what was going on around him.

The family doctor had predicted his demise many times, only to be proven wrong by Grandpaw's tenacious spirit. The last forecast had him departing the world well before Christmas of 1939. In the middle of January, he somehow managed to cling to a life that had been so precious to him, as if it had all been on borrowed time.

Barbara mentioned to George and Mrs. Reese that he looked truly terrible. It was hard to believe that the "tiny rag-pile of loose flesh on bones" had once been her grandfather, that he had fought heroically in the War Between the States. The Aherns knew that they had been blessed by his long life. There could be no regrets, only fond and lasting memories.

As they were musing a sudden gust of wind howled outside the window next to Grandpaw's bed. Apparently, the old lad heard it, too. He opened his eyes and tried to speak, but nothing came out. The wind howled and howled and howled. And then there was nothing but darkness.

Seventy-five years and forty-seven days after being carried off the battlefield at Franklin, drummer boy Danny McCarthy was gone.[12] And with him the Sons of Erin passed forever into American history.

Epilogue

Hero Number Eighteen

A grand ceremony took place on a cold, clear, windy day in Clayton County, Georgia on Saturday, March 12, 1983. Of all of the approximately 700,000 men who had been active in Confederate service between 1861 and 1865, there had been only seventeen winners of the Confederate Medal of Honor, as presented by the Sons of Confederate Veterans.

On that day there would be a recipient number eighteen of the posthumous award which, on this particular occasion, was sponsored by the General Patrick R. Cleburne Camp No. 1361, Sons of Confederate Veterans. Medals were presented only to those individuals who had given their lives for the Southern cause by performing acts far above and beyond the call of duty. It was a glorious day for the Sons of Erin—Hero Number Eighteen had been a member of the Tenth Tennessee! After Pat Cleburne himself, the chosen lad would be remembered as the most decorated Irish-American Southern soldier of them all.

Dignitaries had come from all over the country. A parade, featuring bands and battle flags and folks in colorful period costumes and politicians and clergymen, made their way to the Clayton County Courthouse, Jonesboro, Georgia. At 2:00 p.m. the eighteenth Confederate Medal of Honor was presented to a distinguished Confederate veteran who had been gone for 118 years. The inscription on the monument says it all.

IN MEMORIAM
Dedicated to
Fr. Emmeran Bliemel O.S.B., Chaplain
10th Tennessee Regiment C.S.A.
Killed In Action, August 31, 1864
Battle Of Jonesboro

As it turns out, the most decorated Irish-American Southern soldier of them all wasn't Irish or American or Southern or a soldier.

Randy Mack's Last Gala Ball

The Middle Tennessee Civil War Round Table placed a new marker at the foot of Colonel Randal W. McGavock's grave, laying it flat in front of the family marker. In the shade of towering trees and monuments, some seventy guests gathered for the ceremony at Nashville's Mount Olivet Cemetery. A picnic table stood right on the lawn. Cookies and punch were served. It was July of 1987.

Miss Margaret Lindsley Warden, the great-niece of the colonel, organized and presided over the event. Timothy Burgess explained the trail of the round table from the Raymond graveyard to the presentation of the new marker. Dr. Herschel Gower outlined the life of the leader known to the Sons of Erin as "Randy Mack."[2]

It has been reported in Nashville that when a full moon

appears over Mount Olivet you can still see him riding Tenth Legion, waving his gray red-lined hat with the green feather, bidding his lads a fond farewell.

Jimmy Doyle to Margaret Bailey

The last piece of the legend of the Tenth Tennessee, a unit that technically fought to preserve the institution of slavery, was provided by the granddaughter of a slave, Mrs. Margaret Bailey, 93, of Boston.

It was Thursday, May 30, 1991. The package that had arrived at the tiny village post office of Southwest Suburban Chicago, Oak Lawn, was in response to a letter in the May issue of the *Civil War News*. The package contained the Diary of Jimmy Doyle and the letters that Mrs. Barbara Ahern had sent to Mrs. Margaret Bailey on the occasion of the death of Mrs. Bailey's mother, Mrs. Erlene Reese.

It had been an odd chain of events. Sometime during or after the war, Private Jimmy Doyle passed his diary on to Private Danny McCarthy. When Grandpaw died, George and Barbara Ahern inherited the diary. When Mrs. Reese died, Barbara presented the diary to Mrs. Reese's daughter, Margaret, as a gift. In turn, Mrs. Bailey, with great kindness, sent the diary to the researcher who was investigating the history of the Tenth Tennessee. The final eyewitness source for this book can, therefore, be referred to as Doyle/McCarthy/Ahern/Reese/Bailey.

An Irish Blessing
Dedicated to Margaret Bailey

May the road rise to meet you
May the wind be always at your back,
May the rain fall soft upon your field
And, until we meet again,
May God hold you in the hollow of his hand.

Appendix

Muster Roll

A complete roster of names is a research project in itself and a real adventure. It's a process that begins in the dusty basements of some old buildings, and winds up as oversized postage and phone bills. To understand something about where the names come from, it helps to understand a little about where, when, and how the regiment was developed. The formation of Colonel McGavock's original company is an easy-to-trace example.

On April 15, 1861, the ex-mayor of Nashville announced his intention to raise a volunteer company. As a unit D Company was registered in the Tennessee state militia at Nashville on May 9. One-hundred-twenty-four home guards went up to Dover on May 25 to become the largest company of the future regiment. At Fort Donelson on May 29, Colonel Heiman mustered his men and McGavock's Irish lads individually and collectively into his new state militia regiment. Between July 9 and August 31, thirty-two of the 124 men in D Company, mostly non-Irishmen, transferred to other units.

At Fort Henry on September 1, ninety-two lads of the old state militia company were mustered into regular Confederate service as H Company of the Tenth Tennessee Infantry Regiment Of Volunteers (Irish), Confederate Army. At Clinton, Mississippi, on October 2, 1862, thirty-three of those ninety-two Irishmen registered for three more years of Confederate service as F Company of the reorganized Tenth Tennessee. The same pattern is evident in the other nine companies of the regiment, all going from small to tiny units.

Tennesseans In The Civil War, Part Two, *A Military History Of Confederate And Union Units With Available Rosters Of Personnel,* an incredible alphabetical list of eighty-thousand Tennessee soldiers, is as much a hindrance as a help, due to repetitions, omissions, and mistaken identifications of companies and regiments. To add to the confusion, Stanley Horn and his editors threw in the names of all of the Irish and non-Irish alike who were from the Nineteenth Massachusetts—the Federals who got out of Andersonville by signing up for the Tenth Tennessee in the Confederate Army.

An accurate roster for the Sons of Erin can be pieced together by utilizing original muster rolls and service records from both the National Archives in Washington D.C. and the Tennessee State Library in Nashville. State pension records for veterans and widows are also helpful. This final muster roll includes every member who served at least one day in regular Confederate service within the regiment between September 1, 1861, and May 1, 1865. Those who were home guards only are not included, simply because no muster rolls survive from the time prior to official army service.

Most of Heiman's militiamen between May 29 and August 31, 1861, were Middle Tennessee Irish-Americans. As regulars between September 1, 1861, and October 2, 1862, about half of the commissioned officers were Scotch-Irish or Anglo-Irish, while most of the enlisted lads were Irish. After October 2, 1862, most of the officers and nearly all of the enlisted lads were Irish. Some of the non-Irish transferred to other units throughout the war, although no conflict has ever been reported between Irish and non-Irish members of the regiment.

The segregation of soldiers into ethnic groups was accepted practice in both armies, but much more common in the Union army, because of the immigrant population of the North. Clearly there were non-Irish in the Sons of Erin from the beginning to the end of the conflict. It's a good bet that Privates Luther S. Moore, Knude Olsen, and John Soloman weren't from the seven counties. The actual percentage of Irishmen and Irish-Americans in the regiment is hard to determine because of names such as Bradford, Branerly, Foster, Hanley, Jackson, Lee, Martin, and Parker. Nonetheless, the percentage of Irish is very high.

The company designations used here are from October 2, 1862, to May 1, 1865. Lads who transferred to companies within the regiment are listed under their last designation. The ranks reflect the highest rank earned at any time during the war. At the reorganization many of the farmers from Pulaski defected to other units from their area, but the farmers from McEwen and Clarksville stayed with the Sons of Erin. For instance not a single member of the Irish Clarksville company transferred to the all-Clarksville Fourteenth Tennessee regiment on the Eastern front. Toward the end of the war there were as many lads left in the regiment from McEwen and Clarksville as there were from Nashville.

Some members of the Irish regiment are listed by given names, others by nicknames, and all names and spellings are taken exactly as they appear in the original muster rolls. The rank "master sergeant" is consistently listed on the Tenth Tennessee muster rolls instead of the usual Confederate Army rank of "sergeant major;" the designation preferred by the adjutants of the Irish regiment is used here. The number of Sullivans and Connollys defies all logic, but you can bet that more than a few were related. Glory be to Patrick, Paddy, Patsey, Patt, and Pat!

Muster Roll

Staff Members Without Company Designations (9):
Colonel Adolphus Heiman—Original Commanding Officer
Father Henry Vincent Browne O.P.—Chaplain
Father Emmeran Bliemel O.S.B.—Chaplain
Dr. Sidney W. Franklin (Army Major)—Surgeon
Dr. Joseph M. Plunket (Army Captain)—Surgeon
Dr. A. F. Mallet—Surgeon
Dr. Alfred Voorhies—Surgeon
Dr. Dixon Horton—Surgeon
Dr. J. P. Moore—Surgeon

Original CO=1
Chaplains=2
Doctors=6

Total Non-Designated Lads=9

A Company

Almost Exclusively Country Lads From McEwen Area

Commissioned Officers (7)
Lieutenant Colonel John G. O'Neill
Captain James McMurray
Captain Charles H. Stockell
First Lieutenant James White
Second Lieutenant John Ames
Second Lieutenant William Michael Burke
Second Lieutenant Robert Dansby

Non-Commissioned Officers (8)
Master Sergeant Patrick Kirby
Master Sergeant Michael McAuliffe
Sergeant Daniel McCarty
Sergeant Bernard McMahon
Sergeant Morley O'Shea
Corporal Issac L. Colleen
Corporal Timothy Connor
Corporal John Hughes

Privates (76)

John Barrett	Anson Harrington	Patrick Mulloy
William Bradford	Edmund Hays	James Murray
Patrick Brennan	John Hays	Henry Newman
Patrick Brown	John Higgons	Michael O'Connell
Peter Callahan	Martin Joyce	Cornelius O'Donnell
W. B. Cochran	Erwin Kelly	Michael O'Donnell, No. 1
James Connolly	John Kelly	Michael O'Donnell, No. 2
Peter Connolly	Martin Kelly	David O'Hara
William Connolly	Patrick Kelly	Garrett O'Hara
John Connors	Thomas Kelly	John D. O'Sullivan
Thomas Coody	Thomas Kinney	J. W. Parker
John Cunningham	John McDonald	John Quinn
Michael Cusick	Michael McDonald	Patrick Regan
George E. Day	Mike McDowell	Timothy Regan
Patrick Dolan	John McFarland	Owen Ryan
John Donohoe	Patrick McGivney	Patrick Scanlon
John Donovan	Martin McHale	William Sharkey
Patrick Dunn	Steven McIntyre	Miles Shay
Richard Eagan	William McLane	Morris Shehan
Patrick Farland	Denis McLaughlin	Arthur Sullivan
John Farley	William A. Mentiss	Dennis Sullivan
James Farrell	John Mitchell	John Sullivan
Dennis Fehely	Lawrence Molan	Henry Walsh
Garrett Fitzgearld	Patrick Monohan	Patrick Walsh,No. 1
Patrick Flaherty	Michael Moran	Patrick Walsh,No. 2; Benjamin F. Welch

Commissioned Officers=7
Non-Commissioned Officers=8
Privates=76
Total Lads=91

B Company (Originally K)

Mostly City Lads From Nashville

Commissioned Officers (7)
Lieutenant Colonel Samuel M. Thompson
Captain John W. Bryan
First Lieutenant Felix Abby
First Lieutenant Joseph Phillips
Second Lieutenant John Dewayne
Second Lieutenant Robert Erwin
Second Lieutenant Joseph Evans

Non-Commissioned Officers(6)
Master Sergeant John Curley
Master Sergeant Gregory Glenn
Sergeant John Lee
Sergeant Patrick Long
Sergeant McLaughlin McDonald
Sergeant William McGowan

Privates (55).

Thomas Branerly
Joseph Brannon
Berry Bridges
John Carey
John Carroll
Patrick Coffee
Michael Conell
John Conelly
Patrick Conley
Jack Connelly
Coleman Connolly
Jake Connolly
James Connors
John Costello
Lawrence Costello
Barney Crahans
Dennis Curran
Duncan Duffey
Patrick Dunn

William Feeley
John Ferrans
Paddy Fitzpatrick
Tim Flaherty
Thomas Fury
Virginius Garnett
Patrick Giles
Patrick Gorman
James Harrington
James Hays
Hiram Jepperson
Pat Kean
Patrick Kearnes
George W. Kennedy
Patrick Kinney
Michael Madigan
Edward Magher
Thomas Maher

Dennis McCarty
James McCarty
William McManus
Patrick Monahan
Robert Minnohan
John Mullen
John Murphy
Matt O'Donald
Robert Reynolds
Wiley Rhodes
Sylvester Shea
Patrick Smith
John Soloman
Thomas Sullivan
Martin Toole
Philip Tracy
Michael Wall
Jeremiah Webb

Commissioned Officers=7
Non-Commissioned Officers=6
Privates=55
Total Lads=68

C Company (Originally F)

Mostly City Lads From Nashville

Commisioned Officers(8)
Captain Saint Clair Morgan
Captain Clarence C. Malone
First Lieutenant William Moses Hughes
First Lieutenant Robert Paget Seymour
Second Lieutenant James N. Bradshaw
Second Lieutenant John S. Long
Second Lieutenant John McCullough
Second Lieutenant J. G. Mullen

Non-Commisioned Officers(12)
Master Sergeant Michael Kane
Master Sergeant James Maloney
Sergeant James Farrell
Sergeant John Flannagan
Sergeant William Fletcher
Sergeant Michael Mitchell
Sergeant Coleman Mullen
Sergeant James Sweeney
Corporal Noah Crain
Corporal Patrick Fahey
Corporal John Kinney
Corporal Joseph Moriarity

Privates(49)

Martin Bain	Jesse Dunigan	Patrick McCauley
Patrick Barry	Luke Eagan	Edward McGann
James Bayne	Michael Enright	Francis W. Meeker
Patrick Blye	James Farley	Francis Mooney
Patrick Boyle	Frank E. Fenton	James Murphy
John A. Broderick	James Flowers	John Nugent
Daniel Carroll	Denis Ford	John Purcell
Thomas Clesham	Peter Galvin	John Selinger
John Cloharty	William Glynn	Thomas Shaughnessy
Anselm Cole	William Jackson	David Shay
Adam Collins	James Kelley	John Shea
Thomas Conroy	Michael Kelley	Charles Shields
Patrick Conry	Luke Killion	Dennis Skandling
Dennis Cronan	Thomas Lally	Gideon Sleeper
Thomas Cusham	Patrick Lane	Michael Sullivan, No. 1
James Donegan	Darby Martin	Michael Sullivan, No. 2
		Dennis Sweeney

Commissioned Officers=8
Non-Commissioned Officers=12
Privates=49
Total Lads=69

D Company (Originally G)

Almost Exclusively City Lads From Nashville

Commissioned Officers (4)
Captain Boyd M. Cheatham
Captain William Sweeney
First Lieutenant Bartley Dorsey
Second Lieutenant John Clark

Non-Commissioned Officers (11)
Master Sergeant James Hayes
Master Sergeant Hugh McGuire
Master Sergeant W. A. Wray
Sergeant Edward English
Sergeant S. L. Grult
Sergeant James T. Trumble
Corporal John Bollin
Corporal Jerry Donohoe
Corporal Michael Laffey
Corporal James McCue
Corporal John Morrissey

Privates (63)

Owen Bollin
John Brennan
Patrick Brien
William Burks
Michael Cochran
Peter Collins
Mike Conley
Patsey Connas
Patrick Connell
James Connelly
Jimmy Connolly
John Connoly
Mike Corcoran
Martin Creahan
Michael Deharty
John Delany
W. H.Dempsey
Martin Devaney
William Dolaney
Thomas Donlon
Anthony Doudon

Michael Dougherty
James Dwyer
Edmund Eagan
Anthony Egan
Morris Fitzgerald
William Fitzgerald
Martin Flaherty
Patrick Gallagher
Patrick Hackett
Owen E. Haley
Patrick Haney
Daniel Harrington
James Hartnett
John Joyce
Michael Kelly
John Kenney
Michael Levins
James Loughlin
John Lucas
John Madden
Amable Martin

Walter McAvellay
William R. McGinley
John McGurty
Frank McKenney
Thomas McNichols
Francis J. Mellville
George W. Miller
Timothy Mohan
Michael Mullin
Thomas Mulry
Daniel Murphy
Michael Murphy
P. W. Murphy
Michael O'Sullivan
Pierce Pendergast
Patrick Riley
Michael Riordan
William Roach
John Ryan
Richard Shea
Eugene Sullivan

Commissioned Officers=4
Non-Commissioned Officers=11
Privates=63
Total Lads=78

E Company (Originally B)

City Lads From Nashville And Country Lads From That Area

Commissioned Officers (8)
Colonel William Grace
Captain Leslie Ellis
Captain Thomas Gibson
Captain James P. Kirkman
First Lieutenant R. W. McAvoy
First Lieutenant Theodore Kelsey
Second Lieutenant William Gleason
Second Lieutenant William Isaac Poe

Non-Commissioned Officers(9)
Master Sergeant Bernard McCabe
Sergeant Simon Cremian
Sergeant Samuel Cummings
Sergeant Hugh McCormick
Sergeant Andrew Noonan
Corporal James Kelley
Corporal Patrick King
Corporal William Mullin
Corporal John A. O'Neill

Privates (56)

Patrick Cady
Patrick Carberry
Patrick Carmudy
Dennis Carrigan
Henry Clarey
Johnny Connolly
Thomas Connolly
Timothy Cudery
James Dorsey
John Eagan
William Flaherty
Martin Fleming
John Foley
Thomas Francis
Timothy Galloway
Patrick Garraghan
John Gavin
Patrick Gillaspie
Dennis Grogan

Patrick Hagan
Jeremiah Harrington
James Joyce
Michael Joyce
James Kelly
Thomas Keltcher
John Leddy
Patrick Linskey
Patrick Loftus
Thomas Lynch
James Mahon
John Mahoney
Patrick Manning
Patrick McDerby
Patrick McDermot
Patrick McGee
James Mehan
James Moran
William Muldoon

Thomas Murphy
Nicholas O'Brien
Daniel Pryor
Patrick Roach
James Ryan
Mike Ryan
Eugene Shannon
Barney Shea
Jerry Shea
Patrick Sheehan
Thomas Slattery
John Smith
John Sullivan
Timothy Sullivan
John Tully
James Ward
Francis Williams
Daniel Zelly

Commissioned Officers=8
Non-Commissioned Officers=9
Privates=56
Total Lads=73

F Company (Originally H)

Almost Exclusively City Lads From Nashville

Commissioned Officers (9)
Colonel Randal W. McGavock
Captain Aloysius Berry
Captain William Ford
Captain John E. Johnson
Captain Robert Joynt
First Lieutenant Thomas Connor
First Lieutenant William McGinnis
Second Lieutenant James Finnucane
Second Lieutenant Randal G. Southall

Non-Commissioned Officers (8)
Sergeant Martin Glynn
Sergeant Mike Hoolahan
Sergeant James Hyde
Sergeant Daniel Kelly
Sergeant Frank Robinson
Sergeant Dennis Sullivan
Corporal Michael Carney
Corporal Michael Connors

Privates(75)

William Bernard	Martin Gibbons	Michael McGowan
Adam Bishop	Frank Gibson	John McKeon
Peter Casey	Patrick Glennon	Thomas McKeough
John Clarey	John Griffin	Thomas Meagher
James Coleman	Patrick M. Griffin	Patrick Monohan, No.1
James C. Collins	Daniel Griskey	Patrick Monohan, No. 2
Josiah C. Conley	Henry Guill	Andy Mooney
Thomas Conley	Charles Gushan	Luther S. Moore
Bryan Connolly	Martin Haley	Dennis Murphy
Patrick Corbett	Patrick Hannon	Patrick O'Brien
Patrick Crane	William Houck	John O'Herron
John Curley	Miles Joyce	Knude Olsen
William Donnelly	Peter Joyce	Dennis O'Neil
Jimmy Doyle	Daniel Keagan	Charles J. Owen
Daniel Driscoll	John Keaton	John Quigley
John Duffy	Alfred Keefe	Henry Quinn
Moses Dupree	Edward Kelly	John Quinn
Dominick Dyer	Jack Kennedy	William Quirk
Edward Fahey	Martin Kinncannon	Michael Ryan
William Fairley	Bartley Madden	John Sullivan, No. 1
Thomas Feeney	Florence Mahan	John Sullivan, No. 2
James Flanagan	Patrick M. McCormick	Francis Swindle
Michael Gallagher	William McDonnell	James Tompkill
John Galleher	Harold P. McGinnis	John Welsch
John C. Germain	Mark McGiver	W. W. Wood.

Commissioned Officers=9
Non-Commissioned Officers=8
Privates=75   Total Lads=92

G Company (Originally E)

Mostly City Lads from Nashville

Commissioned Officers (10)
Major Stephen Brandon
Captain John Archibald
Captain George A. Diggons
First Lieutenant W. S. Flippin
First Lieutenant John D. Winston
Second Lieutenant A. H. Bennie
Second Lieutenant William W. Foote
Second Lieutenant E. W. Harlowe
Second Lieutenant Oliver H. Height
Second Lieutenant William R. Lanier

Non-Commissioned Officers (4)
Sergeant John Carr
Sergeant Patrick Kennedy
Sergeant Michael F. Maye
Corporal Jerry O'Donahou

Privates(34)

Patrick Berk
Timothy Burns
Thomas Curran
Patrick Delaney
James Donoho
James Dougherty
Daniel Dunn
John Jones
Thomas Joyce
Martin Judge
Patrick Keaton

Michael Kenney
William Langhan
Mike Lowery
Jeremiah Lyons
Martin Maloney
Patrick Maloney
Dennis McCarthy
Timothy McGurdin
Thomas McLaughlin
John McTigne
Michael Meagher

James Moran
Edward P. Murphy
Jerry Murphy
Thomas O'Brien
Thomas O'Donnell
Dennis O'Sullivan
James O'Sullivan
Thomas Riley
William R. Roberts
James Ryan
Thomas Spellman
Florence Sullivan

Commissioned Officers=10
Non-Commissioned Officers=4
Privates=34
Total Lads=48

H Company (Originally I)

Mostly Country Lads From Pulaski

Commissioned Officers (7)
Major Lafayette McConnico
Captain Joseph Ryan
Captain Lewis T. Waggoner
First Lieutenant John W. Handy
First Lieutenant William McCoy
Second Lieutenant Thomas McClaskey
Second Lieutenant James O'Donnell

Non-Commissioned Officers (8)
Master Sergeant G. B. Ford
Sergeant Patrick Cunningham
Sergeant Edward McFadden
Sergeant Jeremiah Monihan
Corporal Thomas Connolly
Corporal John McCabe
Corporal William Quinlan
Corporal Malachi Ryan

Privates (51)

Mark Burk	Patrick Farrell	Patrick McGettighn
Mick Calley	Michael Finn	John McGrath
John Casey	E. G. Foster	Michael Moran
John Caully	Peter Gallihan	Frank Nelligan
Peter Clancy	David Gorman	Michael Quinihan
Michael Conley	Michael Hanley	Edward Riley
Daniel Connel	John Kain	John Riley
Miles Connolly	John Kavanaugh	Timothy Riley
Patrick Connolly	Michael Kearney	James Searry
William Connolly	Timothy Leary	Michael Shay
Matthew Conoly	James Maloney	Francis Sullivan
John Conway	Mike McAndrew	Jerome Sullivan
Patrick Conway	William McAndrew	Patrick Sullivan
Patrick Costello	Edward McCormick	Timothy Tansey
Richard Diamond	William J. McCready	Frank Welsch
Michael Donlan	Philip McDermott	Patrick Welsch
Michael Eagan	Thomas McFarland	Patrick Whalen

Commissioned Officers=7
Non-Commissioned Officers=8
Privates=51
Total Lads=66

I Company (Originally D)

Almost Exclusively Country Lads From The Clarksville Area

Commissioned Officers (9)
Captain Jacob C. Farrell
Captain William M. Marr
Captain Henry S. Monroe
Captain John L. Prendergast
First Lieutenant Lynch B. Donoho
Second Lieutenant James T. Dunlap
Second Lieutenant William H. Dwyer
Second Lieutenant Polk Harbeson
Second Lieutenant Edward Ryan

Non-Commissioned Officers (12)
Master Sergeant Andrew Dicky
Master Sergeant Morris Griffin
Master Sergeant John Guffey
Sergeant Patrick Dwyer
Sergeant Michael O. O'Neill
Sergeant Roger Sheehy
Corporal James R. Bryant
Corporal John Cannon
Corporal David Gorrell
Corporal Richard McAnany
Corporal James Wall
Corporal Robert D. Wilson

Privates (61)

Gavani Beatty
Thomas Buchanan
James L. Byers
Edmund Byrnes
Dennis Cahill
James Carney
James Carroll
Michael Cowley
Daniel Daley
John Dempsey
Michael Dignan
John Dooley
John Doyle
Daniel D. Dunne
James Dunning
Joseph Dyer
William Farrell
Dennis Flanigan
John Galloway
John E. Gardiner

James Haggerty
Patrick Hanley
Barney Hart
Thomas Healy
Patrick Hogan
Patrick Hurley
Columbus Jacobs
William W. Jenkins
Owen Keenan
Patrick Kelly
James Killane
James Lally
Larry Landrigan
William M. Lovett
W. S. Lunn
Joshua Macey
John Maher
Cain Mahony
Michael Mahony
Thomas McCabe

Daniel McCarthy
John McElroy
Thomas H. McFarland
James McLauflin
Patrick S. McNamara
John Moriarity
Daniel O'Brien
John O'Brien
Patrick O'Keefe
Nathan O'Quinn
James Powers
Michael Roach
James C. Rumbo
John K. Rumbo
Daniel Shea
John Smith
Daniel Sullivan
Denis Sullivan
Jerry Sullivan
J. M. Ticer
Philip Whalen

Commissioned Officers=9
Non-Commissioned Officers=12
Privates=61
Total Lads=82

K Company (Originally C)

Mostly City Lads From Nashville

Commissioned Officers (9)	*Non-Commissioned Officers (8)*
Captain John H. Anderson	Mstr. SergeantPatrickMcLaughlin
Captain Lewis R. Clark	Sergeant William Gallop
Captain Edward Mc Gavock	Sergeant Patrick M. Sullivan
First Lieutenant William F. Beatty	Corporal William Kiley
First Lieutenant L. P. Hagan	Corporal Mike Mc Donald
First Lieutenant John W. McLaughlin	Corporal Patrick Riley
Second Lieutenant Henry Carter	Corporal Patrick J. Sullivan
Second Lieutenant James Conroy	
Second Lieutenant James A. Wiley	

Privates (39)

Patrick Barrett	Mike Killeen	Mike Mullen
Thomas Bourk	John Lamb	John Nolan
John Calhoun	John Lawlor	Patt O'Donnell
John Conlon	Darby Lee	Luke O'Rourke
Daniel Connolly	Martin Leonard	William Parrish
Mark Connolly	Francis Mahoney	Michael Quirk
Barberry Devine	James Mahoney	Patrick Runnells
John M. Divine	Martin Mahoney	Thomas Rush
Michael Falvy	David Maloney	Dennis Shannon
Patrick Farrell	James Molloy	Rufus Smith
Thomas Foley, No. 1	John Moran	Michael Sullivan, No. 1
Thomas Foley, No. 2	Michael Morrissey	Michael Sullivan, No. 2
Andrew Hughes	Thomas Morrissey	Hugh Tonney.

Commissioned Officers=9
Non-Commissioned Officers=8
Privates=39
Total Lads=56

353

Regimental Totals
Staff Without Company Designations (including 3 commissioned officers)=9
Other Commissioned Officers=78
Non-Commissioned Officers=86
Privates=559

Total Lads=732

Totals By Individual Rank
Chaplains=2
Civilian Doctors=4
Colonels=3
Lieutenant Colonels=2
Majors=3
Captains=27
First Lieutenants=17
Second Lieutenants=29
Master Sergeants=15
Sergeants=38
Corporals=33
Privates=559

Total Lads=732

THE COMMISSIONED OFFICERS OF THE SONS OF ERIN BY HIGHEST RANK ACHIEVED

A) Transferred to another unit, or did not reenlist.
B) Resigned due to sickness or personal reasons.
C) Disabled by wounds.
D) Died, killed, or mortally wounded during the war.
E) One of the last survivors.

Colonel Adolphus Heiman (D)
Colonel Randal W. McGavock (D)
Colonel William Grace (D)

Lieutenant Colonel John G. O'Neill
Lieutenant Colonel Samuel M. Thompson(CE)

Major Stephen Brandon (B)
Major (Dr.) Sidney W. Franklin (A)
Major Lafayette McConnico (A)

Captain John H. Anderson (A)
Captain John Archibald (B)
Captain Aloysius Berry (C)
Captain John W. Bryan
Captain Boyd M. Cheatham (A)
Captain Lewis R. Clark (E)
Captain George A. Diggons (C)
Captain Bartley J. Dorsey
Captain Leslie Ellis (A)
Captain J. C. (Jake) Farrell
Captain William Ford (A)
Captain Thomas Gibson (BE)
Captain John B. Johnson (A)
Captain Robert Joynt
Captain James P. Kirkman
Captain Clarence C. Malone(E)
Captain William M. Marr (A)
Captain Edward McGavock (A)
Captain James McMurray
Captain Saint Clair Morgan (D)
Captain Henry S. Monroe
Captain (Dr.) Joseph M. Plunket (B)
Captain John L. Prendergast (C)

Captain Joseph Ryan
Captain Charles H. Stockell (E)
Captain William Sweeney (D)
Captain Lewis T. Waggoner (A)

First Lieutenant Felix Abbey (B)
First Lieutenant William L. Beatty
First Lieutenant Thomas Connor(C)
First Lieutenant Lynch B. Donoho (E)
First Lieutenant W. S. Flippin
First Lieutenant L. P. Hagan
First Lieutenant John W. Handy (A)
First Lieutenant William M.Hughes
First Lieutenant Theodore Kelsey(D)
First Lieutenant John S. Long
First Lieutenant R. W. McAvoy
First Lieutenant William McCoy
First Lieutenant John McLaughlin(A)
First Lieutenant William McGinnis
First Lieutenant Joseph Phillips
First Lieutenant Robert P. Seymour
First Lieutenant John D. Winston (D)

Second Lieutenant John Ames (D)
Second Lieutenant A. H. Bennie
Second Lieutenant J. N. Bradshaw
Second Lieutenant William M. Burke
Second Lieutenant Henry Carter (A)
Second Lieutenant John Clark
Second Lieutenant James Conroy
Second Lieutenant Robert Dansby
Second Lieutenant John Dewayne
Second Lieutenant James T. Dunlap
Second Lieutenant William Dwyer (AD)
Second Lieutenant Robert N. Ervin
Second Lieutenant Joseph Evans
Second Lieutenant James Finnucane
Second Lieutenant William W. Foote (E)
Second Lieutenant William Gleason
Second Lieutenant Polk Harbeson
Second Lieutenant E. W. Harlow
Second Lieutenant Oliver H. Height
Second Lieutenant William R. Lanier
Second Lieutenant Thomas Mc Claskey
Second Lieutenant John McCullough (D)
Second Lieutenant J. G. Mullin
Second Lieutenant James O'Donnell
Second Lieutenant William Isaac Poe
Second Lieutenant Edward Ryan
Second Lieutenant Randal G. Southall (B)
Second Lieutenant James White
Second Lieutenant James A. Wiley

The Top Ten Combat Officers of the Sons of Erin
As Ranked By The Author

1) **Colonel William Grace.** Staff officer at Fort Henry, Fort Donelson, Raymond. Regimental CO at Chickamauga, New Hope Church, Decatur, Utoy Creek, Jonesborough. Huge, striking, powerful, a soldier's soldier. Consistently pugnacious in battle, highly respected by all. An especially strong performance at Utoy Creek. Cited for distinguished service in Army Official Records. Injured at Chickamauga. Mortally wounded in action at Jonesborough.

2) **Lieutenant Colonel John G. O'Neill.** Company CO at Fort Henry, Fort Donelson, Raymond. Staff officer at Chickamauga. Regimental CO at Missionary Ridge, Rocky Face Ridge, Resaca, Franklin, Third Murfreesborough, Nashville. A fine performance as sharpshooter detachment CO at Raymond, and as regimental CO at Missionary Ridge. Popular with the lads. Cited for distinguished service in Army Official Records. Seriously wounded at Resaca.

3) **Captain John L. Prendergast.** An enlisted lad at Fort Henry and Fort Donelson. Company CO at Raymond and Chickamauga. Staff officer at Missionary Ridge. Briefly acting regimental CO at Resaca. Staff officer at New Hope Church, Decatur, Utoy Creek, and Jonesborough. Versatile soldier, equally as skilled as sharpshooter and infantryman. Wounded twice at both Raymond and Chickamauga. Disabled at Jonesborough.

4) **First Lieutenant Thomas Connor.** An enlisted lad at Fort Henry and Fort Donelson. A sharpshooter detachment officer at Raymond and Chickamauga. O'Neill's top gun. Superb long-range shooter. Held in awe by the lads. Disabled at Chickamauga.

5) **Colonel Randal W. McGavock.** Regimental CO at Fort Henry, Fort Donelson, Raymond. Didn't last long enough to rank up there with Grace and O'Neill. Steady under fire at Erin Hollow and Raymond. Much liked and respected leader. Cited for distinguished service in Army Official Records. Killed in action at Raymond.

6) **Captain Saint Clair Morgan.** Company CO at Fort Henry, Fort Donelson, Raymond. Staff officer at Chickamauga. Handsome, distinguished friend of McGavock, highly respected by Grace. Popular with lads. Killed in action at Chickamauga.

7) **First Lieutenant Robert Paget Seymour.** Enlisted lad at Fort Henry and Fort Donelson. Company officer at Raymond. Courier at Chickamauga, Missionary Ridge, Rocky Face Ridge, Resaca, New Hope Church, Decatur, Utoy Creek, Jonesborough, Franklin, Third Murfreesborough, Nashville. Professional soldier, replaced Ted Kelsey as adjutant-courier. Rescued Grace at Chickamauga. Held in high esteem by lads. In spite of high-risk courier assignment, apparently went unscathed in battle.

357

8) **Lieutenant Colonel Samuel M. Thompson.** Company CO at Fort Henry and Fort Donelson. Staff officer at Raymond and Chickamauga. Respected and trusted by both McGavock and Grace. Disabled at Chickamauga.

9) **Second Lieutenant John Ames.** Drill sergeant at Fort Henry and Fort Donelson. Company officer at Raymond. Hard-nosed-front-line soldier, respected and feared by lads. Cited for distinguished service in Confederate Military History. Killed in action at Raymond.

10) **First Lieutenant Theodore Kelsey.** Company officer at Fort Henry and Fort Donelson. Replaced John Handy as adjutant-courier. Performed capably as courier at Raymond and Chickamauga. Respected and trusted by Grace. Cited for distinguished service in Army Official Records. Killed in action at Chickamauga.

THE SIXTY-SIX MEMBERS OF THE IRISH REGIMENT WHO GAVE THEIR
LIVES FOR THE SOUTHERN CAUSE

Battlefield Deaths (30)
KIA = killed in action.
MWIA = mortally wounded in action.

Raymond, Mississippi, May 12, 1863 (8)
Colonel Randal W. McGavock, Regimental Staff, KIA
Second Lieutenant John Ames, A Company, KIA
Sergeant James Hyde, F Company, MWIA
Private Patrick Barrett, K Company, MWIA
Private Thomas Branerly, B Company, KIA
Private Richard Eagan, A Company, KIA
Private Michael Levins, D Company, KIA
Private Darby Martin, C Company, KIA

Chickamauga, Georgia, September 18 to 20, 1863 (11)
Captain Saint Clair Morgan, C Company, KIA
Captain William Sweeney, D Company, KIA
First Lieutenant Theodore Kelsey, E Company, KIA
First Lieutenant John D. Winston, G Company, MWIA
Private James Flowers, C Company, MWIA
Private Patrick McGettighn, H Company, MWIA
Private James Murray, A Company, KIA
Private James Kelly, E Company, MWIA
Private Jeremiah Harrington, E Company, KIA
Private James Mahon, E Company, KIA
Private Thomas Murphy, E Company, MWIA

Missionary Ridge, Tennessee, November 25, 1863 (4)
Second Lieutenant John McCullough, C Company,MWIA
Sergeant Patrick Kennedy, G Company, KIA
Private Philip Mc Dermott, H Company, KIA
Private Patrick Delaney, G Company, KIA

Resaca, Georgia, May 14, 1864 (1)
Private Patrick Flaherty, A Company, MWIA

Decatur, Georgia, July 22, 1864 (2)
Private Patrick Conry, C Company, KIA
Private William A. Mentiss, A Company, MWIA

Jonesborough, Georgia, August 31, 1864 (3)
Colonel William Grace, Regimental Staff, MWIA
Father Emmeran Bliemel, Regimental Staff, KIA
Sergeant James Hayes, D Company, KIA

Franklin, Tennessee, November 30, 1864 (1)
Private Martin Fleming, E Company, KIA

Prison Deaths (26)

Camp Chase, Columbus, Ohio (2)
Private James Haggarty (Franklin) I Company (2-3-65)
Private Patrick O'Donnell (Nashville) K Company, (1-17-65).

Camp Douglas, Chicago, Illinois (24)
Master Sergeant Michael Kane (Fort Donelson) C Company (3-1-62))
Private William Bradford (Chickamauga) A Company (10-12-63)
Private Daniel Connolly (Fort Donelson) K Company (8-8-62)
Private Michael Corcoran (Fort Donelson) D Company (3-3-62)
Private John Dempsey (Fort Donelson) I Company (3-20-62)
Private Edmund Eagan (Fort Donelson) D Company (3-9-62)
Private William Feeley (Fort Donelson) B Company (4-10-62)
Private E. G. Foster (Fort Donelson) H Company (5-1-62)
Private Frank Gibson (Fort Donelson) F Company (9-3-62)
Private Patrick Hackett (Fort Donelson) D Company(3-28-62)
Private John Higgins (Fort Donelson) A Company (7-10-62)
Private William W. Jenkins (Fort Donelson) I Company (8-27–62)
Private John Jones (Fort Donelson) G Company (3-9-62)
Private John Joyce (Fort Donelson) D Company (5-3-62)
Private John Kelly (Fort Donelson) A Company (4-14-62)
Private Darby Lee (Fort Donelson) K Company (5-5-62)

Private William M. Lovett (Fort Donelson) I Company (4-2-62)
Private Edward McCormick (Fort Donelson) H Company (3-13-62)
Private William McLane (Fort Donelson) A Company (4-15-62)
Private John McTigne (Fort Donelson) G Company (3-24-62)
Private John Moriarity (Fort Donelson) I Company (3-20-62)
Private Daniel Pryor (Chickamauga) E Company (10-28-63)
Private William R. Roberts (Fort Donelson) G Company (4-11-62)
Private John Smith (Fort Donelson) I Company (9-10-62)

Deaths From Disease, Mississippi (10)
Colonel Adolphus Heiman, Regimental Staff (11-16-62)
Master Sergeant Hugh McGuire, D Company (11-18-62)
Private John Cloharty, C Company (12-27-62)
Private Patrick Conway, H Company (11-2-62)
Private Michael Donlan, H Company (12-26-62)
Private Michael Finn, H Company (10-2-62)
Private John Keaton, F Company Company (6-7-63)
Private James McLauflin, I Company (12-26-62)
Private John Murphy, B Company (12-27-62)
Private John Smith, E Company (11-17-62)

The above sixty-six lads died while registered in the service of the Sons of Erin. There are another four men buried at Oakwoods Cemetery, Chicago, identified as members of the Tenth Tennessee, who died at Camp Douglas. In reality the quartet served entirely in other units.

Private J. A. C. Fisher, 51st Confederate Regiment, C Company.
Private J. J. Gaurin, 15th Tennessee Regiment, H Company.
Private J. F. Garrison, 47th Tennessee Regiment, H Company.
Private John Stringer, 30th Tennessee Regiment, C Company.

THE SIX CAMPAIGNS OF THE SONS OF ERIN

The River Forts Campaign
February 4 to 15, 1862 (Fort Henry, Fort Donelson)

Department or Army Group-Department of the West (No. 2)
Army CO—General Albert Sidney Johnston
Army Corps CO—General Leonidas Polk
Division CO—General Lloyd Tilghman; General Bushrod R. Johnson
Brigade CO—Colonel Adolphus Heiman
Regiment CO—Lieutenant Colonel Randal W. McGavock

Primary Opposing Regiment—45th Illinois (Erin Hollow)
Engaged—720
Captured, Escaped, Deserted—720
% of Losses—100

Highlight—Defensive stand at Erin Hollow, February 13, 1862

The Battle Of Raymond, Mississippi.
May 12, 1863.

Department or Army Group— Department of Mississippi
and Eastern Louisiana
Army CO—General John C. Pemberton
Detached Brigade CO—General John Gregg
Regiment CO—Colonel Randal W. McGavock; Lieutenant
Colonel James J. Turner

Primary Opposing Regiment— 7th US Missouri
Engaged—254
Killed—8
Wounded—35
Captured—9
Total Losses—52
% of Losses—20

**Highlight—Performance of A Company on O'Neill's Hill,
3:00 to 3:30.**

The Battle Of Chickamauga
September 18 to 20, 1863

Department or Army Group—Army of Tennessee
Army CO—General Braxton Bragg
Army Wing CO—General James Longstreet
Army Corps CO—General John Bell Hood
Division CO—General Bushrod R. Johnson
Brigade CO—General John Gregg; Colonel Cyrus A. Sugg
Regiment CO—Colonel William Grace

Primary Opposing Regiment—113th Ohio (Steedman's Hill)
Engaged—190
Killed—11
Wounded—37 (2 of whom were captured and died in prison)

Total Losses—48
% of Losses—25

Highlight—Capture of the 1st U.S. Missouri Battery at Dyer's Farm, September 20.

The Battle Of Missionary Ridge
November 25, 1863

Department or Army Group—Army of Tennessee
Army CO—General Braxton Bragg
Army Corps CO—General John C. Breckinridge
Division CO—General William B. Bate
Brigade CO—Colonel Robert C. Tyler; Colonel A. F. Rudler; Lieutenant Colonel James J. Turner
Regiment CO—Major John G. O'Neill

Primary Opposing Regiment—11th Michigan
Engaged—104
Killed—4
Wounded—11
Captured—17
Total Losses—32
% of Losses—31

Highlight—Being the last regiment to fall back from the center of the line.

The Atlanta Campaign
May 5 to August 31, 1864
(Rocky Face Ridge, Resaca, New Hope Church, Decatur,
Utoy Creek, Jonesborough)

Department or Army Group—Army of Tennessee
Army CO—General Joseph E. Johnston; General John Bell
Hood
Army Corps CO—General William J. Hardee; General
Stephen D. Lee
Division CO—General William B. Bate; General John Calvin
Brown
Brigade CO—Colonel/General Thomas Benton Smith
Regiment CO—Major John G. O'Neill; Captain John L.
Prendergast (acting CO, Resaca); Colonel William Grace;
Captain Lewis R. Clark (acting CO, Jonesborough)

Primary Opposing Regiment—8th US Tennessee (Utoy Creek)

Engaged—69
Killed—6
Wounded—21
Captured—7
Total Losses—34
% of Losses—49

**Highlight—Counter-assault against the East Tennes-
seans at Utoy Creek, August 6.**

Hood's Tennessee Campaign
November 30 to December 16, 1864
(Franklin, Third Murfreesborough, Nashville)

Department or Army Group—Army of Tennessee
Army CO—General John Bell Hood
Army Corps CO—General B. Franklin Cheatham
Division CO—General William B. Bate
Brigade CO—General Thomas Benton Smith
Regiment CO—Lieutenant Colonel John G. O'Neill

Primary Opposing Regiment—95th Ohio (Nashville)

Engaged—36
Killed—1
Wounded and/or Captured—31
Total Losses—32
% of Losses—89

**Highlight—Skirmishing support of Forrest's Cavalry,
Murfreesborough, December 7.**

INDIVIDUAL BATTLES AT WHICH THE SONS OF ERIN WERE PRESENT

BATTLE	CO	ENGAGED	RESULTS
Fort Henry, Tenn., Feb. 4-6,1862	McGavock	Yes	Yankee Win
Ft. Donelson,Tn., Feb. 12-15, 1862	McGavock	Yes	Yankee Win
Chickasaw Bluffs, Ms., Dec. 29, 1862	McGavock	No	Rebel Win
First Pt Hudson, La., March 14, 1863	McGavock	No	Rebel Win
Raymond, Miss., May 12, 1863	McGavock	Yes	Yankee Win
Chickamauga, Ga., Sept. 18-20, 1863	Grace	Yes	Rebel Win
Mis'onary Ridge, Tenn., Nov. 25, 1863	O'Neill	Yes	Yankee Win
Rocky Face Ridge, Ga., May 5-9, 1864	O'Neill	Yes	Rebel Win
Resaca, Ga., May 14-15, 1864	O'Neill	Yes	Rebel Win
Cassville, Ga., May 19, 1864	Grace	No	Yankee Win
New Hope Ch'ch, Ga., May 23-27,1864	Grace	Yes	Rebel Win
Pine Mountain, Ga., June 14, 1864	Grace	No	Yankee Win
Kennesaw Mountain, Ga., June 27, 1864	Grace	No	Rebel Win
Peachtree Creek, Ga., July 20, 1864	Grace	No	Rebel Win

Atlanta (Decatur), Ga., July 22, 1864	Grace	Yes	Yankee Win
Ezra Church, Ga., July 28, 1864	Grace	No	Rebel Win
Utoy Creek, Ga., Aug. 6, 1864	Grace	Yes	Rebel Win
Jonesborough, Ga., Aug. 31, 1864	Grace	Yes	Yankee Win
Franklin, Tenn., Nov. 30, 1864	O'Neill	Yes	Yankee Win
3RD Murfre'bor'h, Tenn., Dec. 7, 1864	O'Neill	Yes	Yankee Win
Nashville, Tenn., Dec. 15-16, 1864	O'Neill	Yes	Yankee Win
Bentonville, N.C., March 19-21, 1865	O'Neill	Yes	Yankee Win

The Infantry Brigades in which the Sons of Erin Served

Colonel Adolphus Heiman's Brigade at Fort Henry
Twenty-Seventh Alabama Infantry Regiment.
Tenth Tennessee Infantry Regiment.
Forty-Eighth Tennessee Infantry Regiment.

Colonel Adolphus Heiman's Reinforced Brigade at Fort Donelson
Twenty-Seventh Alabama Infantry Regiment.
Tenth Tennessee Infantry Regiment.
Thirtieth Tennessee Infantry Regiment.
Fortieth Tennessee Infantry Regiment.
Forty-Second Tennessee Infantry Regiment.
Forty-Eighth Tennessee Infantry Regiment.
Fifty-Third Tennessee Infantry Regiment.

General John Gregg's Brigade at Raymond
Third Tennessee Infantry Regiment.
Tenth/Thirtieth Tennessee Consolidated Infantry Regiment.
Forty-First Tennessee Infantry Regiment.

Fiftieth Tennessee Infantry Regiment.
Seventh Texas Infantry Regiment.
First Tennessee Infantry Battalion.

Colonel Cyrus Sugg's Brigade at Chickamauga
Third Tennessee Infantry Regiment.
Tenth Tennessee Infantry Regiment.
Thirtieth Tennessee Infantry Regiment.
Forty-First Tennessee Infantry Regiment.
Fiftieth/First Tennessee Consolidated Infantry Regi–
ment.
Seventh Texas Infantry Regiment.

Colonel William Grace's Provisional Brigade at Chickamauga.
Tenth Tennessee Infantry Regiment.
Seventeenth Tennessee Infantry Regiment.
Thirtieth Tennessee Infantry Regiment.
Forty-First Tennessee Infantry Regiment.

Colonel Robert Tyler's Brigade at Missionary Ridge
Thirty-Seventh Georgia Infantry Regiment.
Tenth Tennessee Infantry Regiment.
Fifteenth/Thirty-Seventh Tennessee Consolidated In-
fantry Regiment.
Twentieth Tennessee Infantry Regiment.
Thirtieth Tennessee Infantry Regiment.
Fourth Georgia Battalion Sharpshooters.
First Tennessee Infantry Battalion.

General Benton Smith's Brigade at Atlanta
Thirty-Seventh Georgia Infantry Regiment.
Second Tennessee Infantry Regiment.
Tenth Tennessee Infantry Regiment.
Fifteenth/Thirty-Seventh Tennessee Consolidated In-
fantry Regiment.

Twentieth Tennessee Infantry Regiment.
Thirtieth Tennessee Infantry Regiment.
Fourth Georgia Battalion Sharpshooters.

General Benton Smith's Brigade at Nashville
Thirty-Seventh/Fourth Georgia Consolidated Infantry Regiment.
Second/Tenth/Fifteenth/Twentieth/Thirtieth/Thirty-Seventh Tennessee Consolidated Infantry Regiment.

General Joseph Palmer's Brigade at Bentonville
First/Sixth/Eighth/Ninth/Sixteenth/Twenty-Seventh/Twenty-Eighth/Thirty-Fourth Tennessee Consolidated Regiment.
Eleventh/Twelfth//Thirteenth/Twenty-Ninth/Forty-Seventh/Fiftieth/Fifty-First/Fifty-Fourth Tennessee Consolidated Regiment.
Fourth/Fifth/Nineteenth/Twenty-Fourth/Thirty-First/Thirty-Third/Thirty-Fifth/Thirty-Eighth/Forty-First Tennessee Consolidated Regiment.
Second/Third/Tenth/Fifteenth/Eighteenth/Twentieth/Twenty-Sixth/Thirtieth/Thirty-Second/Thirty-Seventh/Forty-Fifth Tennessee Consolidated Regiment.

Notes

Footnote references to the 127 volumes of *Army Official Records(AOR)* can be needlessly long and confusing to the reader. For example:

United States War Department. Washington, D.C. *War of the Rebellion: Official Records of the Union and Confederate Armies.* Series Number I, Volume Number 24, Part Number 3, Serial Number 38, Page Number 742. Battlefield Report of Lieutenant Colonel James J. Turner, CSA, Commanding Tenth/Thirtieth Tennessee Consolidated Infantry Regiment.

Every single *AOR* note used here is from the same Series I. Volume numbers are misleading and part numbers do not provide enough identity. In point of fact, there can be several books designated by the same "volume" number, each separated by its own "part" number. The only designation that consistently leads the researcher to the correct place in the set is the "serial" number. Each of the 111 books of Series I is listed by its own unique serial number, from serial number 1 through serial number 111.

The author believes it is important to include the officer who filed the report or the officer who wrote the dispatch as a quick and accurate research tool. For these reasons, the abbreviated version of the above example, as posted in the notes, appears in this manner:

AOR, Serial 38, p. 742(Turner).

In addition to *Army Official Records(AOR)*, other abbreviations for military reference materials include the following: *Southern Historical Society Papers(SHSP), Military Annals of Tennessee: Confederate(MATC), Confederate Military History(CMH), Confederate Veteran Magazine(CVM), Campaigns of the Civil War(CCW), Battles and Leaders of the Civil War(BL), Tennessee Historical Quarterly(THQ), Tennessee Historical Magazine(THM), Civil War Times Illustrated(CWTI).*

CHAPTER ONE

SEVEN-HUNDRED-TWENTY-FIVE LADS

The opening section of this initial chapter, concerning the organization of the Tenth Tennessee, was taken almost exclusively from three sources, two of which are contained in the same book—*Pen and Sword: The Journals of R. W. McGavock,* edited by Herschel Gower and Jack Allen. Gower's biography of McGavock is listed as *Pen and Sword;* McGavock's own journals are listed as such. The third source is the diary of Private Jimmy Doyle, which has no title, begins suddenly in the summer of 1861 and ends abruptly in the fall of 1863.

Doyle's references to the mayoral campaign of 1858 and pre-war Nashville, written at Fort Henry in 1861, run so parallel to some of McGavock's entries that it is likely that the private "interviewed" the lieutenant colonel. Doyle claims to have known McGavock slightly before the war, but since McGavock makes no mention of Doyle, it is impossible to verify this. The content and style of Doyle's diary are dramatically different from the content and style of the journals of the educated McGavock, especially as they relate to camp stories of the enlisted men.

The background material about the early military situation in the Western theatre of operations comes primarily from Army of Tennessee historians Stanley Horn and Thomas Lawrence Connelly.

The Sons of Erin: the St. Patrick's Club

1. Gower, *Pen and Sword,* pp. 27-29.
2. Ibid., p 44.
3. Ibid., p. 45.
4. McGavock's journals, p. 290.
5. Ibid., p. 171.
6. As cited in Gower, *Pen and Sword,* p. 51.
7. McGavock's journals, p. 305.
8. Ibid., p. 304.
9. Ibid., p. 384.
10. Gower, *Pen and Sword,* p. 66.
11. Doyle's diary, pp. 19-20.
12. McGavock's journals, p. 488.
13. Ibid.
14. Doyle's diary, p. 19.
15. McGavock's journals, p. 489.
16. Doyle's diary, p. 20.
17. Ibid.
18. Ibid.
19. Gower, *Pen and Sword,* p. 69.

20. Ibid.

21. Ibid., p. 76.

22. Horn, *Army of Tennessee,* pp . 46-47 and Porter, *Confederate Military History: Tennessee,* p. 6.

The Sons of Erin: the Company

23. The flag can be viewed at the Tennessee State Museum, Nashville. A sketch is available though the Milwaukee Public Museum.

24. Doyle's diary, p. 11.

25. Gower, *Pen and Sword,* p. 77.

26. Griffin, "The Famous Tenth Tennessee," *CVM*, vol. 13, p. 553.

27. Doyle's diary, p. 14.

28. Connelly, *Army of the Heartland,* p. 10.

The Sons of Erin: the Regiment

29. Frank, "Adolphus Heiman: Architect and Soldier," *THM*, vol. 5, pp. 35-50.

30. Ibid.

31. Horn, *Army of Tennessee,* p. 80.

32. Doyle's diary, p. 4.

33. Ibid., p. 18.

34. Frank, "Adolphus Heiman: Architect and Soldier," *THM,* vol. 5, p. 51.

35. Connelly, *Army of the Heartland,* pp. 39-40.

36. Doyle's diary, p. 9.

37. Ibid., p. 3, p. 7.

38. Ibid., pp. 6-8.

39. Griffin, "The Famous Tenth Tennessee," *CVM,* vol. 13, p. 553.

40. *AOR*, Serial 7, p. 145.

41. Horn, *Tennesseans in the Civil War,* vol. 1, p. 193.

42. Clark, "Tenth Tennessee Infantry," *MATC*, pp. 282-283.

43. Doyle's diary, p. 16.

44. Ibid., pp. 15-16.

45. Walke, "The Gunboats at Belmont and Fort Henry." *BL*, vol. 1, p. 363.

46. Horn, *Army of Tennessee,* p. 76.

47. Connelly, *Army of the Heartland,* pp. 78-79.

48. As cited in Gower, *Pen and Sword.* pp. 79-80.

49. Horn, *Army of Tennessee,* p. 77.

50. Connelly, *Army of the Heartland,* p. 79.

51. Foote, *The Civil War: A Narrative, Fort Sumter to Perryville,* p. 151.

52. Griffin, "The Famous Tenth Tennessee," *CVM,* vol. 13, p. 553.

CHAPTER TWO

ESCAPE

Confederate infantry movements around Fort Henry are based on *AOR*, especially the detailed deployment reports of the two ranking officers, General Lloyd Tilghman and Colonel Adolphus Heiman. There are several good eyewitness accounts of the naval bombardment in *BL*.

Benjamin Franklin Coolling's *Forts Henry and Donelson* offers a complete description of the engagement on the Tennessee River, using the traditional interpretation that the Confederates were "chased out" of Fort Henry into Fort Donelson. The interpretation used here reflects the Southern view of Tilghman, Heiman, Colonel James D. Porter, McGavock, Doyle, and Private Patrick M. Griffin, namely, that the Confederates "escaped" from Fort Henry to Fort Donelson. This notion of escaping from the clutches of the Federals is strong in the accounts of McGavock, Doyle, and Griffin.

It was while camped at Fort Henry in the winter of 1861-62 that the enlisted men of the Tenth Tennessee began to notice Doyle writing his diary. The entries for this period increasingly became random lists of names concerning the most trivial routines of army life. Also at this time the memoirs of Griffin began to exaggerate the military contributions of the regiment, the first beginnings of the myth of Griffin's "Bloody Tinth."

Christmas Cheers

1. Doyle's diary, p. 22
2. Ibid.
3. Ibid.
4. Ibid., pp. 22-23.
5. Connelly, *Army of the Heartland*, pp. 62-63.
6. Taylor, Jesse. "The Defense of Fort Henry," *BL*, vol. 1, p. 370.
7. Horn, *Army of Tennessee*, pp. 78-82.
8. *AOR*, Serial 7, p. 148.
9. Doyle's diary, p. 26.
10. Ibid.
11. Porter, *CMH Tennessee*, p. 595.
12. McGavock's journals, p. 583.
13. Force, *From Fort Henry to Corinth, CCW*, pp. 27-28.
14. Doyle's diary, p. 27.
15. Ibid.
16. Cooling, *Forts Henry and Donelson*, pp. 45-46.
17. *AOR*, Serial 7, p. 125 (Grant).
18. Catton, *This Hallowed Ground*, p. 86.
19. Warner, *Generals in Blue*, p. 293.
20. Porter, *CMH Tennessee*, pp. 18-20.

Colonel Heiman Versus The United Sates Navy

21. *AOR*, Serial 7, p. 137 (Tilghman).
22. Ibid.
23. Ibid., pp. 148-149 (Heiman).
24. McGavock's journals, p. 583.
25. Doyle's diary, p. 29.
26. Ibid.
27. *AOR*, Serial 7, p. 128 (McClernand).
28. Ibid., p. 149 (Heiman).
29. Ibid.
30. Ibid., p. 138 (Tilghman).
31. Ibid., p. 125 (Grant).
32. Cooling, *Forts Henry and Donelson,* p. 92.
33. McGavock's journals, p. 583.
34. Walke, "The Gunboats at Belmont and Fort Henry." *BL*, vol. 1, p. 362.
35. Doyle's diary, p. 30.
36. *AOR*, Serial 7, p. 122 (Andrew Foote).
37. Force, *From Fort Henry to Corinth, CCW*, p. 31.
38. *AOR*, Serial 7, p. 150 (Heiman).
39. Doyle's diary, pp. 30-31.
40. *AOR*, Serial 7, p. 128 (McClernand).
41. Doyle's diary, p. 31.
42. Ibid.
43. McGavock's journals, p. 583.
44. Ibid.
45. Muster Rolls, frame no. 0165.
46. *AOR*, Serial 7, pp. 138-139 (Tilghman).
47. Doyle's diary, p. 33.
48. Ibid., pp. 33-34.

General Tilghman Versus The United States Navy

49. Cooling, *Forts Henry and Donelson,* p. 101.
50. McGavock's journals, pp. 584-585.
51. *AOR*, Serial 17, p. 124 (Grant).
52. Ibid., p. 146 (Hayes).
53. McGavock's journals, pp. 584-586.
54. Walke, "The Gunboats at Belmont and Fort Henry," *BL*, vol. 1, p. 362.
55. *AOR*, Serial 7, p. 123 (Andrew Foote).
56. Porter, *CMH Tennessee,* p. 19.
57. McGavock's journals, p. 585.

58. Foote, *The Civil War: A Narrative, Fort Sumter to Perryville,* pp. 189-190.

59. Griffin, "The Famous Tenth Tennessee," *CVM,* vol. 13, p. 554.

60. *AOR*, Serial 7, p. 142 (Tilghman); Ibid, p. 123 (Andrew Foote).

61. Force, *From Fort Henry to Corinth, CCW,* pp. 31-32.

62. Walke, "The Gunboats at Belmont and Fort Henry," *BL,* vol. 1, p. 366.

63. McGavock's journals, p. 587.

64. Doyle's diary, pp. 35-36.

65. McGavock's journals, p. 587.

66. Ibid.

67. Catton, *This Hallowed Ground,* p. 113.

68. As Cited in Cooling, *Forts Henry and Donelson,* p. 111.

69. Foote, *The Civil War: A Narrative, Fort Sumter to Perryville,* p. 191.

70. *AOR*, Serial 7, p. 142 (Tilghman).

CHAPTER THREE

THE LEGEND OF ERIN HOLLOW

Fort Donelson is emphasized in this text more than any of the other Western campaigns, because of its importance to the Tenth Tennessee. Dover was the only place where the entire original regiment was in combat together.

The obscure February 13 land engagement at Erin Hollow was reconstructed through the use of three primary sources, the most important of which is the manuscript of historian Edwin C. Bearss, U.S. Fort Donelson Park Service document no. 12, "The Fighting on February 13." The other two works are those of Cooling and James J. Hamilton.

Regimental eyewitnesses were Heiman, McGavock, Doyle, and Griffin. The brief Fort Donelson account of Griffin is presented here because of its colorful nature. However, Griffin's fanciful memoirs are not used to establish any facts in this chapter.

The low esteem for General Sidney Johnston as a Confederate army commander was firmly established by Connelly nearly thirty years ago. The low esteem for the unpopular General Gideon Pillow in regards to just about everything comes from a wide array of sources. McGavock was both amusing and merciless in his judgment of the man. Be it noted that politicians Pillow and McGavock were well known to each other before the war.

Also, be it noted that both General C. F. Smith and Commodore Andrew Foote died shortly after their service at Fort Donelson. In stark contrast, Union General Lew Wallace survived the battle of Dover by forty-three years to become one of America's most prolific writers; his best known book is *Ben Hur*. Confederate General Simon Buckner survived that same battle by fifty-two years to become the last living member of the Southern high command. Ironically, Buckner's son of the same name and of the same rank was the only American general killed in action during World War II.

Friday, February 7 to Tuesday, February 11, 1862

1. Doyle's diary, p. 36.
2. Ibid.
3. McGavock's journals, p. 587.
4. Doyle's diary, p. 37.
5. Williams, *P. G. T. Beauregard: Napoleon in Gray*, p. 118.
6. Ibid., pp. 18-20.
7. *AOR*, Serial 7, p. 360.
8. Ibid.
9. Davis, *Confederate General*, vol. 1, p. 39.
10. Ibid.
11. Doyle's diary, p. 37.
12. As cited in McGavock's journals, p. 589.
13. Ibid.
14. Doyle's diary, p. 38.
15. McGavock's journals, p. 589.
16. Ibid.
17. Davis, *The Orphan Brigade: The Kentucky Confederates Who Couldn't Go Home*, pp. 13-27.
18. Doyle's diary, p. 38.
19. Ibid.
20. Ibid.
21. Connelly, *Army of the Heartland*, p. 113.
22. Ibid.
23. As cited in Wyeth, *That Devil Forrest*, p. 5.
24. Connelly, *Army of the Heartland*, p. 115.
25. Ibid.
26. Ibid.
27. As cited in Foote, *The Civil War: A Narrative, Fort Sumter to Perryville*, p. 195.
28. As cited in Hamilton, *Fort Donelson*, p. 110.
29. As cited in Foote, *The Civil War: A Narrative, Fort Sumter to Perryville*, p. 196.
30. Horn, *Army of Tennessee*, p. 86.
31. As cited in Foote, *The Civil War: A Narrative, Fort Sumter to Perryville*, p. 196.

Wednesday, February 12, 1862

32. Hamilton, *Fort Donelson,* p. 37.

33. *AOR,* Serial 7, p. 366 (Heiman).

34. Hamilton, *Fort Donelson,* p. 37.

35. Bearss, "Troop Movements," Fort Donelson National Park Map.

36. Ibid.

37. Ibid.

38. Hamilton, *Fort Donelson,* p. 20.

39. *AOR,* Serial 7, p. 367 (Heiman).

40. Ibid.

41. Doyle's diary, p. 38.

42. *AOR,* Serial 7, p. 367 (Heiman).

43. Doyle's diary, p. 38.

44. *AOR,* Serial 7, p. 367 (Heiman).

45. Foote, The *Civil War: A Narrative, Fort Sumter to Perryville,* pp. 199-201.

46. Doyle's diary, pp. 38-39.

Thursday, February 13, 1862

47. Ibid.

48. Foote, *The Civil War: A Narrative, Fort Sumter to Perryville,* p. 202.

49. Ibid.

50. Ibid.

51. Ibid.

52. Warner, *Generals in Gray,* p. 123.

53. Wallace, "The Capture of Fort Donelson," *BL,* vol. 1, p. 407.

54. Ibid.

55. Boatner, *Civil War Dictionary,* p. 394.

56. Foote, *The Civil War: A Narrative, Fort Sumter to Perryville,* p. 195

57. *AOR,* Serial 7, Appendix.

58. McGavock's journals, p. 590.

59. *AOR,* Serial 7, p. 367 (Heiman).

60. Bearss, "The Fighting on February 13," p. 18.

61. Ibid.

62. Hamilton, *Fort Donelson,* p. 101.

63. Bearss, "The Fighting on February 13," pp. 24-25.

64. Ibid.

65. Ibid.

66. Ibid.

67. Ibid.

68. Ibid.

69. Ibid.

70. *AOR,* Serial 7, p. 203 (Haynie).

Engagement at Erin Hollow
1:25 to 1:40 PM
Thursday, February 13, 1862
Tennessee Irishmen Versus Illinois Lead Miners

71. Doyle's diary, p. 39.

72. Ibid.

73. Ibid.

74. Crummer, *With Grant at Fort Donelson, Shiloh, and Vicksburg: A Journal,* pp. 27-28.

75. Ibid.

76. Ibid.

77. McGavock's journals, p. 590.

78. Crummer, *With Grant at Fort Donelson, Shiloh, and Vicksburg: A Journal,* p. 28.

79. Ibid.

80. Doyle's diary, p. 39.

81. Tennessee Veterans Pension Application No. 435.

82. Doyle's diary, pp. 39-40.

83. Ibid., p. 40.

84. Porter, *CMH Tennessee,* p. 21.

85. McGavock's journals, p. 590.

86. William Grace, Military Service Record and Doyle's diary, p. 40.

87. McGavock's journals, p. 590.

88. Doyle's diary, p. 40.

89. *AOR,* Serial 7, p. 367 (Heiman). Doyle's page 40 is so similar to Heiman's report on page 367 that the private may well have "interviewed" the colonel sometime after the engagement.

90. Griffin, "The Famous Tenth Tennessee," *CVM,* vol. 13, p. 554.

91. Hamilton, *Fort Donelson,* pp. 107-108.

92. Ibid.

93. Doyle's diary, p. 40.

94. *AOR,* Serial 7, p. 204 (Haynie).

95. McGavock's journals, p. 590.

96. *AOR,* Serial 7, p. 367 (Heiman).

97. Bearss, "The Fighting on February 13," p. 39.

98. McGavock's journals, p. 591.

99. As cited in Connelly, *Army of the Heartland,* p. 118.

100. *AOR,* Serial 7, pp. 368-369 (Heiman).

101. Ibid.

102. Horn, *Army of Tennessee,* p. 89.

103. As cited in Bearss, "The Fighting on February 13," pp. 29-30.

104. Faust, *Encyclopedia of the Civil War,* p. 272.

Friday, February 14, 1862

105. Doyle's diary, pp. 40-41.
106. Ibid., p. 41.
107. Ibid.
108. Walke, "The Western Flotilla at Fort Donelson," *BL*, vol. 1, pp. 433-436.
109. Ibid.
110. Grant, *Memoirs,* vol., 1, pp. 298-304.
111. Doyle's diary, p. 41.
112. *AOR,* Serial 7, p. 369 (Heiman).
113. Hamilton, *Fort Donelson,* Appendix.
114. Wallace, "The Capture of Fort Donelson," *BL,* vol. 1, p. 415.
115. Porter, *CMH Tennessee,* p. 23.
116. Hamilton, *Fort Donelson,* pp. 159-161.
117. McGavock's journals, p. 592.

Saturday, February 15, 1862

118. Force, *From Fort Henry to Cornith, CCW,* pp. 51-52.
119. Ibid.
120. Ibid.
121. Cooling, *Forts Henry and Donelson,* p. 169.
122. Doyle's diary, p. 41.
123. Cooling, *Forts Henry and Donelson,* pp. 169-170.
124. Ibid., p. 170.
125. Ibid.
126. Doyle's diary, p. 41.
127. Ibid.
128. McGavock's journals, p. 592.
129. Warner, *Generals in Blue,* p. 281.
130. Wallace, "The Capture of Fort Donelson," *BL,* vol. 1, p. 417.
131. Ibid., pp. 417-418.
132. Doyle's diary, p. 41.
133. Wyeth, *That Devil Forrest,* pp. 46-47.
134. As cited in Connelly, *Army of the Heartland,* pp. 122-123.
135. Ibid.
136. Force, *From Fort Henry to Corinth, CCW,* p. 57.
137. As cited in Foote, *The Civil War: A Narrative, Fort Sumter to Perryville,* p. 208.
138. Ibid., p. 209.
139. As cited in Hamilton, *Fort Donelson,* pp. 252-253.
140. Wallace, "The Capture of Fort Donelson," *BL,* vol. 1, p. 424.
141. *AOR,* Serial 7, p. 369 (Heiman).

142. McGavock's journals, p. 592.
143. Ibid.
144. Wyeth, *That Devil Forrest,* p. 50.
145. As cited in Foote, *The Civil War: A Narrative, Fort Sumter to Perryville,* pp. 210-211.
146. Ibid.

Sunday, February 16, 1862

147. *AOR,* Serial 7, p. 386 (Forrest).
148. As cited in Hamilton, *Fort Donelson,* p. 319.
149. Ibid.
150. McGavock's journals, p. 593.
151. Ibid.
152. Ibid.
153. Ibid.
154. Ibid., p. 594.
155. Doyle's diary, pp. 41-42.

Consequences.

156. Horn, *Army of Tennessee,* p. 100.
157. Ibid.
158. Meaney, "Valiant Chaplain of the Bloody Tenth," *THQ,* vol. 41, pp. 39-40.
159. Ibid.
160. Ibid.

CHAPTER FOUR

JAILBIRDS IN THE NORTHWESTERN WATERS

Camp Chase: A History of the Prison and Its Cemetery by William H. Knauss provides detailed information about that particular Federal facility. McGavock's lengthy Fort Warren journal presents an excellent insight into the man's ante-bellum vision of life.

The *Report of the Illinois Adjutant General, 1865,* offers an extremely biased "Bloody Shirt" account of Camp Douglas, as seen, of course, from the Union viewpoint. The viewpoint of the Confederate prisoners is presented by Tenth Tennessee eyewitnesses Lewis R. Clark, Griffin, and Doyle, who wrote about their own personal Camp Douglas experiences, all three separate and independent of each other. The three versions are remarkably similar and consistent.

The U.S. War Department records for Camp Douglas can be found at the office of Chicago's historic Oakwoods Cemetery, 67th to 71st streets. A few miles north, within the boundaries of the old campground, is the Camp Douglas Museum on 35th street, an incredible collection of mementos, whose preservation has been the life-long work of Ernest Griffin, the grandson of a black Union camp guard.

Material about the reorganization of the regiment first appeared in Clark's 1886 paper, "Tenth Tennessee Infantry," in *MATC.* Horn and his Tennessee Centennial Commission updated the material in *Tennesseans in the Civil War,* first volume.

Camp Chase

1. Griffin, "The Famous Tenth Tennessee," *CVM,* vol. 13, p. 554.
2. McGavock's journals, p. 597.
3. Ibid.
4. Ibid., p. 598.
5. Ibid., p. 600.
6. Ibid., p. 599.
7. Knauss, *Camp Chase,* pp. 112-113.
8. McGavock's journals, p. 600.

Fort Warren

9. Ibid., pp. 600-601.
10. Ibid., p. 601.
11. Frank, "Adolphus Heiman: Architect and Soldier," *THM,* vol. 5, p. 55.
12. McGavock's journals, p. 636.
13. Ibid., p. 604.
14. Ibid., pp. 604-605.
15. Ibid., p. 616.
16. Ibid., p. 632.
17. Ibid., p. 641.
18. Ibid., p. 626.
19. Ibid., p. 627.
20. Chapman, "A Trophy From Fort Donelson," *New York Herald,* May 14, 1862.
21. A letter dated March 20, 1991 from H. M. Madaus to the author.

22. Ernest Griffin Papers, Camp Douglas Museum.

23. *AOR*, Serial 3, p. 335.

24. Griffin, "The Famous Tenth Tennessee," *CVM*, vol. 13, p. 554.

25. *Report of the Illinois Adjutant General, 1865*, p. 124.

26. Clark, "Tenth Tennessee Infantry," *MATC*, p. 284.

27. Griffin, "The Famous Tenth Tennessee," *CVM*, vol. 13, p. 554.

28. Doyle's diary, p. 42

29. *Report of the Illinois Adjutant General, 1865*, pp. 122-123.

30. Oakwoods Cemetery U.S. War Department Document No. 7.

31. *AOR*, Serial 4, pp. 91-92 and Horn, *Tennesseans in the Civil War*, vol. 1, pp. 193-196.

32. McGavock's journals, p. 657.

Reorganization

33. Ibid., p. 662.

34. Clark, "Tenth Tennessee, Infantry," *MATC*, p. 284.

35. McGavock's journals. p. 672.

36. Clark, "Tenth Tennessee Infantry," *MATC*, p. 285.

37. John G. O'Neill, Military Service Record.

38. Clark, "Tenth Tennessee Infantry," *MATC*, pp. 284-285.

39. Ibid., p. 285.

CHAPTER FIVE

THE BATTLE OF SNYDER'S BLUFF: CALLED ON ACCOUNT OF RAIN

The battles of Chickasaw Bluffs and First Port Hudson represent, by far, the best historical efforts of Griffin's "The Famous Tenth Tennessee," published in the December, 1905, issue of *CVM*. His description of the naval bombardment contains some interesting insights into the little-known Mississippi River engagement. Griffin's knowledge of Union strategy and movements indicate that he may well have been using an early edition of *Navy Official Records(NOR)* to refresh his memory.

The diary of Captain S. R. Simpson, the quartermaster of the Thirtieth Tennessee, mentions Major William Grace, Sergeant Bernard McCabe, Heiman, McGavock, and other members of the Tenth Tennessee. Unlike the accounts of McGavock, Griffin, and Doyle, Simpson's diary can be especially campy; he occasionally records his bowel movements in some detail.

Also unlike McGavock, Griffin, and Doyle, Simpson used racial slurs, two of which are directly quoted in the text. As was typical of ante-bellum Southern farmers, the captain referred to slaves as "niggers" and free blacks as "coloreds." However, his remarks are mild for those times. Racial hostility, in the modern sense, was probably not his intention. In fact, he recalled a farmer friend of his who was a "colored."

Marching in Mississippi

1. McGavock's journals, p. 675.
2. Clark, "Tenth Tennessee Infantry," *MATC,* p. 285.
3. *AOR,* Serial 24, p. 806 (Pemberton).
4. Griffin, "The Famous Tenth Tennessee," *CVM,* vol. 13, p. 554.
5. Simpson's diary, p. 12.
6. Ibid., p. 13.
7. Griffin, "The Famous Tenth Tennessee," *CVM,* vol. 13, p. 554.
8. Muster Rolls, frame no. 0192.
9. Frank, "Adolphus Heiman: Architect and Soldier," *THM,* vol. 5, p. 56.
10. Simpson's diary, p. 14.
11. Clark, "Tenth Tennessee Infantry," *MATC,* pp. 289-290.
12. Horn, *Tennesseans in the Civil War,* vol. 1, p. 194.
13. Doyle's diary, p. 46 and Simpson's diary, p. 15.

The Battle of Chickasaw Bluffs
Monday December 29, 1862
General Pemberton Versus General Sherman

14. Catton, *This Hallowed Ground,* pp. 239-240.
15. Martin, *The Vicksburg Campaign,* pp. 51-52.
16. Greene, *The Mississippi, CCW,* p. 74.
17. Catton, *This Hallowed Ground,* pp. 242-243.
18. Wyeth, *That Devil Forrest,* p. 99.
19. Morgan, "Assault on Chickasaw Bluffs," *BL,* vol. 3, p. 463.
20. *AOR,* Serial 25, p. 677 (Barton).
21. Griffin, "The Famous Tenth Tennessee," *CVM,* vol. 13, p. 554.
22. As cited in Faust, *Encyclopedia of the Civil War,* p. 138.
23. Greene, *The Mississippi, CCW,* p. 77.
24. Griffin, "The Famous Tenth Tennessee," *CVM,* vol. 13, p. 554.
25. Ibid.
26. As Cited in Greene, *The Mississippi, CCW,* p. 80.

The Battle of First Port Hudson
Saturday, Sunday, March 14-15, 1863
General Gardner Versus Admiral Farragut

27. Griffin, "The Famous Tenth Tennessee," *CVM*, vol. 13, p. 554.
28. Ibid., pp. 554-555.
29. Warner, *Generals in Gray*, p. 97.
30. *AOR*, Serial 21, p. 1000, p. 1033.
31. Ibid., pp. 933-934.
32. Simpson's diary, pp. 6-9.
33. Ibid., pp. 14-18.
34. Bernard McCabe, Military Service Record.
35. Foote, *The Civil War: A Narrative, Fredericksburg to Meridian*, pp. 213-214.
36. Griffin, "The Famous Tenth Tennessee," *CVM*, vol. 13, p. 555.
37. Ibid.
38. Ibid.
39. Ibid.
40. Ibid.
41. *AOR*, Serial 21, p. 278.
42, Ibid.
43. Doyle's diary, pp. 47-48.
44. Simpson's diary, p. 21.

CHAPTER SIX

THE GREAT SIEGE OF JACKSON THAT NEVER HAPPENED

Throughout its four-year history, the Tenth Tennessee demonstrated a remarkable affinity for becoming involved in some of the most obscure actions of the war. In spite of the fact that Raymond, Mississippi, is the least know battle of the critical Vicksburg campaign, it nonetheless represented the only action in which the Irish regiment was engaged.

The essentials of the Battle of Raymond are recreated by following four separate works of Bearss, most notably his second volume of *Campaign for Vicksburg*. The chief historian of the National Park Service offers precise information about Tenth Tennessee troop movements.

Clark adds important details about the exploits of individual members of the regiment. The report of Lieutenant Colonel James J.

Turner, Thirtieth Tennessee, in *AOR* is especially helpful concerning the action around O'Neill's Hill. An important source for the interpretation of Turner's battlefield tactics is Porter's Tennessee volume of *CMH.*

Not unexpectedly, the Federal casualty tally for Raymond in Stevenson's brigade of Logan's division of McPherson's corps of Grant's army differs dramatically in the reports of Turner and Union General John D. Stevenson.

Stevenson reported the number 115 as total losses in the three regiments he commanded that day; that is, the Seventh U.S. Missouri, the Thirty-Second Ohio, and the Eighty-First Illinois. Turner, by making a quick count on the field, estimated the number 150 as enemy losses during the half hour at O'Neill's Hill alone. It can be safely assumed that the truth lies somewhere in between. The number of losses suffered by Stevenson was probably smaller than 150 men at O'Neill's Hill and probably higher than 115 men for the entire six-hour confrontation.

Regardless of the exact figures, there is no doubt that Turner's small Tenth/Thirtieth Tennessee consolidated regiment severely damaged the future combat viability of three Union regiments.

General Grant's Spring Offensive

1. Bearss, "The Vicksburg Campaign and Siege," *Battlefield Guide,* p. 127.
2. Ibid.
3. Grant, "The Vicksburg Campaign," *BL* vol. 3, p. 503.
4. Simpson's diary, p. 22.
5. *AOR,* Serial 38, p. 862 (Pemberton).
6. Ibid., p. 737.
7. Ibid.
8. Bearss, "The Battle of Raymond," *Jackson Clarion,* January 12, 1958.
9. Ibid.
10. Ibid.

The Battle of Raymond, Mississippi
Tuesday, May 12, 1863, 10:00 AM - 4:00 PM
General Gregg Versus General McPherson

11. Bearss, *Campaign for Vicksburg,* vol. 2, p. 492.
12. Ibid., pp. 492-493.
13. Ibid.

14. Ibid, pp. 494-495.

15. Grant, "The Vicksburg Campaign," *BL*, vol. 3, p. 503.

16. Carter, *The Final Fortress,* p. 190.

17. Bearss, *Campaign for Vicksburg,* vol. 2, p. 499.

18. Ibid.

19. Ibid.

20. Clark, "Tenth Tennessee Infantry," *MATC*, p. 286.

21. Ibid.

22. Bearss, "The Battle of Raymond," *Jackson Clarion,* January 26, 1958.

23. Doyle's diary, p. 50. and Clark, "Tenth Tennessee Infantry," *MATC,* p. 286.

24. *AOR*, Serial 38, p. 741(Turner).

25. Ibid., pp. 741-742.

26. Doyle's diary, pp. 50-51.

27. *AOR,* Serial 38, p. 742 (Turner).

28. Doyle's diary, p. 51.

29. Ibid.

30. *AOR,* Serial 38, p. 742, p. 760.

31. Bearss, "The Battle of Raymond," *Jackson Clarion*, February 12, 1958.

32. Ibid.

33. Ibid.

34. Porter, *CMH Tennessee,* p. 82.

35. Bearss, "Raymond," *Battlefield Guide*, p. 140.

36. *AOR,* Serial 38, p. 742 (Turner).

37. Horn, *Tennesseans in the Civil War,* vol. 1, p. 194.

38. Porter, *CMH Tennessee,* p. 83.

39. *AOR*, Serial 36, p. 862, p. 955 (Pemberton).

40. Timothy Burgess Papers, "Raymond Losses" and Bearss, *Campaign for Vicksburg,* vol. 2, p. 515.

41. Clark, "Tenth Tennessee Infantry," *MATC,* p. 286.

42. *AOR,* Serial 38, p. 741 (Turner).

43. Gower, *Pen and Sword*, pp. 89-90.

A Tale of Two Rebellious Padres

44. Griffin, "The Famous Tenth Tennessee," *CVM*, vol. 13, p. 556.

45. Ibid.

46. Ibid.

47. Ibid., p. 557.

48. Ibid.

49. Meaney, "Valiant Chaplain of the Bloody Tenth," *THQ,* vol. 41, p. 41.

50. Ibid.

51. Griffin, "The Famous Tenth Tennessee," *CVM,* vol. 13, p. 559.

The Fall of Vicksburg

52. Carter, *The Final Fortress,* pp. 191-192.

53. Grant, "The Vicksburg Campaign," *BL*, vol. 3, p. 505.

54. Porter, *CMH Tennessee,* pp. 83-84.

55. Greene, *The Mississippi, CCW,* pp. 147-148.

56. Boatner, *Civil War Dictionary,* p. 429.

57. Foote, *The Civil War: A Narrative, Fredericksburg to Meridian,* pp. 363-365.

58. Simpson's diary, p. 25.

59. Horn, *Tennesseans in the Civil War,* vol. 1, p. 195, and Doyle's diary, p. 53.

60. Clark, "Tenth Tennessee Infantry," *MATC,* p. 290.

61. Long, *The Civil War: An Almanac 1861-1865,* p. 562.

62. Clark, "Tenth Tennessee Infantry, *MATC,* p. 290.

63. Warner, *Generals in Gray,* p. 306.

64. Simpson's diary, p. 30.

65. Ibid., p. 37.

66. Muster Rolls, frame no. 0190.

67. Clark, "Tenth Tennessee Infantry," *MATC,* p. 287.

68. Horn, *Tennesseans in the Civil War,* vol. 1, p. 195.

69. Ibid.

CHAPTER SEVEN

RIVER OF BLOOD

Between the morning of Friday, September 18, and the evening of Sunday, September 20, the Tenth Tennessee participated in most of the Confederate troop movements during the Battle of Chickamauga. The regiment was engaged in operational successes at Pea Vine Ridge, Reed's Bridge, Lee and Gordon's Mills, Brotherton's Farm, and Dyer's Farm. The regiment was engaged in operational failures at the Lafayette road and at Steedman's Hill. Since only a few paragraphs have ever been written about the Tenth Tennessee at Chickamauga, a wide variety of military reference materials are needed here.

In *AOR,* the detailed and scholarly report of General Bushrod R. Johnson contains valuable information concerning the action on all three days. The report of Lieutenant Colonel Watt W. Floyd, Seventeenth Tennessee, is helpful about activities on September 19; the report of Colonel Cyrus A. Sugg, Fiftieth Tennessee, provides needed facts for September 20. Several Union reports are essential in piecing together the action around Steedman's Hill.

Other important military eyewitness accounts include the papers of Colonel Archer Anderson and Captain James Dinkins in the *SHSP,* and the paper of General Harvey Hill in *BL.* At the regimental level, Tenth Tennessee eyewitnesses were Clark, Doyle, and Griffin; Thirtieth Tennessee eyewitnesses were Turner and Simpson. In spite of his habit of inflating the casualty figures of the Irish regiment, Clark does well in describing the battlefield deeds of Grace, Captain John L. Prendergast and First Lieutenant Robert Paget Seymour.

McCabe was the only enlisted man of the regiment to be mentioned somewhere in every single eyewitness account of the Tenth Tennessee. Because of his personal popularity, the off-beat story of his "wound" is found in four different sources—Porter, Simpson, Doyle, and McCabe's own military service record. Porter places the commissary sergeant's heroics at Raymond, while the other three accounts describe in some detail the scenario used in the text. Unlike Porter, General Frank Cheatham's chief-of-staff, who wrote his book thirty years after the war, diarists Doyle and Simpson were closely associated with McCabe in 1863.

Chickamauga casualty figures from the army level all the way down to the regimental level were gathered from seven sources: Thomas Livermore; Timothy Burgess; Muster Rolls; Military Service Records; *AOR; Tennesseans in the Civil War;* Pension Applications.

The Chickamauga Campaign
Thursday, September 17, 1863
General Bragg Versus General Rosecrans

1. Dinkins, "The Battle of Chickamauga," *SHSP* vol. 32, pp. 306-309.
2. Hill, "Chickamauga: The Great Battle of the West," *BL,* vol. 3, p. 639.
3. Horn, *Army of Tennessee,* p. 283.
4. As cited in Ibid.
5. Connelly, *Autumn of Glory,* p. 204.
6. "Opposing Forces at Chickamauga," *BL* vol. 3, pp. 672-676.

7. Hill, "Chickamauga: The Great Battle of the West," *BL,* vol. 3, p. 639.

8. Horn, *Army of Tennessee,* pp. 239-241.

9. Korn, *The Fight for Chattanooga,* pp. 32-42.

10. Abazzia, *The Chickamauga Campaign,* p. 49.

11. *AOR,* Serial 51, p. 17.

12. Ibid.

13. Ibid., Serial 53, p. 516

14. Ibid., Serial 51, pp. 468-469.

15. Livermore, *Numbers and Losses,* p. 105.

The Chickamauga Campaign
Friday, September 18, 1863
Pea Vine Ridge, Reed's Bridge, Lee and Gordon's Mills
General Bushrod Johnson Versus Colonel Wilder

16. Anderson, "Campaign and Battle of Chickamauga," *SHSP,* vol. 9, p. 404.

17. Hill, "Chickamauga: The Great Battle of the West," *BL,* vol. 3, p. 647.

18. *AOR,* Serial 50, p. 447 (Wilder).

19. Ibid., p. 451 (Miller).

20. Ibid., p. 923 (Minty).

21. Ibid., Serial 51, pp. 451-452 (B. Johnson).

22. Doyle's diary, p. 55.

23. *AOR,* Serial 51, p. 452 (B. Johnson).

24. Ibid.

25. Ibid., Serial 50, p. 923 (Minty).

26. Doyle's diary, pp. 55-56.

27. *AOR,* Serial 51, p. 452 (B. Johnson).

28. Hill, "Chickamauga : The Great Battle of the West," *BL* , vol. 3, p. 649.

29. Ibid.

30. *AOR,* Serial 51, p. 472 (W. W. Floyd).

31. Clark, "Tenth Tennessee Infantry," *MATC,* p. 287.

32. Ibid.

33. Doyle's diary, p. 56.

34. Connelly, *Autumn of Glory,* pp. 199-201.

The Battle of Chickamauga, First Official Day
Saturday, September 19, 1863
The Lafayette Road and the Widow Glenn's Farm
General Hood Versus General Wood

35. Horn, *Army of Tennessee,* p. 258.

36. Doyle's diary, p. 56.

37. Anderson, "Campaign and Battle of Chickamauga," *SHSP,* vol. 9, p. 405.

38. As cited in Korn, *Fight for Chattanooga,* p. 44.

39. Cist, *Army of the Cumberland, CCW,* p. 197.

40. Ibid.

41. Porter, *CMH Tennessee,* p. 99.

42. Horn, *Tennesseans in the Civil War,* vol. 1, p. 195.

43. Clark, "Tenth Tennessee Infantry," *MATC,* p. 287.

44. *AOR,* Serial 51, p. 481 (W. W. Floyd).

45. Ibid. p. 473 (Fulton).

46. Porter, *CMH Tennessee,* p. 99.

47. *AOR,* Serial 51, p. 481 (W. W. Floyd).

48. Doyle's diary, p. 57, and Clark, "Tenth Tennessee Infantry," *MATC,* p. 287.

49. *AOR,* Serial 51, p. 481 (W. W. Floyd).

50. Ibid.

51. Ibid., pp. 453-454 (B. Johnson).

52. As cited in Abazzia, *The Chickamauga Campaign,* p. 77.

53. *AOR,* Serial 50, p. 692 (Harker).

54. Ibid., Serial 51, p. 454 (B. Johnson).

55. Simpson's diary, p. 46.

56. *AOR,* Serial 51, p. 481 (W.W. Floyd).

57. Doyle's diary, pp. 57-58.

58. Porter, *CMH Tennessee,* p. 595; Bernard McCabe, Military Service Record; Doyle's diary, p. 57, and Simpson's diary, p. 46.

59. Doyle's diary, p. 58.

60. Anderson, "Campaign and Battle of Chickamauga," *SHSP,* vol. 9, p. 409.

61. *AOR,* Serial 51, p. 481 (W. W. Floyd).

62. Buck, *Cleburne and His Command,* pp. 144-145.

63. Ibid.

64. Doyle's diary, pp. 58-59.

The Battle of Chickamauga, Second Official Day
Sunday, September 20, 1863, 11:30 AM - 3:30 PM
Brotherton's Farm and Dyer's Farm
Colonel Sugg Versus First Lieutenant Schueler

65. Anderson, "Campaign and Battle of Chickamauga," *SHSP,* vol. 9 p. 409.

66. "Opposing Forces at Chickamauga," *BL,* vol. 3, pp. 672-676.

67. Ibid.

68. Ibid.

69. Foote, "The Civil War: A Narrative, Fredericksburg to Meridian, p. 731.

70. Dinkins, "The Battle of Chickamauga," *SHSP,* vol. 32 pp. 303-304.

71. As cited in Cist, *Army of the Cumberland, CCW,* p. 222.

72. Thurston, "Crisis at Chickamauga," *BL,* vol. 3, pp. 663-665.

73. Ibid.

74. Doyle's diary, p. 59.

75. *AOR,* Serial 51, p. 495 (Sugg).

76. As cited in Cist, *Army of the Cumberland, CCW,* p. 222.

77. Foote, *The Civil War: A Narrative, Fredericksburg to Meridian,* pp. 746-747.

78. *AOR,* Serial 51, p. 495 (Sugg).

79. "Opposing Forces at Chickamauga," *BL,* vol. 3, pp. 672-676.

80. *AOR,* Serial 51, pp. 457-458 (B. Johnson).

81. Ibid., pp. 495-496 (Sugg).

82. Doyle's diary, p. 59.

83. *AOR,* Serial 51, p. 467 (B. Johnson).

84. Clark, "Tenth Tennessee Infantry," *MATC,* p. 287.

85. Clarence C. Malone, Military Service Record.

86. *AOR,* Serial 51, p. 458 (B. Johnson).

87. Foote, *The Civil War: A Narrative, Fredericksburg to Meridian,* p. 741.

88. *AOR,* Serial 51, p. 481 (Sugg).

89. Connelly, *Autumn of Glory,* p. 223.

The Battle of Chickamauga, Second Official Day
Sunday, September 20, 1863, 3:30 - 9:00 PM
The Fight for Steedman's Hill
Colonel Grace Versus Lieutenant Colonel Warner

90. Cozzens, "This Terrible Sound," *CWTI,* September, October, 1992, pp. 32-33.

91. *AOR,* Serial 51, p. 482 (W.W.Floyd).

92. Korn, *The Fight for Chattanooga,* pp. 64-65.

93. *AOR,* Serial 50, p. 855 (Granger).

94. Hill, "Chickamauga: The Great Battle of the West," *BL,* vol. 3, p. 659.

95. Abazzia, *The Chickamauga Campaign,* p. 107.

96. As cited in Ibid.

97. *AOR,* Serial 51, p. 496 (Sugg).

98. Horn, *Army of Tennessee,* p. 267.

99. Fullerton, "Reinforcing Thomas at Chickamauga," *BL,* vol. 3, pp. 665-666.

100. *AOR,* Serial 50, p. 860 (Steedman).

101. Anderson, "Campaign and Battle of Chickamauga," *SHSP,* vol. 9, p. 415.

102. *AOR* Serial 50, p. 867 (Mitchell) and Ibid., Serial 51, p. 463 (B. Johnson).

103. Doyle's diary, p. 60.

104. *AOR,* Serial 50, p. 809 (VanVleck) and Ibid., Serial 51, p. 496 (Sugg).

105. Doyle's diary, p. 62.

106. As cited in Foote, *The Civil War: A Narrative, Fredericksburg to Meridian,* p. 768.

107. Dinkins, "The Battle of Chickamauga," *SHSP,* vol. 32, pp. 306-309.

108. Connelly, *Autumn of Glory,* p. 226.

Lew Clark and Stanley Horn
The Myth of the Bloody Tenth

109. Clark, "Tenth Tennessee Infantry," *MATC,* p. 287.

110. Timothy Burgess Papers, "Chickamauga Losses."

111. Horn, *Tennesseans in the Civil War,* vol. 1, p. 195.

112. Clark, "Tenth Tennessee Infantry," *MATC,* p. 290.

113. Livermore, *Numbers and Losses,* pp. 105-106.

114. *AOR,* Serial 51, p. 467 (B. Johnson) and Ibid., p. 497 (Sugg).

115. Clark, "Tenth Tennessee Infantry," *MATC,* p. 287.

116. Horn, *Tennesseans in the Civil War,* vol. 1, p. 195; *AOR,* Serial 51, p. 467 (B. Johnson); Muster Rolls, frame nos. 0022, 0024, 0026, and Military Service Records.

117. Horn, *Army of Tennessee,* p. 273.

118. Horn, *Tennesseans in the Civil War,* vol. 1, p. 195.

119. Wyeth, *That Devil Forrest,* pp. 243-245.

120. Ibid., p. 246.

121. Grant, "Chattanooga," *BL* vol. 3, pp. 698-699.

CHAPTER EIGHT

FIGHTING FOR CLOUDS

Clark's seven-page narrative contains the one and only paragraph ever written about the skirmish line of the Tenth Tennessee atop Missionary Ridge. Fortunately, Clark's brief description squares completely with the eyewitness data about the Tyler brigade in Turner's account of the Thirtieth Tennessee. General William B. Bate's report in *AOR* must be blended with the reports of Union regimental officers in order to trace the movements of the Tenth Tennessee in proper sequence.

In reference to the center position of General John C. Breckinridge's corps, historians firmly assert that Bate's division, which included Major John G. O'Neill and the Irish regiment, fought harder and longer than any of the other Confederate units in that sector. The primary source for the background material is James Lee McDonough's work, *Chattanooga: A Death Grip on the Confederacy.*

Since Doyle and Griffin were by now out of the picture, specific information about individual soldiers of the Tenth Tennessee is almost entirely missing for the Battle of Missionary Ridge, except for a few references found in the regimental muster rolls and military service records, especially concerning O'Neill and Captain Clarence C. Malone. Even if O'Neill's long-lost battle report should ever be discovered, it is doubtful that his deployment details would add much to those offered by Clark and Turner.

Be it noted that Union First Lieutenant Arthur MacArthur, Jr., later a lieutenant general in the regular U.S. Army, was the father of General of the Army Douglas MacArthur.

The Battles for Chattanooga
General Bragg Versus General Grant

1. Muster Rolls, frame nos. 0022, 0024, 0026.
2. Patrick M. Griffin, Military Service Record.
3. Barbara Ahern's letters to Margaret Bailey, 1949.
4. Horn, *Tennesseans in the Civil War,* vol. 1, p. 195.
5. As cited in McDonough, *Chattanooga: A Death Grip On The Confederacy,* p. 277.
6. Grant, "Chattanooga," *BL,* vol. 3, pp. 698-699.
7. Ibid.
8. *AOR,* Serial 55, p. 739 (Bate).
9. Grant, "Chattanooga," *BL,* vol. 3, pp. 703-704.

10. Buck, "Cleburne and His Division," *SHSP* vol. 8, pp. 465-467.

11. McDonough, *Chattanooga: A Death Grip On The Confederacy,*pp. 174-186.

12. Ibid.

13. Ibid.

14. Muster Rolls, frame no. 0028 and Clark, "Tenth Tennessee Infantry," *MATC,* pp. 287-288.

15. *AOR*, Serial 55, pp. 739-740 (Bate).

16. Ibid.

17. Catton, *This Hallowed Ground,* pp. 365-366.

18. *AOR*, Serial 55, p. 189 (Sheridan).

The Battle of Missionary Ridge
Wednesday, November 25, 1863, 4:00 - 9:00 PM
Major O'Neill Versus Captain Keegan

19. Ibid., p. 741 (Bate).

20. As cited in Cist, *Army of the Cumberland, CCW,* pp. 254-255.

21. As cited in Fullerton, "The Army of the Cumberland at Chattangooga," *BL,* vol. 3, p. 725.

22. *AOR,* Serial 55, p. 195 (F. Sherman).

23. Ibid., p. 741 (Bate).

24. McDonough, *Chattanooga: A Death Grip On The Confederacy,* p. 199.

25. Porter, *CMH Tennessee,* p. 116.

26. Clark, "Tenth Tennessee Infantry," *MATC,* p. 288.

27. *AOR,* Serial 55, p. 459 (R. W. Johnson) and Ibid., pp. 480-481 (Stoughton).

28. Ibid., p. 464 (Carlin) and Ibid., p. 743 (Bate).

29. Ibid., p. 482 (Moore).

30. Ibid., p. 484 (Raffin) and Ibid., p. 483 (Moore).

31. Ibid., p. 486 (Hanna), and Ibid., p. 743 (Bate).

32. Ibid., p. 485 (Keegan).

33. Ibid., p. 483 (Moore); Ibid., p. 485 (Keegan); and Ibid., p. 743 (Bate).

34. Clark, "Tenth Tennessee Infantry," *MATC,* p. 288.

35. Ibid. and *AOR,* Serial 55, p. 743 (Bate).

36. Connelly, *Autumn of Glory,* p. 276.

37. Muster Rolls, frame nos. 0048, 0050.

38. Porter, *CMH Tennessee,* p. 116.

39. Korn, *The Fight for Chattanooga,* pp. 148-149.

40. Buck, "Cleburne and His Division," *SHSP*, vol. 8, pp. 470-475.

41. Ibid.

42. Warner, *Generals in Gray*, pp. 312-313.
43. Clark, "Tenth Tennessee Infantry," *MATC*, p. 288.
44. Ibid. and Timothy Burgess Papers, "Missionary Ridge Losses."
45. Clarence C. Malone, Military Service Record.
46. Clark, "Tenth Tennessee Infantry," *MATC*, p. 290.
47. *AOR*, Serial 56, pp. 825-826.
48. Ibid., p. 886.

CHAPTER NINE

I NEVER KNEW HIS NAME

Because the role played by the Tenth Tennessee during the Atlanta campaign was so minor, the complete movements of the regiment could not possibly be traced without Captain Ed Porter Thompson's huge nineteenth century work, *History of the Orphan Brigade, 1861-1865.* Thompson's massive single volume is more of an overview of the war in the West than a unit history.

It is fortunate for the purposes of this book that Thompson provided details about all four of the Confederate brigades in Bate's division and not just details about the Kentucky brigade alone. The modern study of William C. Davis concentrates on the subject matter of the Kentucky Orphans. Thompson, however, remains a valuable research tool for information about the three brigades commanded by Generals Jesse Finley, Henry Jackson, and Thomas Benton Smith.

Once again, it was the fate of the Tenth Tennessee to participate in some of the most obscure engagements of the war. The skirmish at Utoy Creek is a classic example. Not even mentioned in some histories of the Atlanta campaign, the Union version of Utoy Creek can be found in the *AOR* reports of Generals Jacob D. Cox and James W. Reilly, plus Cox's fuller description in his *Atlanta,* published in 1882.

The Confederate version is limited to one paragraph in one newspaper story, and one paragraph in Thompson. A good summary of the various skirmishes along the creek can be found in Mark Boatner's *Civil War Dictionary.*

After exaggerating the losses of his own regiment at Chickamauga, Clark exaggerated enemy losses at Utoy Creek: "Occupying the field, we found that we had killed, wounded, and captured more men than we had in our entire brigade." Not so. There were 306 Federal losses and about six-hundred men in the reinforced Confederate brigade. Therefore, Clark was off by about three-hundred losses, which was some one-hundred more than in his discrepancy at Chickamauga.

The author makes a determined effort to reintroduce Father

Emmeran Bliemel to the Civil War community by quoting just about every word ever printed about him. Members of the Benedictine Order have sorted out the misspellings of his name and the misinformation about their fellow priest, put the few known facts together, and preserved his memory. The article, papers, and letters of Father Peter J. Meaney O.S.B. are the most recent and best of the materials.

Be it noted that an American Catholic army chaplain was reported to have been killed by bandits at the time of the Mexican War. Be assured, however, that the statement made in the text is historically accurate and verifiable. Bliemel was, indeed, the first American Catholic military chaplain killed in action *on a battlefield* in the history of the United States.

Confederate Benedictine Monk

1. Meaney, "Valiant Chaplain of the Bloody Tenth," *THQ,* vol. 41, pp. 42-43.

2. Ibid.

3. Doyle's diary, p. 9.

4. Meaney, "Valiant Chaplain of the Bloody Tenth," *THQ,* vol. 41 pp. 43-44.

5. Ibid.

6. Roberts, "Tribute to a Chaplain," *Nashville Daily American.* May 16, 1889.

7. O'Connor, "The Life and Times of Father Abram J. Ryan." *Immaculate Conception Catholic Church, Its People, Its History,* p. 23.

8. Robert Paget Seymour, Military Service Record.

The Great Siege of Dalton

9. Thompson, *Orphan Brigade,* p. 239.

10. As cited in Losson, *Tennessee's Forgotten Warriors: Frank Cheatham and His Confederate Division,* p. 137.

11. Bernard McCabe, Military Service Record.

12. Horn, *Army of Tennessee,* p. 315.

The Battles *for* Atlanta
Rocky Face Ridge, Resaca, New Hope Church
General Joe Johnston Versus General Sherman

13. "Opposing Forces in the Atlanta Campaign," *BL* , vol. 4, pp. 284-292 and Livermore, *Numbers and Losses,* p. 120.

14. Thompson, *Orphan Brigade,* pp. 244-246.

15. Ibid.

16. *AOR,* Serial 56, p. 886 and Serial 74, p. 640.

17. Cox, *Atlanta, CCW*, pp. 33-42.

18. Johnston, "Opposing Sherman's Advance to Atlanta", *BL*, vol. 4, p. 265.

19. Thompson, *Orphan Brigade,* pp. 244-246.

20. Ibid.

21. Clark, "Tenth Tennessee Infantry," MATC, p. 288.

22. Muster Rolls, frame no. 0032.

23. Veterans Pension Application No. 4357.

24. Ibid.

25. Timothy Burgess Papers, "Resaca Losses."

26. *AOR,* Serial 74, p. 662.

27. Porter, *CMH Tennessee*, p. 129.

28. Thompson, *Orphan Brigade,* p. 258.

29. Ibid., p. 250.

30. Porter, *CMH Tennessee,* p. 130.

31. Thompson, *Orphan Brigade,* p. 258.

32. Ibid.

33. Ibid.

34. Porter, *CMH Tennessee,* p. 130.

35. Bailey, *The Battles for Atlanta,* pp. 71-72.

36. Ibid.

37. Thompson, *Orphan Brigade,* p. 260.

38. As cited in Porter, *CMH Tennessee*, p. 130.

39. As cited in Bailey, *The Battles for Atlanta*, p. 74.

40. Connelly, *Autumn of Glory,* p. 431.

The Battles *of* Atlanta
Decatur, Utoy Creek, Jonesborough
General Hood Versus General Sherman

41. Thompson, *Orphan Brigade,* p. 261.

42. Roy, "General Hardee and the Military Operations Around Atlanta," *SHSP,* vol. 8, pp. 359-361.

43. Thompson, *Orphan Brigade,* p. 261.

44. Ibid., p. 263.

45. Roy, "General Hardee and the Military Operations Around Atlanta," *SHSP,* vol. 8, p. 366.

46. Ibid.

47. Thompson, *Orphan Brigade,* p. 263.

48. Livermore, *Numbers and Losses,* p. 123.

49. Muster Rolls, frame no. 0034.

50. Clark, "Tenth Tennessee Infantry," *MATC,* p. 288.

51. Muster Rolls, frame no. 0034.

52. AOR, Serial 74, p. 662.

53. Ibid.

54. Horn, *Tennesseans in the Civil War,* vol. 1, p. 176.

55. *AOR,* Serial 74, pp. 676-682.

56. Cox, *Atlanta, CCW,* p. 190.

57. "Tennesseans in Georgia," *Nashville Dispatch,* Monday, August 22, 1864.

58. *AOR,* Serial 73, p. 689 (Cox).

59. Ibid., Serial 74, p. 662.

60. Ibid., Serial 73, p. 705 (Reilly) and 'Tennesseans in Georgia," *Nashville Dispatch,* Monday, August 22, 1864.

61. *AOR,* Serial 73, pp. 705-706 (Reilly).

62. Ibid., p. 689 (Cox).

63. Thompson, *Orphan Brigade,* p. 264.

64. Ibid.

65. "Tennesseans in Georgia," *Nashville Dispatch,* Monday, August 22, 1864.

66. Thompson, *Orphan Brigade,* p. 264.

67. "Tennesseans in Georgia," *Nashville Dispatch,* Monday, August 22, 1864.

68. *AOR* Serial 73, p. 690 (Cox).

69. "Tennesseans in Georgia," *Nashville Dispatch,* Monday, August 22, 1864.

70. Clark, "Tenth Tennessee Infantry," MATC, p. 289.

71. *AOR,* Serial 74, p. 765 (S. D. Lee).

72. Ibid., Serial 73, p. 707 (Reilly).

73. Muster Rolls, frame no. 0034.

74. Connelly, *Autumn of Glory,* p. 395.

75. Roy, "General Hardee and the Military Operations Around Atlanta," *SHSP,* vol. 8, p. 372.

76. Bailey, *The Battles of Atlanta,* p. 151.

77. Ibid.

78. Ibid.

79. Porter, *CMH Tennessee*, p. 141.

80. Meaney, "Valiant Chaplain of the Bloody Tenth," *THQ,* vol. 41, p. 45.

81. Ibid.

82. Ibid.

83. Father Peter J. Meaney Papers.

84. William Grace, Military Service Record.

85. Clark, "Tenth Tennessee Infantry," *MATC,* p. 289.

86. Muster Rolls, frame no. 0032.

87. Veterans Pension Application, No. 2010.

88. Muster Rolls, frame nos. 0032, 0034.

89. Meaney, "Valiant Chaplain of the Bloody Tenth," *THQ,* vol. 41, p. 45.

90. Robert Paget Seymour, Military Service Record.

91. Meaney, "Valiant Chaplain of the Bloody Tenth," *THQ*, vol. 41, p. 46.

92. Mount Olivet, Nashville, Cemetery Records.

93. Meaney, "Valiant Chaplain of the Bloody Tenth," *THQ*, vol. 41, p. 46.

94. Cooper, "Reminiscence of Two Gallant Regiments," *CVM*, vol. 17, p. 113.

95. Clark, "Tenth Tennessee Infantry," *MATC*, p. 289.

96. Thompson, *Orphan Brigade*, p. 274.

97. Wiley, *Embattled Confederates*, p. 189.

98. Baptist, "Father Blemill and Captain Gracie," *CVM*, vol. 17, p. 186.

99. Porter, *CMH Tennessee*, p. 141.

100. Davis, *The Orphan Brigade: The Kentucky Confederates Who Couldn't Go Home*, pp. 232-233.

101. Horn, *Tennesseans in the Civil War*, vol. 1, p. 195.

CHAPTER TEN

FOUR LADS

In order to limit his account to seven pages, Clark summarized the last six months of the war in one sentence, stating that the Tenth Tennessee participated in the battles of Franklin, Nashville, and Bentonville, sustaining "heavy casualties." Nothing more is added. As a result there is no regimental eyewitness testimony for this period. Scant information is available from service records, muster rolls, pension applications, prison camp documents, and cemetery records.

The military movements of the Tenth Tennessee can be traced by using a combination of Horn and Porter. Background material is based mainly on Connelly's *Tennessee Civil War* and Union Colonel Henry Stone's article in *BL*.

Note that the original 1860s spellings appear in the text for Jonesborough, Murfreesborough, and Greensborough. The modern spelling of these towns is Jonesboro, Murfreesboro, and Greensboro.

A Footnote to History

1. Horn, *Tennesseans in the Civil War*, vol. 1, p. 195.
2. Ibid., vol. 2, pp. 9-450, and Muster Rolls, frame no. 0190.

The Confederate Counter-Offensive Into Tennessee
Franklin, Third Murfreesborough, Nashville
Lieutenant Colonel Shy Versus Colonel McMillen

3. Connelly, *Tennessee Civil War*, p. 28.

4. Porter, *CMH Tennessee,* p. 156.

5. Ibid.

6. Stone, "Repelling Hood's Invasion of Tennessee," *BL* vol. 4, pp. 433-435.

7. Porter, *CMH Tennessee,* pp. 156-157.

8. Ibid., p. 157-158.

9. Warner, *Generals in Gray*, p. 54.

10. Timothy Burgess Papers, "Franklin Losses."

11. Barbara Ahern's letters to Margaret Bailey, 1949.

12. Wyeth, *That Devil Forrest*, p. 485.

13. Ibid.

14. Porter, *CMH Tennessee,* p. 162, p. 295, p. 333.

15. John G. O'Neill, Military Service Record.

16. Porter, *CMH Tennessee,* p. 162, p. 295.

17. Horn, *Tennesseans in the Civil War* vol. 1, p. 195.

18. Ibid. and Stone, "Repelling Hood's Invasion of Tennessee," *BL,* vol. 4, pp. 463-464.

19. Warner, *Generals in Gray,* p. 284.

20. Ibid., p. 19.

21. Livermore, *Numbers and Losses,* p. 133.

22. Timothy Burgess Papers, "Nashville Losses."

23. Knauss, *Camp Chase,* p. 373, p. 375.

Surrender in North Carolina

24. Horn, *Tennesseans in the Civil War,* vol. 1, p. 195.

25. Ibid.

26. Muster Rolls, frame no. 0040.

27. Ibid; Horn, *Tennesseans in the Civil War,* vol. 1, pp. 195-196 and Bernard McCabe, Military Service Record.

28. Muster Rolls, frame nos. 0040, 0042.

29. Clark, "Tenth Tennessee Infantry," *MATC,* p. 282.

30. Porter, *CMH Tennessee,* p. 595.

The Last Toll

31. Clark, "Tenth Tennessee Infantry," *MATC*, pp. 289-290; Horn, *Tennesseans in the Civil War,* vol. 1, pp. 195-196, vol. 2, pp. 9-450; Veterans Pension Applications; Timothy Burgess Papers; Military Service Records; Muster Rolls.

POSTSCRIPT

1. Frank, "Adolphus Heiman: Architect and Soldier," *THM,* vol. 5, p. 57.

2. Gower, *Pen and Sword*, pp. 90-91.

3. Clark, "Tenth Tennessee Infantry," *MATC*, p. 285.

4. Meaney, "Valiant Chaplain of the Bloody Tenth," *THQ*, vol. 41, pp. 46-47.

5. Veterans Pension Application No. 153.

6. Griffin, "The Famous Tenth Tennessee," *CVM,* vol. 13, p. 556.

7. May 29, 1949 Letter from Barbara Ahern to Margaret Bailey, and Porter, *CMH Tennessee,* p. 595.

8. Griffin, "The Famous Tenth Tennessee," *CVM*, vol. 13, p. 553.

9. Widows of Veterans Pension Application nos. 3048, 5946, 6894, 5587, 7536, 7181, 11086.

10. Gower, *Pen and Sword,* pp. 92-93, and September 28, 1991, Letter from Herschel Gower to the author.

11. *Tennessee Civil War Veterans Questionnaires,* vol. 4, pp. 1400 - 1401.

12. May, June, 1949 Letters from Barbara Ahern to Margaret Bailey.

EPILOGUE

1. *Clayton News Daily,* March 14, 1983; *National Catholic Reporter.* March 18, 1983; *America Magazine,* March 26, 1983; *CVM,* March, 1983; and other materials from Father Peter J. Meaney.

2. *The Sunday Tennessean,* July 19, 1987.

BIBLIOGRAPHY

MANUSCRIPTS

Camp Douglas Museum, Chicago, Il.
    Ernest Griffin. "The Confederate Mound at Oakwoods," 1979.
Chicago Historical Society, Chicago, Il.
    Nathan Bedford Forrest Papers, no date.
Confederate Museum, Richmond, Va.
    Congress of the Confederate States of America, "Facts and Incidents of the Siege, Defense, and Fall of Fort Donelson." Huntsville, Al. 1863.
Fort Donelson National Battlefield, Dover Tn.
    Park Service Maps, "Troop Movements," no date.
Middle Tennessee Civil War Roundtable, White House, Tn.
    Timothy Burgess. "Tenth Tennessee Death, Cemetery, and Casualty Records," 1991.
Mississippi Chapter of the Daughters of the Confederacy, Jackson, Ms.
    Battle of Raymond Papers, May 12, 1963.
Mount Olivet Cemetery Records, Nashville, Tn, 1981.
National Archives, Washington, D.C.
    Muster Rolls. Tenth Tennessee Infantry Regiment of Volunteers(Irish) CSA. Military Reference Branch, Confederate Record Group 109. 190 microfilm frames. 1911.
State of Illinois, General Headquarters, Office of the Adjutant General. Springfield, Il. "Official Report on Camp Douglas." June, 1865.
Tennessee State Library, Department of Archives, Nashville, Tn.
    Tenth Tennessee Infantry (CSA) Military Service Records, no date.
Tennessee State Library, Department of Archives, Nashville, Tn.
    Tenth Tennessee Infantry (CSA) Veterans and Widows of Veterans Pension Applications, no date.
United States. Department of the Interior. National Park Service, Denver Service Center. Chickamauga and Chattanooga Battlefield Park Documents, nos. 3008 and 3010. "Chattanooga Campaign," no date.
United States. Department of the Interior, Washington, D.C.
    National Park Service, Denver Service Center. Fort Donelson Battlefield Park Document no. 11. Edwin C. Bearss, "Fortifications at Fort Donelson," 1959.
_____. National Park Service, Denver Service Center. Fort Donelson Battlefield Park Document no. 12. Edwin C. Bearss, "The Fighting on February 13," 1959.

_____. National Park Service, Denver Service Center. "Kennesaw Mountain Battlefield Park documents, nos. 2068 and 2069. *Atlanta Campaign,* no date.

United States. War Department, District of the Lakes, Chicago, Il. A Ledger of the Confederate Dead, Camp Douglas, 1912.

United States. War Department, District of the Lakes, Detroit, Mi. Camp Douglas Burial Documents, 1867-1900.

GOVERNMENT PUBLICATIONS

United States. Bureau of the Census. *Eighth Census of the United States, 1860.* 4 vols. Washington, D.C. Government Printing Office, 1860.

United States. Department of the Navy. *War of the Rebellion: Official Records of the Union and Confederate Navies.* 30 vols. and index. Washington, D.C., Government Printing Office, 1894-1927.

United States. War Department. *Official Military Atlas of the Civil War.* Washington, D.C., Government Printing Office, 1891-1896.

_____. *War of the Rebellion: Official Records of the Union and Confederate Armies.* 127 vols. plus index. Government Printing Office, 1880-1901.

DIARIES AND LETTERS

Ahern, Barbara. Letters to Margaret Bailey. Boston, Ma., May, June 1949. Author's collection.

Bearss, Edwin C. Letters written to the author by the Vicksburg historian from Washington, D.C., 1991. Author's collection.

Cooling, Benjamin Franklin. Letters written to the author by the Forts Henry and Donelson historian from Washington, D.C., 1992. Author's collection.

Doyle, Jimmy. Diary, 1861-1863. Private collection of Margaret Bailey.

Gower, Dr. Herschel. Letters and papers written to the author by the McGavock biographer from Dallas, Tx., 1991-1993. Author's collection.

Griffin, Ernest. Letters written to the author by the Camp Douglas Museum curator from Chicago, Il., 1990-1991. Author's collection.

Levy, Dr. George. Letters and papers written to the author by the Camp Douglas historian from Chicago, Il. 1991. Author's collection.

Madaus, Howard Michael, Letters and documents sent to the author by the Confederate Battle Flags historian from Milwaukee, Ws., 1991. Author's collection.

Malone, Clarence C. Letters. Atlanta, GA., dated October 26, 1864, January 23, 1865 from the personal collection of John M. Vaughn, III.

Meaney, Father Peter J., O.S.B. Letters, with newspaper and magazine clippings, sent to the author by the Bliemel biographer from Morristown, NJ., 1991-1993. Author's collection.

Simpson, Captain S.R. Diary, 1862-1863 Mississippi Department of History and Archives.

NEWSPAPERS

Charleston [S.C.] *Mercury*
Clarion Ledger Daily American, (Jackson, Ms.)
Clayton County [Georgia] *Daily News*
Nashville Banner
Nashville Daily American
Nashville Dispatch
New York Herald
New York Tribune
Sunday Tennessean, [Nashville, Tn.]

ARTICLES AND ESSAYS

Ambrose, Steven E. "Fort Donelson: A Disastrous Blow to the South." *Civil War Times Illustrated* (June, 1966): pp. 4-24.

Anderson, Archer. "Campaign and Battle of Chickamauga." *Southern Historical Society Papers* (September, 1881): vol. 9, pp. 385-418.

Baptist, N.W. "Father Blemill and Captain Gracie." *Confederate Veteran Magazine* (April, 1909): vol. 17, p. 186.

Bell, Patricia. "Gideon Pillow: A Personality Profile." *Civil War Times Illustrated* (October 1967): pp. 12-19.

Buck, Irving A. "Cleburne and His Division at Chickamauga and Ringgold Gap." *Southern Historical Society Papers* (November, December, 1880): vol. 8, pp. 465-467.

Castel, Albert. "Black Jack Logan." *Civil War Times Illustrated* (November 1976): pp. 4-11.

Castel, Albert. "Union Fizzle at Atlanta: the Battle of Utoy Creek." *Civil War Times Illustrated* (February, 1978): pp. 26-32.

Clark, Lewis R. "Tenth Tennessee Infantry." Memoirs in *Military Annals of Tennessee: Confederate.* Nashville, Tn. edited and privately published by John B. Lindsley, M.D., 1886.

Cooling, Benjamin Franklin. "Union Victory on the Twin Rivers."

Blue and Gray (February, 1992): pp. 10-20; pp. 45-53.

Cooper, James L. "Reminiscence of Two Gallant Regiments." *Confederate Veteran Magazine* (March, 1909): vol. 17, p. 113.

Cozzens, Peter. "This Terrible Sound: the Battle of Chickamauga." *Civil War Times Illustrated (* September, October 1992): pp. 30-39; pp. 63-64.

Crownover, Sims. "The Battle of Franklin." *Tennessee Historical Quarterly* (December, 1955.): vol. 14, pp. 291-322.

Dinkins, James. "The Battle of Chickamauga." *Southern Historical Society Papers* (September, 1904): vol. 32, pp. 306-309.

Eichenlaub, Richard. "Storm on the Cumberland." *America's Civil War* (March, 1990): pp. 26-33.

Frank, John G. "Adolphus Heiman: Architect and Soldier." *Tennessee Historical Society Magazine* (Annual, 1946): vol. 5, pp. 35-57.

Fullerton, Joseph S. "Reinforcing Thomas at Chickamauga." *Battles and Leaders of the Civil War* (1887-1889): vol. 3, pp. 665-667.

_____. "The Army of the Cumberland at Chattanooga." *Battles and Leaders of the Civil War* (1887-1889): vol. 3, pp. 719-726.

Grant, U.S. "Chattanooga." *Battles and Leaders of the Civil War* (1887-1889): vol. 3, pp. 679-711.

_____. "The Vicksburg Campaign." *Battles and Leaders of the Civil War.* (1887-1889): vol. 3, pp. 493-539.

Griffin, Patrick M. "The Famous Tenth Tennessee." Memoirs in *Confederate Veteran Magazine.* Nashville, Tn. December, 1905.

Haskew, Michael, "Valley of the Shadow." *America's Civil War* (September, 1990): pp. 18-24.

Hill, D. H. "Chickamauga: the Great Battle of the West." *Battles and Leaders of the Civil War* (1887-1889): vol. 3, pp. 638-663.

Horn, Stanley. "Nashville During the Civil War." *Tennessee Historical Quarterly* (March, 1945): vol. 4, pp. 3-22.

Johnston, Joseph E. "Opposing Sherman's Advance to Atlanta." *Battles and Leaders of the Civil War* (1887-1889): vol. 4, pp. 260-277.

Kegley, Tracy M. "Bushrod Rust Johnson: Soldier and teacher." *Tennessee Historical Quarterly* (September, 1948): vol. 7, pp. 249-258.

Kelly, Dennis. "Back in the Saddle: the War Record of William Bate." *Civil War Times Illustrated* (December, 1988): pp. 27-33.

McWhiney, Grady. "Braxton Bragg and Confederate Defeat." *Civil War Times Illustrated (April, 1972):* pp. 4-7; pp. 42-48.

Meaney, Peter J., O.S.B. "Valiant Chaplain of the Bloody Tenth." *Tennessee Historical Quarterly* (Spring, 1982): pp. 37-47.

Morgan, George W. "Assault on Chickasaw Bluffs." *Battles and Leaders of the Civil War* (1887-1889): vol. 3, pp. 462-470.

O'Connor, Cornelia, "The Life and Times of Father Abram J. Ryan." in *Immaculate Conception Catholic Church, Its People, Its History* (1980): pp. 17-25.

Plaisance, Aloysius. O.S.B., "Emmeran Bliemel, O.S.B. Heroic Confederate Chaplain." *American Benedictine Review* (June, 1966): vol. 17, pp.
209-216.

Robertson, William Glenn. "Rails to the River of Death." *Civil War
Society Magazine* (November December 1991): pp. 50-55; pp. 70-71.

Roy, T.R. "General Hardee and the Military Operations Around Atlanta," *Southern Historical Society Papers* (September, October,
1880): vol. 8, pp. 337-387.

Stone, Henry. "Repelling Hoods's Invasion of Tennessee." *Battles and
Leaders of the Civil War* (1887-1889): vol. 4, pp. 440-464.

Stonesifer, Toy P. "Gideon Pillow: A study in Egotism." *Tennessee
Historical Quarterly* (Winter, 1966): vol. 25, pp. 340-350.

Taylor, Jesse. "The Defense of Fort Henry." *Battles and Leaders of the
Civil War* (1887-1889): vol. 1, pp 368-372.

Thurston, Gates P. "The Crisis at Chickamauga." *Battles and Leaders of
the Civil War* (1887-1889): vol. 3, pp. 663-665.

Tucker, Glenn. "The Battle of Chickamauga." *Civil War Times* (May,
1969): vol. 8, pp. 4-54.

Turner, James J. "Thirtieth Tennessee Infantry." Memoirs in *Military
Annals of Tennessee: Confederate.* Nashville, Tn. edited and privately
published by John B. Lindsley, M.D., 1886.

Walke, Henry. "The Gunboats at Belmont and Fort Henry." *Battles and
Leaders of the Civil War* (1887-1889): vol. 1, pp. 358-367.

_____. "The Western Flotilla at Fort Donelson," *Battles and Leaders of
the Civil War* (1887-1889): vol. 1, pp. 430-452.

Walker, Peter Franklin. "Command Failure: the Fall of Forts Henry
and Donelson." *Tennessee Historical Quarterly* (December, 1957):
vol. 16, pp. 335-360.

Wallace, Lewis. "The Capture of Fort Donelson," *Battles and Leaders of
the Civil War* (1887-1889) vol. 1, pp. 398-428.

Weller, J. C. "Nathan Bedford Forrest: An Analysis of Untutored Military
Genius." *Tennessee Historical Quarterly* (September, 1959): vol. 18,
pp. 213-251.

Woodworth, Steven E. "Formula for Disaster." *Civil War Society Magazine* (January, February 1992): pp. 34-39; p. 53.

Wukowits, John F. "Decks Covered with Blood." *America's Civil War*
(March, 1992): pp. 40-45.

BOOKS

Abbazia, Patrick. *The Chickamauga Campaign.* New York: Gallery Books, 1988.

Bailey, Ronald H. *The Battles for Atlanta: Sherman Moves East.* Alexandria, Virginia: Time-Life Books, 1988.

Battles and Leaders of the Civil War. 4 vols. New York: Century Magazine Publishers, 1887-1889.

Bearss, Edwin C. *The Campaign for Vicksburg.* 3 vols. Dayton: Morningside Bookshop, 1986.

Boatner, Mark M., III. *Civil War Dictionary.* New York: David McKay, 1959.

Brown, Alexander D. *The Galvanized Yankees.* Champaign: University of Illinois Press, 1963.

Bryan, Charles W. Jr., *The Civil War in East Tennessee.* Knoxville: University of Tennessee Press, 1978.

Bryan, T. C., *Confederate Georgia.* Athens: University of Georgia Press, 1953.

Buck, Irving A. and Thomas R. Hay. *Cleburne and his Command.* [by Buck], *Pat Cleburne: Stonewall Jackson of the West.* [by Hay] Jackson, Tennessee: published together in a single volume by McCowat-Mercer Press, 1959.

Campaigns of the Civil War. 16 vols. New York: Charles Scribner's Sons, 1882-1883.

Carter, Samuel III. *The Final Fortress: The Campaign for Vicksburg 1862-1863.* New York: St. Martin's Press, 1980.

Catton, Bruce. *This Hallowed Ground.* New York: Washington Square Press Pocket Books, 1963.

_____. *Terrible Swift Sword.* New York: Washington Square Press Pocket Books, 1963.

Cist, Henry M. *Army of the Cumberland.* New York: Charles Scribner's Sons, 1882-1883.

Confederate Military History. 17 vols. and 2 vol. index. Atlanta: Confederate Publishing Company, 1899.

Confederate Veteran. 40 vols. and 3 vol. index. Nashville: published by *Confederate Veteran Magazine,* 1893-1932.

Connelly, Thomas L. *Army of the Heartland: Army of Tennessee 1861-1862.* Baton Rouge: Louisiana State University Press, 1988.

_____. *Autumn of Glory: Army of Tennessee 1862-1865.* Baton Rouge: Louisiana State University Press, 1988.

_____. *Civil War Tennessee.* Baton Rouge: Lousiana State University Press, 1988.

Cooling, Benjamin Franklin. *Forts Henry and Donelson: Key to the Confederate Heartland.* Knoxville: University of Tennessee Press, 1987.

Cox, Jacob D. *Atlanta.* New York: Charles Scribner's Sons, 1882-1883.

Cross, Wallace Jr. *Ordeal by Fire.* Clarksville, Tennessee: Clarksville Montgomery County Museum Bookshop, 1990.

Crummer, Wilbur F. *With Grant at Fort Donelson, Shiloh, and Vicksburg: A Journal.* Oak Park, IL published privately, 1915.

Davis, William C. *Confederate Generals.* 6 vols. Washington: National Historical Society, 1991-1992.

_____. *The Orphan Brigade: The Kentucky Confederates Who Couldn't Go Home.* New York: St. Martin's Press, 1980.

Eaton, Clement. *Jefferson Davis.* New York: Free Press, 1977.

Elliot, Colleen Morse, and Louise Armstrong Moxley. *Tennessee Civil War Veterans Questionnaires.* 5 vols. Nashville: Southern Historical Society Press, 1922.

Faust, Patricia L. *Historical Times Illustrated: Encyclopedia of the Civil War,* New York: Harper and Row, 1986.

Flint, Roy Kenneth. *The Battle of Missionary Ridge.* Tuscaloosa: University of Alabama Press, 1960.

Foote, Shelby. *The Civil War: A Narrative, Fort Sumter to Perryville.* New York: Vintage Books, 1986.

_____. *The Civil War: A Narrative, Fredericksburg to Meridian.* New York: Vintage Books, 1986.

_____. *The Civil War: A Narrative, Red River to Appomattox.* New York: Vintage Books, 1986

Force, M.F. *From Fort Henry to Cornith.* New York: Charles Scribner's Sons, 1882-1883.

Gower, Herschel and Jack Allen. *Pen and Sword: the Life and Journals of Randal W. McGavock.* Jackson, Tn. McCowat Mercer Press, 1960.

Grant, U.S. *Personal Memoirs.* 2 vols. New York: Charles L. Webster and Company, 1886.

Greene, F. V. *The Mississippi.* New York: Charles Scribner's Sons, 1882-1883.

Hamilton, James J. *The Battle of Fort Donelson.* Cranbury, New Jersey: Thomas Yoseloff Publishers, 1968.

Horn, Stanley, Chairman, Civil War Centennial Commission. *Tennesseans in the Civil War: A Military History of Confederate and Union Units With Available Rosters of Personnel.* 2 vols. Knoxville: University of Tennessee, 1964-1965.

———. *Army of Tennessee.* Indianapolis: Bobbs-Merrill, 1941.

Immaculate Conception Catholic Church. Its People, Its History. Clarksville, Tennessee: published privately, 1980.

Johnston, Joseph E. *Narrative of Military Operations During the Late War.* New York: Appleton Press, 1874.

Kennedy, Frances H. *Civil War Battlefield Guide.* Boston: Houghton Mifflin, 1990.

407

Knauss, William H. *Camp Chase: A History of the Prison and its Cemetery.* Nashville: Methodist Episcopal Church Printers, 1906.

Korn, Jerry. *The Fight for Chattanooga: Chickamauga to Missionary Ridge.* Alexandria, Virginia: Time-Life Books, 1988.

Livermore, Thomas L. *Numbers and Losses in the Civil War.* Bloomington: Indiana University Press, 1957.

Long, E. B. *Civil War Day by Day: An Almanac 1861-1865.* New York: Doubleday, 1971.

Losson, Christopher. *Tennessee's Forgotten Warriors: Frank Cheatham and His Confederate Division.* Knoxville: University of Tennessee Press, 1989.

Madaus, Howard M. and Robert D. Needham. *The Battle Flags of the Confederate Army of Tennessee.* Milwaukee: Public Museum Printers, 1976.

Martin, David. *The Vicksburg Campaign.* New York: Gallery Books, 1990.

McDonough, James Lee. *Chattanooga: A Death Grip On The Confederacy.* Knoxville: University of Tennessee Press, 1984.

McMurray, W. J. *History of the Twentieth Tennessee Regiment Volunteer Infantry.* Nashville: Elder's Bookstore, 1976.

Porter, James D. *Confederate Military History: Tennessee.* Atlanta: Confederate Publishing Company, 1899.

Roller, David C. and Robert W. Twyman, *Encyclopedia of Southern History.* Baton Rouge: Louisiana State University Press, 1979.

Savas, Theodore P. and David A. Woodbury. *The Campaign for Atlanta and Sherman's March to the Sea.* vol. I. Campbell, California: Savas Woodbury Publishers, 1992.

Southern Bivouac. 6 vols. Louisville: published by the Kentucky branch of the Southern Historical Society, 1882-1887.

Thompson, Ed Porter. *History of the Orphan Brigade 1861-1865.* Louisville: Charles T. Dearing Press, 1898.

Warner, Ezra J. *Generals in Blue.* Baton Rouge: Louisiana State University Press, 1984.

_____. *Generals in Gray.* Baton Rouge: Louisiana State University Press, 1983.

Wiley, Bell Irving. *Embattled Confederates.* New York: Bonanza Books, 1964.

Williams, T. Harry. *P.G.T. Beauregard: Napoleon in Gray.* Baton Rouge: Louisiana State University Press, 1981.

Wyeth, Dr. John Allan. *That Devil Forrest.* New York: Harper Brothers, 1959.

INDEX

Note: An asterisk after a number indicates that a photo appears on that page.

The author, a single resident of the Chicago suburb of Oak Lawn, is a research historian with a Master of Arts degree. Two of his ancestors served in the Confederate Army, and as a result of that, he has developed a special interest in the Civil War. One of his latest projects is a detailed report prepared for Chicago's Oakwoods Cemetery of the 4,039 Camp Douglas prisoners buried in the cemetery.

Ed Gleeson is a member of the Sons of Confederate Veterans, the Civil War Society, and the Chicago Historical Society. Although *Rebel Sons of Erin* is his first book, he has plans to author other books on the subject of Irish Confederates.